Engaging Indonesia

Critical Dialogues on Culture and Society

Series Editors
Manneke Budiman, Universitas Indonesia, Depok, Indonesia
Melani Budianta, Universitas Indonesia, Depok, Indonesia
Abidin Kusno, York University, Toronto, Canada
Rita Padawangi, Singapore University of Social Sciences, Singapore, Singapore

Engaging Indonesia brings together current debates in social and cultural studies relating to the study of Indonesia, with the aim of giving voice to both leading and emerging Indonesianists. Critical and interdisciplinary, the books in the series contribute to knowledge formation by addressing pressing issues facing the country - cultural, social, and political - from contemporary and historical perspectives. Works may include research-based monographs, edited volumes, handbooks, and translations of both recent, and seminal/historical works. The series is particularly welcoming of topics relating to issues of urban and environmental change, to questions of identity and place, to problems of governance and conflicts, to the politics of representation, language, and performances, and to the global and postcolonial contexts in which these are addressed. Special consideration is given to studies that cover underrepresented regions and marginalized voices, as well as those that seek to recover lost archives, uncounted political events, or forgotten historical figures. Relevant to students and scholars from a broad range of disciplines in the humanities and social sciences with a particular interest in researching Indonesia, the series champions intellectual engagement with the archipelago's rapidly changing landscape - from within, and beyond.

Richmond Stroupe · Lilie Roosman
Editors

Applied Linguistics in the Indonesian Context

Society, Culture and Language

Springer

Editors
Richmond Stroupe
Graduate School of Letters
World Language Center
Soka University
Hachiōji, Tokyo, Japan

Lilie Roosman
Department of Linguistics
Faculty of Humanities
Universitas Indonesia
Depok, Jawa Barat, Indonesia

ISSN 2948-2909　　　　　　　ISSN 2948-2917　(electronic)
Engaging Indonesia
ISBN 978-981-97-2335-5　　　ISBN 978-981-97-2336-2　(eBook)
https://doi.org/10.1007/978-981-97-2336-2

© The Editor(s) (if applicable) and The Author(s) 2025. This book is an open access publication.

Open Access This book is licensed under the terms of the Creative Commons Attribution 4.0 International License (http://creativecommons.org/licenses/by/4.0/), which permits use, sharing, adaptation, distribution and reproduction in any medium or format, as long as you give appropriate credit to the original author(s) and the source, provide a link to the Creative Commons license and indicate if changes were made.
The images or other third party material in this book are included in the book's Creative Commons license, unless indicated otherwise in a credit line to the material. If material is not included in the book's Creative Commons license and your intended use is not permitted by statutory regulation or exceeds the permitted use, you will need to obtain permission directly from the copyright holder.
The use of general descriptive names, registered names, trademarks, service marks, etc. in this publication does not imply, even in the absence of a specific statement, that such names are exempt from the relevant protective laws and regulations and therefore free for general use.
The publisher, the authors and the editors are safe to assume that the advice and information in this book are believed to be true and accurate at the date of publication. Neither the publisher nor the authors or the editors give a warranty, expressed or implied, with respect to the material contained herein or for any errors or omissions that may have been made. The publisher remains neutral with regard to jurisdictional claims in published maps and institutional affiliations.

This Springer imprint is published by the registered company Springer Nature Singapore Pte Ltd.
The registered company address is: 152 Beach Road, #21-01/04 Gateway East, Singapore 189721, Singapore

If disposing of this product, please recycle the paper.

Foreword

Ever since its independence on 17 August 1945, Indonesia has grappled with issues concerning languages. Throughout the decades up to early 2000s, the publication of book-length monographs or edited volumes on languages in the country was in accordance with the language discourse characterising the political regimes governing the nation. Soekarno's administration (ruling from 17 August 1945 to 11 March 1967) and Soeharto's New Order (12 March 1967–21 May 1998) shared the same emphasis on Indonesian as the national language, hence accentuating its importance as the unifying language of a highly diverse nation. Book-length publications appearing during the long timeline of the two regimes reflected this discourse, focusing on the grammar and linguistic development of the Indonesian language (see Alisjahbana, 1949; Dardjowidjojo, 1978) and the role of Indonesian as a unifying language (e.g., Abas, 1987). Even those using language policy as their central theoretical framework also placed a great emphasis on the Indonesian language; for example, strategies for linguistic modernisation (Alisjahbana, 1976) and approaches for Indonesia's development and cultivation (Moeliono, 1986). Three diverging discourses appeared in the 1990s: one that critically examined the role of the Indonesian language in maintaining power (e.g., Heryanto, 1995; Latif & Ibrahim, 1996), another questioning the impact of linguistic favouritism of Indonesian on identity, interaction, and ethnic marginalisation (e.g., Errington, 1998; Kuipers, 1998); and a third which scrutinised the role of Indonesian language policy in education (see Alwasilah, 1997).

As Indonesia entered the new millennium, emphasis on the Indonesian language was no longer as great as it used to be under the linguistic machinery of the New Order's powerful language planning agency, the *Badan Bahasa* (see Moeliono, 1986 for the role of the *Badan Bahasa* during Soeharto's New Order regime). Indeed, interest in the Indonesian language persisted until the early 2000s, which saw the publication of books focusing on the historical development of the language (Sneddon, 2003) and the emergence of its diglossic, colloquial variety in metropolitan Jakarta (Sneddon, 2006). However, acknowledgement of Indonesia's superdiversity gained immediate and somewhat greater traction. Thus, book-length research studies have focused most notably on the employment of mobile, fluid linguistic features in superdiverse Indonesia, both in the context of Indonesians living within the nation's political borders as well as those overseas (see Goebel, 2010, 2015). Foulcher, Moriyama, and Budiman (2012) are exemplary in its examination of the fluid transitions emerging amidst the dramatic shifts in Indonesian politics, culture, and society during the Reform Era, which enabled freedom of expression using languages spoken by indigenous peoples and those once politically marginalised ethnics such as the Chinese. Other book-length publications focus on diversity of language practices; for example, translanguaging practices involving Indonesian, Javanese, and English (Zentz, 2017) and how such practices give rise to intersubjectivity (Djenar, Ewing, & Manns, 2018). More emphasis on Indonesia's superdiversity appears in Zein (2020), leading to conceptualisation of new theories. Accounting for all elements in Indonesia's linguistic ecology, including Indonesian and regional lingua francas, the book identifies the nation as a dynamic, complex, and polycentric sociolinguistic environment, called *superglossia*. Meanwhile, its examination of language endangerment in the country leads to the conceptualisation of *revitalisation planning* as a holistic, integrated, and systematic theory of language preservation, which ensures the conservation of biodiversity, linguistic and cultural diversity, political stability, spiritual and religious sustenance, sustainable development, as well as the empowerment of minoritised indigenous communities. Critical examination of English as a global language also appears in Zein (2020), in addition to the works of prolific scholars such as Setiono Sugiharto (see e.g., Sugiharto, 2015). Given the proliferation of research into English language education in Indonesia in the past few years (Zein, Sukyadi, Hamied, & Lengkanawati, 2020), many have argued to redirect the focus from English as a foreign language (EFL) to English as a lingua franca (ELF), and realign teacher education accordingly (see Zein, 2018). Overall, those recent publications have portrayed not only the fact that the linguistic landscape and sociolinguistic concerns have truly changed from the time the eminent scholar Sutan Takdir Alisjahbana conceptualised Indonesian modern grammar (see Alisjahbana, 1949) but also outlined challenges in contemporary Indonesia.

This present edited volume, *Applied Linguistics in the Social Sciences and in the Indonesian Context*, is a welcome addition to scholarship amidst the emerging challenges. The editors, Richmond Stroupe and Lilie M. Roosman, have successfully pulled the strings together to discuss various facets of applied linguistics in the Indonesian context. This volume takes a broad perspective of applied linguistics as an academic discipline. It offers fresh insights into applied linguistics in Indonesia in its discussion of educational linguistics, corpus linguistics, critical discourse analysis and clinical linguistics. Contributions range from the diffusion of English as a medium of instruction, to students' learning motivation, to semantic cognitive analysis, to authorship analysis, the persuasion of advertisements, to translanguaging and identities, to discourse and cohesion in Alzheimer's patients, among others. This approach at the onset marks a significant departure from previous book publications which were either sociolinguistically-, methodologically- or politically-oriented. Consequently, the volume opens doors for new, insightful discussions in the rich context of Indonesia's sociolinguistic environment.

I welcome this edited volume, which makes a case for an academic text in higher education in the country and beyond. Further, I sincerely hope the volume will serve as an impetus for further research, inspiring graduate students, scholars and researchers alike to investigate a plethora of questions worth examining in new forms of applied linguistics research that are analytically rigorous and methodologically robust.

December 2023   Subhan Zein
Universitas Pendidikan Indonesia
Bandung, Indonesia

References

Abas, H. (1987). *Indonesian as a unifying language of wider communication: A historical and sociolinguistic perspective*. Pacific Linguistics, ANU Press.
Alisjahbana, S. T. (1949) *Tatabahasa Baru Bahasa Indonesia*. Dian Rakyat.
Alisjahbana, S. T. (1976). *Language planning for modernization: The case of Indonesia and Malaysia*. De Gruyter Mouton.
Alwasilah, A. C. (1997). *Politik bahasa dan pendidikan*. Rosdakarya.
Dardjowidjojo, S. (1978). *Sentence patterns in Indonesian*. University of Hawai'i Press.
Djenar, D., Ewing, M., & Manns, H. (2018). *Style and intersubjectivity in youth interaction*. De Gruyter Mouton.
Errington, J. J. (1998). *Shifting languages: Interaction and identity in Javanese Indonesia*. Cambridge University Press.
Foulcher, K., Moriyama, M., & Budiman, M. (Eds.). (2012). *Words in motion: Language and discourse in Post-New Order Indonesia*. Research Institute for Languages and Cultures of Asia and Africa.
Goebel, Z. (2010). *Language, migration, and identity neighbourhood talk in Indonesia*. Cambridge University Press.
Goebel, Z. (2015). *Language and superdiversity: Indonesians knowledging at home and abroad*. Oxford University Press.
Heryanto, A. (1995). *Language of development and development of language: The case of Indonesia*. Pacific Linguistics, ANU Press.
Kuipers, J. C. (1998). *Language, identity, and marginality in Indonesia: The changing nature of ritual speech on the island of Sumba*. Cambridge University Press.
Latif, Y., & Ibrahim, I. S. (Eds.) (1996). *Bahasa dan kekuasaan: Politik wacana di panggungOrde Baru*. Mizan.
Moeliono, A. (1986). *Language development and cultivation: Alternative approaches in language planning*. Pacific Linguistics, ANU Press.
Sneddon, J. (2003). *The Indonesian language: Its history and role in modern society*. The University of New South Wales Press.
Sneddon, J. (2006). *Colloquial Jakartan Indonesian*. ANU Pacific Linguistics.
Sugiharto, S. (2015). Disentangling linguistic imperialism in English language education: The Indonesian context. In M. Bigelow & J. Ennser-Kananen (Eds.), *The Routledge handbook of educational linguistics* (pp. 224–236). Routledge.
Zein, S. (Ed.). (2018). *Teacher education for English as a lingua franca: Perspectives from Indonesia*. Routledge.
Zein, S. (2020). *Language policy in superdiverse Indonesia*. Routledge.

Zein, S., Sukyadi, D., Hamied, F. A., & Lengkanawati, N. S. (2020). English language education in Indonesia (2011–2019): A review of research. *Language Teaching, 53*(4), 491–523. 10.1017/S0261444820000208

Zentz, L. (2017). *Statehood, scale and hierarchy: History, language and identity in Indonesia.* Multilingual Matters.

Contents

Part I Introduction

1 **Applied Linguistics in the Social Sciences and the Indonesian Context** 3
Richmond Stroupe and Lilie M. Roosman

Part II Education and Linguistics

2 **The Diffusion of English-Medium Instruction at Higher Education in Indonesia: Towards English as an Academic Lingua Franca** 15
Syariful Muttaqin, Hsueh-Hua Chuang, and Han-Chin Liu

3 **The Indonesian Assessment of Early Grade Reading (EGRA) and Beginning Reading Evaluation** 35
Harwintha Anjarningsih

4 **Students' Motivation in Learning English as a Foreign Language Through Discovery Learning** 51
Sabrina Asrianty Putri and Sisilia Setiawati Halimi

5 **Analysis of the Indonesian Cultural Elements in Secondary School English Textbooks Published by KEMENDIKBUD** 79
Alemina Br. Perangin-angin, Desri Maria Sumbayak, Lara Desma, Siti Patimah, and Indah Putri Tamala

6 **A Preliminary Report: Examining Pre-service Teacher Education, Teaching Practices, and Linguistic Diversity in the Indonesian Context** 97
Richmond Stroupe and Sisilia Setiawati Halimi

Part III Corpus Linguistics

7 **Semantic Cognitive Analysis of Chinese Language VO Collocation** 117
Symphony Akelba Christian and Hermina Sutami

8 **Collocation of Preposition *Terhadap* in Indonesian Language: A Corpus-Based Analysis** 137
Raya Jayawati Ratnawilis Amanah Notonegoro and Totok Suhardijanto

9 **Claiming Importance of Research: A Corpus Linguistics Analysis on Indonesian Students' Research Papers** 155
Risa Rumentha Simanjuntak

10 **N-gram Based Authorship Analysis in Indonesian Text: Evidence Case Study in Authorship Dispute Cases** 181
Devi Ambarwati Puspitasari, Adi Sutrisno, and Hanif Fakhrurroja

Part IV Critical Discourse Analysis

11 **The Persuasive Power of Advertisements: An Analysis of Structure and Context in Javanese in 1935–1953** 199
Diah Mardiningrum Joyowidarbo, Atin Fitriana, and Dwi Puspitorini

12 **Understanding Promises from the Perspective of Argumentation: The Cases from Presidential Debates** 223
Dwi Purwanto and Filia

13 **The Development of the Uses of the Word *dengan* from Indonesian Newspaper Period 1910–2010** 239
Gita Ayodhiya Sanarta and Dien Rovita

14 **Connecting Texts and Thoughts: How Translanguaging and Multilingual Writings Reflect Hybrid Identities in Colonial Times** 261
Afwa Zakia Al Azkaf, Nurenzia Yannuar, Yazid Basthomi, and Yusnita Febrianti

Part V Clinical Linguistics

15 Superstructure of Discourse and Cohesion in Narratives Spoken by People with Alzheimer's 279
Nailah Azkiya and Untung Yuwono

16 Time Reference and Telicity in Agrammatic Aphasia in Bahasa Indonesia 291
Siti Eka Soniawati, Harwintha Anjarningsih, and Myrna Laksman-Huntley

Contributors

Afwa Zakia Al Azkaf Department of English, Universitas Negeri Malang, Malang, Indonesia

Harwintha Anjarningsih Linguistics Departement, Faculty of Humanities, Universitas Indonesia, Depok, Jawa Barat, Indonesia

Nailah Azkiya Indonesian Study Program, Faculty of Humanities, Universitas Indonesia, Jakarta, Indonesia

Yazid Basthomi Department of English, Universitas Negeri Malang, Malang, Indonesia

Symphony Akelba Christian Linguistics Department, Faculty of Humanities, Universitas Indonesia, Depok, Indonesia

Hsueh-Hua Chuang National Sun Yat-Sen University, Kaohsiung, Taiwan

Lara Desma Faculty of Cultural Sciences, Universitas Sumatera Utara, Medan City, Indonesia

Hanif Fakhrurroja Research Center for Language, Literature, and Community, National Research and Innovation Agency of Republic Indonesia, Jakarta, Indonesia

Yusnita Febrianti Department of English, Universitas Negeri Malang, Malang, Indonesia

Filia Universitas Indonesia, Jakarta, Indonesia

Atin Fitriana Faculty of Humanities, Javanese Literature, Universitas Indonesia, Jakarta, Indonesia

Sisilia Setiawati Halimi Univesitas Indonesia, Depok, Indonesia; Linguistics Department, Faculty of Humanities, Universitas Indonesia, Jawa Barat, Indonesia

Diah Mardiningrum Joyowidarbo Faculty of Humanities, Javanese Literature, Universitas Indonesia, Jakarta, Indonesia

Myrna Laksman-Huntley Linguistics Departement, Faculty of Humanities, Universitas Indonesia, Depok, Indonesia

Han-Chin Liu National Chiayi University, Chiayi City, Taiwan

Syariful Muttaqin Universitas Brawijaya, Malang, Indonesia

Raya Jayawati Ratnawilis Amanah Notonegoro Indonesian Language and Literature Department, Faculty of Humanities, Universitas Indonesia, Depok, Indonesia

Siti Patimah Faculty of Cultural Sciences, Universitas Sumatera Utara, Medan City, Indonesia

Alemina Br. Perangin-angin Faculty of Cultural Sciences, Universitas Sumatera Utara, Medan City, Indonesia

Dwi Purwanto Universitas Indonesia, Jakarta, Indonesia

Devi Ambarwati Puspitasari Research Center for Language, Literature, and Community, National Research and Innovation Agency of Republic Indonesia, Jakarta, Indonesia

Dwi Puspitorini Faculty of Humanities, Javanese Literature, Universitas Indonesia, Jakarta, Indonesia

Sabrina Asrianty Putri English Studies Program, Faculty of Humanities, Universitas Indonesia, Jawa Barat, Indonesia

Lilie M. Roosman Linguistics Department, Faculty of Humanities, Universitas Indonesia, West Java, Indonesia

Dien Rovita Department of Linguistics, Faculty of Humanities, University of Indonesia, Jakarta, Indonesia

Gita Ayodhiya Sanarta Indonesian Studies, Faculty of Humanities, University of Indonesia, Jakarta, Indonesia

Risa Rumentha Simanjuntak Research Interest Group Digital Language and Behavior, Bina Nusantara University, Kebon Jeruk, Indonesia;
English Department, Faculty of Humanities, Bina Nusantara University, Jakarta, Indonesia

Siti Eka Soniawati Linguistics Departement, Faculty of Humanities, Universitas Indonesia, Depok, Indonesia

Richmond Stroupe Graduate School of Letters, World Language Center, Soka University, Hachiōji, Tokyo, Japan

Totok Suhardijanto Linguistics Department, Faculty of Humanities, Universitas Indonesia, Depok, Indonesia

Desri Maria Sumbayak Faculty of Cultural Sciences, Universitas Sumatera Utara, Medan City, Indonesia

Hermina Sutami Linguistics Department, Faculty of Humanities, Universitas Indonesia, Depok, Indonesia

Adi Sutrisno Faculty of Cultural Sciences, Universitas Gadjah Mada, Yogyakarta, Indonesia

Indah Putri Tamala Faculty of Cultural Sciences, Universitas Sumatera Utara, Medan City, Indonesia

Nurenzia Yannuar Department of English, Universitas Negeri Malang, Malang, Indonesia

Untung Yuwono Indonesian Study Program, Faculty of Humanities, Universitas Indonesia, Jakarta, Indonesia

Part I
Introduction

Chapter 1
Applied Linguistics in the Social Sciences and the Indonesian Context

Richmond Stroupe and Lilie M. Roosman

Abstract The field of applied linguistics has developed out of traditional linguistics research with a unifying focus on the relationship between theory and practice. This introductory chapter discusses how the field of applied linguistics has broadened to encompass multidisciplinary research while investigating practical language issues with the goal of addressing "real-world" problems. Researchers in the field now investigate diverse, contemporary topics such as language education, corpus linguistics, second language acquisition, English as a lingua franca, and the intersection of language with culture, gender, media, and other social variables and constructs. This introductory chapter highlights recent contributions to the field by local researchers, and also presents how the sections in this volume further contribute to the body of applied linguistics knowledge, providing insights from the multilingual, multicultural context of Indonesia. The authors in these sections focus on research areas including the relationship between linguistics and education, corpus linguistics, language use in society and media, and clinical linguistics. This volume provides an opportunity to raise the awareness of non-Western perspectives and research in applied linguistics, enriches understanding in the field, and offers insight into the diverse social and linguistic contexts of Indonesia.

Keywords Applied linguistics · Language, culture and society · Multicultural and multilingual · Applied linguistics in Indonesia · Non-Western research perspectives

---

R. Stroupe (✉)
Graduate School of Letters, World Language Center, Soka University, Hachiōji, Tokyo, Japan
e-mail: richmond@soka.ac.jp

L. M. Roosman
Linguistics Department, Faculty of Humanities, Universitas Indonesia, West Java, Indonesia
e-mail: liliemroosman@ui.ac.id

1.1 Introduction

Language permeates every aspect of our personal lives, communities, and interactions and relationships. At the same time, our use of language does not exist in a vacuum but is rather influenced by purpose and intention, both implicit and explicit, as well as social, cultural, and educational variables, among others. In multicultural and multilingual contexts, such variables can have an even more complex interplay. Examining this diverse landscape in which language is used can lead to better understanding and potentially answer questions and offer solutions to problems regarding language use and its influence on individuals and groups. It is this academic space that linguistics and applied linguistics aim to strengthen.

The field of applied linguistics has grown out of other academic fields, most notably linguistics, which has stimulated ongoing discussions and debates about its place and purpose in academic research. A literature survey indicates no distinct, agreed-upon definition of applied linguistics (Candlin & Sarangi, 2004; Davies, 2007; Michieka, 2011). This lack of consensus has often been criticized especially by researchers who focus on traditional linguistics (Davies, 2007; Harris, 2001). One consistent characteristic that has been highlighted when describing the field of applied linguistics seems to be the "relationship between knowledge, theory, and practice in the field of language" (McCarthy, 2001, as cited by Sánchez, 2007, p. 99). While there appears to be a broad agreement that the ability of research to inform "practice" is a central component of applied linguistics (Harris, 2002; Sánchez, 2007), even here, the role of "practice" remains unclear. Whether practice informs theory or vice versa remains a point of discussion and contention in the literature (Harris, 2002). Nevertheless, studies that focus on how practice can address real-world problems seems to be a driving factor for the field of applied linguistics (Al Alami, 2015; Davies, 2007; Michieka, 2011; Sánchez, 2007).

Applied linguistics emerged in the middle of the last century, when university campuses established programs with this focus (Davies, 2007; Harris, 2002; Li, 2014). What followed was the establishment of academic journals and professional associations that cater to this field of inquiry, the most prominent of which were the International Association of Applied Linguistics (AILA), the British Association for Applied Linguistics (BAAL), and the American Association for Applied Linguistics (AAAL) (Harris, 2002). Yet the development of a concise definition of applied linguistics becomes especially difficult when considering the specific research areas of these organizations, including language education, corpus linguistics, young learner education, culture, and society, research methodology, second-language acquisition, English as a lingua franca, English as an additional language, language and gender/sexuality, media, sports, and academic English (American Association for Applied Linguistics, 2021; International Association of Applied Linguistics, 2021; British Association for Applied Linguistics, 2021). Emerging from a field that primarily focused on language acquisition and educational pedagogy (Davies, 2007; Marqués-Pascual & Spencer-Rodgers, 2016), applied linguistics has broadened to include an array of topic areas. At the same time, the central focus remains that inquiry in the field is based on multidisciplinary research that aims to offer strategies to solve real-world problems and address real-world issues (Al Alami, 2015; Bocanegra-Valle, 2020; Candlin & Sarangi, 2004; Davies, 2007; Li, 2014; Michieka, 2011; Sánchez, 2007).

This edited volume does not intend to resolve the debate on the place of applied linguistics in the broader definition of related academic fields. Rather, the authors of the chapters seek to enrich the body of knowledge within linguistics and applied linguistics, providing insights into the specific context of Indonesia and raising awareness of non-Western-centric research being conducted in what Kachru termed as the expanding circle of countries using English (Kachru, 1985). Growing out of traditional research within these fields and being enhanced by the multilingual and multicultural context of Indonesia, research on these areas in this region is vibrant and extensive. Indeed, studies have been prolific in the areas covered by this specific volume, namely, education in linguistics, society and linguistics, and clinical linguistics.

As a primary focus of applied linguistics, the relation between education and linguistics in the Indonesian context has been well researched. The learning environments associated with the motivation of second-language learners (Baroto, 2016), the use of scaffolding techniques (Isnaini et al., 2015), error correction and feedback in grammar instruction (Dofir, 2018), and the implementation of project-based learning approaches (Handrianto & Rahman, 2018) have been examined in connection with educational practices within Indonesian classrooms. Scholars have also investigated culture with a focus on developing intercultural communicative competence (Permatasari & Andriyanti, 2021) and the extent to which English language education and associated cultural aspects intersect with Indonesian culture (Yamin, 2017). Recent publications have shifted their focus toward instruction centering on critical thinking skills, including an emphasis on assessment (Damaianti et al., 2020), teachers' question formation (Gozali et al., 2021), metacognitive thinking processes (Murtadho, 2021), development of reasoning skills (Suharno & Setyarini, 2021), literature analysis (Mufidah, 2017), and the adoption of a critical literacy approach in a study of Indonesian short stories (Halimah et al., 2020). Highlighting the urgency to implement online learning during the recent coronavirus pandemic, Widyaningsih (2018) investigated methods of providing corrective feedback through online technologies, and Suryadi (2021) examined how teaching materials must be revised to meet students' needs in online learning environments. The investigation of specific aspects of teaching practice in the Indonesian context remains an important focus and contribution of research in this field.

With regard to media and how language is used in society, studies have investigated the occurrence of code-switching in advertisements (Saputra, 2018), lexical and contextual meaning in sports articles (Sucihati, 2021), and language use in Indonesian newspapers (Rafida, 2017; Rahman, 2019; Santosa et al., 2014). Specifically, with respect to research journal articles, Kurniawan and Sabila (2021) and Tocalo (2021) examined the extent of prevalence of move patterns and other linguistic features in abstracts. Regarding actual journal articles, Kurniawan et al. (2019) explored how logical connectors were used in research writing. Culture and language diversity remains a key research area in the field, exemplified by an investigation of the influences of regional languages and how Indonesia's different language systems shape language acquisition (Zen, 2020).

One characteristic of a clinical linguistics approach is the investigation of language disorders. Scholars have often discussed the development of effective educational approaches and teaching practices when working with autism spectrum disorder students. Lasintia et al. (2021), Padmadewi and Artini (2017), Farihat (2020), and Yufrizal et al. (2020) examined effective teaching strategies and practices that address the needs of this unique group of learners and facilitate their academic achievement. Likewise, Friantary et al. (2020) investigated how best to support dyslexic students when acquiring Indonesian reading skills, and Desmita and Machrus (2019) studied the potential benefits of role model strategies for hyperactive children studying English. In a more general sense, Wibowo and Muin (2018) reviewed studies that focus on the development of inclusive schools in response to Indonesian government initiatives, while Efendi (2018) evaluated schools that provide appropriate facilities and support for learners. Finally, language issues related to specific disorders, such as *latah*, have also been investigated (Mubarok et al., 2020). This volume builds on these studies and contributes to the knowledge in the field in these areas.

The first section of this volume discusses research on applied linguistics conducted in educational settings. Syariful Muttaqin, Hsueh-Hua Chuang, and Han-Chin Liu (**Chap. 2**) examined the increasing prevalence of English-medium instruction (EMI) at Indonesian universities. Using quantitative and qualitative data, the perceived advantages and disadvantages of EMI, and students' attitudes towards such instruction, were investigated, concluding in results that indicated these factors were related to students' intentions to enroll in such courses. Harwintha Anjarningsih (**Chap. 3**) determined whether the Reading Meaningful Words subtest of the Indonesian Assessment of Early Grade Reading (EGRA) effectively assesses the decoding skills of primary-age learners. Working with 15 3rd graders, the author analyzed assessment scores and determined that the EGRA would benefit from several recommended revisions. Focusing on teaching pedagogy, Sabrina Asrianty Putri, and Sisilia Setiawati Halimi (**Chap. 4**) investigated the impact of discovery-based English language learning on students' motivation. Adopting quantitative and qualitative data analyses, the authors provided insights into learners' motivation and recommended the implementation of a discovery learning approach to improve English language learning and teaching. Alemina Br. Perangin-angin, Desri Maria Sumbayak, Lara Desma, Siti Patimah, and Indah Putri Tamala (**Chap. 5**) considered the cultural elements present in secondary school English textbooks published by KEMENDIKBUD (Ministry of Education, Culture, Research, and Technology). Their findings indicated that the images used in the English textbooks illustrate aspects of Indonesian culture, including the social organization of nuclear families and communities, living equipment and technology, art represented by musical instruments and narrative folklore, and the religious system represented by Muslim culture. Focusing on secondary teacher preparation and secondary teaching practice, Richmond Stroupe and Sisilia Setiawati Halimi (**Chap. 6**) investigated novice teachers' readiness to work effectively with students in the multilingual and multicultural Indonesian context. The

1 Applied Linguistics in the Social Sciences and the Indonesian Context

beliefs and practices of current teachers and educational leaders (principles, etc.) were examined to determine the extent to which translanguaging pedagogy, the use of multiple languages, and the implementation of 21st-century skills that are being integrated into teaching practice based on the current national curriculum. Considering these contributions as a whole, several useful recommendations have been provided that could address some challenges faced by teachers, learners, and the educational system as a whole in Indonesia.

The second section in this volume highlights research in the area of corpus linguistics. Focusing on Chinese VO collocations, Symphony Akelba Christian and Hermina Sutami (**Chap. 7**) observed differences that affect the formation of VO collocations. They concluded that their findings could provide useful insights for teachers, students, and material designers. In addition, Raya Jayawati Ratnawilis Amanah Notonegoro and Totok Suhardijanto (**Chap. 8**) conducted corpus-based analyses utilizing the Korpus Universitas Indonesia to examine the collocation patterns of the preposition *terhadap*. Again, the researchers stated that their results would benefit not only other linguistic researchers but also the field of language education. Risa Rumentha Simanjuntak (**Chap. 9**) utilized corpus analysis to identify the lexical use and context of the use of rhetorical markers by students. The results of this study identified the most frequent strategies students used to claim importance of their research, and the author recommended providing students with additional lexical strategies to demonstrate the rigor of their research and improve the quality of their writing. N-gram tracing was utilized to determine the authorship of anonymous texts in the research conducted by Devi Ambarwati Puspitasari, Adi Sutrisno and Hanif Fakhrurroja (**Chap. 10**). Through determining, tracing, and computing N-grams in texts both at the character and word levels, defining characteristics of authors' profiles could be distinguished, thereby demonstrating the possible importance of such analyses in legal cases. The chapters in this section demonstrate how corpus linguistics can be utilized in a variety of research contexts.

The third section of the volume highlights research in the area of critical discourse analysis. The first chapter, authored by Diah Mardiningrum Joyowidarbo, Atin Fitriana, and Dwi Puspitorini (**Chap. 11**), examines advertisements in the Javanese language magazine *Panjebar Semangat* from 1935 to 1953. The authors' analysis of persuasive power, which covers the period before and after independence, indicated that Dutch influence was evident in the former period whereas national ideas were more prevalent in advertisements in the latter period. Based on data collected from the debates during the 2019 Indonesian presidential election, Dwi Purwanto and Filia (**Chap. 12**) investigated argumentative commitments and determined that in a political context, promises may consist of both the commitment indicator and backing. The content of Indonesian newspapers from 1910 to 2010 provides the basis for the next chapter in this section. Here, Gita Ayodhiya Sanarta and Dien Rovita (**Chap. 13**) explained how their findings shed light on the use of the preposition *dengan* and its associated collocations. The final chapter in this section examines how hybrid identities during the colonial period are demonstrated through authors' translanguaging and multilingual writings. Afwa Zakia Al Azkaf, Nurenzia Yannuar, Yazid Basthomi and Yusnita Febrianti (**Chap. 14**) based their research on textual data from Indonesian newspapers published in the 1930s and 1970s, and demonstrated how a writer utilized different languages in different contexts, thereby illustrating his hybrid self identity while maintaining loyalty to one primary identity. From historical as well as more contemporary perspectives, the chapters in this section highlight results which can emerge from the use of critical discourse analysis.

The final section of this volume focuses on clinical linguistics. In a submission that examines the superstructure of discourse and cohesion evident in spoken narratives provided by patients with Alzheimer's, Nailah Azkiya and Untung Yuwono (**Chap. 15**) observe that encouraging patients to describe their memories allows medical practitioners to better support them. Patients with mild Alzheimer's could minimize the degeneration process of their disease when they recall memorable events or situations in their past. The final chapter in this section is by Siti Eka Soniawati, Harwintha Anjarningsih, and Myrna Laksman-Huntley (**Chap. 16**), who investigated the degree of difficulty experienced by agrammatic speakers in argument structure and time reference. This clinical focus on linguistic research could provide insight into the best ways to support and work with patients with these diagnoses.

This volume presents a small sample of ongoing dynamic studies in the fields of linguistics and applied linguistics within the academic community in Indonesia. With its rich multilingual and multicultural background, Indonesia's unique context allows for a further investigation of the relation among language, education, society, and clinical applications, as well as other research areas. The editors and authors of this text believe that the research and findings included in the current volume strengthen the overall body of knowledge in these fields and highlight the contemporary opportunities and investigative possibilities not only in Indonesia but also in the broader Southeast Asian and Asian regions.

References

Al Alami, S. A. (2015). Research within the field of applied linguistics: Points to consider. *Theory and Practice in Language Studies*, *5*(7), 1330–1337. https://doi.org/10.17507/tpls.0507.03

American Association for Applied Linguistics. (2021). *About AAAL*. American Association for Applied Linguistics. https://www.aaal.org/about-us

Baroto, M. A. A. (2016). The effects of language input, learning environment, and motivation toward second language acquisition. *LET: Linguistics, Literature and English Teaching Journal*, *6*(2). https://doi.org/10.18592/let.v6i2.1456

Bocanegra-Valle, A. (Ed.). (2020). *Applied linguistics and knowledge transfer*. Peter Lang. https://doi.org/10.4000/asp.7522

British Association for Applied Linguistics. (2021). *Special interest groups (SIGs)*. British Association for Applied Linguistics. https://www.baal.org.uk/what-we-do/special-interest-groups/

Candlin, C. N., & Sarangi, S. (2004). Making applied linguistics matter. *Journal of Applied Linguistics and Professional Practice*, *1*(1), 1–8. https://doi.org/10.1558/japl.v1.i1.1

Damaianti, V. S., Abidin, Y., & Rahma, R. (2020). Higher order thinking skills-based reading literacy assessment instrument: An Indonesian context. *Indonesian Journal of Applied Linguistics*, *10*(2), 513–525. https://doi.org/10.17509/ijal.v10i2.28600

Davies, A. (2007). *An introduction to applied linguistics* (2nd ed.). Edinburgh University Press.

Desmita, N., & Machrus, M. A. (2019). His strength is my strategies: Experience of an English teacher in Indonesia teaching English for hyperactive students in inclusive class. *Journal of Advanced Research in Social Sciences and Humanities*, *4*(2), 66–73. https://doi.org/10.26500/JARSSH-04-2019-0204

Dofir, D. (2018). Second language acquisition based on grammatical rule for the first semester of Tadris Bahasa Inggris Department at STAI Mempawah. *LET: Linguistics, Literature and English Teaching Journal*, *8*(2), 177–188. https://doi.org/10.18592/let.v8i2.2398

Efendi, M. (2018). The implementation of inclusive education in Indonesia for children with special needs: Expectation and reality. *Journal of ICSAR*, *2*(2), 142–147. https://doi.org/10.17977/um005v2i22018p142

Farihat, W. N., & Chairudin, C. (2020). The portrait of autism language disorder of Indonesian students (linguistics study). *SELL Journal: Scope of English Language Teaching, Linguistics, and Literature*, *5*(1), 58–66. http://194.59.165.171/index.php/SL/article/view/359

Friantary, H., Afriani, Z. L., & Nopitasari, Y. (2020). The implementation of Indonesian language learning for dyslexic in children at elementary schools in Bengkulu. *Linguists: Journal of Linguistics and Language Teaching*, *6*(2), 23–29. https://doi.org/10.29300/ling.v6i2.3750

Gozali, I., Lie, A., Tamah, S. M., & Jemadi, F. (2021). HOTS questioning ability and HOTS perception of language teachers in Indonesia. *Indonesian Journal of Applied Linguistics*, *11*(1), 60–71. https://doi.org/10.17509/ijal.v11i1.34583

Halimah, H., Mulyati, Y., & Damaianti, V. S. (2020). Critical literacy approach in the teaching of literary appreciation using Indonesian short stories. *Indonesian Journal of Applied Linguistics*, *10*(1), 84–94. https://doi.org/10.17509/ijal.v10i1.24992

Handrianto, C., & Rahman, M. A. (2018). Project based learning: A review of literature on its outcomes and implementation issues. *LET: Linguistics, Literature and English Teaching Journal*, *8*(2), 110–129. https://doi.org/10.18592/let.v8i2.2394

Harris, T. (2002). Linguistics in applied linguistics: A historical overview. *Journal of English Studies*, *3*(2), 99–114. https://doi.org/10.18172/jes.72

International Association of Applied Linguistics. (2021). *AILA research networks*. International Association of Applied Linguistics. https://aila.info/about/

Isnaini, Y., Saukah, A., & Prayogo, J. A. (2015). Using scaffolding technique to improve the writing ability of the 11th graders of SMAN 5 Mataram. *LET: Linguistics, Literature and English Teaching Journal*, *5*(2), 95–113. https://doi.org/10.18592/let.v5i2.1444

Kachru, B. B. (1985). Standards, codification and sociolinguistic realism: The English language in the outer circle. In R. Quirk & H. G. Widowson (Eds.), *English in the world: Teaching and learning the language and literatures* (pp. 11–30). Cambridge University Press.

Kurniawan, E., & Sabila, N. A. A. (2021). Another look at the rhetorical moves and linguistic realizations in international and Indonesian journal articles: A case of tourism research. *Indonesian Journal of Applied Linguistics*, *11*(2), 318–329. https://doi.org/10.17509/ijal.v11i2.32055

Kurniawan, E., Ruswan, D., & Cahyowati, A. (2019). Exploring logical connectors in journals with different indexing levels: A comparison between international and national indexed journals. *Indonesian Journal of Applied Linguistics*, *9*(1), 76–84. https://doi.org/10.17509/ijal.v9i1.16088

Lasintia, M., Prihantoro, P., Edy, S., & Ariani, D. (2021). English language teaching strategy for ASD (Autism Spectrum Disorder) students. *Linguists: Journal of Linguistics and Language Teaching*, *7*(1), 77–93. https://doi.org/10.29300/ling.v7i1.4247

Li, F. (2014). Current situation and development trend of applied linguistics. Advances in social science, education and humanities research. In *Proceedings of the 2014 international conference on education technology and social science* (pp. 132–136). Atlantis Press. https://doi.org/10.2991/icetss-14.2014.28

Marqués-Pascual, L., & Spencer-Rodgers, J. (2016). Applied linguistics research at the service of classroom practices: Bridging connections. *Journal of New Approaches in Educational Research, 5*(2), 64–65. https://doi.org/10.7821/naer.2016.7.200

Michieka, M. M. (2011). Language in education and the role of applied linguistics in Kenya. *Journal of Language, Technology and Entrepreneurship in Africa, 3*(1), 1–18. https://doi.org/10.4314/jolte.v3i1.66559

Mubarok, A., Rahman, F., & Fajrianor, F. (2020). Latah: A clinical linguistic review. *LET: Linguistics, Literature and English Teaching Journal, 10*(1), 66–85. https://doi.org/10.18592/let.v10i1.3845

Mufidah, N. (2017). The study of naturalism on a thousand splendid sun novel. *LET: Linguistics, Literature and English Teaching Journal, 3*(2), 95–105. https://doi.org/10.18592/let.v3i2.1390

Murtadho, F. (2021). Metacognitive and critical thinking practices in developing EFL students' argumentative writing skills. *Indonesian Journal of Applied Linguistics, 10*(3), 656–666. https://doi.org/10.17509/ijal.v10i3.31752

Padmadewi, N. N., & Artini, L. P. (2017). Teaching English to a student with autism spectrum disorder in regular classroom in Indonesia. *International Journal of Instruction, 10*(3), 159–176. https://doi.org/10.12973/iji.2017.10311a

Permatasari, I., & Andriyanti, E. (2021). Developing students' intercultural communicative competence through cultural text-based teaching. *Indonesian Journal of Applied Linguistics, 11*(1), 72–82. https://doi.org/10.17509/ijal.v11i1.34611

Rafida, T. (2017). The English blending words in Indonesian's newspapers. *LET: Linguistics, Literature and English Teaching Journal, 6*(2). https://doi.org/10.18592/let.v6i2.1457

Rahman, Y. A. (2019). Lexical cohesion of English language newspapers in Indonesia. *Jurnal Akrab Juara, 4*(1), 161–168.

Sánchez, W. (2007). On the nature of applied linguistics: Theory and practice relationships from a critical perspective. *GIST Education and Learning Research Journal, 1*, 98–114. https://latinjournal.org/index.php/gist/article/view/563

Santosa, R., Priyanto, A. D., & Nuraeni, A. (2014). Genre and register of antagonist's language in media: An appraisal study of Indonesian newspapers. *Kata, 16*(1), 23–36. https://doi.org/10.9744/kata.16.1.23-36

Saputra, M. (2018). An analysis of code-switching used in Honda advertisements in Indonesia. *IOSR Journal of Humanities and Social Science (IOSR-JHSS), 23*(4), 16–22.

Sucihati, T. B. (2021). An analysis of lexical and contextual meaning on sport news in Jawa Pos Newspaper (Linguistics Study). *BRIGHT: A Journal of English Language Teaching, Linguistics and Literature, 4*(1), 40–47. https://doi.org/10.29100/bright.v4i1.1816

Suharno, S., & Setyarini, S. (2021). Promoting EFL junior secondary students' critical thinking skills through analogical reasoning in narrative text. *Indonesian Journal of Applied Linguistics, 11*(1), 211–220. https://doi.org/10.17509/ijal.v11i1.34660

Suryadi, S. B. (2021). Needs analysis on English online learning in Informatics Technology Department, State Polytechnic of Malang. *BRIGHT: A Journal of English Language Teaching, Linguistics and Literature, 4*(2), 61–69. https://doi.org/10.29100/bright.v4i2.2064

Tocalo, A. W. I. (2021). Move structures and their rhetorical verbs of research article abstracts across Englishes. *Indonesian Journal of Applied Linguistics, 11*(1), 1–10. https://doi.org/10.17509/ijal.v11i1.34593

Wibowo, S. B., & Muin, J. A. (2018). Inclusive education in Indonesia: Equality education access for disabilities. *KnE Social Sciences, 3*(5), 484–493. https://doi.org/10.18502/kss.v3i5.2351

Widyaningsih, T. L. (2018). An analysis of online corrective feedback implementation in writing class. *BRIGHT: A Journal of English Language Teaching, Linguistics and Literature, 2*(1), 63–78. https://doi.org/10.29100/bright.v2i1.740

Yamin, M. (2017). English with Indonesia taste: Dominant culture shift to local culture. *LET: Linguistics, Literature and English Teaching Journal, 4*(1), 20–30. https://doi.org/10.18592/let.v4i1.1397

Yufrizal, H., Susanti, R. D., & Effendi, L. S. (2020). Language learning by autism spectrum disorder in an inclusive school in Indonesia. *Hamdard Islamicus, 43*(1), 369–384. http://repository.lppm.unila.ac.id/22252/

Zen, E. L. (2020). Role of regional language background and speech styles on the production of Voice Onset Time (VOT) in English among Indonesian multilinguals. *Indonesian Journal of Applied Linguistics, 10*(2), 359–368. https://doi.org/10.17509/ijal.v10i2.28604

Richmond Stroupe has worked with university and professional language learners from Asia since 1989. He a Ph.D. in International Comparative Education from the University of Southern California and has been involved in the development of language learning programs in a number of contexts. He is a professor at Soka University in Tokyo, Japan where he is currently the Chair of the Master's Program in International Language Education: TESOL. He is also an advisor of doctoral students in Applied Linguistics and English Language Teaching Pedagogy in the Graduate School of Letters at Soka University. Richmond has been active in a number of English teaching associations, including TESOL International, and he is the former President of the Japan Association for Language Teaching (JALT). Richmond regularly conducts workshops, publishes and presents on a variety of professional activities and research projects, which include teacher education practices, curriculum and professional development, and developing learners' critical thinking skills. Most recently, his research activities focus on developing frameworks for successful secondary education in limited resource areas, enhancing Global Citizenship Education, and the integration of Artificial Intelligence (AI) into language learning approaches.

Open Access This chapter is licensed under the terms of the Creative Commons Attribution 4.0 International License (http://creativecommons.org/licenses/by/4.0/), which permits use, sharing, adaptation, distribution and reproduction in any medium or format, as long as you give appropriate credit to the original author(s) and the source, provide a link to the Creative Commons license and indicate if changes were made.

The images or other third party material in this chapter are included in the chapter's Creative Commons license, unless indicated otherwise in a credit line to the material. If material is not included in the chapter's Creative Commons license and your intended use is not permitted by statutory regulation or exceeds the permitted use, you will need to obtain permission directly from the copyright holder.

Part II
Education and Linguistics

Chapter 2
The Diffusion of English-Medium Instruction at Higher Education in Indonesia: Towards English as an Academic Lingua Franca

Syariful Muttaqin, Hsueh-Hua Chuang, and Han-Chin Liu

Abstract There is an increasing trend in adopting English-medium instruction (EMI) as an academic lingua franca in response to higher education internationalization. Considered as an innovation in content teaching, its adoption rate at Indonesian higher education remains questionable. Using the Diffusion of Innovation (DOI) frameworks, this paper aims to explore the EMI attributes regarding its relative advantage, compatibility, complexity, trialability, and observability and to examine the relationships between the EMI perceived attributes and the attitudes and behavioral intention towards EMI among university students in the Indonesian context. This study is a mixed-method study. The quantitative data were collected using Likert-scale questionnaires from 125 students from two reputable universities, while the qualitative data were obtained through focus-group discussions. The quantitative data were statistically analyzed using *SmartPLS* to address the research problems. Thematic analysis was employed for the qualitative data for explaining and clarifying the quantitative findings. The findings show that EMI is considered very highly advantageous and compatible, highly observable and trialable, and surprisingly low in complexity to learn content courses. In addition, the EMI perceived relative advantages and compatibility that were predictive to the students' attitudes toward EMI. Finally, perceived relative advantages, trialability, and observability of EMI were predictive to the students' behavioral intention to enroll in EMI. EMI is therefore worth applying at higher education institutions in Indonesia as an approach to enhance both students' content understanding and English competence and to support Indonesian universities' internationalization vision.

S. Muttaqin (✉)
Universitas Brawijaya, Malang, Indonesia
e-mail: smuttaqin@ub.ac.id

H.-H. Chuang
National Sun Yat-Sen University, Kaohsiung, Taiwan
e-mail: hsuehhua@g-mail.nsysu.edu.tw

H.-C. Liu
National Chiayi University, Chiayi City, Taiwan
e-mail: hanchinliu@etech.ncyu.edu.tw

© The Author(s) 2025
R. Stroupe and L. Roosman (eds.), *Applied Linguistics in the Indonesian Context*, Engaging Indonesia, https://doi.org/10.1007/978-981-97-2336-2_2

Keywords English-medium instruction · Diffusion of innovation · Attitudes · And behavioral intention

2.1 Introduction

English-medium instruction (EMI) as an innovation has become more popular and has been widely used to teach content subjects in higher education institutions (HEIs) (Galloway et al., 2017). As English is now more positioned as a lingua franca, especially in academic settings, the promotion of EMI is considered crucial in response to globalization (Jenkins et al., 2011; Marlina & Xu, 2018). Aimed to expand students' knowledge of different academic disciplines (Macaro et al., 2018; Pecorari & Malmström, 2018; Wanphet & Tantawy, 2018), develop students' English professional expertise (Dearden, 2014), prepare students to take part in the international community (Doiz et al., 2011), and develop students' English, as a learning by-product (Wanphet & Tantawy, 2018), EMI has been diffused with quite different rates of adoption as an innovation (Macaro et al., 2018). This is due to some challenges faced by both teachers and students (Wu, 2006), such as insufficient levels of English proficiency (Shiamuchi, 2018), lack of infrastructure support facilities (Floris, 2014), and lack of clear guidelines (Dearden, 2014). A more fundamental step therefore should be directed to see how students perceive EMI's attributes, namely relative advantage, compatibility, complexity, trialability, and observability (Rogers, 2003) and how their perceived attributes affect their attitude and intentions towards adopting by using a Technology Acceptance Model (TAM) (Davis, 1989).

As warned by Venkatesh and Davis (2000), newly introduced systems will be useless, if the innovations, such as EMI, are not adopted or accepted by the intended users. In the Indonesian higher education context, EMI has been preferred to equip the university students with necessary knowledge and language skills, as well as intercultural skills to have a better future, especially in specific employment sectors, such as economics, business, or engineering (Dewi, 2017; Ibrahim, 2001; Simbolon, 2017). However, considering the status of English as a foreign language in Indonesia, students' decision to adopt EMI to develop their disciplinary knowledge is worthy of research due to the concern that content knowledge should not be sacrificed by the use of English rather than the Indonesian language in content delivery. Therefore, to investigate behavioral intent to adopt EMI by the students at an Indonesian university is worth studying by incorporating Rogers' (2003) DOI theory of attributes of innovation, namely relative advantage, compatibility, complexity, trialability, observability, and Davis' (1989) Technology Acceptance Model (TAM).

In addition, innovation adoption can be determined by the degree of attitudes of the adopters (Al-Zaidiyeen et al., 2010; Davis, 1989). According to Fishbein and Ajzen (1975) attitude is a tendency of someone in responding to an idea or an object as either valuable or unvaluable. With its intended purposes along with its complexities, EMI surely leads to different attitudes of its adopters, especially students as they are the actors in the EMI implementation. Furthermore, Venkatesh and Davis (2000) argued the role of attitude in influencing the adoption of a new system. In addition, attitude is important to determine behavioral intention (Mkhize et al., 2016), in this case towards taking EMI, among the students during their content learning. Furthermore, lecturers' readiness to apply EMI, such as their knowledge, skills, abilities, and attitudes, has been revealed in non-English speaking countries, like in Malaysia (Lo & Othman, 2023); however, a more important study should be geared towards looking at students' readiness to take EMI as they are the main agent in an EMI implementation (Dafouz & Smit, 2020).

Based on the abovementioned statements, this paper aims to examine the extent how EMI is perceived regarding its attributes, namely relative advantage, compatibility, complexity, trialability, and observability among the Indonesia university students and how the EMI perceived attributes affect the attitudes and behavioral intention of the university students towards adopting EMI.

2.2 Literature Review

2.2.1 English as a Lingua Franca in Academic Settings

As the world is becoming more globalized, the position of English turns into English as a lingua franca (ELF) which is defined as a contact language that is used by speakers from different language backgrounds (Jenkins et al., 2011). Here, speakers now converse, utilizing different varieties of English, in different contexts, which has become more acceptable without considering the necessity of native speaker equivalence (Marlina & Xu, 2018), such as in business, tourism, or academic settings. According to Mauranen (2003), one specific area of ELF in academic settings is English as a lingua franca in academic settings (ELFA). The adoption of ELFA has been driven by the prevalence and need of English as a medium of instruction in response to increased globalization, characterized by the more mainstream English, rather than native English (Jenkins et al., 2011). The phenomena of international publications, staff and student mobility, and academic collaboration thus require English to be more positioned as a lingua franca rather than as a learned subject in the higher education context. The emergence of English-medium instruction marks the stronger position of English as a lingua franca in an academic setting, especially in a university context, such as is the case in Europe (Jenkins et al., 2011) with the adoption of English-medium instruction at higher education institutions, as stated in the Bologna Process (Dafouz & Smit, 2020). As considered relatively new in Indonesia, a careful investigation on the diffusion of EMI is a worth taking study, which can indicate how Indonesian higher education institutions are moving towards adopting EMI as an approach to teach content courses for enhancing internationalization as in other Asian countries, such as Japan, Korea, China, and Taiwan.

2.2.2 EMI as an Innovation in Content Subject Teaching

Content teaching and learning is moving towards using English-medium instruction (EMI) in academic settings in non-English speaking countries (Dearden, 2014; Genesee, 1994). EMI is thus an *innovation,* that is an idea, practice, or object that is perceived as new by an individual or other unit of adoption (Rogers, 2003). Dearden (2014) defines EMI as "The use of the English language to teach academic subjects in countries or jurisdictions where the first language (L1) of the majority of the population is not English" (p. 2). Proponents of EMI argue that English in today's EFL teaching approach should be acquired in context (naturally) rather than just learned formally as a compulsory subject (Galloway et al., 2017; Pecorari & Malmström, 2018) for more meaningful and contextual learning with interactivity and authenticity in both input and output (Dearden, 2014). EMI is also a reinvention, a change or modification by a user in the process of adoption and implementation (Rogers, 2003), of previous models, namely content and language integrated learning (CLIL) in Europe (Genesee, 1994), immersion in Canada (Hau et al., 2000), bilingual teaching, and content-based instruction (CBI) (Galloway et al., 2017).

In spite of its practical benefits, such as intercultural understanding and global awareness/citizenship (Wanphet & Tantawy, 2018), a greater number of job opportunities, and job acceptance (Galloway et al., 2017), and added English improvement (Wanphet & Tantawy, 2018), a critical point should be addressed to respond to the possible difficulty of comprehending lectures, longer study completion time or even drop out, low class interaction, and rejection of EMI (Doiz et al., 2011).

2.2.3 Theoretical Framework

This study applied a trilogy of affect, cognition, and conation stated by Fishbein and Ajzen (1975), which have been much researched in relation to behavioral actions (Teo et al., 2009). Affect refers to a person's feeling toward and evaluation of some object, person, issue, or event; cognition denotes his knowledge, opinions, beliefs, and thoughts about the object; and conation refers to his behavioral intentions and his actions with respect to or in the presence of the object (Fishbein & Ajzen, 1975). These three domains are very important for measuring the adoption of an innovation, in this case EMI, as a breakthrough for content subject teaching. In addition, the English as a foreign language (EFL) context in Indonesia really matters in the use of English as a lingua franca in an academic or higher education interaction setting.

Then, attributes can be characterized by any trait, property, quality, characteristic, outcome or event related to an object (Fishbein & Ajzen, 1975). Regarding diffusion of EMI as an approach in teaching content subjects, whether to adopt or not and then how the rate of adoption will be, attributes of innovations have been seen as influential factors for innovation adoption (Dingfelder & Mandell, 2011). The term adoption is here then referred as behavioral action (Teo et al., 2009) to use EMI in learning content subjects either the students, in teaching the subjects by the lecturers, or in EMI policy making by university authorities. Thus, the degree of the perceived attributes of EMI are measures to determine the attitudes and the intention to adopt EMI by university students.

2.2.3.1 Diffusion of Innovation (DOI) Theory

According to Rogers (2003), diffusion is aimed to provide the users of innovation with necessary knowledge of the innovation that can determine the adoption process. Innovation attributes have been influential factors for adoption (Dingfelder & Mandell, 2011). Rogers (2003) proposed five attributes to the adoption of diffusions which consist of relative advantage (RA), compatibility (CP), complexity (CL), trialability (TR), and observability (OB).

Relative advantage is the degree to which an innovation is perceived as better than the idea being superseded, regarding economic, social, prestige, or convenience factors (Rogers, 2003). Realizing this advantage is related to taking any further action in the diffusion of innovation (Mkhize et al., 2016). Tanye (2016) recognized these as incentives for the acceptance of an innovation. In general, the greater the perceived relative advantage, the more rapid its rate of adoption will be (Rogers, 2003). The next attribute is compatibility which is the degree to which an innovation is perceived as being consistent or compatible with the existing values, past experiences, and needs of potential adopters (Rogers, 2003), and is highly correlated with the attitude towards an innovation (Mkhize et al., 2016). In addition, Duan et al. (2010) showed that compatibility significantly affected the adoption of an innovative learning system in a positive way.

Another attribute is complexity, which is the degree to which an innovation is perceived as difficult to understand and use (Rogers, 2003) due to being different from the mainstream practices or complicated. This is similar to Davis' (1989) technology acceptance model (TAM) concept, that is, ease-of-use concept to innovation acceptance. The more complicated an innovation, the slower the adoption will be as the innovation requires new skills and understandings (Rogers, 2003). Trialability is defined as the degree to which an innovation may be experimented with on a limited basis, with faster adoption being obtained when innovations are trialable (Rogers, 2003). Trialability is related to whether an innovation can be tried out in real practice or tested to see its applicability by conducting action research or experiments (Osborne, 2016). Finally, observability is the degree to which the results of an innovation are visible to others, where the more visible the results of an innovation are, the more likely they are to be adopted (Rogers, 2003), and is considered important in any innovative learning situation (Osborne, 2016). HEI policy makers or educators can enhance the degree of adoption of new teaching innovation by making explicit to their colleagues the innovations they are trialing (Osborne, 2016). The above attributes can determine the acceptance of an innovation, in this case EMI approach, as a breakthrough in teaching content courses in an English as a foreign language (EFL) context.

2.2.3.2 Technology Acceptance Model (TAM)

The Technology Acceptance Model (TAM) can be used to measure the adoption of technology by its potential users (Davis, 1989; Davis et al., 1989; Venkatesh & Davis, 2000) which refers to Theory of Reasoned Action (TRA) proposed by Fishbein and Ajzen (1975) stating how beliefs and attitudes are related to intentions to perform, in this case to adopt EMI. The model integrates both ease of use and usefulness as the basic determinants of innovation adoption (Davis, 1989). In the EMI context, along with the increasing attention to EMI students' intention to adopt EMI to ensure its effectiveness in the content teaching and learning needs to be emphasized. TAM is parsimonious as a model describing the interaction among personal beliefs (perceptions), attitudes, and intentions (Teo et al., 2009).

Therefore, based on TAM theory, the attributes consist of (1) usefulness, the extent to which a person believes that using the system will enhance his or her job performance, and (2) ease of use, the extent to which a person believes that using a system will be free of effort (Venkatesh & Davis, 2000) In addition, the behavioral intention (BI) covers many domains. The first is subjective norms, which is a person's perception that most people who are important to him think he should or should not perform the behavior in question (Fishbein & Ajzen, 1975). The next domain is voluntariness and compliance with social influence. Here, the potential adopters are aware that it is not compulsory to accept an innovation (Moore & den Benbasat, 1991). Then, BI requires internalization of social influence. This is the process in which an adopter of a system incorporates an important referent promoting that an innovation should be used (Warshaw, 1980). In addition, BI will influence someone's image and social status. Here, an adoption of a new system can increase the adopters' image and status in a society (Moore & den Benbasat, 1991). Another important factor is job relevance, that is the degree to which the target system is applicable to his or her job (Venkatesh & Davis, 2000). In addition, BI is also determined by the output quality, whether a system is capable of performing certain tasks and the degree to which those tasks are related to or match the job goals (Venkatesh & Davis, 2000). Finally, BI is affected by result demonstrability, which is the "tangibility of the results of using the innovation" (Moore & den Benbasat, 1991). Adopting these two most referred theories, this study therefore used four DOI attributes, relative advantage, compatibility, complexity, and observability as these are compatible with the TAM attributes.

2.2.3.3 Attitude

Attitude is "a learned predisposition to respond to an object or class of objects in a consistently favorable or unfavorable way" (Fishbein & Ajzen, 1975, p. 6) which can be positive or negative, depending on how an innovation adopter perceives an innovation. Attitude is believed as a key factor in innovation adoption (Al-Zaidiyeen et al., 2010; Davis, 1989; Venkatesh & Davis, 2000). Attitude was found to be correlated with attributes of innovation with compatibility as the strongest, compared to relative advantage and complexity which could be used to determine behavioral intention towards an innovation (Mkhize et al., 2016). Further, attitude was jointly determined by perceived usefulness and ease of use (Davies et al., 1989). Therefore, EMI policy makers are really supposed to accommodate students' attitude towards any policy in their educational activities, as positive attitude was contributive in students' success in learning (Gardner, 1985). However, little has been done to see how attitude has been influenced by students' perceived attributes and then affects students' intention in taking EMI course.

2.2.3.4 Behavioral Intention

Using the TRA concept, behavioral intention (BI) is believed to be determined by subjective attitude and subjective norms (Davis, 1989). BI is a measure of the strength of one's intention to perform a specified behavior (Fishbein & Ajzen, 1975). Meanwhile, SN is "the person's perception that most people who are important to him think he should or should not perform the behavior in question" (Fishbein & Ajzen, 1975, p. 302). Attitude and behavioral intention relationship implies that innovation adopters form intentions to perform behaviors toward which they have positive effect (Davies et al., 1989). Therefore, behavioral intention is determined by the perceived usefulness and attitude towards an innovation (Davis et al., 1989). Accordingly, a research model is proposed based on the theories and existing research findings (Fig. 2.1).

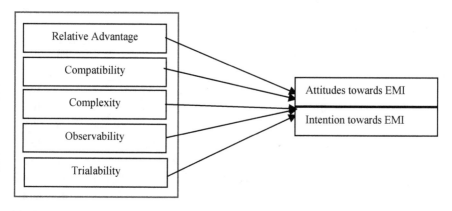

Fig. 2.1 Research model

2.3 Method

This research applied a mixed-methods approach. The quantitative data was obtained using a survey conducted online to the students at two reputable universities in East Java applying English medium instruction. The population of this study were the students from the two universities who were either enrolled in or not enrolled in an EMI class. They were from five study backgrounds: humanities, engineering, economics, agriculture, and social science fields. The sample was collected using purposive sampling with the aim to get more representative participants according to the purposes of this study to allow the fulfillment of specific criteria used to select the participants in the study. The distribution of the sample is presented in Table 2.1.

The survey instrument was designed by incorporating Rogers' (2003) theory of DOI attributes integrated with TAM consisting of four constructs, namely relative advantage, compatibility, complexity, and observability complemented by attitude and behavioral intention adopted from Davis (1989), as presented in Table 2.2.

The scale used five-point Likert scales from 1 (strongly disagree) to 5 (strongly agree). Expert and peer-reviews were conducted in order to construct a valid and reliable instrument followed by a pilot study to measure the degree of reliability of the instrument which was measured using Cronbach alpha (0.85). The questionnaire for this study was an online questionnaire, using a Google form platform. The students were invited to participate online to fill in the questionnaire of the study by distributing the link to the questionnaire along with the consent form statement of the students as participants and statement of the purpose of the study.

Table 2.1 Distribution of sample

Variables	Description	N	%
Gender	Female	88	70.4
	Male	37	29.6
Study program	English language	50	40.0
	Engineering	13	10.4
	Economics and business	26	20.8
	Agriculture	17	13.6
	Social sciences	19	15.2
Enrolled in EMI	No	42	33.6
	Yes	83	66.4
English proficiency	Basic	11	8.8
	Pre-intermediate	9	7.2
	Intermediate	47	37.6
	Upper intermediate	38	30.4
	Advanced	19	15.2
	Experts	1	0.8
Total		125	100

Table 2.2 Interconnection between DOI and TAM

DOI	TAM
Relative advantage (RA)	Usefulness Job relevance Output quality
Compatibility (COMPT)	Image and social influence Internalization of social influence Voluntariness and compliance with social influence Subjective norms
Complexity (COMPL)	Ease of use
Trialability (TRI)	
Observability (OBS)	Result demonstrability

The data of this study were transferred to an Excel file and were then transformed into an SPSS file for reliability check and *SmartPLS* software for data analysis. Data cleaning and coding were performed for different types of analysis. The two types of data analysis included were descriptive statistics to gain a better understanding of the data and inferential statistics performed to address the objectives of the study. The reliability of the data was shown to be high with the score of Cronbach Alpha 0.8 from the SPSS Analysis, indicating that the data were reliable for further analysis. Finally, multiple regression analysis was conducted to analyze the relationships of different constructs in the proposed model using *SmartPLS*.

The qualitative data were collected through a focus group discussion (FGD) involving 10 students from those answering the questionnaire and willing to participate in the discussion. These 10 students were from two majors: (1) humanities, and (2) social and political sciences. The FGD was intended to further explain and confirm the findings based on the quantitative findings. The FGD was recorded and then transcribed for further analysis. Using thematic analysis, the quantitative findings were explained and confirmed through the participants' responses to the questions in the FGD. Trustworthiness was obtained through peer checking of the transcribed data and participant debriefing for confirmation. Participants' names were pseudonyms to maintain confidentiality. The use of qualitative data was also necessary for triangulation of data collection and analysis of this study.

2.4 Findings

2.4.1 The Perceived Attributes of EMI

Regarding the EMI attributes, its relative advantages were perceived as the highest, with the mean of 4.22. Among taking EMI advantages, "EMI class helps me to improve my English." was considered the highest, followed by "I can widen my understanding about content subjects in my study", then "Taking EMI will enable me to accomplish my dream job more quickly", and finally "Taking EMI gives me higher prestige" (Table 2.3).

From the qualitative data, the EMI program has been confirmed as beneficial for the students as the theories in their classes mostly still used English texts, so they can learn more updated and wider knowledge. They also have more global perspectives in relation to their field of study, as stated by one of the participants below.

Brian: In my opinion, their understanding becomes more comprehensive, as there are a lot of references using English such as journal articles. So, when we have a basic in English in our course, that will develop our global perspectives.

In terms of language, the students also learned new vocabularies, new terms, and concepts, especially related to their disciplinary knowledge. Their listening and speaking skills were also improved as they were more involved in classroom interaction using English. The English references they have used in their EMI classes also helped them improve their reading ability. They also felt that their English proficiency score, such as CEPT, improved after some semesters following an EMI class. Finally, they expressed the benefit of following an EMI program for their future career. They stated that multinational companies require employees to be able to present in their job-related activities in English. Therefore, the experience in taking an EMI class was believed to increase their confidence in using English for their future career.

The next attribute considered very high was EMI compatibility with the mean of 4.09. EMI's compatibility regarding "EMI class is a response to face globalization" was the highest, followed by "Taking EMI can strengthen my understanding of other cultures", "My previous English learning experience enhances my EMI Class" and finally "Taking EMI fits with my study needs" (Table 2.4).

From the focus group discussion, EMI was believed to be compatible with the demand for the requirement to succeed in globalization era, that is to be able to communicate in English, not only for daily interaction, but for academic purposes. This is due to the fact that English is the lingua franca among the academics worldwide, but a more important emphasis is on how to deliver ideas, present arguments, express opinions, in global academic and job-related interactions. In addition, the social media platforms enable students and employees to interact interculturally and in being involved in interdisciplinary encounters, which requires being proficient in English, as stated by two of FGD participants below.

Table 2.3 Perceived relative advantage of EMI

Attributes	M	SD
I can widen my understanding about content subjects in my study	4.30	0.66
EMI class helps me to improve my English	4.54	0.559
Taking EMI will enable me to accomplish my dream job more quickly	4.05	0.714
Taking EMI gives me higher prestige	3.99	0.732
Overall mean	4.22	

Table 2.4 Perceived compatibility of EMI

Attributes	M	SD
EMI class is a response to face globalization	4.38	0.641
Taking EMI can strengthen my understanding of other cultures	3.96	0.709
My previous English learning experience enhances my EMI class	3.86	0.701
Taking EMI fits with my study needs	4.17	0.678
Overall mean	4.09	

Galih: Related to globalization, if we are talking about academic settings, we must be able to express our arguments either by supporting our ideas or strengthen our arguments when we present or argue with others.

Toni: Well, when we get information from international media or websites, such as CNN or BBC, which are in English, one of the first thing to use the information is that we have to understand the language used.

The next attribute was its trialability with the mean of 3.59 (Table 2.5). Related to EMI trialability, "Mixed use between English and Indonesian should be applied in EMI class" was considered the highest, followed by "I have opportunities to try different learning strategies in EMI class", then "My university prepares me in taking EMI" and finally "Before taking EMI at my university I have experienced EMI in high school".

From the focus group discussion, EMI students were required to have a specific strategy to use English, one of which is by trying to think and express ideas in English directly, rather than to translate from Indonesian to English. Another strategy was using movies, daily vlogs, or YouTube to develop their speaking skills which are important in arguing, such as in debating. Self-practice in speaking by him or herself or doing monologue was also useful to develop their English, especially speaking. They felt that they had to force themselves to use English, as stated by one of the participants below.

Table 2.5 Perceived trialability of EMI

Attributes	M	SD
Before taking EMI at my university, I have experienced EMI in high school	3.14	1.076
I have opportunities to try different learning strategies in EMI class	3.75	0.755
My university prepares me in taking EMI	3.67	0.827
Mixed use between English and Indonesian should be applied in EMI class	3.78	0.796
Overall mean	3.59	

Gilang: Well, I then preferred monologue, though not in front of a mirror, so I asked myself first, then I answered myself, though it looked strange, but I felt I become more natural in speaking English.

In addition, the use of advanced information and technology has provided the students with opportunities to select applications of media for language learning, such as Duo Lingo. The social media platform has also helped them to have international friendship that will help them develop their English.

The next attribute was EMI observability with the mean of 3.51 (Table 2.6). Here, "EMI students show ability to present topics in English' was considered the highest, followed by "I notice EMI graduates are successful in their job", and the last "EMI students show wider understanding of the content subject compared to L1MI".

From the FGD the EMI students were observed to excel in their English performance. EMI students were observed to use their English for discussing issues about politics, NATO, and UN that are the topics in a political study as stated by one of the participants below.

Desty: Yesterday I observed from my friends they were using political terms to discuss issues about NATO and United Nations, using English, well it was such an upgrade.

Brian: So, not only in the communication aspect, but also in building opinion, it was shown how different the EMI students, from regular students, from their vocabulary uses and the way they communicate.

EMI students were also found to speak more spontaneous, fluent, and smooth compared to regular class students that used Indonesian as a medium of instruction. The method the EMI students developed ideas or ways of thinking, such as in developing arguments and choices of vocabulary that were more accurate and more communicative in the specific field, compared to those from the regular class. In addition, EMI students were observed to be more confident in using their English, as seen from some international competitions they followed, with excellent public speaking ability that could elaborate their ideas well.

Finally, related to EMI complexity (Table 2.7), the students perceived that its complexity was low with the mean of 2.9. It was shown that "I find it difficult to read references in English" was considered the most complex attribute, followed by "I find myself not confident in interacting with my friends by using English", then

Table 2.6 Perceived observability of EMI

Attributes	M	SD
Observability		
EMI students show ability to present topics in English	3.68	0.70
EMI students show wider understanding of the content subject compared to L1MI	3.35	0.940
I notice EMI graduates are successful in their job	3.50	0.744
Overall mean	3.51	

Table 2.7 Perceived complexity of EMI

Attributes	M	SD
I find it confusing to understand contents in EMI courses	2.6	0.912
I find it difficult to read references in English	3.21	1.038
I find it difficult to follow my teachers' explanation in English	2.76	0.975
I find myself not confident in interacting with my friends by using English	3.05	1.158
Overall mean	2.90	

"I find it difficult to follow my teachers' explanation in English", and finally "I find it confusing to understand contents in EMI courses".

From the FGD findings EMI students were challenged to understand academic terms. The academic terms are different from academic terms sometimes, thus causing the students to get difficulties in comprehending English texts as stated by the following participants.

Brian: But, in some situations, sometimes we find difficulties in comprehending the language used, such as in the teachers' intonation and teaching methods.

Desta: So, in my opinion, academic terms are different from daily languages. So, when we want to take EMI, the students must be equipped with adequate English skills, so that they will not be afraid or discouraged in using English in class, such as they will be shy to speak if they do not understand and are afraid of making mistakes.

Then, using English as a foreign language requires cognitive skills in comprehending and at the same time producing English utterances, both in reading and in speaking. This was due to the way the students usually applied translation when they read or spoke in English. Therefore, cognitive ability was required, which even made speaking English more difficult. However, as they become more exposed to and more involved in an EMI program, they felt speaking English was more natural and automatic. In addition, the lecturers' pronunciation was sometimes difficult for the students to understand, due to unstandardized pronunciation. Their prior education also, according to the FGD participants, did not prepare them to use English for delivering content knowledge, as the focus of the high school was more on having high scores in school examinations.

2.4.2 Students' Attitudes and Behavioral Intention Towards EMI

Regarding students' attitudes about EMI, the respondents showed a very positive attitude towards EMI with the mean score of 4.3. According to the students, EMI was perceived as a positive, useful, and interesting to learn content subject. Finally, the students showed high behavioral intention to take EMI with the mean of 3.58.

Table 2.8 Students' attitudes and behavioral intention towards EMI

Attitudes	M	SD
Taking EMI is very useful for me	4.33	0.63
Taking EMI is a positive step for me	4.38	0.617
Taking EMI is interesting for me	4.18	0.773
Overall mean	4.30	
Behavioral intention		
I will continue to take EMI course	3.82	0.78
I will suggest my friends to take EMI course	3.84	0.72
Indonesian-medium instruction/IMI students should transfer to EMI course	3.10	0.686
Overall mean	3.59	

According to the students, they had a high intention to take EMI and suggested their friends from regular classes to enroll in EMI courses and for those already enrolled in an EMI course to further continue their program. Table 2.8 shows the details of these findings.

2.4.3 Do the Perceived Attributes Affect Their Attitudes?

From the analysis, the perceived attributes by students were then seen in their effects towards their attitudes on taking EMI. From the finding among the five attributes, two attributes, namely relative advantage and compatibility, were found to have significant effects towards attitudes of the students, though with weak effect coefficients at 0.383 and 0.241 respectively. The other attributes, complexity, trialability, and observability, were not significantly predictive towards the attitudes. The detailed results of the path coefficient are shown in Table 2.9.

Regarding the effects of EMI perceived attributes on the students' behavioral intention, three attributes, relative advantages, observability, and trialability were significant predictors on the students' behavioral intention. The coefficient values

Table 2.9 Path Coefficient of the Effects of Perceived Attributes to Attitudes

Variables	Original sample (O)	Sample mean (M)	Standard deviation (STDEV)	T statistics (|O/STDEV|)	P values
C->AT	0.392	0.383	0.095	4.141	0.000
CL->AT	−0.047	−0.059	0.082	0.581	0.561
OB->AT	0.114	0.125	0.067	1.685	0.092
RA->AT	0.234	0.241	0.073	3.204	0.001
TR->AT	0.106	0.12	0.088	1.208	0.227

Table 2.10 Path coefficient of the effects of perceived attributes to behavioral intentions

Variables	Original sample (O)	Sample mean (M)	Standard deviation (STDEV)	T statistics (IO/STDEVI)	P values
C->BI	0.077	0.082	0.092	0.838	0.402
CL->BI	−0.199	−0.194	0.111	1.788	0.074
OB->BI	0.28	0.279	0.066	4.213	0.000
RA->BI	0.278	0.276	0.076	3.64	0.000
TR->BI	0.181	0.189	0.086	2.097	0.036

were at 0.276 ($p < 0.001$), 0.279 ($p < 0.001$), and 0.189 ($p < 0.05$). The other attributes were not significant predictors of their behavioral intentions. The finding indicates that real learning benefits and feasibility of taking EMI were drivers towards taking EMI programs which might not be achieved if taking regular undergraduate programs that uses Indonesian language as the medium of instruction. The path coefficients can be shown in Table 2.10.

2.5 Discussion

This study has found that the students perceived EMI positively, to be specific at a high to very high level. As a newly implemented content teaching approach EMI is considered useful, suitable, feasible, and more common to be applied at higher education institutions in Indonesia. This is in line with Simbolon's (2017) and Dewi's (2017) findings that EMI helped students develop their disciplinary knowledge and English skills along with intercultural skills to prepare them for their future career. This is also supported by the fact that more universities are adopting EMI as a means for their internationalization (Macaro et al., 2019). The position of English as a lingua franca strengthens the urgency of EMI promotion at higher education institutions. English and content subjects are then supposed to be more integrated in course delivery in the classroom to provide a more conducive environment for English language development (Genesee, 1994) due to meaningful and contextual features of EMI (Dearden, 2014). This is supported by the students' perception that EMI is not such a complex teaching approach as the EMI complexity attribute is relatively at a low level. This is contradictory to some findings that complexity was found in EMI implementation caused by English language issues (Chang, 2010; Wu, 2006). In addition, despite many issues to be addressed regarding content lecturers' English and pedagogical competence (Lamb et al., 2021) and possibly poorly planned EMI programs (Pecorari & Malmström, 2018), EMI is a favorable option for university students. This can be due to their awareness that in global competition, the role of English is becoming more vital for both academic and work success.

Furthermore, the attitude of the students towards EMI was shown to be very high. Attitude is very crucial for the adoption of any innovation, in this case EMI teaching (Venkatesh & Davis, 2000). Students' attitudes is considered a positive approach to provide both content and English language enhancement (Wanphet & Tantawy, 2018). In addition, positive attributes to EMI are important for students' success in second language learning (Gardner, 1985). Despite EMI's context in non-English speaking countries, the positive attitude can be a driving force for policy makers to develop their existing EMI programs. One of the issues to be addressed is the minimum support by EMI policy makers, such as lack of professional development (Muttaqin & Chuang, 2022).

Regarding the students' behavioral intention, that is one's intention to perform a specified behavior (Fishbein & Ajzen, 1975, p. 288), the study found that the students' intention to take EMI was relatively high. This shows that EMI is considered a preferred approach in learning their disciplinary knowledge. This indicates that they are willing to take EMI classes, instead of regular Indonesian class with the attributes already stated by them. They even suggest that non-EMI students should enroll in EMI classes. As stated by Fishbein and Azjen (1975), those with high intention tend to perform a certain behavior. From the findings presented here, there is, however, a possibility that students may hesitate to enroll in EMI programs, which may be caused by their lack of confidence in taking an EMI program. This then suggests that policy makers should assure that an EMI program be well planned and designed so that the EMI students will learn their content courses with ease despite the use of English as a foreign language, instead of the Indonesian language, as a means of instruction in their classes.

The next finding of this study is that two of the perceived attributes affect the students' attitudes towards EMI, namely relative advantage and compatibility. This supports Mkhize et al. (2016) finding that relative advantage and compatibility are two determining factors towards attitudes among EMI students. This can be explained that EMI aiming towards content understanding and English improvement attracts university students as they are planning for their future career or further academic pursuit. This is further strengthened by TAM theory (Davies et al., 1989) that both usefulness and ease of use are determining factors for the high degree of attitude towards adoption of EMI. Referring to the fact that high degree of attitude will lead to success in foreign language, and surely other fields, learning (Gardner, 1985), policy makers at universities can promote EMI as beneficial and feasible as long as with clear guidelines of pedagogical strategies to assure the linguistic barriers are not a hindrance.

The last finding of this study shows that three attributes were predictive to behavioral intention to take EMI, namely relative advantages, observability, and trialability. This confirms that EMI with its usefulness is the strongest driver for the students in taking an EMI program, as stated by Davis et al. (1989). Furthermore, observability and trialability attributes indicate that EMI is a feasible program for the Indonesian students. This finding contradicts the criticisms put forward by Hamid et al. (2013) suggesting that the EMI approach may harm students' understanding of content instruction due to their limited English language skills. Therefore, the crucial question now is how the university has to design an EMI program in a clear, well-planned, and manageable manner so that EMI can be implemented smoothly, catering to both pedagogical and linguistics issues, along with the appropriate infrastructure support.

2.6 Conclusion

This study has revealed that in an English as an academic lingua franca context, especially at higher education institutions, EMI has been perceived as highly positive in its advantages, with students' content, language, and intercultural enhancement. The approach is also a feasible and strategic approach to help university students develop their disciplinary knowledge for further career or academic pursuits. That taking an EMI program is a complex teaching and learning approach is refuted here, as shown by the perceived low complexity of EMI. Furthermore, EMI usefulness, applicability, flexibility are keys for enhancing the university students' attitudes and eventually intention to take an EMI program. This has provided an optimistic perspective, instead of perceiving EMI as harmful for students' content understanding and unclear English improvement. Having these all, in an academic setting, English can surely be promoted as an academic lingua franca for disciplinary knowledge construction, especially for those who want to achieve not only content knowledge, but also English, professional, and intercultural competences. By so doing, Indonesian academics can be more open to the world advancement in all fields, and cope with the highly demanding globalization. The main critical take away now is how well an EMI program is designed to suit the university students' disciplinary knowledge learning objectives. The EMI policy makers at universities then need to meet and agree with those in the micro level, such as lecturers, students, and parents about what to prepare and how to improve as EMI is relatively newly adopted in the Indonesian higher education context. In addition, by knowing what is needed to further improve an ongoing EMI program implementation, the students will maximize the EMI learning benefits and the institutions can gradually achieve their internationalization vision. To further elaborate the findings, future studies can include more qualitative and fieldwork data by conducting teaching and learning observations to reveal more real EMI practices. This will surely provide further insights on the EMI attributes in relation to attitudes, behavioral intention, as well as real practices of the lecturers to diffuse EMI at higher education institutions in Indonesia.

Acknowledgements We are deeply grateful to all the following: Faculty of Cultural Studies, Universitas Brawijaya, Indonesia for providing funding for our research project, Prof. Ali Saukah for the constructive input, and Dr. Subhan Zein, for the fruitful discussions and great encouragement, thus making this article possible. We also thank all who have been actively involved in the data collection and analysis for this project.

References

Al-Zaidiyeen, N. J., Mei, L. L., & Fook, F. S. (2010). Teachers' attitudes and levels of technology use in classrooms: The case of Jordan school. *International Education Studies, 3*(2), 211–218.

Chang, Y. Y. (2010). English-medium instruction for subject courses in tertiary education: Reactions from Taiwanese undergraduate students. *Taiwan International ESP Journal, 2*(1), 53–82.

Dafouz, E., & Smit, U. (2020). ROAD-MAPPING English medium education in the internationalised university. *Palgrave Macmillan.* https://doi.org/10.1007/978-3-030-23463-8

Davis, F. D. (1989). Perceived usefulness, perceived ease of use, and user acceptance of information technology. *MIS Quarterly, 13*(3), 319–340.

Davis, F. D., Bagozzi, R. P., & Warshaw, P. R. (1989). User acceptance of computer technology: A comparison of two theoretical models. *Management Science, 35*(8), 982–1003.

Dearden, J. (2014). *English as a medium of instruction-a growing global phenomena.* British Council.

Dewi, A. (2017). English as a medium of instruction in Indonesian higher education: A study of lecturers' perspectives. In B. Fenton-Smith, P. Humpsreys, & I. Wilkinshaw, *English medium instruction in higher education in Asia Pacific: From policy to Pedagogy* (pp. 241–258). Springer.

Dingfelder, H. E., & Mandell, D. S. (2011). Bridging the research-to-practice gap in autism intervention: An application of diffusion of innovation theory. *Journal of Autism and Developmental Disorders, 41*(5), 597–609.

Doiz, A., Lasagabaster, D., & Sierra, J. M. (2011). Internationalisation, multilingualism and English-medium instruction. *World Englishes, 30*(3), 345–359.

Duan, Y., He, Q., Feng, W., Li, D., & Fu, Z. (2010). A study on e-learning take-up intention from an innovation adoption perspective: A case in China. *Computers & Education, 55*(1), 237–246.

Fishbein, M., & Ajzen, I. (1975). *Belief, attitude, intention, and behavior: An introduction to theory and research.* Addison-Wesley Publishing Company.

Floris, F. D. (2014). Learning subject matter through English as the medium of instruction: Students' and teachers' perspectives. *Asian Englishes, 16*(1), 1–13.

Galloway, N., Kriukow, J., & Numajiri, T. (2017). *Internationalisation, higher education and the growing demands for English: An investigation into the English medium of instruction (EMI) movement in Japan and China.* British Council.

Gardner, R. (1985). *Social psychology and second language learning: The role of attitude and motivation.* Edward Arnold.

Genesee, F. (1994). *Integrating language and content: Lessons from immersion. NCRCDSLL educational practice reports.* Center for Research on Education, Diversity and Excellence, UC Berkeley.

Hamid, M. O., Nguyen, H. T., & Baldauf, R. B. (2013). Medium of instruction in Asia: Context, processes and outcomes. *Current Issues in Language Planning, 14*(1), 1–15.

Hau, K.-T., Marsh, H. W., Kong, C.-K., & Poon, A. C.-S. (2000). *Late immersion and language of instruction (English vs. Chinese) in Hong Kong high schools: Achievement growth in language and nonlanguage subjects.* The Annual Meeting of the American Educational Research Association.

Ibrahim, J. (2001). The implementation of EMI (English medium instruction) in Indonesian universities: Its opportunities, its threats, its problems, and its possible solutions. *Kata, 3*(2), 121–137.

Jenkins, J., Cogo, A., & Dewey, M. (2011). Review of developments in research into English as a lingua franca. *Language Teaching, 44*(3), 281–315. https://doi.org/10.1017/S0261444811000115

Lamb, M., Kuchah, H., Coleman, H, Hadisantosa, N., Waskita, D., & Ahmad, N. F. (2021). *The state of English as medium of instruction (EMI) in higher education institutions in Indonesia.* Research Report by the Indonesian Ministry of Education and Culture and the British Council, The British Council, Indonesia. https://www.britishcouncil.id/sites/default/files/the_state_of_english_as_me dium_of_instruction_in_heis_in_indonesia_full_report_final.pdf

Lo, Y. Y., & Othman, J. (2023). Lecturers' readiness for EMI in Malaysia higher education. *PLoS ONE, 18*(7), e0284491. https://doi.org/10.1371/journal.pone.0284491

Macaro, E., Curle, S., Pun, J., An, J., & Dearden, J. (2018). A systematic review of English medium instruction in higher education. *Language Teaching, 51*(1), 36–76.

Macaro, E., Akıncıoğlu, M., & Han, S. (2019). English medium instruction in higher education: Teacher perspectives on professional development and certification. *International Journal of Applied Linguistics, 30*, 144–157. https://doi.org/10.1111/ijal.12272

Marlina, R., & Xu, Z. (2018). English as a lingua franca. In J. I. Liontas (Ed.), *TESOL encyclopedia of English language teaching: Teaching English as an international language* (pp. 1–13). John Wiley & Sons.

Mauranen, A. (2003). The corpus of English as lingua franca in academic settings. *TESOL Quarterly, 37*(3), 513–527. https://doi.org/10.2307/3588402

Mkhize, P., Mtsweni, S., & Buthelezi, P. (2016). Diffusion of innovations approach to the evaluation of learning management system usage in an open distance learning institution. *International Review of Research in Open and Distributed Learning, 17*(3), 295–312.

Moore, G. C., dan Benbasat, I. (1991). Development of an instrument to measure the perceptions of adopting an information technology innovation. *Information Systems Research, 2*(3), 192–222.

Muttaqin, S., & Chuang, H. H. (2022). Variables affecting English-medium instruction students' achievement: Results of a multiple regression analysis. *International Journal of Educational Research Open, 3*(2022), 100152. https://doi.org/10.1016/j.ijedro.2022.100152

Osborne, M. (2016). How can innovative learning environment promote the diffusion of innovation? *Teachers and Curriculum, 16*(2), 11–17.

Pecorari, D., & Malmström, H. (2018). At the crossroads of TESOL and English medium instruction. *Tesol Quarterly, 52*(3), 497–515.

Rogers, E. M. (2003). *Diffusion of innovations*. Free Press.

Shiamuchi, S. (2018). English-medium instruction in the internationalization of higher education in Japan: Rationales and issues. *Educational Studies in Japan: International Yearbook*, 77–90.

Simbolon, N. E. (2017). Partial English instruction in English-medium (EMI). In J. Valcke (Ed.), *Integrating content and language in higher education: Perspectives on professional practice: Perspectives from lecturers in a University in Indonesia* (pp. 167–186). Peter Lang.

Tanye, H. A. (2016). Perceived attributes of Innovation: Perceived security as and additional attribute to Roger's diffusion of innovation theory. *International Journal of Multicultural and Multireligious Understanding, 3*(6), 6–18.

Teo, T., Lee, C. B., Chai, C. S., & Wong, S. L. (2009). Assessing the intention to use technology among pre-service teachers in Singapore and Malaysia: A multigroup invariance analysis of the Technology Acceptance Model (TAM). *Computers & Education, 53*(3), 1000–1009.

Venkatesh, V., & Davis, F. D. (2000). A theoretical extension of the technology acceptance model: Four longitudinal field studies. *Management Science, 46*(2), 186–204.

Wanphet, P., & Tantawy, N. (2018). Effectiveness of the policy of English as a medium of instruction: Perspectives and outcomes from the instructors and students of university science courses at a university in the UAE. *Educational Research for Policy and Practice, 17*, 145–172.

Warshaw, P. R. (1980). A new model for predicting behavioral intentions: An alternative to Fishbein. *Journal of Marketing Research, 17*(2), 153–172. https://doi.org/10.2307/3150927

Wu, S. W. (2006). Students' attitude toward EMI: Using Chung Hua University as an example. *Journal of Education and Foreign Language and Literature, 4*, 67–84.

Syariful Muttaqin Ph.D. is an assistant professor at the Department of Languages and Literature at Universitas Brawijaya, Malang, Indonesia. He has earned his B.A. in English Education from State University of Malang, M.A. in TESOL studies from the University of Queensland, Australia, and Ph.D. in Education and Human Development, from National Sun Yat-sen University, Taiwan.

His research and publication areas are English-medium instruction (EMI), higher education internationalization, language learning strategies, ELT, morphology, and syntax.He can be contacted at: smuttaqin@ub.ac.id.

Hsueh-Hua Chuang is a professor of Center for Teacher Education and Graduate Institute of Education at National Sun Yat-sen University in Taiwan. Her expertise ranges from information literacy and cyber ethics, Subject Matter and pedagogy for language arts / English and Qualitative Research Methods. Address for correspondence: Center for Teacher Education/Graduate Institute of Education, National Sun Yat-sen University. 70 Lien-hai Road, Kaohsiung Taiwan, 80424. She can be contacted at: hsuehhua@g-mail.nsysu.edu.tw or hsuehhua@g-mail.nsysu.edu.tw

Han-Chin Liu is an assistant professor at the Department of E-Learning Design and Management at the National Chiayi University in Taiwan. His research interests includeInstructional Technology, technology integrated learning, and multimedia learning. He can be contacted at: hanchinliu@etech.ncyu.edu.tw

Open Access This chapter is licensed under the terms of the Creative Commons Attribution 4.0 International License (http://creativecommons.org/licenses/by/4.0/), which permits use, sharing, adaptation, distribution and reproduction in any medium or format, as long as you give appropriate credit to the original author(s) and the source, provide a link to the Creative Commons license and indicate if changes were made.

The images or other third party material in this chapter are included in the chapter's Creative Commons license, unless indicated otherwise in a credit line to the material. If material is not included in the chapter's Creative Commons license and your intended use is not permitted by statutory regulation or exceeds the permitted use, you will need to obtain permission directly from the copyright holder.

Chapter 3
The Indonesian Assessment of Early Grade Reading (EGRA) and Beginning Reading Evaluation

Harwintha Anjarningsih

Abstract The importance of being able to read for children's future is beyond doubt. In Indonesia, on the one hand, a standardized linguistically-based test is needed to identify reading milestones and the Tes Membaca Satu Menit (TMSM) is a pioneer in that respect. In other countries, such tests have existed for a long time, such as the Een Minuut Lesetest in the Netherlands. On the other hand, the Early Grade Reading Assessment had existed and been used before by education authorities and practitioners, although it needs to be informed by results of a standardized linguistically-based test. Therefore, this research asks the question whether the Reading Meaningful Words (RMW) subtest of the EGRA is sufficient to evaluate children's decoding skills. The current investigation builds on previous research looking into the effects of orthographic depth, syllabic complexity, word length, and use of sub-lexical clusters in Bahasa Indonesia beginning reading. In the first month of the school year, third grade children's (n = 15) reading performance is recorded on the TMSM and EGRA. Results show that the RMW subtest (n = 50 words) was read 99% correctly in less than 60 s by the third-grade participants. However, in the same time duration, the children are able to read on average 30 words correctly in the TMSM with some mistakes, namely producing words with at least 50% of the sounds in the target words (visual miscues), and regularizations of diphthongs, digraphs and consonant clusters. If the results of EGRA are used to inform educators and authorities in charge of curriculum development to map the stages of reading in Indonesian and devise methods of intervention for the children lagging behind in reading development, it is suggested that the EGRA is not sufficient. Item analysis shows that 40 of the words in the RMW subtest are disyllabic, 9 are trisyllabic, and only 6 of the words contain digraphs, 1 contain diphthongs, and none contains consonant clusters. Yet, three- or four-syllable words are also common in the children's reading materials, and diphthongs, digraphs, and consonant clusters are common Grapheme Phoneme Correspondence (GPC) in the Indonesian orthography. The design of this subtest, hence, does not facilitate the children to show what they have and have not mastered. The key finding shows children's reading milestones are influenced by word length

---

H. Anjarningsih (✉)
Linguistics Department, Faculty of Humanities, Universitas Indonesia, Jawa Barat, Indonesia
e-mail: harwintha@ui.ac.id

and easiness of mapping between phonemes and graphemes and the EGRA needs to incorporate linguistically-based manipulations.

Keywords Reading in Indonesian · Beginning reading · Normal reading · Reading milestones · Assessment of early grade reading (EGRA)

School children's reading ability has been assessed using standard educational tests throughout the world (e.g., in Malawi (Mejia, 2011a); in Ghana (Mejia, 2011b); in Liberia (Piper & Korda, 2009)) in cooperation with the countries' Ministry of Education. In Indonesia, the Assessment of Early Grade Reading (EGRA; RTI International, 2013) has been used and one of the purposes of EGRA is to inform classroom literacy instruction (Dubeck & Gove, 2015). In RTI International (2013) it is reported that the EGRA was administered to third grade elementary school students in Indonesia in the months of November and December, 2012.

Children's reading ability is also customarily assessed by means of linguistically-based test such as the Een Minuut Lesetest in the Netherlands (Brus & Voeten, 1972). In such tests, reading norms based on age have been established and one child's reading performance can be compared to the norms. In Indonesia, Tes Membaca Satu Menit (TMSM) is a pioneer test whose test items are controlled based on orthographic depth, syllabic complexity, use of sub-lexical clusters, and word length in Bahasa Indonesia beginning reading (Anjarningsih, 2016, 2018; see Seymore et al., 2003). In order to capture objectively what children can and cannot read (yet), a word-reading test must contain all syllabic patterns in Indonesian and varied word lengths and is administered with a time limit. Educational policies with far-reaching consequences must be developed based on results from such a test because if a test is too easy and limited, the results will give a false impression that all is well. While previous studies have discussed Indonesian word- reading, they focused on different age groups (e.g., Hasanah & Risa, 2017), foreign students studying Indonesian (e.g., Prasetiyo, 2019), or the development of tools that were not meant to be used as a nation-wide test (e.g., Borleffs et al., 2018). To fill the gap, the current research compares and contrasts primary school children's reading performance using two materials: the Indonesian version of the the Real Word Reading (RMW) subtest of the EGRA, which was developed by educators without any linguistic variables and the TMSM, which was developed based on linguistic considerations. It aims at suggesting what improvements could be made to this subtest to make it more objective in assessing children's word-reading.

3.1 Word Decoding in Transparent Languages

Children's success in reading is influenced by the Grapheme Phoneme Correspondence (GPC) in their orthography. Opaque orthographies such as that of English make it longer for children to master reading familiar words than transparent orthographies such as that of Italian or Spanish (Seymore et al., 2003). Children learning to read English need to understand that graphemes do not map in a one-to-one fashion to phonemes and phonemes also have a one to many mapping to graphemes. For example, the grapheme < a > is /æ/ in 'apple,' /eI/ in 'paper,' /ɑː/ in 'last' and the phoneme /ʌ/ is spelled with the grapheme < u > in 'b*u*t,' graphemes < ou > in 'en*ou*gh,' and < oo > in 'bl*oo*d' (Cambridge Online Dictionary, 2019). Indonesian orthography is relatively transparent with just a few irregularities. However, it is precisely the irregularities that have been shown to influence children's reading success (Colenbrander et al., 2020). In other words, mastering the irregularities shows that children are progressing in their reading, especially in understanding the GPC of the Indonesian orthography. The irregularities are defined as the diphthongs, digraphs, and consonant clusters by Anjarningsih (2016, 2018).

Furthermore, Indonesian children's reading miscues are a key to their reading development. They progress from making substitution miscues (e.g., reading 'mama' as 'kaki') to making regularization miscues (e.g., reading 'krisis' as 'kirisis' or 'kisis'), which shows a move from guessing the words that are read to knowing all the graphemes composing the words despite still unsure about reading the irregularities such as the consonant cluster *kr* in the word '*kr*isis.' Previous studies on Italian, also a language with transparent orthography, show that beginning readers of a transparent orthography are affected by word length (Zoccolotti et al., 2005) such that words with more letters take more time to read than words with fewer letters. This length effect is claimed to show the operation of sub-lexical reading or reading at the level below a word. In addition, length effect indicates a reading process that takes place between the visual presentation of a word and its identification by readers (Van den Boer et al., 2013). At second grade, lexical procedure is already dominant, making readers less prone to length effect (Zoccolotti et al., 2005). In other words, reading long or short words takes the same or similar time starting from second grade.

What kind of performance may indicate reading problems in transparent orthographies such as that of Indonesian? Previous research suggests that slow reading is a good candidate. In German, Dutch, and Finnish this slow reading has been shown to be persistent (Marinus et al., 2012; Huemer et al, 2010), but reading accuracy remains good throughout. In other words, poor readers read all words correctly, but it takes longer for them to read the words. In Indonesian reading tests, therefore, reading speed has to be measured and controlled as well to ensure that children's reading progress is evaluated correctly.

3.2 Educational Challenges in Indonesia

The implementation of education and the process to reach the goals mentioned in the curriculum has to be discussed in relation to the reality faced by students. In the field, Indonesia faces a lot of educational challenges, the greatest of which is the country's vast geography and a lot of remote areas (Luschei & Zubaidah, 2012). Febriana et al. (2018) mentioned that in the country's border and underdeveloped regions, a lot of schools that they researched had to be reached by inadequate road conditions and means of transportation. This made it difficult for the teachers and students to come regularly to the schools. Indeed, the difficult access has resulted in teachers' absenteeism in Papua and West Papua (Prouty, 2012).

Other challenges that influenced the academic progress of students are lack of facilities and lack of teachers. These facilities include electricity, text books, dictionaries, classroom condition, chairs and desks, blackboards, chalks, and internet (Febriana, et al., 2018; Malaikosa & Sahayu, 2019). This condition has caused teachers to rely on their skills and knowledge that oftentimes resulted in less than maximal lessons (Febriana, et al., 2018). In addition, this is made worse by the shortage of teachers that happen in remote areas, leading to courses taught by teachers who do not have the competency to teach them, such as history taught by a mathematics teacher (Hidayah & Marhaeni, 2016). Taken together, the challenges affect not only the day-to-day educational process but also the resulting quality of the students graduating from schools facing them. Although schools in urban areas are obviously not challenge-free, poor access road condition, inadequate public transportation, lack of electricity, and teacher shortage are in general much less of an issue than in remote areas.

3.3 Adequacy of the Rmw Subtest of the Egra to Assess Children's Decoding

Taking a look at the Indonesian EGRA (RTI International, 2013), it is interesting to connect the subtests in the EGRA with what has been discussed in the literature in order to see their linguistic underpinnings and investigate children's reading performance in the subtests in an urban area very close to Jakarta, the country's capital city.. The Reading Meaningful Words (RMW) subtest of the EGRA is one that needs attention because a casual inspection reveals an abundance of words with two syllables and words with simple syllable structure, namely Consonant–Vowel-Consonant–Vowel structure without any irregularities in the spelling. Choosing this subtest to scrutinize is based on two reasons: 1. Word level decoding has been extensively discussed in the literature and there are preliminary results from Indonesian as well; 2. Children's performance in decoding single words needs to be tested with a valid test in order for it to provide an accurate picture of decoding that influences children's later reading (e.g., sentence level reading and comprehension, discourse level reading and comprehension). The choice of an urban area was made under the consideration of a possible relationship between school location and children's reading performance and prediction to results in more remote, less-facilitated schools.

Based on the discussion in the previous sections, this research asks the question whether the Reading Meaningful Words (RMW) subtest of the EGRA is sufficient to evaluate children's word decoding skills.

3.4 Methodology

To start the methodology section, essential information from the tests (Anjarningsih, 2018; RTI International, 2013) pertinent to this research extracted from the RMW subtest of the EGRA and TSMS is given in Table 3.1.

From Table 3.1, we can see that the RMW subtest of the EGRA have predominantly 2-syllable words and words with simple syllable complexity such as 'lalu,' 'sudah' and 'melihat.' For the TMSM, there are comparable number of 2-syllable words and 3-syllable words; the number of 4-syllable words is about a quarter of the number of the 2-syllable and 3-syllable words. For the syllabic complexity, there are comparable number of words with simple structure, diphthongs, digraphs, and consonant clusters (e.g., bagi, tun*ai*, ta*ny*a, and g*r*atis, respectively). The simple syllabic structure has been found to be the earliest to be mastered by children, followed by the diphthongs, digraphs and consonant clusters (Anjarningsih, 2016).

Fifteen third grade elementary school children studying in the city of Depok, Indonesia, which is a suburb of the capital city Jakarta, read aloud the RMW subtest of the EGRA in the first month of the academic year (end of July-end of August 2019). The average age is 8 years 5 months and 9 were girls and 6 were boys. All children were reported to have no history of language problems by parents and teachers.

Both tests are to be carried out in maximum 1 min per participant. Children are instructed to read the words the best they can with their own speed. For the RMW, the test is discontinued if the children do not read correctly any of the first five words (in the first row). For the TMSM, the test is stopped after 1 min regardless of the children's reading performance.

Children's reading was audio-taped and transcribed orthographically. Miscues were later identified as substitution (produced word shares less than 50% similarity with target words), visual (target word shares at least 50% of graphemes with produced word), or regularization (the diphthongs, digraphs and consonant clusters in target word are read as just one of the composing graphemes in the produced word, or a vowel is inserted between/among the letters in the consonant clusters) miscues. Miscues were also classified whether they occurred in one-, two, three- or four-syllable words.

Table 3.1 Important information from RMW subtest of the EGRA and TSMS

RMW EGRA (n = 50 words)					TMSM (n = 91 words)				
Number of syllables	234 words	316 words	40 words		242 words	341 words	49 words	
Syllabic complexity	Simple 41 words	Diphthongs 1 word	Digraphs 8 words	Consonant clusters 0 words	Simple 26 words	Diphthongs 20 words	Digraphs 23 words	Consonant clusters 22 words

3.5 Results: Beginning Reading Performance

3.5.1 Performance on the Reading Meaningful Words Subtest of the EGRA

In general, the children read the RMW in less than 1 min with a high degree of success (Table 3.2).

Table 3.2 Reading performance for the RMW subtest of the EGRA

Participant	Duration (s)	Correct (in words)	Miscue details
P1	31	50	–
P2	29	50	–
P3	40	50	–
P4	29	50	–
P5	32	50	–
P6	27	50	–
P7	32	50	–
P8	51	48	'menyanyi' read as 'menyayangi' (visual error, target word shares at least 50% of graphemes with produced word) 'jawab' read as 'jawaban' (visual error, target word shares at least 50% of graphemes with produced word)
P9	48	50	–
P10	29	50	–
P11	59	48	'kamu' read as 'mau' (visual error, target word shares at least 50% of graphemes with produced word) 'balon' read as 'kalon' (visual error, target word shares at least 50% of graphemes with produced word)
P12	34	49	'bisa' read as 'biasa' (visual error, target word shares at least 50% of graphemes with produced word)
P13	40	48	'menyanyi' read as 'menyayangi' (visual error, target word shares at least 50% of graphemes with produced word) 'karena' read as 'krena' (visual error, target word shares at least 50% of graphemes with produced word)
P14	42	50	–
P15	50	49	'menyanyi' read as 'menyayangi' (visual error, target word shares at least 50% of graphemes with produced word)
	Average = 38.2	Average = 49.5	

The high degree of success (8 miscues in 750 words or 99% correctly read words) seems to be related to the preponderance of simple 2 syllable words in the RMW subtest of the EGRA. All the miscues or errors that are committed are visual errors, showing that the children had a good command of the graphemes and could read the syllables containing the graphemes well. Furthermore, regarding the number of syllables in the miscued words, a comparable number of words with 2 syllables and words with 3 syllables were miscued (4 versus 4). Therefore, in this subtest of the EGRA, we do not see effects of number of syllables on children's reading performance. However, we have to keep in mind that this subtest does not represent the number of syllables and syllabic complexity in Indonesian words well.

3.5.2 Performance on the Tes Membaca Satu Menit (TMSM)

In Table 3.3, the children's reading performance on the TMSM is given. For the TMSM, analysis is limited in the time duration in which the children use in completing the RMW subtest of the EGRA in order to give a comparable performance.

Overall, from Table 3.3, it is observed that no miscue was committed on the words with simple syllable structure. The 39 miscues that were committed were spread among the words containing diphthongs, words containing digraphs and words containing consonant clusters (n total = 465 words). In other words, the incorporation of diphthongs, digraphs and consonant clusters unravels a difficulty with 8.4% of words that the children attempted to read.

The 39 miscues that occurred are of only two types: visual and regularization. For diphthongs the visual miscues outnumber the regularization ones (14 versus 3), for the digraphs the number is comparable for the two types (vis = 3, and reg = 3), and for the consonant clusters, visual miscues are much fewer in number that the regularization miscues (5 versus 11). Comparing the number of syllables in the miscued words, overall words with 3 syllables or more were more prone to miscues than words with 2 syllables as proven by 59% of the miscued words have 3 syllables or more, and 41% have 2 syllables.

In terms of speed, in the average 38.2 s, participants could read 28.4 words correctly. If rounded up to 29 words, and included the words number 1 to 29 in the TMSM, we have the following breakdown in terms of number of syllables: 19 two-syllable words, 8 three-syllable words, and 2 four-syllable words. In terms of syllable complexity, those 29 words were composed of 9 words with simple syllable structure, 7 words with diphthongs, 9 words with digraphs, and 4 words with consonant clusters. Taken together, the results indicated that in the average time of 38.2 s the participants were 91.6% successful in reading the stimulus in the TMSM, and none of the miscues were on words with simple syllable structure. When given materials with varying syllable lengths, participants showed that 3–4 syllable words were more difficult than those with 2 syllables, showing traces of sub-lexical procedure that was still utilized by them.

Table 3.3 Reading performance for the TMSM

Participant	Duration (s)	Correct (in words)	Miscue details
P1	31	31	'pegawai' read as 'pengawai' (visual error, target word shares at least 50% of graphemes with produced word)
P2	29	39	'pegawai' read as 'pengawai' (visual error, target word shares at least 50% of graphemes with produced word) 'samur*ai*' read as 'samur*a*' (regularization error, the diphthong in target word is read as just one of the composing graphemes in produced word)
P3	40	25	'pegawai' read as 'pengawal' (visual error, target word shares at least 50% of graphemes with produced word) '*br*utal' read as '*beru*tal' (regularization error, the consonant cluster in target word is read with an extra sound in the middle of the two composing graphemes in produced word)
P4	29	31	–
P5	32	23	'kaisar' read as 'ka-i-sar' (regularization error, the diphthong in target word is read as two single graphemes in produced word) 'pegawai' read as 'pewangi' (visual error, target word shares at least 50% of graphemes with produced word) '*sy*arat' read as '*say*ara' (regularization error, the digraph in target word is read with an extra sound in the middle of the two composing graphemes in produced word) '*kr*itik' read as '*kar*tika' (regularization error, the consonant cluster in target word is read with an extra sound in the middle of the two composing graphemes in produced word) 'samurai' read as 'samuarai' (visual error, target word shares at least 50% of graphemes with produced word) 'distribusi' read as 'distributi' (visual error, target word shares at least 50% of graphemes with produced word)
P6	27	30	–
P7	32	31	–

(continued)

Table 3.3 (continued)

Participant	Duration (s)	Correct (in words)	Miscue details
P8	51	20	'k*ai*sar' read as 'k*i*sar' (regularization error, the diphthong in target word is read as just one of the composing graphemes in produced word) 'insinyur' read as 'insisur' (visual error, target word shares at least 50% of graphemes with produced word) '*kr*itik' read as '*keri*tik' (regularization error, the consonant cluster in target word is read with an extra sound in the middle of the two composing graphemes in produced word) 'syarat' read as 'sayarat' (regularization error, the digraph in target word is read with an extra sound in the middle of the two composing graphemes in produced word) 'harim*au*' read as 'harim*o*' (visual error, target word shares at least 50% of graphemes with produced word) 'distribusi' read as 'disetribusi' (visual error, target word shares at least 50% of graphemes with produced word) 'strategi' read as 'seterategi' (regularization error, the consonant cluster in target word is read with an extra sound in the middle of the three composing graphemes in produced word)
P9	48	22	'kaisar' read as 'kaisa' (visual error, target word shares at least 50% of graphemes with produced word) 'pegawai' read as 'penggawai' (visual error, target word shares at least 50% of graphemes with produced word) 'distribusi' read as 'disitribusi' (visual error, target word shares at least 50% of graphemes with produced word) 'cenderung' read as 'cendurung' (visual error, target word shares at least 50% of graphemes with produced word) '*br*utal' read as '*bur*tal' (regularization error, the consonant cluster in target word is read with an extra sound in the middle of the two composing graphemes in produced word) '*kr*itik' read as '*keri*tik' (regularization error, the consonant cluster in target word is read with an extra sound in the middle of the two composing graphemes in produced word)
P10	29	36	'pegawai' read as 'pengawai' (visual error, target word shares at least 50% of graphemes with produced word) 'strategi' read as 'seterategi' (regularization error, the consonant cluster in target word is read with an extra sound in the middle of the three composing graphemes in produced word)

(continued)

3 The Indonesian Assessment of Early Grade Reading (EGRA) ...   45

Table 3.3 (continued)

Participant	Duration (s)	Correct (in words)	Miscue details
P11	59	24	'pegawai' read as 'pengawai' (visual error, target word shares at least 50% of graphemes with produced word) 'brutal' read as 'brutai' (visual error, target word shares at least 50% of graphemes with produced word) 'punya' read as 'puya' (regularization error, the digraph in target word is read as just one of the composing graphemes in produced word) 'kritik' read as 'keritik' (regularization error, the consonant cluster in target word is read with an extra sound in the middle of the two composing graphemes in produced word) 'distribusi' read as 'distiribusi' (regularization error, the consonant cluster in target word is read with an extra sound in the middle of the two composing graphemes in produced word)
P12	34	23	'pegawai' read as 'pengawai' (visual error, target word shares at least 50% of graphemes with produced word) 'distribusi' read as 'distriubusi' (visual error, target word shares at least 50% of graphemes with produced word)
P13	40	31	'pegawai' read as 'pengawai' (visual error, target word shares at least 50% of graphemes with produced word)
P14	42	30	'brutal' read as 'berutal' (regularization error, the consonant cluster in target word is read with an extra sound in the middle of the two composing graphemes in produced word) 'kritik' read as 'keritik' (regularization error, the consonant cluster in target word is read with an extra sound in the middle of the two composing graphemes in produced word)
P15	50	30	'pegawai' read as 'pegamai' (visual error, target word shares at least 50% of graphemes with produced word) 'pulau' read as 'pulai' (visual error, target word shares at least 50% of graphemes with produced word) 'cenderung' read as 'cederung' (visual error, target word shares at least 50% of graphemes with produced word)
	Average = 38.2	Average = 28.4	

3.6 Discussion

Reading is an essential skill in today's society and governments throughout the world have utilized standardized tests to assess children's reading performance. With the comparison of Indonesian third grade children's performance in two decoding tests presented here, we have tried to show types of reading miscues committed when reading the words in the tests. We outlined the specific characteristics of this transparent orthography and described how the two tests have incorporated them, i.e., orthographic depth, syllabic complexity, use of sub-lexical clusters, and word length. Having tested the third-grade students, we noted a higher percentage of miscues in the TSMS than in the RMW subtest.

Irregularities in the spelling, namely diphthongs, digraphs and consonant clusters were shown to be difficult for the children. This is in line with previous studies (e.g., Colenbrander et al., 2020) showing that irregularities in spelling have a negative effect on children's reading performance. However, on the one hand, this difficulty was not evident in the RMW because very few words there contained digraphs and diphthongs, and none contained consonant clusters. On the other hand, the miscues on the TMSM were visual and regularization, showing that the young participants had basic skills to decode the Grapheme Phoneme Correspondence (GPC) but were still struggling with and used sub-lexical procedure in reading the words with digraphs, diphthongs and consonant clusters. Based on this, to further improve the adequacy of the RMW subtest of the EGRA, we suggest adding words with digraphs, diphthongs, and consonant clusters. They should also be embedded in words with two, three and four syllables.

Our results seemed to suggest that the difficulties could be even greater in less urban areas with less access to adequate materials, teachers, and facilities. If this is indeed the case, there is an urgent need to modify the RMW subtest so that the difficulties could be assessed and appropriate actions could be taken. For example, it would be easier to link difficulties in sentence reading if we had objective data about word reading and to target the syllable structure and word length for treatment. Otherwise, difficulties in sentence reading could be misunderstood and mistreated, and the children could continue to perform poorly.

3.7 Conclusion

This current research aimed to observe whether the Reading Meaningful Words (RMW) subtest of the EGRA is sufficient to evaluate children's word decoding skills. Based on the results in the previous section, it seems that the answer is no. The RMW of the EGRA seems too easy for the participants and the success of the participants in the subtest actually masked the decoding problems that they still had. The results show that as with other transparent orthographies, irregularities in the spelling and word length (number of syllables) are two factors that should be in reading tests to evaluate children's reading progress. Therefore, the conclusion offered by the developers of Indonesian EGRA for the RMW subtest, in that "the results would suggest that most children in grade 3 are sufficiently automatic with words that are commonly used in Bahasa Indonesia (RTI International, 2013, p. 26)" needs to be treated with caution. Linguistic considerations such as those applied in the TMSM should be incorporated in the RMW subtest to improve this subtest to make it more objective in assessing children's word-reading.

Compared to Italian young readers (Zoccolotti et al., 2005), Indonesian third-grade readers in this research seem to take longer to master the lexical procedure. This is despite comparable ages and grade (mean age of 8.7 years in Zoccolotti et al., 2005). While differences in the teaching and learning process remain to be investigated, this finding serves as a reminder that the quality and outcome of primary education in Indonesia still needs to be enhanced. This is also in line with the meager 2019 Programme for International Student Assessment (PISA) reading results obtained by Indonesia, ranked 72 from 77 countries (Kurnia, 2019). The current results are more important if the diversities in children's education and environments in Indonesia are taken into account. Indonesia, with its many provinces and various geographical conditions, presents challenges for educators and children alike. The more remote or rural the areas where the schools are, usually the fewer facilities the schools have and the farther they are from the where the students live. If the participants of the current study who live in an urban area still have decoding problems that are not captured by the RMW subtest, it can be reasoned that the problems are worse in rural or isolated areas. Surely, a subtest in a test that is used to guide nationwide policies needs to incorporate linguistically relevant variables to capture children's reading progress objectively. If left untreated by teachers, at the third grade level, the children may be hampered in the next reading skills, such as those for reading comprehension and analytical skills (Caravolas et al., 2019; Kendeou et al., 2009). This is precisely the next set of skills to be investigated in a larger sample of children to develop an objective test of reading so that the factors and skills contributing to the ultimate aim of reading, comprehension, are fully and correctly explored. Other subtests of the EGRA also need to be checked linguistically before they can validly be used to guide educational policy development in Indonesia.

Appendix: The Reading Meaningful Words Subtest of the Assessment of Early Grade Reading (RTI International, 2013)

selalu	pulang	yang	ketika	adalah
ibu	ada	melihat	tiga	dengan
emas	tidak	kamu	menyanyi	mereka
kakak	akan	sudah	kata	ikan
balon	ia	uang	guru	telah
sekolah	saat	bisa	sangat	kelas
anak	dia	kalau	semua	karena
tanya	itu	aku	orang	lalu
jawab	ini	dari	namun	dapat
rumah	untuk	dalam	air	hari

References

Anjarningsih, H. Y. (2016). Characterising the reading development of Indonesian children. In Y. Yanti (Ed.), *Proceedings of KOLITA 14: Konferensi Linguistik Tahunan Atma Jaya Keempat Belas* (pp. 156–159).

Anjarningsih, H. Y. (2018) Read, miscue, and progress: A preliminary study in characterizing reading development in shallow Indonesian orthography. In XXX (Eds.), *Proceedings of the tenth conference on applied linguistics and the second english language teaching and technology conference in collaboration with the first international conference on language, literature, culture, and education–volume 1: CONAPLIN and ICOLLITE* (pp. 839–843).

Borleffs, E., Glatz, T. K., Daulay, D. A., Richardson, U., Zwarts, F., & Maassen, B. A. (2018). GraphoGame SI: The development of a technology-enhanced literacy learning tool for Standard Indonesian. *European Journal of Psychology of Education, 33*(4), 595–613. https://doi.org/10.1007/s10212-017-0354-9

Brus, B., & Voeten, M. (1972) *Eén minuut test. Schoolvorderingen voor het lezen, bestemd voor voor het tweede t/m vijfde leerjaar van de lagere school.* Berkhout bv..

Caravolas, M., Lervåg, A., Mikulajová, M., Defior, S., Seidlová-Málková, G., & Hulme, C. (2019). A cross-linguistic, longitudinal study of the foundations of decoding and reading comprehension ability. *Scientific Studies of Reading, 23*(5), 386–402. https://doi.org/10.1080/10888438.2019.1580284

Colenbrander, D., Wang, H.-C., Arrow, T., & Castles, A. (2020). Teaching irregular words: What we know, what we don't know, and where we can go from here. *The Educational and Developmental Psychologist, 37*(2), 97–104. https://doi.org/10.1017/edp.2020.11

Dubeck, M. M., & Gove, A. (2015). The early grade reading assessment (EGRA): Its theoretical foundation, purpose, and limitations. *International Journal of Educational Develeopment, 40*, 315–322. https://doi.org/10.1016/j.ijedudev.2014.11.004

Febriana, M., Nurkamto, J., Rochsantiningsih, D., & Muhia, A. (2018). Teaching in rural Indonesian schools: Teachers' challenges. *International Journal of Multicultural and Multireligious Understanding, 5*(5), 11–20.

Hasanah, M., & Risa, Y. (2017). Correlation between reading literacy ability and achievement in learning indonesian language in grade X. ISLLAC.

Hidayah, I., & Marhaeni, P. A. T. (2016). Reinforcement of professional teacher candidates in Indonesia through program of graduates educating in the frontier, outermost, and disadvantaged regions (SM-3T). *International Journal of Research in Education and Science, 2*(1), 166–171.

Huemer, S., Mikko, A., Landerl, K., & Lyytinen, H. (2010). Repeated reading of syllables among Finnish-speaking children with poor reading skills. *Scientific Studies of Reading, 14*(4), 317–340. https://doi.org/10.1080/10888430903150659

Kendeou, P., van den Broek, P., White, M., & Lynch, J. S. (2009). Predicting reading comprehension in early elementary school: The independent contributions of oral language and decoding skills. *Journal of Educational Psychology, 101*, 765–778.

Kurnia, T. (2019). Skor Terbaru PISA: Indonesia Merosot di Bidang Membaca, Sains, dan Matematika. *Liputan6*. https://www.liputan6.com/

Luschei, T. F., & Zubaidah, I. (2012). Teacher training and transitions in rural Indonesian schools: A case study of Bogor, West Java. *Asia Pacific Journal of Education, 32*(3), 333–350.

Malaikosa, C. A., & Sahayu, W. (2019). Teachers' challenges on implementing EFL curriculum in Indonesian rural area. *Journal of Foreign Language Education and Technology, 4*(1), 61–71.

Marinus, E., de Jong, P., & van der Leij, A. (2012). Increasing word-reading speed in poor readers: No additional benefits of explicit letter-cluster training. *Scientific Studies of Reading, 16*, 166–185. https://doi.org/10.1080/10888438.2011.554471

Mejia, J. (2011a). *Malawi early grade reading assessment: National baseline report.* Prepared by the Malawi Teacher Professional Development Support (MTPDS) activity implemented by Creative Associates International, Inc., RTI International, and Seward Inc., for USAID/Malawi and the Ministry of Education, Science, and Technology.

Mejia, J. (2011b). *NALAP formative evaluation report, Ghana.* Prepared by RTI International for USAID/Ghana.

Piper, B., & Korda, M. (2009) *Data analytic report: EGRA Plus: Liberia baseline assessment.* Prepared by RTI International for USAID.

Prasetiyo, A. E. (2019) Developing an Indonesian reading proficiency text for BIPA learners. *IRJE: Indonesian Research Journal in Education, 3*(2), 265–279.

Prouty, R. (2012) *"We Like Being Taught" a study on teacher Absenteeism in Papua and West Papua.* UNCEN–UNIPA–SMERU–BPS–UNICEF.

RTI International. (2016). *Early grade reading assessment (EGRA) toolkit* (2nd ed.). United States Agency for International Development.

RTI International. (2013). *Baseline monitoring report, volume 3: An assessment of early grade reading—How well children are reading.*

Seymour, P. H. K., Aro, M., & Erskine, J. M. (2003). Foundation literacy acquisition in European orthographies. *British Journal of Psychology, 94*, 143–174.

Stern, J. M. B., Dubeck, M. M., & Dick, A. (2018). Using Early Grade Reading Assessment (EGRA) data for targeted instructional support: Learning profiles and instructional needs in Indonesia. *International Journal of Educational Development, 61*, 64–71. https://doi.org/10.1016/j.ijedudev.2017.12.003

Van den Boer, M., de Jong, P. F., & Haentjens-van Meeteren, M. (2013). Modeling the length effect: Specifying the relation with visual and phonological correlates of reading. *Scientific Studies of Reading, 17*, 243–256. https://doi.org/10.1080/10888438.2012.683222

Zoccolotti, P., De Luca, M., Di Pace, E., Gasperini, F., Judica, A., & Spinelli, D. (2005) Word length effect in early reading and in developmental dyslexia. *Brain and Language, 93*, 369–373.
https://dictionary.cambridge.org/dictionary/english/

Harwintha Anjarningsih born in Kebumen, 2 March 1981, completed her doctoral study in Neurolinguistics/Aphasiology at the University of Groningen, the Netherlands. A faculty member in the English Study Program and Linguistics Department, Faculty of Humanities, Universitas Indonesia, her research interests span from phonetics/phonology, morphology, syntax, psycholinguistics, language impairments across ages, bilingual language processing, and education for children with special needs. Website: harwintha.blogspot.com.

Open Access This chapter is licensed under the terms of the Creative Commons Attribution 4.0 International License (http://creativecommons.org/licenses/by/4.0/), which permits use, sharing, adaptation, distribution and reproduction in any medium or format, as long as you give appropriate credit to the original author(s) and the source, provide a link to the Creative Commons license and indicate if changes were made.

The images or other third party material in this chapter are included in the chapter's Creative Commons license, unless indicated otherwise in a credit line to the material. If material is not included in the chapter's Creative Commons license and your intended use is not permitted by statutory regulation or exceeds the permitted use, you will need to obtain permission directly from the copyright holder.

Chapter 4
Students' Motivation in Learning English as a Foreign Language Through Discovery Learning

Sabrina Asrianty Putri and Sisilia Setiawati Halimi

Abstract In Indonesia, the Curriculum 2013 encourages teachers to use discovery learning for teaching English. The effects of discovery-based learning have also been analyzed from various perspectives. However, limited studies have been specifically conducted to represent both female and male students' motivation toward their discovery-based English language learning experiences. Therefore, this study looked into the students' motivational introspections and orientations toward their discovery-based English language learning. The subjects in this study were the students of Senior High School in Jakarta, Indonesia. The study collected both quantitative and qualitative data that were gathered through a survey and interviews. The results of the survey were analyzed using the Independent-Sample T-test and descriptive analysis. Meanwhile, the verbatim transcriptions of the interviews were analyzed using the grounded theory analysis. The quantitative data reveal that extrinsic goal orientation became the most motivating factor for the students to implement discovery learning in studying English. In addition, the qualitative data explains how the students perceived the six motivational factors differently. The findings also suggest some ways to enhance English language learning and teaching through discovery learning. Thus, this study is highly relevant to give teachers ideas on how to motivate students in learning English as a Foreign Language (EFL).

Keywords Learning motivation · English as a foreign language (EFL) · Discovery learning · High school students · Indonesia

---

S. A. Putri
English Studies Program, Faculty of Humanities, Universitas Indonesia, Jawa Barat, Indonesia

S. S. Halimi (✉)
Linguistics Department, Faculty of Humanities, Universitas Indonesia, Jawa Barat, Indonesia
e-mail: ss_halimi@ui.ac.id; sshalimi@gmail.com

4.1 Introduction

About 1.5 billion out of 7.5 billion people speak English in this world (Lyons, 2017). That makes English have a significant role in facilitating people's cross-cultural communication worldwide. The government of Indonesia seems to be aware of the need to master this 'international language' to join today's global competition. In response to that, the latest curriculum, which is Curriculum 2013, recommends several ways of learning and teaching English that generally focus on developing student-centered learning experiences (Indonesia Ministry of Education & Culture, 2016b). The recommendation includes discovery/inquiry-based learning, expository learning, problem-based learning, and project-based learning.

Discovery learning method was firstly introduced in the 1960s by Jerome Bruner, whose view becomes a timeless reference in defining discovery learning. There is a myriad definition of discovery-based learning in literature. Gradually, as suggested by Alfieri et al. (2010), discovery learning (Bruner, 1961) is widely known as a way of learning that encourages students to independently formulate their understanding toward the target information within the confines of the task and its material. To make the students as autonomous and self-propelled is the primary purpose of discovery learning (Alfieri et al., 2010; Bruner, 1961; Thorsett, 2002). Concerning the purpose, as suggested in Alfieri et al. (2010), well-prepared mind before discovering a new course material is essential; therefore, teachers are required to give guidance and structured instruction based on the level of difficulty in discovering the target information.

There has been an increasing number of studies analyzing the effects of discovery-based English language learning from various perspectives in the past decade. Honomichl and Chen (2012) investigated the importance of strategic guidance in children's discovery learning. In the same year, Singaravelu's study (2012) revealed that the students' discovery learning is more effective than traditional methods in learning English grammar. In 2015, Achera et al. (2015) investigation indicated the students using a guided discovery approach performed better in Geometry and Mathematics than the participants who were taught through the traditional lecture method. Also, Chase and Abrahamson (2018) pointed out discovery learning as an appropriate solution for a heuristic, technology-based learning models. In early 2020, Musdizal and Hartono's (2020) research indicated a significant effect of discovery learning on the students' writing skill. Most recently, Purnamasari and Argawati (2020) also recommended discovery learning to be used for teaching the students how to write recount text.

Meanwhile, the success of a learning method, in fact, has so many contributing factors. Motivation is one of the most well-known psychological factors responsible in explaining the reason why the success among learners, including the second language learners, can vary (Brown, 2007; Dornyei & Ushioda, 2011; Ghazvini & Khajehpour, 2011; Gilakjani et al., 2012). Many notable scholars have tried to define motivation for language learning from various perspectives. According to the constructivist view, for instance, motivation has a greater emphasis on social context and individual personal choices. This view also comes from Bruner who introduced the term 'discovery learning' at first (1961 as cited in Brown, 2007). He sees motivation as the 'autonomy of self-reward' that is one of the most effective ways to encourage a learner in any age to think and eventually learn something new thoroughly. Gardner and Lambert (1972), with one of their historically well-known studies of motivation, come up with dichotomous clusters of motivation from several different kinds of attitudes which are instrumental and integrative orientations. Later on, Gardner (2001) defines motivation in language learning as a compromising of effort and desire to achieve the learning's objectives and a pleasant attitude. The other widely known motivational research, Dornyei (1998) sees second language classroom motivation as a relevant construct to draw a long succession of second language acquisition.

In the last five years, there were studies attempted to portray the relationship between motivation and discovery learning. Carroll and Beman (2015) looked into the effect of inquiry-based learning in enhancing male students' motivation in an Australian school. The results showed an increased level of the students' willingness to engage and develop their insight through inquiry-based learning. In 2018, Arkhipova et al. (2018) researched on the motivation of learning English as a foreign language (EFL) in a Russian university. The results proved that students' interest in learning English is episodic due to their fear of academic criticism and problems. Besides, Niaz et al. (2018) found out that there was no significant difference in the motivational level of English language learners regarding gender. Unfortunately, limited studies have been conducted to represent both female and male students' motivation toward their discovery-based English language learning experiences.

Therefore, this study using both qualitative and quantitative research methodology aims to shed more lights on how female and male students' motivation is toward the discovery-based English language learning. Furthermore, this study also aims to answer the question of how the students' motivational introspections and orientations affecting their experiences in learning EFL through discovery learning. The results of this study are expected to reveal the most significant motivational factor. Hence, recommendations are proposed to create a motivating discovery-based English language learning and teaching in a classroom setting.

4.2 Motivated Language Strategy Questionnaire

To measure the success of language pedagogy in foreign language classroom, this research observed the student's self-report over their motivation for a particular learning strategy. Thus, survey research using written motivational questionnaire is widely known to be the most effective way to understand students' motivation (Dornyei & Taguchi, 2010; Dornyei & Csizer, 2012). One of the most used questionnaires on motivational research in a foreign language classroom setting is Motivated Language Strategy Questionnaire (MLSQ). MSLQ was first introduced in 1986. Initially, it was a self-report instrument designed by Pintrich and his colleagues to assess college students' motivational orientations and learning strategies for a college course (Credé & Phillips, 2011; Pintrich & Garcia, 1991; Stoffa et al., 2010). MSLQ has been adapted and translated into many languages worldwide to investigate learners' motivation and learning strategies in classroom settings. MSLQ uses the principles of a general cognitive view of motivation and learning strategies. There are 31 statements and three scales that attempt to assess students' motivational orientations toward a course. The scales include three theoretical components; they are 'value beliefs', 'expectancy', and 'affect'.

Value beliefs have three subscales that asses the level of students' motivation in their intrinsic goal orientation, extrinsic goal orientation, and task value. The goal orientations, overall, show the students' reasons why they keep doing the language learning process. In the intrinsic goal orientation, the statements refer to "the students' internal factors that make them persistence in participating in the academic task and mastering the language" (Credé & Phillips, 2011, p. 2). The subscales can show how the students perceive the challenges during the learning process, become curious, and have desire to focus on mastering the language. Meanwhile, the extrinsic goal orientation concerns with "the degree to which the students participate in the language learning process for obvious reasons: acknowledgment, approval, good grades, or rewards from other people" (Credé & Phillips, 2011, p. 2). Thus, extrinsic goal orientation can be considered as a complement to the intrinsic goal orientation in language learning. Besides the goal orientations, the task value assesses "the degree to which the students have a belief that the course material is interesting and worth learning" (Credé & Phillips, 2011, p. 2). Their views regarding the course materials' importance and utility can be portrayed through the statements in this subscale.

In the expectancy component, there are control of learning beliefs and self-efficacy for learning and performance as the subscales—both exhibit the students' belief that they have control over their level of achievement in a learning situation (Credé & Phillips, 2011). The control of learning beliefs features akin to the students' locus of control. Its statements depict the students' belief that their efforts during the learning process will eventually result positively. Hence, the higher the students believe in their opportunity to create a good result, the more the students are likely to give their efforts to study and complete their assignment. On the other hand, the eight-item self-efficacy for learning and performance is "a self-appraisal of someone's confidence that a task can be performed" (Credé & Phillips, 2011, p. 2). The subscale's statements deal with the students' belief of their controlling skill as a useful tool to have an excellent learning performance and to eventually master the course material.

Last but not least, the affective domain consists of test anxiety. The subscale attempts to look into "the learners' degree of anxiety and fear" (Credé & Phillips, 2011, p. 2). The students' concern toward their ability to perform in an assignment or examination potentially affects their learning performance negatively. Thus, every student needs to train him/herself to have effective learning strategies and test-taking skills.

According to the studies above, motivation is a complex and vital factor in the success of second language acquisition. In this study, the six motivational subscales of

MSLQ are explored to examine the most motivating factor for the students' discovery-based English language learning process.

4.3 Collecting the Students' Self-Report

The participants in this study are a teacher and the students of a Senior High School in Jakarta, Indonesia. The school has been implementing the discovery learning since the Curriculum 2013 was implemented. The students participating in this research were all 12th-grade students who were in their first semester of their study. Most of them came from middle to lower-income families living in South Jakarta and Depok. Out of 324 registered students in the school, there were more female students than male students. The students who participated in the survey came from the three classes taught by the same teacher. According to the teacher, they share similar average score for the English language subject; thus, the derived data is expected to be homogenous.

At first, a preliminary survey with yes/no questions was conducted. The preliminary survey investigated the existence of the discovery learning in the school and the students' awareness of its implementation in the English language learning process. There were 14 questions in the preliminary survey and they were derived from the principles of discovery learning. Before the questionnaire was distributed, it was firstly back-translated, and pilot tested. As the school allowed information gathering from the 12th grade students, this preliminary survey successfully collected 144 participants' valid answers. It means 44.44% of all 12th-grade students participated in this preliminary survey. The result indicated the existence of discovery learning in English language learning and teaching in the school as can be seen in Fig. 4.1.

Based on the preliminary survey, as seen in Fig. 4.1, most of the students were aware of the practices of discovery learning in their English learning process at school. This result shows that it is feasible to conduct the next step of the research at this High School.

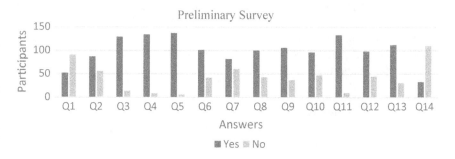

Fig. 4.1 The result of preliminary survey

After the preliminary survey, a cross-sectional survey with the introspection method was prepared to investigate the students' motivation in learning EFL through discovery learning. The main questionnaire was adapted from the MLSQ by Pintrich et al. (1991). The statements in the questionnaire include the six constructs: (a) intrinsic construct, (b) extrinsic construct, (c) task value, (d) control of learning beliefs, (e) self-efficacy for learning and performance, and (f) test anxiety. It uses a 5-point Likert scale start from strongly disagree to strongly agree (see Appendix 1).

First, the questionnaire was translated into Indonesian. After that, it was pilot tested to 10 students from XII Social Science 4–6 classes who shared similar characteristics with the targeted participants in XII Social Science 1–3 classes. The pilot test gave suggestions on how to distribute the questionnaire and revealed several parts that needed revisions before its distribution. Then, the revised questionnaire was distributed in two days to follow the participating classes' schedules as permitted by the school. The students from XII Social Sciences 1–3 classes voluntarily participated in this survey. To increase the survey result's accuracy, the participants listened to the brief explanation about discovery learning first before reflecting on their learning motivation in the survey. Besides, in order to have their actual and natural motivational reflection, they were asked to respond to the questionnaire directly in their classroom.

Each class that took part in the survey consisted of 36 students. However, at the time of the data collection, there were only 105 students participated from the three classes. The result was analyzed into a neat data file through IBM SPSS Statistics 22. During the data processing, 10 participants' data were found to be invalid, so they were excluded from the next step of the data process. Hence, the 95 valid data involved 53 female and 42 male participants as sum up in Table 4.1.

The participants' motivational introspection of the 31 MSLQ's adapted statements was then quantitatively processed through IBM SPSS Statistics 22. The purpose was to see the most motivating factor from both female and male students. The Independent-Samples T-test was conducted to compare the regressed data of MSLQ's six motivational factors as can be seen in Table 4.2.

With minimum dispersion around the mean, the standard deviation in Table 4.2 represents the degree to which individuals within the sample differ from the sample mean. Both female and male students share a standard deviation that is close between the two groups of gender. The standard error in Table 4.2 also estimates a little difference from the population mean. This means that the results can be claimed to represent the 12th-grade students in the High School. There is no statistical difference between female and male students in the results of data processing. The extrinsic

Table 4.1 The number of female and male participants

		Frequency	Percent	Valid percent	Cumulative percent
Valid	Female	53	55,8	55,8	55,8
	Male	42	44,2	44,2	100,0
	Total	95	100,0	100,0	

Table 4.2 The results of the survey

Motivational factors	Gender	N	Mean	Std. deviation	Std. error mean	t-value	Sig
Intrinsic goal oriented	Female	53	3.4670	0.65603	0.09011	0.211	0.103
	Male	42	3.4405	0.54328	0.08383		
Extrinsic goal oriented	Female	53	4.0755	0.50380	0.06920	−0.253	0.737
	Male	42	4.1012	0.47517	0.07332		
Task value	Female	53	3.2987	0.67650	0.09292	−0.021	0.596
	Male	42	3.3016	0.60288	0.09303		
Control of learning beliefs	Female	53	3.7311	0.62567	0.08594	2.077	0.679
	Male	42	3.4702	0.58488	0.09025		
Self-efficacy for learning and performance	Female	53	3.3160	0.71371	0.09804	−0.379	0.307
	Male	42	3.3690	0.62953	0.09714		
Test anxiety	Female	53	3.2189	0.65312	0.08971	−0.039	0.316
	Male	42	3.2238	0.54317	0.08381		

goal orientation, however, shares the highest value for both male and female students. Table 4.2 also shows the means of intrinsic goal orientation, task value, control of learning beliefs, self-efficacy for learning and performance, and test anxiety. The range is from 3.2189 to 3.7311. This illustrates that the level of motivation for those five motivational factors is relatively moderate. A descriptive analysis was used to investigate the students' responses, which mostly ranged between the scale 'neutral' and 'agree'.

The other research instrument used in this study was interview. The researchers interviewed the teacher and the participating students' representatives. The interviews aim to exhibit the unrevealed factors from the survey. The semi-structured interview was conducted with a list of questions as a guideline (see Appendix 2 for the teacher and student interview questions). The interviews were conducted in Indonesian to lessen any potential misunderstanding. Since the teacher taught English to the three participating classes, this interview was resourceful in gathering the information about: how the discovery learning was going on in the school, what kind of challenge(s) that the teacher had found in implementing it, and, most importantly, how it affected the overall students' motivation in learning English. The face-to-face interview with the teacher was not recorded as required by her. In order to decrease any potential bias, the teacher's answers were written in notes when the interview was conducted. With the teacher's consent, the interview notes were then rewritten into a neat report and were also translated into English.

Moreover, to get a deeper understanding of the students' perspectives, interviews were also conducted with 30 selected students as representatives. They were chosen based on the regressed quantitative data to represent the three participating classes, gender, and level of motivation. The number of students interviewed is 30% of the subjects participating in this study (Nunan & Bailey, 2009). The interviews were conducted by phone and recorded with mutual consent. They were conducted in Indonesian to decrease any possibility of misunderstanding. The results of the interviews were then transcribed into true verbatim transcriptions—a conversion of the spoken word into text by including every word, sound, and non-verbal communication to deliver the way it has been spoken (Indian Scribes, 2018). The names of the participants who became the interviewees were presented as pseudonyms to protect their identities as promised in the consent forms.

Both the teacher's interview notes and the students' transcripts were analyzed through grounded theory—a well-known approach that seeks to generate a research's finding(s) by systematically gathering and inductively analyzing the collected data (Brinkmann, 2013; Bryman, 2012). One of the essential processes in grounded theory, according to Bryman (2012), is coding. In data-driven qualitative research, it involves reviewing transcripts or field notes and clustering the findings based on their potential theoretical significance.

4.4 Unveiling the Unwritten Self-Report Details

This part presents the results of the interview with the teacher and interviews with the students. At first, the English language teacher, A. M., found a great number of definitions about discovery learning (A.M., personal communication, November 12, 2018). Then, the teacher inferred that discovery learning is a way to find something which is assigned to the students before she eventually teaches them the course material. In the interview on November 12, 2018, the teacher also stated, "I have never explained the definition of discovery learning." The reason was that the English class's syllabus in the Curriculum 2013 does not require it (Indonesia Ministry of Education & Culture, 2016a). This condition implied one of the reasons why not all of the students knew the definition of discovery learning in the preliminary survey.

The teacher found her students' interest in learning English through discovery learning was quite good (A.M., personal communication, November 12, 2018). However, the students' assignment or examination results were not always able to fulfil the school's expectations. Although the results were not positive, the teacher noticed her students were enthusiastic in exploring the course materials, sharing their opinions and arguments, and helping one another when they were encouraged to figure out the materials on their own first. In the interview on November 12, 2018, the teacher also stated that the implementation of discovery learning could be easy and difficult depending on certain conditions. It was easy when the students were enthusiastic in improving their English. In addition, the students had the opportunities to solve their problems, answered their own questions, and shared their discoveries. The teacher believed that her students would have a brighter future if they continuously did discovery-based English language learning. It was because the method prepares students to be more independent in the future; and therefore, they will be able to solve their problems by themselves and learn the course material based on their preferences.

However, the teacher also had to deal with some challenges while implementing this method (A.M., personal communication, November 12, 2018). First, discovery learning was not applicable in every course material so that the teacher needed to combine it with other learning methods. Besides, it was challenging to make sure that every student shares a similar understanding of the course material because of their different learning pace. Moreover, the lesson's allocated time was often insufficient to fully implement the discovery learning. Hence, the teacher often ended up teaching with the traditional method to deliver the materials faster.

While the questions for the teacher mainly focused on teaching experiences, the questions for the students were meant to obtain a more in-depth understanding of the survey results. The results of the average means of the 30 students' motivation can be seen in Table 4.3 below:

The level of motivation (high, moderate or low) was derived from quartile (Q) 1–3 based on the students' means resulted in the Independent Samples t-Test. Besides their class and gender, the 30 participants were chosen based on their means of motivation compared to the value spread between the quartile. The interviewees were categorized as low-motivated when their means were equal or less than Q1 (Female = 3.30303 and Male = 3.31845). If their means were around Q2 (Female = 3.39150

Table 4.3 The interview results related to motivation and gender

Class	Average means of motivation	Gender	Total
XII Social science 1	High	Female	2
		Male	1
	Moderate	Female	1
		Male	3
	Low	Female	2
		Male	1
XII Social science 2	High	Female	1
		Male	3
	Moderate	Female	2
		Male	0
	Low	Female	2
		Male	2
XII Social science 3	High	Female	2
		Male	0
	Moderate	Female	1
		Male	4
	Low	Female	2
		Male	1
Total of the students' representative			30

and Male $= 3.31845$), they would be considered to have moderate motivation. Meanwhile, the highly motivated interviewees had the average mean which was equal or more than Q3 (Female $= 3.66508$ and Male $= 3.46728$).

In response to the first question about the term 'discovery learning', most of the interviewed students were quite familiar with the practices, especially in English language classes. They found their English language teacher had applied the principles of discovery learning. Thus, they were able to define discovery learning when the questionnaire was distributed.

According to their understanding, discovery learning is a learning method that requires them to independently study the course material with minimal guidance from the teacher before sharing their thoughts to others. Their teacher finally led the sharing session in order to draw the right conclusion of the course material. Therefore, the students recognized the high-demand of active participation of this learning method. The students' answers to question numbers 2–7 resulted in a further explanation of MSLQ's six motivational factors. They are summarized below:

1. Intrinsic Goal Orientation

The four statements in the intrinsic goal orientation look into the students' internal factors that make them persistence in mastering the language from inside themselves (Credé & Phillips, 2011). In the interviews, most students with high to moderate motivation found the discovery learning enjoyable. They were persistent in completing the language learning process for various reasons, such as curiosity, freedom, and self-fulfillment. The highly motivated students seemed to enjoy the freedom in exploring the materials about which they were curious. Six out of 11 moderately motivated students also said that discovery learning made them feel more confident in learning because they had figured out the material before discussing it in the class. Meanwhile, the other moderately motivated interviewees thought that discovery learning was enjoyable only in certain conditions such as when they were eager to study, the course material and its media were fun for them, or the teacher was ready to do more interactions with the students. Seven out of nine low-motivated students found that discovery learning was difficult because they did not understand English well.

2. Extrinsic Goal Orientation

Credé and Phillips (2011) stated that the extrinsic goal orientation concerns with how the students perceive themselves to be a part of the language learning process for obvious reasons such as acknowledgment, competition, evaluation, grades, and rewards from the others. Based on the data in Table 4.2, it is clear that these reasons became the highest motivating factors for both female and male students. The means of male and female participants is above 4.0. The qualitative data confirmed that the high-motivated students were enthusiastic in learning English through discovery because they wanted to be more knowledgeable than the other fellow students. Meanwhile, the moderately motivated students' awareness of global competition and the need to prepare their future were two of the most apparent motivating factors for them to like learning English through discovery learning. The low-motivated students also agreed with the need to be an independent learner in the future, which is the purpose of discovery-based English language learning. Even so, the fear of bad evaluation seemed to dominate their motivation that they preferred the traditional teaching.

The interviewees also shared diverse opinions about discovery learning. All of them, regardless of their level of motivation, thought that their close friends have both positive and negative views on discovery learning. The proponents found that it was more fun to learn by themselves than to depend on what the teacher taught. In contrast, those who were against the implementation of discovery learning thought that their teacher's guidance was insufficient to help them understand the targeted course material. Also, most of the interviewees did not find the opinions of people surrounding them could affect them significantly. However, three moderately motivated students and three low motivated students found that their study partners' opinions might affect them. As an illustration, they would feel encouraged to perform better than the other students if they were part of an ambitious team.

3. Task Value

Task value assesses the degree to which the students engage in the task(s) given during the language learning process (Credé & Phillips, 2011). The students with high to moderate motivation mostly thought that discovery learning method in English subject was applicable to be used in other subjects, necessary for their future, and engaging. They believed they easily remembered the course material when they followed their teacher's instructions in implementing discovery learning. Therefore, they tried to give their best performance. In contrast, two out of the nine highly motivated students sometimes found the time allocation was insufficient for them to thoroughly understand the course material through the assigned task(s). Also, male and female students with low motivation still believed that discovery learning helped them memorizing the course material better than the traditional approach. Even so, the low-motivated students still felt the urgency to learn through direct-teaching.

4. Control of Learning Beliefs

According to Credé and Phillips (2011), control of learning beliefs features how the students believe that the efforts they have given during the learning process will eventually bring positive results. The students with high motivation believed that their efforts during the learning process would eventually bring positive outcomes. They optimistically thought of having a brighter future by using discovery learning to master English, the 'international language'. Meanwhile, seven out of 11 students with moderate motivation believed that they could eventually learn better because they had learned the course material 'twice' through the discovery learning steps. In contrast, the low-motivated students thought that their efforts in discovery learning would not bring positive results. They did not believe they had the power in controlling their learning performance.

5. Self-Efficacy for Learning and Performance

Self-efficacy for learning and performance is a self-appraisal of someone's ability to complete a task and eventually master the course material (Credé & Phillips, 2011). The interview results from the high to moderately motivated students portrayed that they believed in their capability to have a better learning performance while doing the discovery-based English language learning. However, this kind of result did not come from the low-motivated students. They immediately saw themselves incompetent to master English through discovery learning.

6. Test Anxiety

According to Credé and Phillips (2011), test anxiety demonstrates the learners' fear and worry toward a given task or examination. The students with high to moderate motivation generally exhibit mild anxiety about their learning performance that is common to happen in everyday life. When the course material(s) that they had learned through discovery learning turned into an assignment or even an examination, they did not find negative thoughts dominating their mind. Hence, they were quite optimistic about performing well. On the other hand, the low motivated students felt more anxious about making mistakes when they were taught through discovery learning. They eventually chose to be directly taught by the teacher instead of discovering the course material on her own. Even so, two out of 10 low-motivated students thought that they might have performed better in the assignment or examination if they had followed the discovery-based English language learning. Interestingly, two highly motivated students and two moderately motivated students shared similar opinion with the low motivated students. They thought the course material taught through discovery learning added more work to them in answering the questions in the assignment or examination.

4.5 The Students' Diverse Motivational Introspections and Orientations

This part discusses the data presented in the previous part of the chapter. From the survey, it is clear that no significant difference was seen between female and male students regarding the implementation of discovery learning. Of the six motivational factors being investigated, the extrinsic goal oriented holds the highest value as depicted in Table 4.2. In the same way, the qualitative data confirmed that most of the students perceived external factors as their motivation. The participants' focus was still on the competition that they had to face and it was not directly related to the learning process. The findings also point out a competitive yet rewarding learning situation as the main stimulation for the students in discovery-based English language learning. This condition indicates that the implementation of discovery learning in the Senior High School has not reached its ultimate goal; that is, to prepare students to be autonomous and self-propelled learners as claimed by Bruner (1961), Thorsett (2002), and Alfieri et al. (2010).

Meanwhile, the other five motivational factors share similar means in both female and male participants. However, the semi-structured interviews revealed that various situations during the discovery-based English language learning affected the students' level of motivation differently. The intrinsic goal orientation of the students with high to moderate motivation tended to see their participation in the discovery learning as an end in itself. Thus, they enjoyed the learning process and trusted the course material as worth learning. In addition, the highly to moderately motivated students considered the discovery-based English language learning as a promising way to have a brighter future. They believed that having faith in their own ability in independently figuring out the course material and gradually having an excellent learning performance will help them a lot in their future study.

On the contrary, the low-motivated students shared pessimistic views in most of their answers. They saw themselves incompetent to master English through discovery learning in most of their answers. Often, they thought their efforts in discovery learning would only bring negative results. They preferred direct-teaching since they were afraid of drawing the wrong conclusion if it was solely based on their discoveries. Their fear of making mistakes illuminates their confidence; hence, they believed they would perform better only through direct-teaching. Even so, some of them still believed in the usefulness of discovery learning when the course material is more readily accessible to retrieve. The easy access to materials is really highlighted by Bruner (1961), Thorsett (2002), and Alfieri et al. (2010) if we want the implementation of discovery learning to be successful.

The findings in the interviews also point out some challenges that both the teacher and students encountered. The first challenge was the time constraint to apply every step of discovery learning thoroughly. The time constraint could be one of the factors that affected the negative result of discovery learning because it made the students unable to formulate the best conclusion from the course material. The second challenge was the students' different level of independence and willingness to learn a new English course material on their own. It was difficult to thoroughly apply discovery learning because the students in every class had varied preferences. While the low motivated students demanded the learning to start with the traditional teaching, the students with high to moderate enjoyed the discovery learning. Thus, the way of teaching in discovery learning should be designed to fairly compromise and facilitate all students regardless of their level of motivation. Last but not least, it should be troublesome for a teacher to motivate more than 30 students in every class and make sure they correctly understand the course material at the same time. That was one of the reasons why the students had a different level of motivation even though the same English language teacher taught them.

Uncontrollable factors might affect the level of a student's motivation in discovery-based English language learning. To lessen the probability of uncontrollable factors to happen, an effective lesson plan can facilitate students' explorations effectively. For instance, to mitigate the time limitation, the teacher can mix the learning methods so that the learning process runs smoothly. Besides that, assistance or guidance from the teacher to every student, especially during the discussion, is essential. In line with Alfieri, et al. (2010) and Honomichl and Chen (2012), the level of assistance or guidance should be designed based on each class's characteristics and the course material's level of difficulty. Thus, sufficient interactions between a teacher and students are crucial in discovery-based English language learning. In addition, a competitive yet rewarding learning situation in the class is still relevant to stimulate the students' motivation. Indeed, an English teacher should be able to arrange and manage the competition and the rewarding system in a class that implements discovery-based teaching and learning.

4.6 Conclusion

The students' self-report in the questionnaire and semi-structured interviews depict various introspections on their motivations and orientations in learning English through discovery learning. The 5-point Likert scale questionnaire is adapted from the MLSQ by Pintrich, Smith, Garcia, and McKeachie (1991) that focus on six constructs: (a) intrinsic construct, (b) extrinsic construct, (c) task value, (d) control of learning beliefs, (e) self-efficacy for learning and performance, and (f) test anxiety. In addition to the questionnaire, semi-structured interviews were conducted to further examine the findings in the survey.

As depicted in Table 4.2, there is no significant difference in the female and male students' motivation. However, the statistical findings show that the extrinsic goal orientation as the highest value. The extrinsic goal orientation, as clarified in the interviews, included external acknowledgment, competition, evaluation, grades, and rewards from the others. This result contrasts the purpose of discovery learning, which was insisted by Bruner (1961), Thorsett (2002) and Alfieri et al. (2010); that is, to promote a self-regulated learning experience from within the learners. Therefore, when this study was conducted, the implementation of discovery learning in the Senior High School had not achieved the ultimate goal, which aims to develop student-centered learning experiences in the Curriculum 2013.

The findings in this study also show the significance of the other five motivational factors. Each factor contributed differently toward the level of students' motivation. There were some conditions such as individual preferences and time allocation that varied the students' level of motivation. Hence, there should be innovative ways to prepare students to be independent, self-propelled, and successful English learners. An effective lesson plan, appropriate amount of guidance, and a supportive discovery-based English language learning situation should be devised to achieve this.

As for the future, the research on the implementation of discovery learning in English language learning and teaching should be continued, especially in EFL countries. The modified replication of this study would be beneficial for English language pedagogy in the future. Since the questionnaire used in this study only covers several variables of motivation, future research should use a different set of questions to detect different possible effects of a learning and teaching's method. Moreover, gathering a larger sample size from more schools will create a more representative result of English language learning and teaching, especially in Indonesia.

Acknowledgements This work was supported by Universitas Indonesia's Research Grant (PITMA B 2019) managed by DRPM UI/Indonesian Ministry of Research, Technology, and Higher Education's Research Grant (PDUPT 2019) managed by DRPM UI

Appendix 1

Motivational Introspection Questionnaire

The following questions ask about your motivation for the English language class. Remember there are no right or wrong answers, so just answer as accurately as possible. Use the scale below to answer the questions by ticking each column that represents your thought. If you strongly agree with the statement, tick (√) in the column 5; if you strongly disagree with the statement, tick (√) in the column 1. If you more or less agree with the statement, tick (√) the column that best describes your choice between the columns 1 and 5.

Statement		Scale				
		1 Strongly disagree	2 Disagree	3 Neutral	4 Agree	5 Strongly agree
1. In an English language class like this, I prefer to do discovery learning for course material that really challenges me, so I can learn new things	1. *Dalam sebuah kelas bahasa Inggris seperti ini, saya lebih suka melakukan* discovery learning *untuk mempelajari materi pelajaran yang sangat menantang bagi saya, sehingga saya dapat mempelajari hal baru*					
2. If I study in appropriate ways of discovery learning, then I will be able to learn English language course material in this class	2. *Jika saya belajar dengan cara-cara yang benar dari metode* discovery learning, *maka saya akan mampu mempelajari materi pelajaran bahasa Inggris di kelas ini*					
3. When I am taking an English language test in this class, I think about how poor my discovery learning compared with other students	3. *Ketika saya sedang ujian bahasa Inggris di kelas ini, saya berpikir tentang seberapa buruk* discovery learning *saya dibandingkan dengan siswa-siswa lainnya*					

(continued)

(continued)

Statement		Scale				
		1 Strongly disagree	2 Disagree	3 Neutral	4 Agree	5 Strongly agree
4. I think I will be able to use what I have learned in English language course which implements discovery learning to other courses	4. Saya berpikir saya bisa menggunakan apa yang telah saya pelajari di kelas bahasa Inggris yang menerapkan discovery learning di mata pelajaran lainnya					
5. I believe I will receive a good score in this English language class by doing discovery learning	5. Saya mempercayai bahwa saya akan mendapatkan nilai yang baik di kelas bahasa Inggris ini dengan melakukan discovery learning					
6. Through discovery learning, I'm certain that I can understand the most difficult course material presented in the readings for this English language class	6. Melalui discovery learning, saya yakin bahwa saya bisa memahami materi pelajaran yang paling sulit yang ada dalam bahan bacaan dari kelas bahasa Inggris ini					
7. Getting a good score in English language class which implements discovery learning is the most satisfying thing for me right now	7. Mendapatkan nilai yang baik dalam kelas bahasa Inggris yang menerapkan discovery learning adalah hal yang sangat memuaskan bagi saya saat ini					

(continued)

(continued)

Statement		Scale				
		1 Strongly disagree	2 Disagree	3 Neutral	4 Agree	5 Strongly agree
8. When I am taking an English language test in this class, I keep thinking about items that I have not learned through discovery learning so that I have trouble answering the question	8. *Ketika saya sedang ujian bahasa Inggris di kelas ini, saya terus memikirkan tentang hal-hal yang belum saya pelajari melalui* discovery learning *jadi saya kesulitan menjawab pertanyaannya*					
9. It is my own fault if I don't learn the English language course material in this class through discovery learning	9. *Adalah kesalahan saya pribadi jika saya tidak mempelajari materi pelajaran bahasa Inggris di kelas ini melalui* discovery learning					
10. It is important for me to learn English language course material in this class by implementing discovery learning	10. *Adalah sesuatu yang penting bagi saya untuk mempelajari materi pelajaran bahasa Inggris di kelas ini dengan menerapkan* discovery learning					

(continued)

(continued)

Statement		Scale				
		1 Strongly disagree	2 Disagree	3 Neutral	4 Agree	5 Strongly agree
11. The most important thing for me right now is improving my overall average score, so my goal in an English language class is getting a good score especially in a class which implements discovery learning like this class	11. Hal yang paling penting bagi saya saat ini adalah meningkatkan keseluruhan nilai rata-rata saya, sehingga tujuan saya dalam sebuah kelas bahasa Inggris adalah mendapatkan nilai yang bagus terutama dalam kelas yang menerapkan discovery learning seperti kelas ini					
12. I feel confident that I can learn the basic concepts taught in this English language course by conducting discovery learning	12. Saya merasa percaya diri bahwa saya bisa mempelajari konsep-konsep dasar yang diajarkan dalam mata pelajaran bahasa Inggris ini dengan melakukan discovery learning					
13. If I can, I want to get better score than most of other students in English language class which implements discovery learning like this class	13. Jika saya bisa, saya ingin mendapat nilai yang lebih baik daripada kebanyakan siswa lainnya di kelas bahasa Inggris yang menerapkan discovery learning seperti kelas ini					

(continued)

(continued)

Statement		Scale				
		1 Strongly disagree	2 Disagree	3 Neutral	4 Agree	5 Strongly agree
14. When I was taking an English language test which testifies the course material learned through discovery learning, I think of the possibilities of failing	14. *Ketika saya sedang tes bahasa Inggris yang menguji materi pelajaran yang dipelajari melalui discovery learning, saya berfikir tentang kemungkinan untuk gagal*					
15. I feel confident that I can understand the most complex material taught by the teacher in this English language course after doing discovery learning	15. *Saya merasa percaya diri bahwa saya bisa memahami materi yang paling kompleks yang diajarkan oleh guru dalam mata pelajaran bahasa Inggris ini setelah saya melakukan discovery learning*					
16. In an English language class like this, I prefer to do discovery learning for course material that arouses my curiosity even though it is difficult to be learned	16. *Dalam sebuah kelas bahasa Inggris seperti ini, saya lebih suka melakukan discovery learning untuk mempelajari materi pelajaran yang menimbulkan rasa ingin tahu saya walaupun itu sulit untuk dipelajari*					

(continued)

(continued)

Statement		Scale				
		1 Strongly disagree	2 Disagree	3 Neutral	4 Agree	5 Strongly agree
17. I am very interested in finding out the contents of this English language class by myself at first	17. *Saya merasa sangat tertarik untuk menemukan konten-konten dari kelas bahasa Inggris ini oleh diri saya sendiri terlebih dahulu*					
18. If I try my best to do discovery learning, then I will understand the English language course material well	18. *Jika saya mencoba dengan sebaik mungkin untuk melakukan discovery learning, maka saya akan mengerti materi pelajaran bahasa Inggris dengan baik*					
19. I feel uneasy, upset when I was taking an English language exam which examines the course material learned through discovery learning	19. *Saya merasakan perasaan tidak enak, kecewa ketika saya sedang ujian bahasa Inggris yang menguji materi pelajaran yang dipelajari melalui* discovery learning					
20. I feel confident that I can do the assignments and tests in this English language course after conducting discovery learning	20. *Saya merasa percaya diri bahwa saya bisa mengerjakan tugas-tugas dan tes dalam mata pelajaran bahasa Inggris ini setelah melakukan* discovery learning					

(continued)

(continued)

Statement		Scale				
		1 Strongly disagree	2 Disagree	3 Neutral	4 Agree	5 Strongly agree
21. I hope to succeed in this English language class because I have done discovery learning	21. *Saya berharap bisa berhasil di kelas bahasa Inggris ini karena saya sudah melakukan discovery learning*					
22. The most satisfying thing for me in learning the English language through discovery learning is trying to understand the material as completely as possible by myself first	22. *Hal yang paling memuaskan bagi saya dalam belajar bahasa Inggris melalui discovery learning adalah mencoba untuk memahami materi selengkap mungkin oleh diri sendiri terlebih dahulu*					
23. I think the course material in the English language class which implements discovery learning is very useful for me to learn	23. *Saya berpikir materi pelajaran di kelas bahasa Inggris yang menerapkan discovery learning itu sangat berguna untuk saya pelajari*					

(continued)

(continued)

Statement		Scale				
		1 Strongly disagree	2 Disagree	3 Neutral	4 Agree	5 Strongly agree
24. When I have the opportunity to learn the English language through discovery learning, I choose the assignment that I can learn by myself even though it doesn't guarantee a result with good score	24. *Ketika saya mendapat kesempatan untuk belajar bahasa Inggris melalui discovery learning, saya memilih tugas yang bisa saya pelajari sendiri walaupun tidak menjamin hasil dengan nilai yang baik*					
25. If I don't understand the English language course material, it is because I didn't try my best in doing discovery learning at first	25. *Jika saya tidak mengerti materi pelajaran bahasa Inggris, itu karena saya tidak mencoba dengan sebaik mungkin dalam melakukan discovery learning di awal*					
26. I like the course material of this English language class because of discovery learning	26. *Saya menyukai materi pelajaran dari kelas bahasa Inggris ini karena discovery learning*					
27. Understanding the course material from this English language class through discovery learning is very important to me	27. *Memahami materi pelajaran dari kelas bahasa Inggris ini melalui discovery learning itu sangat penting bagi saya*					

(continued)

(continued)

Statement		Scale				
		1 Strongly disagree	2 Disagree	3 Neutral	4 Agree	5 Strongly agree
28. I feel my heart beating fast when I was taking an English language exam which examines the course material learned through discovery learning	28. Saya merasa jantung saya berdegup kencang ketika saya sedang ujian bahasa Inggris yang menguji materi pelajaran yang dipelajari melalui discovery learning					
29. I'm certain that I can master various skills being taught in this English language class because I have done discovery learning	29. Saya merasa yakin bahwa saya dapat menguasai berbagai keterampilan yang diajarkan di kelas bahasa Inggris ini karena saya sudah melakukan discovery learning					
30. I want to do the best in English language class which implements discovery learning like this class because it is important to show my ability to my family, friends, or others	30. Saya ingin melakukan yang terbaik dalam kelas bahasa Inggris yang menerapkan discovery learning seperti kelas ini karena penting bagi saya untuk menunjukkan kemampuan saya kepada keluarga saya, teman-teman saya, dan lainnya					

(continued)

(continued)

Statement		Scale				
		1 Strongly disagree	2 Disagree	3 Neutral	4 Agree	5 Strongly agree
31. By considering the difficulty of the course material, the teacher, and my skills, I think I will do the best in this English language class after conducting discovery learning	31. *Dengan mempertimbangkan kesulitan dari materi, gurunya, dan keterampilan saya, saya berpikir saya akan melakukan yang terbaik di kelas bahasa Inggris ini setelah melakukan discovery learning*					

Appendix 2

Teacher Interview Questions

1. Can you explain what discovery learning is?
2. How would you describe your experience of teaching English language through discovery learning?
3. Did you find teaching English through discovery learning was easy or difficult?
4. Do you believe or think that your students will have a brighter future if they study English language primarily through discovery learning?

Student Interview Questions

1. Have you ever known about the discovery learning before participating in this research?
2. What is discovery learning according to your understanding?
3. How would you describe your experience of studying English through discovery learning? Was it difficult or easy? Was it enjoyable or suffering?
4. Do you believe or think that you will have a brighter future if you study English language through discovery learning? Why?
5. How are the closest people to you, like family member or friend, view on this matter? Do their views affect you?

6. Are there any other reasons, beside your teacher's instruction or the curriculum 2013, that make you want to study English through discovery learning?
7. How does discovery learning affect your confidence in learning English language especially when you are doing your assignment or examination?

References

Achera, L. J., Belecina, R. R., & Garvida, M. D. (2015). The effect of group guided discovery approach on the performance of students in geometry. *International Journal of Multidisciplinary Research and Modern Education, 1*(2), 331–342. http://rdmodernresearch.org/wp-content/upl oads/2016/05/208.pdf
Alfieri, L., Brooks, P. J., Aldrich, N. J., & Tenenbaum, H. R. (2010). Does discovery-based instruction enhance learning? *Journal of Educational Psychology, 103*(1), 1–18.
Arkhipova, M. V., Belova, E. E., & Shutova, N. V. (2018). On motivation of learning English as a foreign language: Research experience in Russian university context. In A. Filchenko, & Z. Anikina (Eds.), *Linguistic and cultural studies: Traditions and innovations. LKTI 2017. Advances in Intelligent Systems and Computing* (p. 677).
Brinkmann, S. (2013). *Qualitative interviewing*. http://booksdescr.org/item/index.php?md5=1FE 7199195A417DFCDEB1C AD40ECA795
Brown, H. D. (2007). *Principles of language learning and teaching*. Pearson Education, Inc.
Bruner, J. S. (1961). The act of discovery. *Harvard Educational Review, 31*, 21–32.
Bryman, A. (2012). *Social research methods* (4th Ed.). https://www.researchgate.net/profile/You sef_Shahwan4/post/What_is_the_best_and_the_most_recent_book_in_medical_research_met hodology/attament/59d6525179197b80779aa90f/AS%3A511717807321088%401499014441 133/download/Social+Research+Methods.pdf
Carroll, J., & Beman, V. (2015). Boys, inquiry learning and the power of choice in a middle school English classroom [Abstract]. *Australian Journal of Middle Schooling, 15*(1), 4–17. https://res earchbank.acu.edu.au/fea_pub/3424/
Credé, M., & Phillips, L. A. (2011). A meta-analytic review of the motivated strategies for learning questionnaire. *Learning and Individual Differences, 21*, 337–346. https://www.sciencedirect. com/science/article/pii/S1041608011000379
Dörnyei, Z., & Ushioda, E. (2011). *Teaching and researching motivation*. Pearson Education.
Dörnyei, Z., & Csizér, K. (2012). How to design and analyze surveys in SLA research? In A. Mackey & S. M. Gass (Eds.), *Research methods in second language acquisition: A practical guide* (pp. 74–94). Wiley-Blackwell Publishing Ltd.
Dörnyei, Z., & Taguchi, T. (2010). *Questionnaires in second language research*. Routledge.
Dörnyei, Z. (1998). Motivation in second and foreign language learning. *Language Teaching, 31*, 117–135. https://www.cambridge.org/core/journals/language-teaching/article/motivation-in-second-and-foreign-language-learning/CF6301F6C401F2CB511529925B298004
Gardner, R. C. (2001). Integrative motivation and second language acquisition. In Z. Dörnyei & R. Schmidt (Eds.), *Motivation and second language acquisition* (pp. 1–19). University of Hawaii Press.
Gardner, R., & Lambert, W. (1972). *Attitudes and motivation in second language learning*. https:// eric.ed.gov/?id=ED081270
Ghazvini, S. D., & Khajehpour, M. (2011). Attitudes and motivation in learning English as a second language in high school students. *Procedia Social and Behavioral Sciences, 15*, 1209–1213. https://www.sciencedirect.com/science/article/pii/S1877042811004435

Gilakjani, A. P., Leong, L., & Sabouri, N. B. (2012). A study on the role of motivation in foreign language learning and teaching. *Modern Education and Computer Science, 7,* 9–16. http://www.mecs-press.org/ijmecs/ijmecs-v4-n7/IJMECS-V4-N7-2.pdf

Honomichl, R. D., & Chen, Z. (2012). The role of guidance in children's discovery learning. *Wiley Interdisciplinary Reviews: Cognitive Science, 3,* 615–622. https://doi.org/10.1002/wcs.1199

Indian Scribes. (2018, November 12). 4 rules of verbatim transcription. https://www.indianscribes.com/4-rules-of-verbatim-transcription/

Indonesia Ministry of Education and Culture. (2016a). *High school subject syllabus: English lesson.* Indonesia Ministry of Education and Culture Printing Office. https://app.buku.kemendikbud.go.id/pencetak-kurikulum-k13

Indonesia Ministry of Education and Culture. (2016b). *Standard process of primary and secondary education* (No.22, the Year 2016). Retrieved October 24, 2018, from https://bsnp-indonesia.org/wp-content/uploads/2009/06/Permendikbud_Tahun2016_Nomor022_Lampiran.pdf

Lyons, D. (2017). How many people speak English, and where is it spoken? [Blog post]. https://www.babbel.com/en/magazine/how-many-people-speak-english-and-where-is-it-spoken/

Musdizal, & Hartono, R. (2020). The influence of discovery learning method and video on students' writing skill. *International Journal of Scientific and Technology Research, 9(1),* 1152–1155. http://www.ijstr.org/final-print/jan2020/-The-Influence-Of-Discovery-Learning-Method-And-Video-On-Students-Writing-Skill.pdf

Niaz, S., Memon, N., & Umrani, S. (2018). Gender differences in motivation level for learning English as an L2. *International Research Journal of Arts and Humanities, 46(46),* 27–33. https://www.academia.edu/38909559/Gender_Differences_in_Motivation_Level_for_Learning_English_as_an_L2

Nunan, D., & Bailey, K. M. (2009). *Exploring second language classroom research: A comprehensive guide.* Cengage Learning.

Pintrich, P. R., Smith, D. A. F., Garcia, T., & McKeachie, W. J. (1991). *A manual for the use of the motivated strategies for learning questionnaire (MSLQ).* https://eric.ed.gov/?id=ED338122

Pintrich, P. R., & Garcia, T. (1991). Student goal orientation and self-regulation in the college classroom. In M. L. Maehr & P. R. Pintrich (Eds.), *Advances in motivation and achievement* (pp. 371–402). JAI Press.

Purnamasari, A., & Argawati, N. O. (2020). The use of discovery learning method in teaching writing recount text to the tenth grade of SMAN Ngamprah. *Professional Journal of English Education, 3(4),* 470–476. https://pdfs.semanticscholar.org/bd5b/f7a929dc0ecc332c4d7a497e0c83635e771d.pdf

Singaravelu, G. (2012). Discovery learning strategies in English. *Journal on English Language Teaching, 2,* 57–62. https://eric.ed.gov/?id=EJ1070208

Stoffa, R., Kush, J. C., & Heo, M. (2010). Using the motivated strategies for learning questionnaire and the strategy inventory for language learning in assessing motivation and learning strategies of generation 1.5 Korean Immigrant Students. *Education Research International, 2011,* 1–8. https://doi.org/10.1155/2011/491276

Thorsett, P. (2002). Discovery learning theory: A primer for discussion. *EPRS, 8500–09*(09), 02.

Sabrina Asrianty Putri is alumnus of English Studies Program. She earned her bachelor degree from Faculty of Humanities, Universitas Indonesia in 2019. She has a keen interest in looking into development issues, including education.

Sisilia Setiawati Halimi is a senior lecturer at the Faculty of Humanities, Universitas Indonesia. Her research interests include language assessment, English for Specific Purposes (ESP), and teacher professional development. She is the member of the Cooperation Division of Teaching English as a Foreign Language in Indonesia (TEFLIN) association.

Open Access This chapter is licensed under the terms of the Creative Commons Attribution 4.0 International License (http://creativecommons.org/licenses/by/4.0/), which permits use, sharing, adaptation, distribution and reproduction in any medium or format, as long as you give appropriate credit to the original author(s) and the source, provide a link to the Creative Commons license and indicate if changes were made.

The images or other third party material in this chapter are included in the chapter's Creative Commons license, unless indicated otherwise in a credit line to the material. If material is not included in the chapter's Creative Commons license and your intended use is not permitted by statutory regulation or exceeds the permitted use, you will need to obtain permission directly from the copyright holder.

Chapter 5
Analysis of the Indonesian Cultural Elements in Secondary School English Textbooks Published by KEMENDIKBUD

Alemina Br. Perangin-angin, Desri Maria Sumbayak, Lara Desma, Siti Patimah, and Indah Putri Tamala

Abstract Culture is a vital aspect of human development, and education should incorporate local cultural content in textbooks, such as secondary school English textbooks. Teachers play a crucial role in character-building learning and should incorporate multicultural education and value education in history learning. This study aims to identify cultural elements in English textbooks from the KEMENDIKBUD (Ministry of Education, Culture, Research and Technology) for secondary school 7–9th grade. The research uses a descriptive qualitative method, focusing on text and images containing cultural elements. The analysis reveals four elements of local culture in the textbook: the existence of social organizations in nuclear families and communities, a system of living equipment and technology in images of daggers, food, clothing, and bags, art in the form of *angklung* as a musical tool and *"Tangkuban Perahu"* narrative as a folklore, and a religious system in images using Muslim culture. These components suggest that the KEMENDIKBUD English textbooks for secondary school students reflect aspects of Indonesian culture.

Keywords Cultural elements · Textbooks · Secondary school · Multimodal · KEMENDIKBUD

A. Br. Perangin-angin · D. M. Sumbayak (✉) · L. Desma · S. Patimah · I. P. Tamala
Faculty of Cultural Sciences, Universitas Sumatera Utara, Medan City, Indonesia
e-mail: desrimariasumbayak@usu.ac.id

A. Br. Perangin-angin
e-mail: alemina@usu.ac.id

I. P. Tamala
e-mail: Indahputritamala19@students.usu.ac.id

© The Author(s) 2025
R. Stroupe and L. Roosman (eds.), *Applied Linguistics in the Indonesian Context*, Engaging Indonesia, https://doi.org/10.1007/978-981-97-2336-2_5

5.1 Introduction

In our increasingly interconnected world, the significance of cross-cultural comprehension and communication cannot be overstated. The field of education holds immense power in shaping the perceptions and attitudes of future generations, making the content of textbooks a vital aspect of transmitting culture. In Indonesia's educational landscape, the KEMENDIKBUD (Ministry of Education and Culture) has been influential in determining the curriculum and shaping the content of secondary school English textbooks. As Indonesia strives to equip its youth for the challenges of the twenty-first century, it becomes crucial to examine how Indonesian cultural elements are portrayed and integrated within these English textbooks.

Meanwhile, the relationship between language and culture has become more important in EFL (English as First Language) teaching, and learning as the phenomenon in English Language Teaching (ELT) is transitioning from communicative competence to intercultural communicative competence. Because of the effects of globalization, ELT can transcend national and ethnic borders and be seen in a globalized and broader context (Risanger, 2018). The position of English as an international language (EIL) necessitates reforms in the ELT culture dimension. It is supposed to teach students how to use English as a lingua franca while also developing their intercultural sensitivity and understanding (Stevanović, 2018).

Research in China has examined how native cultural elements are represented in English-language textbooks used in secondary education in China and Mongolia. The researchers used a content analysis approach to quantitatively examine the multimodal native cultural content in the chosen textbooks. The results of the analysis revealed that both sets of textbooks contain diverse multimodal native cultural content. However, there was a significant imbalance between the representation of visible Big 'C' and more implicit Small 'c' categories in each set (Li et al., 2023). The article concludes with implications for textbook design and classroom teaching, and calls for further studies on teachers' and learners' perceptions of multimodal native cultural content.

In the Indonesian context, research has been conducted to address the cultural dimensions in English textbooks in Indonesia. The research includes a qualitative study of the 2017 grade 10 English textbook, which consists of reading passages, dialogues, and images. The analysis employs Byram's checklist, which provides eight cultural dimensions. The findings reveal that cultural elements are represented in varying degrees in the textbooks, with some aspects being more dominant than others. For example, stereotypes and national identity are found to be prevalent in textbooks, while minority groups are less represented (Ariawan, 2020). Other researchers have utilized Bennett's four multicultural dimensions to analyze the values portrayed in the textbook. The findings revealed that the textbook represented three dimensions of multicultural values: acceptance and appreciation of cultural diversity, respect for human dignity and universal human rights, and respect for the earth (Pratama et al., 2021).

From both of the previous studies mentioned above, we can see that the research to investigate Indonesian local culture in an English textbook published by KEMENDIKBUD (Ministry of Education and Culture) has been conducted for senior high school grades. There has also been research to analyze English textbooks for secondary schools. Prihatiningsih et al. (2021) examined the cultural representation in English as a Foreign Language (EFL) textbooks for seventh graders. The researchers used a qualitative content analysis and a multimodal social semiotic approach to analyze two textbooks. The findings showed that the textbooks had an imbalance in the representation of cultural types, with a focus on the source culture. This could hinder students' ability to learn about other cultures and become effective intercultural communicators. The study suggests that teachers should choose textbooks carefully and supplement them with additional materials to address these issues.

Another study with the aim to analyze the representation of local culture in the Indonesian junior high school English textbook titled *When English Rings a Bell* for grade 8 utilizes a qualitative research approach and applies content analysis as the research method. The researcher analyzes the textbook using a cultural dimensions framework (Moran, 2001), which includes four components: product, practice, perspective, and person. The findings of the study reveal that the English textbook contains representations of local culture through the dimensions of product and perspective such as institutions, art forms, places, lives, and intellectual value.

However, the research above was addressed solely based on a single English textbook published by KEMENDIKBUD (Ministry of Education and Culture) and there is no study using Koentjaraningrat (2005) cultural dimension theory. Thus, this research aims to comprehend the representation, portrayal, and integration of Indonesian culture in secondary school English textbooks published by KEMENDIKBUD (Ministry of Education and Culture) based on multimodal theories and Koentjaraningrat (2005) cultural elements theory.

5.2 Method

The research method used in this study is descriptive qualitative, where the researchers describe the research data consisting of images and text from textbooks. The research findings are examined in detail using multimodal theories. The data sourced from English textbooks for Seventh grade *When English Rings a Bell* (Wachidah et al., 2017a), Eighth grade English textbooks *When English Rings a Bell* (Wachidah et al., 2017a), and Ninth grade English textbooks "Think Globally Act Locally" (Wachidah et al., 2018) published by KEMENDIKBUD (Ministry of Education and Culture). The data was analyzed and categorized into cultural elements based on Koentjaraningrat's (2005) explanation of the seven universal constituent elements of culture: religious systems and ceremonies, civic systems and organizations, knowledge systems, language, art, livelihood systems, and technology systems and equipment.

5.3 Analysis

5.3.1 Social System

According to Koentjaraningrat (2005), every group of people has customs and rules that govern their lives and the various forms of unity in their environment. These rules are both written and unwritten norms that already govern every human life. Koentjaraningrat (2005) stated that the closest and most intimate social unity is the unity of kinship, which includes the immediate nuclear family and other relatives. Other relatives include friends, neighbors, communities within villages, and even between nations.

In Fig. 5.1, an image depicts a youngster partaking in the celebration of their birthday. The child has extended invitations to both relatives and friends, resulting in an atmosphere of joy and happiness shown on the faces of the attendees. The occasion is marked by the provision of cakes and *Nasi Tumpeng* rice, acting as sustenance to commemorate this festive occasion.

Nasi Tumpeng, also known as cone-shaped rice, holds significant cultural value in Indonesian society, frequently being presented during birthday festivities and several other celebratory occasions. This dish symbolizes expressions of gratitude and joy. *Nasi Tumpeng* is traditionally presented by arranging a central mound of rice in a conical shape, which is then accompanied by an assortment of side dishes and vegetables. Typically, *Nasi Tumpeng* is prepared with yellow rice accompanied by *orek tempe* (scrambled tempeh), telur balado (spicy eggs), fried chicken, fresh

Fig. 5.1 *Nasi Tumpeng*, Indonesian traditional food

veggies, and other ingredients as desired. *Nasi Tumpeng* embodies a philosophical concept that serves as a symbolic portrayal of the intricate interplay between the divine and human beings, as well as the interconnectedness among individuals. The human perception of the concept of God is characterized by its association with grandiosity, elevation, and supremacy. Consequently, the emergence of the belief in deities at Mahameru Peak might be attributed to Mount Meru, a volcanic cone located in East Java, Indonesia. Mount Semeru holds the distinction of being the tallest peak located on the Java island.

The *Nasi Tumpeng* rice then assumed the symbolic role of a mountain summit or the embodiment of the divine notion. In addition to rice, the accompanying items offered with *Nasi Tumpeng* also possess their own symbolic significance. *Nasi Tumpeng* is typically accompanied by a selection of seven different types of side dishes. In the Javanese language, the numerical value of seven is represented by the term "pitu," which is derived from the abbreviation "pitulungan," meaning assistance or aid. Furthermore, the hue of the rice adorning the *Nasi Tumpeng* holds significant symbolic connotations. Yellow rice signifies the hue of gold, serving as a representation of regal magnificence. *Nasi Tumpeng* serves as a symbolic representation of beseeching divine protection, security, and gratification for many aspirations in life. In addition to this, the hues of *Nasi Tumpeng* rice predominantly consist of yellow and white, each carrying distinct symbolic connotations. The color white of *Nasi Tumpeng* rice is emblematic of purity, while the color yellow signifies affluence and elevated ethical standards. The idea underlying the inclusion of side dishes, such as salted fish, in the *Nasi Tumpeng* dish exemplifies the principle of mutual cooperation. Boiled eggs are often associated with the concept of resolve, while chicken meat is commonly regarded as a symbol of obedience to a higher power.

Figure 5.2 displays a group of seven high schooled children who are attired with school uniforms, as seen from their blue skirt and pants and white shirts, which are accompanied by ties. Uniforms are mandatory for students at all levels of education in Indonesia. For instance, students enrolled in high school commonly adhere to a dress code policy that requires them to wear uniforms consisting of white and gray attire during their attendance at school. The utilization of these clothes has been mandated by the governing authorities. In addition to conventional school uniforms, the Regional Government possesses the jurisdiction to govern the attire of students in school, including the regulation of traditional clothes. The Decree governs the prescribed uniform colors that are to be worn uniformly across all educational levels in Indonesia. The Decree additionally includes a clarification of its interpretation. The color red is believed to have the potential to foster a mindset conducive to dedicated and focused academic pursuits. In the context of junior secondary school students, the utilization of white and dark blue hues might be interpreted as symbolic representations of qualities such as independence and self-assurance. The utilization of white and gray hues in senior secondary school uniforms symbolizes the transition of students into the realm of puberty.

Figure 5.3 depicts a nuclear family: a paternal figure, a maternal figure, a male offspring, and a female offspring. The practice of family planning imposes a restriction on the number of offspring to a maximum of two children. The Family Planning

Fig. 5.2 Indonesian uniform for secondary school

(KB) program implemented by the Indonesian government is an initiative undertaken by the government to regulate the pace of population expansion and foster the development of high-quality households. The Family Planning (KB) program is a governmental initiative aimed at managing population growth rates and promoting the establishment of high-quality households. The primary aim of family planning is to foster societal well-being, particularly for mothers and children, while also managing population growth in alignment with the Happy Prosperous Small Family Norms (NKKBS). This is achieved through the regulation of birth rates. The efficacy of the family planning program is vital in shaping the overall well-being of families. This program plays a crucial role in safeguarding women's lives and enhancing maternal health, primarily by mitigating the occurrence of unintended pregnancies, promoting appropriate intervals between births, and diminishing the likelihood of infant mortality.

The three images above depict the presence of social connections that occur within both the community and the heart of the family. Figure 5.1 suggests a gathering to celebrate a birthday, with not only the immediate family in attendance but also friends or neighbors who may be partaking in their own special occasion. Figure 5.2 signifies social interactions within a school setting, as evidenced by the holding of hands and shared laughter, indicating a positive bond between individuals. Figure 5.8 captures a complete nuclear family, with vibrant colors and gazes directed toward one another, symbolizing a strong familial connection. Both parents and children exemplify social systems. These three images collectively showcase Indonesian culture, wherein individuals actively engage in social lives within their nuclear families and the surrounding environment.

Fig. 5.3 Family planning

5.3.2 Living Equipment Systems and Technology

The initial attention of anthropologists in understanding human culture is based on the technological elements used by a society in the form of objects used as a living equipment with simple forms and technology. Thus, the discussion of cultural elements included in the living equipment and technology is a discussion of physical culture.

Figure 5.4 depicts a traditional weapon commonly referred to as a *keris*. The term *"keris"* originates from the Javanese language, specifically from the word *"ngiris"* which means to pierce. The *keris* was utilized from the 9th to the fourteenth centuries. It holds a significant position in Indonesian culture, particularly the renowned *keris* which features wavy and jagged patterns. A dagger can be categorized into three parts: the blade (knife), *hulu* (handle), and *werangka* (scabbard). Each part of the dagger carries its own artistic meaning. Daggers were meticulously carved and crafted using various materials such as precious metals, wood, ivory, and even gold. The aesthetic value of a keris can be determined by its age and place of origin. *Keris* is a distinctive weapon commonly associated with regions inhabited by Malay or Malay-related communities, including Sumatra, Java, Malaysia, Brunei, Thailand, and the Philippines. However, currently, the *keris* is predominantly recognized in the Indonesian region, particularly Java. In the past, daggers served multiple purposes such as weapons, heirloom tools, accessories for traditional attire, and spiritual objects. Due to the belief in their magical properties, daggers are often considered lucky charms and utilized as amulets. In folklore, legendary daggers are often depicted as possessing supernatural and extraordinary powers, such as *Mpu Gandring's keris* and *Kiyai Condong* mixed.

Figure 5.5 illustrates a number of bright red chili peppers, which serve as the basic ingredient in the making of *sambal uleg* (crushed chili sauce). *Sambal* is a condiment derived from the crushing of chili peppers, resulting in the release of their aqueous

Fig. 5.4 *Keris* (dagger) traditional weapon from Indonesia

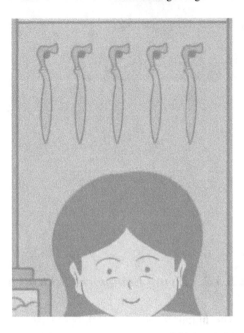

content and the subsequent manifestation of a pungent flavor profile. Upon the use of various spices, the resultant flavor profile will exhibit a piquant quality, thereby serving as a delectable catalyst for stimulating one's hunger. There exist multiple variations of chili sauce. Every variation necessitates a diverse array of ingredients and spices. *Sambal* is a customary Indonesian culinary accompaniment originating from the island of Java. It has been part of the dietary practices of the ancient Javanese population since the tenth century AD. Prior to the introduction of contemporary chili varieties to the archipelago, Javanese individuals relied on indigenous chili varieties, such as Javanese chilies or *puyang* chilies (*Piper retrofractum*), as well as pepper (*Piper nigrum*) and ginger, for the preparation of *sambal*.

In Fig. 5.6 fried *kepok* is depicted as a representative example of a traditional snack in Indonesia. The fried *kepok* holds significant popularity as a snack within the Indonesian culinary landscape. It is commonly enjoyed during leisurely moments in the afternoon, frequently complemented by a cup of coffee or sweet tea. Fried *kepok* are frequently consumed as a breakfast option by individuals who want a lighter morning meal. Fried *kepok* typically consist of bananas, with the specific variety used being a seasonal variation. These bananas are commonly coated with a blend of flour, sugar, and eggs, and subsequently fried in heated oil until they acquire a brown appearance.

Being a multicultural country with a vast amount of diversity, Indonesia's national identity also encompasses various elements. One of these elements includes regional specialties, as every region has its own unique culinary culture. This diversity in food contributes to the strength of Indonesia's national character and showcases the

Fig. 5.5 Sambal Uleg

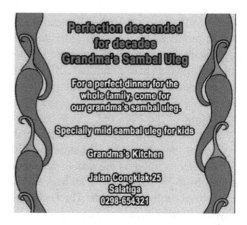

Fig. 5.6 Fried *Kepok*

cultural differences that exist within the country. Additionally, food holds a significant place in everyday life and is greatly influenced by the changing times. It serves as a means to connect individuals with all living beings and serves as a reflection of cultural identity. Moreover, culinary practices in Indonesia represent a multicultural identity that is recognized globally. The cuisine of Indonesia is incredibly diverse, spanning across the entire archipelago due to its strategic location. Examples of typical Indonesian foods include *Sambal Uleg* and fried *Kepok*. These dishes symbolize the plants found in Indonesia that are transformed into iconic Indonesian dishes.

Clothing serves as a form of protection during daily activities for humans, but it also holds aesthetic value by enhancing appearance. Moreover, clothing can indicate a person's origin, thus becoming part of their identity. Traditional clothing, such as the *ulos* of the Batak Toba tribe, plays a significant role in showcasing the culture within a community (see Fig. 5.7). The *ulos*, which means blanket, is made using looms and its colors hold specific meanings. *Ulos* woven cloth represents a customary textile produced by the Batak tribe through the process of weaving. The *ulos* hold significant functional and symbolic significance. *Ulos*, a customary textile, is an integral component of a multitude of traditional ceremonies encompassing significant life events such as births, weddings, deaths, and various other rituals. In relation to color, *ulos* fabric consistently exhibits a predominant trichromatic composition, consisting of the hues red, black, and white. In addition to its utilitarian use as clothing, *ulos* holds significant ceremonial value as a customary gift, serving as a symbol of the esteemed social standing within the Batak tribe.

Another example is the *noken*, The *noken* is a distinctive indigenous bag originating from Papua, crafted with bark fibers primarily sourced from *nenduam* trees, *nawa* trees, or forest orchids. The functions of *noken* exhibit a wide range of diversity. Nevertheless, *noken* is commonly employed for the transportation of many

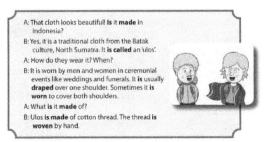

Fig. 5.7 Indonesia traditional cloth

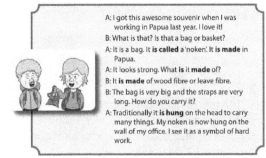

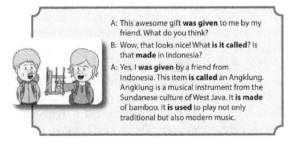

Fig. 5.8 *Angklung*, a Sundanese musical instrument

commodities, including firewood, harvested plants, and even groceries. Typically, little *noken* are employed for the purpose of transporting personal essentials. In addition to its practical uses, *noken* is also employed in ceremonial contexts and serves as a commemorative item for visitors. The *noken* device has the ability to elevate items weighing up to 20 kg. The manner in which it is worn is subject to regional customs. Two well-known types of *noken* are the Wamena *noken* and Raja Ampat *noken*, which have gained significant recognition. On December 4, 2012, UNESCO officially acknowledged Wamena *noken* as an intangible cultural treasure due to its exceptional characteristics. The presences of *ulos* from Batak ethnic group and *noken* from Papua as two traditional living artifacts highlight the presence of Indonesian culture within the book's context.

5.3.3 Arts

Anthropologists' attention to art stems from ethnographic research into the artistic activities of a traditional society. The descriptions collected in the study contain objects or artifacts that contain elements of art, such as sculptures, carvings, and decorations. Early ethnographic writing about elements of art in human culture was more about the engineering and process of making these art objects. In addition, the initial ethnographic description also examines the development of music, dance, and dramatic arts in society.

In the image in Fig. 5.8 is the traditional musical instrument from Indonesia known as the *angklung*. The *angklung* is a traditional Indonesian musical instrument commonly encountered in the region of West Java. The aforementioned musical instrument is crafted using bamboo tubes. The auditory quality of this instrument is generated through the vibrational impact of the bamboo tubes when they are shaken. The term *angklung* derives from the Sundanese language, specifically from *angkleung-angkleung* which signifies the player's synchronized movements with the rhythm. *Klung* on the other hand, represents the melodious tone produced by this instrument. Remarkably, each note is emitted through the varying sizes of bamboo tubes, resulting in a harmonious melody that captivates the listener's senses. The *angklung* is traditionally performed by gripping the lower part of its frame with one hand, while the other hand is responsible for oscillating the instrument horizontally, resulting in the production of successive tones. One notable characteristic of the *angklung* is its limited capacity to produce a single note, necessitating collaborative efforts to generate a comprehensive melodic composition.

Typically, the *angklung* is crafted using black bamboo (*Awi wulung*) or string bamboo (*Awi temen*), which, upon drying, displays a distinctive whitish-yellow hue. To construct an *angklung*, two to four bamboo tubes of different dimensions are collected and securely bound together using rattan. Historical records suggest that the Sundanese have been acquainted with the *angklung* for generations. This enchanting instrument finds its purpose in a multitude of occasions, particularly during agricultural festivities, where it acts as a means of summoning *Dewi Sri* or *Dewi Kesuburan*.

Following the conversion of the people to Islam, this art was utilized to accompany circumcisions and marriages. On November 16, 2010, UNESCO formally recognized the Indonesian *angklung* as a global cultural treasure originating from Indonesia. The recognition of *angklung* by UNESCO was not arbitrary, but rather based on its fulfillment of the requirements for inclusion on the Representative List of Intangible Cultural Heritage of Humanity.

Another finding in terms of arts is from a narrative folklore '*Tangkuban Perahu*' with main characters *Dayang Sumbi* and *Sangkuriang* (Fig. 5.9). The following examples of from this narrative folktale are illustrative:

He didn't know she was *Dayang Sumbi*.

Knowing that *Dayang Sumbi* had deceived him, *Sangkuriang* became very angry.

The moral message from the Legend of Mount *Tangkuban Perahu's* Origin is that people should be honest since it will bring you goodness and happiness in the future. Cheating is harmful to yourself and can result in disaster for you or others.

The presence of Indonesian culture in this textbook is demonstrated by the example of naming a character taken from one of the folklore stories in Indonesia. When students study English as a foreign language, they can better comprehend their own culture. Because they are familiar with the cultural material, the students can grasp the language more quickly. Local folklore supports not just the government's educational purpose, but also other important aspects of language acquisition, such as learning the target language faster (Taylor, 2000).

5.3.4 Religious System

The core value of Pancasila, as the foundation of existence for the Indonesian nation, is unity in diversity. For the Indonesian people, Pancasila signifies a strong foundation that fortifies our shared sense of national identity. As the foundational tenet of the nation and a blueprint for progress, Pancasila influences each facet of human existence. We strengthen unity in the midst of diverse cultural, ethnic, and religious diversity by adhering to Pancasila. Indonesia's motto, "*Bhinneka Tunggal Ika*," which has multiple interpretations but is still one, reflects the relationship between unity and variety. For a nation with a diverse community to prevent division and conflict, the relationship between unity and diversity is crucial. Thousands of islands make up the unified nation of Indonesia. The diversity of Indonesia is influenced by its vast territory. Diversity stems from this state and can be found in things like color, class, ethnicity, religions and culture. The six different religions (Confucianism, Buddhism, Hinduism, Christianity, Islam, and Catholic) that people in Indonesia follow are recognized, demonstrating the diversity of the country's religious practices. Figure 5.10 depicts the friendship of a girl who wears a hijab and her female friend who does not, as well as the friendship of a female who wears a hijab and a

Paragragh 3
1. He fell in love with her at the first sight.
2. She could never get older because she was granted eternal youth by the gods.
3. There he met a beautiful young woman.
4. He did not know that she was Dayang Sumbi.
5. One day Sangkuriang went back to his village.
6. He was big and strong.

Paragraph 4
1. Then she got an idea.
2. Dayang Sumbi saw the bad scar on his forehead.
3. She gave him a task which she thought was impossible for him to do.
4. She told him the truth again and again but he would not believe her.
5. One day he approached Dayang Sumbi to propose her.
6. She asked him to make her a lake and a boat in one night.
7. She soon realized that he was her own son, Sangkuriang.
8. She was thinking hard to find a way not to marry him.
9. She did not know Sangkuriang had genies to help him to do the task.

Paragraph 5
1. Knowing Dayang Sumbi cheated him, Sangkuriang got very angry.
2. Dayang Sumbi got very worried.
3. She was thinking hard again to find a way to fail him.
4. The genies thought that the morning was almost broken.
5. It is now known as Mount Tangkuban Perahu.
6. By dawn both the lake and the boat were almost done.
7. She asked the people in the village to burn the woods in the east, so that the light made all the cocks in the village crow.
8. They ran away as fast they could, leaving the boat unfinished.
9. Then she had an idea.
10. He kicked the boat so hard that it went upside down.

Fig. 5.9 Paragraphs from the narrative folklore *Tangkuban Perahu*

boy from Papua. The hijab is a depiction of Muslim women. This image represents the diversity of religions and ethnic groupings in the Indonesian context.

Koentjaraningrat (2005) asserted that the issue of religious functioning in society stems from the question of why humans believe in a higher supernatural power and why they engage in various methods to communicate and establish connections with these supernatural forces. From the image provided, we can observe a character dressed in Muslim attire. Muslim fashion is closely associated with followers of the Islamic faith. Religion holds great significance in Indonesian society and the everyday lives of its residents. Indonesia boasts the largest Muslim population globally; however, millions of individuals in this country adhere to alternative religions

Siti: "Are you mopping the floor again? You've just finished mopping it, haven't you?"

Dayu: "Well, I tripped over the stool and fell and spilled my milk all over the floor."

Edo: "Where are the others? They are not having lunch now?"

Siti: "No. They are all in the library. They're looking for some texts about animals and plants in the encyclopedia. Let's go and join them."

Fig. 5.10 The diversity of religions and ethnic groupings in the Indonesian context

and animist beliefs. Moral values as social norms may shape individuals' thinking, feeling and behavior (Widodo, 2018). One of the educational goals in the educational landscape is to cultivate those moral values (Lovat, 2017).

5.4 Conclusion

According to Koentjaraningrat (2005), there are seven key elements that contribute to Indonesian culture, namely language, knowledge, social structure, living equipment and technology, livelihood, art, and religion. Remarkably, the English textbook used in secondary schools covers four out of the seven cultural elements, making it an excellent resource for understanding Indonesian culture in its entirety. These four elements include the utilization of the depiction of social organizations through images of nuclear families and the local community, the representation of living equipment and technology systems through illustrations of daggers, food, clothing, and bags, the showcasing of art in the form of *angklung* as a musical instrument and a folklore *Tangkuban Perahu*, and the depiction of religious systems through images of various religious practices. The incorporation of these cultural elements in the KEMBDIKBUD secondary school English textbook is a testament to the importance of preserving Indonesian culture. It highlights the need to impart this knowledge to the younger generation, and textbooks serve as an effective medium for achieving this purpose. By utilizing books as a means of passing on Indonesian culture, the next generation will have a deeper understanding and appreciation for their own heritage, ensuring its longevity for years to come. The diversity of Indonesian culture is of great significance as foreign cultures continue to infiltrate the country. In order to ensure that the rich Indonesian heritage is passed on to future generations, various methods are employed, with textbooks playing a crucial role in spreading cultural knowledge.

References

Ariawan, S. (2020). Investigating cultural dimensions in EFL textbook by using Byram checklist. *Register Journal, 13*(1), 123–152. https://doi.org/10.18326/rgt.v13i1.123-152

Koentjaraningrat. (2005). *Pengantar Antropologi I*. Rineka Cipta.

Li, Z., Zeng, J., & Nam, B. H. (2023). A comparative analysis of multimodal native cultural content in english-language textbooks in China and Mongolia. *SAGE Open, 13*(2), 1–15. https://doi.org/10.1177/21582440231178195

Lovat, T. (2017). Values education as good practice pedagogy: Evidence from Australian empirical research. *Journal of Moral Education, 46*(1), 88–96.

Moran, P. (2001). Defining culture. *Teaching culture: Perspectives in practice*.

Prihatiningsih, F., Petrus, I., & Silvhiany, S. (2021). Cultural representation in EFL textbooks for the seventh graders: A multimodal analysis. *Lingua Cultura, 15*(1), 121–133. https://doi.org/10.21512/lc.v15i1.7319

Risanger, K. (2018). *Representations of the world in language textbooks*. Multilingual Matters.

Stevanović, G. (2018). Comparative analysis of the representation of cultural content in ELT textbooks used in eight grades of primary schools in the Federation of Bosnia and Herzegovina. *Školski Vjesnik: Časopis Za Pedagogijsku Teoriju I Praksu, 67*(3), 389–404.

Taylor, E. K. (2000). *Using folktales*. Cambridge University Press.

Wachidah, S., Gunawan, A., Diyantari, & Khatimah, Y. R. (2017). *Bahasa Inggris, when english rings a bell*. Kementerian Pendidikan dan Kebudayaan.

Wachidah, S., Gunawan, A., Diyantari, & Khatimah, Y. R. (2018). *Bahasa Inggris, think globally act locally*. Kementerian Pendidikan dan Kebudayaan.

Widodo, H. P. (2018). A critical micro-semiotic analysis of values depicted in the Indonesian Ministry of National Education-endorsed secondary school English textbook. In *Situating moral and cultural values in ELT materials* (pp. 131–152). Springer.

Alemina Br. Perangin-angin received a bachelor's degree in English literature from the Universitas Sumatera Utara in 2003, a master's degree in humanities from Universitas Negeri Medan in the Applied English Linguistics Program in 2008, and a doctoral in linguistics from the Universitas Sumatera Utara in 2018. As the lecturer in the Magister English Program at the Universitas Sumatera Utara, she is interested in anthropological linguistics, cultural studies, critical discourse analysis, and gender studies who can be contacted at aleminaperanginangin@gmail.com.

Desri Maria Sumbayak is a senior lecturer at the English Department, Faculty of Cultural Sciences, Universitas Sumatera Utara. She graduated from the Faculty of Letters, Universitas Sumatera Utara, in 1997. She started her teaching experience at the Faculty of Teacher Training and Education, Universitas Riau, in 1998. In the same year, she continued her master's degree in the area of literary studies at Universitas Indonesia and finished the study in 2000. To improve her knowledge of teaching, she pursued her second master's degree in TESOL at the University of Canberra, Australia (2007-2009). At the moment, her areas of research and interest are cultural studies, literature, and teacher training, and teaching methodologies.

Lara Desma is a teacher in SMA Negeri 1 Namurambe. She received her master degree in humanities from Universitas Sumatera Utara in Applied Linguistics Program in 2021. Her interests are nn education, anthropolinguistics and Neuro Linguistics.

Siti Patimah received her master degree in humanities from Universitas Sumatera Utara in the Applied Linguistics Program in 2021. She is interested in critical discourse analysis (CDA) and Indonesian Culture, specifically about the religious system.

Indah Putri Tamala is a student in the English Literature Department Faculty of Cultural Sciences, Universitas Sumatera Utara. She took part as a secretary in the Student Association for more than half a year of successful experience in providing secretarial and administrative support. At the moment, she is doing her thesis analysis about speaking disfluency.

Open Access This chapter is licensed under the terms of the Creative Commons Attribution 4.0 International License (http://creativecommons.org/licenses/by/4.0/), which permits use, sharing, adaptation, distribution and reproduction in any medium or format, as long as you give appropriate credit to the original author(s) and the source, provide a link to the Creative Commons license and indicate if changes were made.

The images or other third party material in this chapter are included in the chapter's Creative Commons license, unless indicated otherwise in a credit line to the material. If material is not included in the chapter's Creative Commons license and your intended use is not permitted by statutory regulation or exceeds the permitted use, you will need to obtain permission directly from the copyright holder.

Chapter 6
A Preliminary Report: Examining Pre-service Teacher Education, Teaching Practices, and Linguistic Diversity in the Indonesian Context

Richmond Stroupe and Sisilia Setiawati Halimi

Abstract Covering an area of approximately 1.8 million square kilometers, and including a vast number of ethnic and linguistic groups, encompassing approximately 700 indigenous and minority languages, from varying cultural backgrounds, Indonesia presents a unique opportunity to examine how its education system addresses such a variety of needs across such a diverse context. Any second language education including English presents unique challenges in such a linguistically diverse landscape. Examining how such an education system addresses these challenges would be useful for policy makers, administrators, teacher educators, and teachers throughout the region as these stakeholders are faced with similar challenges in other Asian countries and beyond. In order to investigate how the Indonesian educational system prepares and responds to such a complex environment, participants for the current ongoing research project are drawn from four groups: Current preservice language educators, teacher educators, graduated/practicing teachers, and institutional leaders (principles, headmasters, etc.). In-depth individual or group interviews were conducted with members of each of the four groups. Classroom observations were also conducted with practicing teachers and are used to confirm information gathered through interviews as to actual practice in the language-learning classroom. The results of such research could be instrumental in providing a better understanding of the current situation of English language teacher education and teaching practice in Indonesia, as well as how to plan for future curricular developments. The results could also not only be valuable to policymakers and planners in Indonesia and across the Asian region but beyond in other contexts where learners represent a variety of linguistic and cultural backgrounds.

R. Stroupe (✉)
Soka University, Tokyo, Japan
e-mail: richmond@soka.ac.jp

S. S. Halimi
Univesitas Indonesia, Depok, Indonesia
e-mail: sshalimi@gmail.com; ss_halimi@ui.ac.id

Keywords Translanguaging · National curriculum · Language education · Teacher education

6.1 Introduction

As a member of the Association of Southeast Asian Nations (ASEAN), Indonesia represents one of the most diverse countries in the region. Covering an area of approximately 1.8 million square kilometers, and including a vast number of ethnic and linguistic groups, encompassing approximately 700 indigenous and minority languages, from varying cultural backgrounds (Australian Government, 2017; Goebel, 2018; Hadisantosa, 2010; Riza, 2008; Zein, 2018b, Zein et al., 2020), Indonesia presents a unique opportunity to examine how that education system addresses such a variety of needs across such a diverse landscape. Likewise, within an educational system that services such a linguistically and culturally diverse student population, any second language education including English presents unique challenges. Examining how such an education system addresses these challenges would be useful for policy makers, administrators, teacher educators, and teachers throughout the region as these stakeholders are faced with similar challenges in other ASEAN countries and beyond (Kirkpatrick, 2017; Stroupe & Maggioli, 2018; Zein, 2018a, 2018b). Such a focus is timely as educational reforms are being implemented or revised, the scope of English language education is being broadened, and the transition from English as a Foreign Language (EFL) to English as a Lingua Franca (ELF) is in process in some countries in the ASEAN region (Stroupe, 2018; Stroupe & Maggioli, 2018; Zein et al., 2020).

This chapter presents preliminary findings from a larger research project that investigated preservice teacher education programs and secondary teaching practices across seven regions of Indonesia. Data analysis and findings included in this preliminary investigation will focus on data gathered from pre-service teacher education students at the university level, their educators, current secondary teachers and educational leaders and classroom observations in Kalimantan, Bali and Padang.

6.2 Background

In an educational context as varied and differentiated as that which exists in Indonesia, a variety of variables should be considered. For the purposes of the current paper, diverse linguistic and cultural characteristics, teacher beliefs and language of instruction, impact of national curricular requirements, and professional development of secondary and preservice teachers in the English language education context will be considered.

In general, most practicing secondary teachers must follow officially government approved national curricula. In some cases, this can be challenging related to the relevancy of the curricula to the local context, and how national requirements can be practically implemented given the time constraints and resources at the local level (Mangali & Hamdan, 2015). As a result, secondary teachers face an array of difficulties when implementing the national curriculum in Indonesia (Retnawati et al., 2016). Teachers often find implementing the curriculum challenging given the time allowed. Also, there is a lack of effective professional development, there may be inadequate teaching resources and materials and some teachers report a lack of student motivation. In particular relevant to implementation of English language curricula, teachers' English proficiency is often cited as a challenge (Gultom, 2016; Malik et al., 2021; Mattarima & Hamdan, 2011; Renandya et al., 2018; Retnawati et al., 2016; Songbatumis, 2017; Sulistiyo, 2016).

Language of instruction, home and national culture, and learners' first language (L1) can have an impact on the extent to which EFL learners are able to achieve language-learning goals successfully in an educational environment. Language educators in the classroom are at the forefront of addressing these challenges. How they address these needs, and how they are prepared to do so through preservice teacher education programs, can have a significant impact on the success of educational systems (Adnyani, 2015; Asfihana, 2017; Hendayana, 2007; USAid, 2001; Zhao & Zhang, 2017). When educational systems are diverse, these challenges can become more complex. Learners and teachers representing a variety of linguistic and cultural backgrounds such as those present in Indonesia add complexity to the teaching and learning process (Amery, 2019; Musgrave, 2014; Rasman, 2018). Other variables that contribute to the complex decision-making process on the part of teachers are national curricular requirements, often related to official national language, as well as their own personal teaching beliefs and linguistic backgrounds.

One recent innovative approach to investigating communication in multilingual contexts in general and in language learning classrooms in particular is a focus on translanguaging. This term refers to the techniques, strategies and language practices used by bilinguals to communicate in multilingual contexts (Garcia & Lin, 2017; Palmer et al., 2014; Turnbull, 2018; Zein, 2018b). This approach to communication allows for the use of multiple languages in order to convey meaning while at the same time allowing learners to exert their own voice and identity in the language classroom. While such strategies and abilities are becoming more common in bilingual literature, and in research related to second language teaching pedagogy, this remains a focus that has been underutilized. Research in Indonesia provides a unique opportunity to observe how preservice teacher education programs can prepare teachers to address the diverse needs of learners by utilizing diverse linguistic resources through incorporating national, foreign, official, indigenous and minority languages into learning environments (Rasman, 2018; Zein et al., 2020).

The influence of language learning on learners, identity, and local cultures has been discussed extensively (Norton, 1997; Pennycook, 1994, 2007). More recently, how this complex interaction affects the practical language learning classroom has also been the topic of research (Butler, 2015; Littlewood, 2007; Nieto, 2001; Tsui & Tollefson, 2017). Furthermore, how to integrate cultural understanding into the language-learning classroom has also been a topic of research and investigation.

The impact of culture on language learning as well as the importance of introducing not only the target language culture but also a variety of cultures into the language-learning context has been well established. This integration is particularly relevant in the context of Indonesia where the possible adoption of English as a lingua franca (ELF) intersects with cultural and linguistic integration (Zein et al., 2020). Within national borders where diverse cultures exist, how teachers in the Indonesian context address cultural understanding and the sharing of cultural perspectives in a language-learning context could be instrumental to other teachers as they strive to reach a balance between culture and language learning in their own classrooms.

In addition to English language proficiency and content knowledge, as learners move into an increasingly globalized context, a new range of twenty-first century skills are required. Dealing with extensive amounts of information, developing critical thinking skills, increasing cultural understanding and intercultural commutative confidence are all skills that are becoming more and more valued in the global community (Bellanca & Brandt, 2010; Beers, 2011; Bourn, 2011; Gamble et al., 2010; Stroupe, 2018; MacDonald et al., 2011; Stroupe, 2017, 2018). Specific to the context of Indonesia, how these skills are reconciled with local/Indonesian values rather than western stereotypes is important. Likewise, how these skills complement the focus on the "character building" aspect of recent Indonesian educational initiatives is also important (Zein et al., 2020). Lastly, how these skills can be integrated into English language learning environments in order to support learners as they graduate and enter the global community, whether at the local, national, or international level, is an important aspect of curriculum development and teaching methodology.

Preservice teacher education programs are extensive in Indonesia. Based on the Law on Teachers and Lecturers (Law No. 14 2005) all teachers are required to graduate with a bachelor's degree, and to receive official certification, with a government target of 2015 to have all current teachers fully certified. While this alone is a monumental task, quality assurance issues remain. In some cases, there is little data to support the assumption that certified teachers have a greater positive impact on learning outcomes than uncertified teachers (OECD/Asian Development Bank, 2015). Preservice teacher education programs also face challenges as they strive to prepare novice teachers for the classroom, including developing necessary teaching and classroom management skills, providing sufficient practicum supervision, and transferring the study of effective pedagogical approaches into effective real world teaching practices (Asfihana, 2017; Kuswandono, 2014; Mudra, 2018; Polim, 2021; Riesky, 2013; Sulistiyo et al., 2017; Zein, 2016).

6.3 Methodology

The current ongoing research focuses on how local teachers navigate the complex interplay between linguistic diversity, cultural diversity, required national curriculums and other aspects and trends in English language education in Indonesia. More specifically, the following research questions underpin the study:

1. How do secondary teachers navigate the linguistic complexities of their teaching contexts, and how do their beliefs affect their choice of language of instruction?
2. To what extent are communicative, student-centered approaches, implemented in Indonesian English language learning classrooms?
3. Do secondary teachers make use of translanguaging pedagogy in their language learning classrooms?
4. Are teachers familiar with and actively implementing 21st-century skills into their teaching curricular?
5. How does the nationally required curriculum affect teaching practice in diverse locales within Indonesia?

In order to answer the research questions above, a qualitative research design was implemented. Participants from preservice teacher education programs and secondary schools were identified through professional contacts at Universitas Indonesia and also through the Association for the Teaching of English as a Foreign Language in Indonesia (TEFLIN). Initial contacts were made with teacher educators in university preservice teacher education programs, and through those contacts, access to preservice teachers, secondary schools, and local educational leaders was established. Efforts were made to collect data from participants in non-centrally located schools, in suburban and more rural contexts, where possible. Of the seven regions in Indonesia, participants from Kalimantan, Bali and Padang are included in the current chapter.

Data collection consists of interviews and classroom observations. Interviews were led by the lead researcher, conducted individually or in groups, and depending on the needs of the participants, were conducted primarily in English or in Bahasa Indonesia with the aid of available translators. Class observations were conducted based on the availability of English language courses in the schedule on the day of specific school visits. Each classroom observation also included a pre- and post-observation interview with the teacher. Detailed notes were taken during the observation as well as photographs and videos where possible. As the observer, the lead researcher did not actively participate in the class sessions.

All interviews were transcribed and then initially coded based on categorization derived from extensive review of the literature. Additional categories and subcategories were added as they emerged from the data, frequencies of responses were calculated based on the type of participant and locale, resulting in specific and overall totals.

6.4 Results

Interviews were conducted with 64 secondary level English language teachers from public, private and vocational secondary schools (Kalimantan, N = 30; Bali, N = 27; Padang, N = 7). In addition, 18 educational leaders were interviewed (Kalimantan, N = 7; Bali, N = 9; Padang, N = 2) serving in the roles of principal (or headmaster), vice principal (of curriculum, finance, facilities, etc., or assistant headmaster) or curriculum advisor. Regarding preservice teacher preparation, both preservice teacher university students (Total = 41; Kalimantan, N = 15; Bali, N = 26; Padang, N = 0) and university teacher educators (Total = 16; Kalimantan, N = 11; Bali, N = 4; Padang, N = 1) were interviewed. This resulted in a total of 22.1 h of recorded interviews that were transcribed and coded. In addition, classroom observations were conducted (Total = 7; Kalimantan, N = 5; Bali, N = 2; Padang, N = 0). Classroom observation notes were taken at the time of the observation and coded.

The key themes of the data collection of the current preliminary study center on teachers' methodological approaches, secondary level curricula, and language of instruction. Related to teaching methodology, teachers across the regions included in this preliminary report exhibited a strong foundation of methodological knowledge. While in some cases a teacher centered approach was still dominant, most teachers did utilize group and pair work along with interesting games and activities for the learners in their classes. Many teachers made use of PowerPoint presentations when technology was available, and made use of whiteboards, realia, and simple games and activities in contexts where resources were more limited. Learners in most classrooms observed were largely engaged, responded well to the teachers, and seemed to show general interest in the content of the lessons. In the vast majority of classes observed, there was clear evidence of pedagogical understanding and previous professional development that manifested in teachers' classes. However, as the examples of two teachers in Kalimantan and preservice teachers below illustrate, this understanding of methodology and teaching practice may not have reached the level necessary for many teachers to make appropriate decisions on how to most effectively adapt and use these methodologies beyond simply implementing activities that they may have learned in professional development sessions.

6.4.1 Teaching Methodology

While a strong foundation of pedagogical knowledge was evident in teachers' practice in the classes observed, there also seemed to be a limit to the ability of teachers to adapt and to apply underlying principles to a variety of learning situations in their classes. Two class observations in different cities in Kalimantan provide an effective contrast. Both classes were made up of predominantly Indonesian, Muslim students, both male and female. Both schools were equally resourced, and both teachers, one male and one female, shared similar experience and enthusiasm for teaching. Both teachers exhibited a strong foundation in the presentation of their content and the activities during their classes, but one was able to reach a higher level of sophistication of teaching methodology than the other.

In the case of a female teacher, this teacher provided slips of paper with corresponding English and Bahasa Indonesia vocabulary. The class was divided into groups, representatives from each group came up to pick up the materials, and the task before the students was to match the vocabulary based on meaning. Students were clearly engaged, enjoying the activity, and responded very positively to the encouragement of the teacher. The teacher spoke predominately in English when instructing the class, and students also spoke in English when addressing the teacher while they depended more on local languages when working in their groups. During the post-observation interview, the teacher was asked if she could have assessed if the students could actually understand the vocabulary in order to complete the task. The teacher responded positively; however, this was in fact doubtful, as the teacher had left a PowerPoint slide with the correct matching vocabulary in view of the students at the front of the room during the activity. Rather than relying on students' ability to understand vocabulary, what could have been a successful group work activity resulted in a visual matching game of lexical items that were presented at the front of the room. While the understanding of the usefulness and effectiveness of group work that this teacher had gained was evident, in addition to the fact that her students were responding positively to that approach, the sophistication to implement that approach effectively to encourage and support true understanding and communication on the part of her learners was missing.

In a second example, the male teacher, also observed in Kalimantan, conducted a class of similar size, with a similar make up of students, focusing on discussing different aspects of a photograph of a group of ethnically diverse students studying in a class in Singapore. The teacher began the activity by showing this large picture to students, asking the students who they thought were in the picture, what were the characters in the picture doing, and to summarize the context in which the picture was taken. Students were engaged, eagerly volunteering information and working collaboratively when instructed to do so by the teacher. The entire class was conducted in English, and students also responded and communicated with each other predominantly in English. The teacher continued to ask questions of students that required them to demonstrate their understanding, express their ideas and opinions, and to communicate that information in English. In addition, the teacher went further, beyond asking simply who was in the picture, but asked why such a diverse group of students were studying together in this particular context. In this way, the teacher moved beyond simple information questions, and moved towards higher order critical thinking questions, to which the students readily responded and offered their own explanations and judgments.

The cases of these two teachers were indicative of a number of classroom observations that occurred across the regions included in this preliminary report. Teachers utilized English in their classroom, made use of pair and group work when possible, and learners responded positively and in large part were engaged with the content in the classes. However, there was a clear distinction between teachers who were able to move beyond the simple implementation of a game that they may have seen in a professional development workshop, and those who seemed to have a greater understanding of the underlying principles of a successful activity, and were able to generalize and utilize those principles with other activities successfully.

Such a difference between the approach of some teachers may in part be based on the type of professional development that is a commonplace for teachers in Indonesia and similar contexts. In many instances, professional development activities center around short-term training programs where activities or approaches are introduced, and discussed over a limited period of time. Although such approaches to professional development can be useful, they often lack the time necessary for teachers to experiment with such approaches, reflect on failures and successes, and gain a deeper understanding of the underlying principles of successful approaches. Such extended professional development programs are rare because of logistical, scheduling, and budgetary restraints. Nevertheless, such long-term interrelated professional development is necessary for teachers to be able to gain a greater understanding of the complexities and sophistication of underlying principles that can then be generalized to a variety of teaching activities and learning experiences for their learners.

6.4.2 Influences of National Curriculum

Closely related to teachers' methodology is the influence of the national curriculum. Through interviews with teachers as well as principles, the national curriculum is clearly the driving force behind instruction in English language classrooms in Indonesia. That being said, fully 100% of the teachers included in this preliminary report indicated that completing the goals and objectives and covering the content specified in the national curriculum was either extremely difficult or impossible. While principals and other educational leaders seemed sympathetic to these difficulties, they often replied that completing the curriculum as specified is a requirement and must be achieved. Even with principles and educational leaders, there seems to be a realization that truly achieving the curriculum as specified would oftentimes not be possible, but to be seen as attempting to do so was extremely important. In addition, standardized national exams were based on the curriculum, and scores received by students on these exams were crucial for promotion to subsequent grades and continuation of education or seeking employment after secondary level courses. When questioned as to why certain content or specific information was included in a particular lesson, the response was often because "it is in the required curriculum" or in other additional supporting teaching materials.

Observing classes are useful to illustrate this influence of the national curriculum. The first of two class observations which provide some insight was conducted by two female preservice teachers as part of their practicum. These preservice teachers were completing their practicum at a rural lower secondary school with approximately 13 students, both male and female. The two preservice teachers had clearly prepared their class materials well, were utilizing PowerPoint slides and also demonstrated a very strong positive rapport with the students in their class. The class began with the analysis of an email presented in the text which focused on exchanging information in the form of introductions. The learners had read the materials, the preservice teachers elicited information from the class, and all students were actively engaged. However, there are many examples of vocabulary in the introductory email that were largely irrelevant and difficult for the learners in this particular context to understand.

For example, the author of the email used as the content of this particular lesson indicated that she wanted to work as a park ranger for the "National Park Service" in the future. Such information was quite culturally bound, and difficult for the students in this particular class to grasp, even though the preservice teachers struggled to help them understand. From this point, the materials in the class proceeded to questions about what is the meaning of an email, compared to the meaning of a personal letter, and the generic structure of emails and letters. As the preservice teachers progressed through this aspect of the curriculum, students gradually begin to lose interest in the content of the lesson, and by the closing of the lesson, we are no longer paying attention in the class. In the post-observation meeting, when the preservice teachers were questioned as to why they included this information which seemed largely irrelevant to their students, the response was "because it's in the required curriculum." The preservice teachers in this particular situation could have built on the positive rapport and interest evident in their learners at the beginning of their lesson, adapted some of the more irrelevant vocabulary, and focused on content more relevant to their learners. Learners at this level, lower secondary, would be much more familiar with and interested in communicating via social media rather than emails or personal written letters. This was a missed opportunity on the part of these preservice teachers to critically consider the content presented in the materials, and adapt those materials, while still achieving the necessary competencies of the curriculum and introducing content that is more interesting and relevant to their learners.

In other examples, teachers again demonstrated a very positive rapport with their students, in arguably challenging contexts in vocational secondary schools where English proficiency is rarely an intrinsic goal for the learners. Nevertheless, two teachers observed in two different cities were very effective in engaging their students and increasing the interest level of their classes. However, in both cases, one through PowerPoint, and the other through the use of a whiteboard, students were presented with an overload of functions and vocabulary. In one case, where the content of the course was focusing on asking for and sharing opinions, 24 different functions were presented to students, whereas the competencies could have been achieved through the presentation of only five or six. In a second case, and a single PowerPoint slide, learners were presented with 36 items in a word bank, comprising English, pronunciation, and the Bahasa Indonesia equivalent. The learners in this particular class, who initially had been engaged, were quickly overwhelmed and lost interest when presented with so much information at one time, facing the nearly impossible task of remembering all this information.

In both of these examples, teachers again exhibit positive rapport with their students, familiarity with strong methodological approaches, but are driven by the requirements of the curriculum, regardless of their need to critically analyze the relevancy or appropriateness of what may be presented in a text or a teacher's handbook and the needs or abilities of their learners. As mentioned earlier, such sophistication relating to critical reflection are skills that are developed over time, and would not be apparent in professional training related to simply how to implement a curriculum rather than being able to adapt materials so that they are more relevant to their learners while still meeting the competencies required in the national curriculum as well as the national standardized examinations.

6.4.3 Integrating Culture

Indonesia is unique in the diversity of culture and language across the country. Regarding culture, the national curriculum allows flexibility to focus on local culture in general as well as within the English language curriculum. Teachers from all regions reported that they make use of a variety of local cultural activities as topics of communication as well as content for materials development in their classes. A number of teachers indicated that they used traditional and local folktales as content for reading activities. Other teachers described using festivals or traditional ceremonies, such as wedding ceremonies, as topics of discussion, comparison, or description. Local cuisine is used to describe processes as students report or actually cook in class using local recipes. More so than in many other areas of the curriculum, teachers seemed to take the opportunity to exercise their autonomy in developing local materials, being creative, and bringing the context of the students' community into the English language classroom. This was a point of much pride on the part of many of the teachers included in this research. In fact, focusing on local culture was encouraged by local leaders as well as the government. A unique example was in Bali, when government workers, including teachers, and students across the island wear traditional Balinese dress and school uniforms on particular days to celebrate their local culture.

6.4.4 Language of Instruction, Teacher Beliefs and Translanguaging

Related to the language of instruction, there seemed to be an interplay between three important variables: Teacher beliefs related to appropriate language of instruction, emphasis of Bahasa Indonesia in the national curriculum, and teacher beliefs related to their own English language proficiency. Local linguistic diversity did not seem to be leveraged as often or as effectively as an educational tool in the English language learning classroom or otherwise. On one hand, the extensive ability of all Indonesians to converse with others across the many islands and linguistic communities of the country in Bahasa Indonesia is rightfully a significant accomplishment and a source of national pride. Bahasa Indonesia is the official language of the country, and therefore also the official language of instruction in all schools at the secondary level. At the same time, in the English language learning classroom, teachers do shift among English, Bahasa Indonesia, and at times local languages. Teachers often reported that they believed that attempting to teach classes in English was important, but often shifted to Bahasa Indonesia in order to ensure clarity, or assist with comprehension of instructions or classroom management. Some teachers believed that they should use English as much as possible in their classes, noting that if students were not exposed to English in their classrooms, the likelihood of any exposure would be very limited. Other teachers focus predominantly on using Bahasa Indonesia. These teachers believed that this was an important focus as this is the national language, and its use was expected in a formal situation such as the educational classroom.

At the same time, the range of teachers' language choice in the classroom was reported from approximately 5% of the time in English up to even as high as 90% of the time in English. When questioned, teachers referred to a number of variables that affected their decisions: the English proficiency level of their students, the motivation level of their students, the content of the particular lesson, or when during the term a course was being taught. However, when observed, many teachers used very limited English during their classes. While there were notable exceptions, many teachers may have used English initially, to introduce or provide instructions for an activity, but rather than allowing time for understanding, these teachers would quickly shift to Bahasa Indonesia and repeat the same instructions, even when students seemingly had already understood the information delivered in English. In such a situation, when students know that instructions will be delivered in Bahasa Indonesia after those in English, there is little motivation to try to understand the content in the target language. When discussing this observation with teachers, on one hand there was a desire on the part of the teachers to ensure clarity and understanding for the students, but also importantly, many teachers reported being rushed to complete assignments in a timely fashion in order to remain on schedule with the curriculum. As a result, little time could be allowed for students to process and confirm understanding of instructions and classroom activities in English. What often results; therefore, is a classroom where English is the focus of study yet not the language of instruction or interaction.

Local languages were rarely used. Teachers stated that they believed that Bahasa Indonesia was the appropriate language for the educational context. In many cases, teachers also believe that they may not be fluent in their students' first or local languages. When local languages were used, the purposes included building rapport between the students and teachers, interjecting humor, and much less frequently, clarifying information.

In such a linguistically diverse context, this approach falls short of what Garcia (2009) has termed translanguaging. Garcia (2018) describes a translanguaging approach that respects the social spaces of different languages but at the same time recognizes that learners can utilize an extensive repertoire of languages present in their own communities. Far beyond code-switching or code-mixing, translanguaging pedagogy challenges the notion of maintaining separation of languages (for example only English in the English language classroom, or the dominance of solely the national language in educational settings), but allows learners to leverage their entire linguistic repertoire for making meaning, communicating and understanding. Such a rich educational tool, not unlike culture, was surprisingly absent from the English language classroom in Indonesia. Many teachers remained staunch in their belief that local languages are inappropriate for a formal setting such as school, and as the national curriculum dictates, Bahasa Indonesia should be the language of instruction.

Nevertheless, there was variation in this rigid linguistic segregation of languages. There seemed to be a continuum present from the national capital of Jakarta, to other prefectural urban centers, to more rural areas that coincided with the emphasis on local languages. Whereas Bahasa Indonesia was clearly dominant in Jakarta, local languages began to play a more minimal role in provincial capitals, and at times played a leading role in rural contexts where local student populations may not have developed sufficient proficiency so that teachers could use Bahasa Indonesia as the language of instruction at all times. What results is a complex set of variables on which teachers base their choice of language in the classroom, which is influenced not only by teacher beliefs and local linguistic characteristics but also geographic distance from urban centers.

6.4.5 Professional Development

Overall, the dedication and skill of Indonesian teachers is impressive. Clearly professional development activities have had an impact on instruction that is delivered across the country. At the same time, there are clear needs for improvement. While professional development has had an impact, oftentimes that has seemed limited to the replication of specific activities, or implementation of prescribed lesson plans provided in teacher support materials or manuals. Although effective activities are being utilized, a greater understanding of the principles underlying those activities, which in turn could be used to adapt activities and utilize different materials, seems to be lacking. This may be in part due to the type of professional development that is often commonplace: a master teacher or expert delivering limited workshops or professional development activities over a limited period of time, without time for teachers' experimentation, reflection, and discussion. The development and evaluation of more long-term professional development activities that support teachers beyond a single workshop could be more effective.

6.4.6 Development of 21st-Century Skills

When considering the implementation of 21st-century skills, most teachers interviewed were unfamiliar with this term. When using alternative terms, such as critical thinking skills or computer literacy skills, etc., some teachers responded that they had heard of HOTS, i.e., higher order thinking skills, but had had little or no training or professional development related to implementing activities designed to develop these skills with their students. A small number of teachers responded that they had heard of 21st-century skills or critical thinking skills, and understood some activities to promote these skills in the class. However, when pressed to provide examples, the activities they used to exemplify the development of critical thinking skills were in fact examples of activities that only required lower order thinking skills. This demonstrated a significant lack of information related to both 21st-century skills and critical thinking skills, or even a misunderstanding of the concept and how such activities could be utilized in the classroom.

The single notable exception to this observation was recorded during interviews with the principal and secondary teachers at a public secondary school in Bukittinggi, Padang, a secondary municipality in the mountainous region of the province. Surprisingly, during the interviews with the secondary teachers at this particular school, they fully understood 21st-century skills, the role of critical thinking, the distinction between higher order and lower order thinking skills, and provided examples of how they integrated these skills into their regular classroom practice in an effort to develop these skills with their learners. Furthermore, when the teachers were asked through which method had they gained this understanding of 21st-century skills, they responded that they had learned these concepts through professional development workshops that had been organized by their principal at their school. In a follow up interview with the principal, he was asked about these professional development workshops, and responded that he undertook the organization of these professional development workshops based on his own initiative. As the principal of the school, he recognized the importance of 21st-century skills for his students, and for his community, in order to maintain a competitive advantage for his students as they moved through the educational system and eventually sought to obtain employment. Of all the teachers interviewed for this preliminary report, only these teachers at this single school were familiar and were able to implement activities focusing on the development of 21st-century skills and critical thinking in their classes. This is a clear indication of how the initiative of an educational leader can have a direct and substantial impact on both the teachers and students within his institution.

6.5 Conclusion

Indonesia presents a unique opportunity to examine how pre-service teacher preparation programs, secondary teachers, and educational leaders can address issues that emerge from working with students from multicultural and multilingual backgrounds, from different economic backgrounds, and from vastly different resourced rural and urban areas. What is most notable about the results from the current research is how all those involved rose to these challenges, making use of the resources available, and seeking out professional development and assistance when possible. When available, such professional development can have significant positive impacts on the learning environment for students from each of these diverse backgrounds. In order to realize these impacts, teachers must be appropriately supported. Professional development that lacks depth, consistency, or follow-up will be unlikely to provide the support necessary, and may rather result in frustration on the part of teachers and educational leaders alike.

National curricula can maintain unity and provide for equal opportunity for all students across diverse contexts. At the same time, such curricula should provide flexibility for teachers who are familiar with local needs and conditions. Clearly, Indonesian teachers make use of the existing flexibility in the national curriculum to introduce different aspects of local culture. At the same time, nearly all teachers struggle with completing prescribed curriculum, particularly in more rural areas where resources, support, and educational opportunities may be more limited. In addition, unlike culture, the utility and effectiveness of providing space in the educational context for local languages and students' linguistic repertoire is quite limited, and is an educational tool that has yet to be leveraged. A broader understanding of translanguaging pedagogy could significantly improve the learning environments of many students in Indonesia, particularly those from communities where the local language remains dominant.

As in the case of the secondary school principal in Bukittingi, Padang, the impact of an effective educational leader cannot be overstated. Nevertheless, few professional development opportunities directly target educational leaders in an effort to provide them with the skills and insights necessary to result in lasting impacts in their respective schools and institutions. In a follow up study, Stroupe, Ardi, Delfi, Santosa, and Siregar (2021) sought to identify the characteristics of successful and impactful educational leaders in the Indonesian context. Utilizing an Indonesian leadership model developed by Raihani (2008), the researchers identified specific characteristics of successful leaders, and propose a professional development model design to support educational leaders.

In such a diverse country as Indonesia, there remain many areas for further research. The extent to which local languages can be integrated into the curriculum, differing experiences of teachers in different regions of the country, and innovative examples of teachers thriving in educational environments with limited resources are areas the current research project will continue to investigate. In addition, research could be focused on the impact of different languages of instruction and how cultural and linguistic variables in educational settings affect student identity and performance. International comparative studies of curricular influence based on language of instruction and pedagogy related not only to translation but to other variables across multiple international contexts could also lead to interesting and significant findings. What is clear is that educational leaders and teachers in Indonesia are dedicated to developing effective educational programs for their students. What may need further attention are the professional development activities and other means of support provided to these educators in order for them to be successful in their endeavors.

Acknowledgements The authors would like to thank the following colleagues, without whose assistance, this research would not have been possible: Professor Ikhsanudin Ikhsanudin, Universitas Tanjungpura, Pontianak, Kalimantan; Professor Maskota Delfi, Andalas University, Padang, West Sumatra; and Professor Made Hery Santosa, Universitas Pendidikan Ganesha, Singaraja, Bali.

References

Adnyani, D. P. D. P. (2015). *Professional development for pre-service teacher: A case study of professional development program for pre-service teacher in State University in Central Indonesia*. [Doctoral dissertation, Stockholm University]. https://www.diva-portal.org/smash/get/diva2:815811/FULLTEXT01.pdf

Amery, R. (2019). Language is more than communication: Why we should maintain the mother tongue and promote linguistic diversity. *Proceedings of EEIC, 2*, 1–5.

Asfihana, R. (2017). The implementation of English teaching practicum at al istiqamah boarding school banjarmasin. *LET: Linguistics, Literature and English Teaching Journal, 4*(2), 94–106.

Australian Government Department of Foreign Affairs and Trade. (2017). Indonesia. https://dfat.gov.au/trade/resources/Documents/indo.pdf

Beers, S. (2011). *Teaching 21st century skills: An ASCD action tool*. Assn for Supervision & Curriculum.

Bellanca, J. A., & Brandt, R. (Eds.). (2010). *21st century skills: Rethinking how students learn*. Solution Tree Press.

Bourn, D. (2011). Global skills: From economic competitiveness to cultural understanding and critical pedagogy. *Critical Literacy: Theories and Practices, 6*(1), 3–20.

Butler, Y. G. (2015). English language education among young learners in East Asia: A review of current research (2004–2014). *Language Teaching, 48*(3), 303–342. https://doi.org/10.1017/s0261444815000105

Gamble, N., Patrick, C., & Peach, D. (2010). Internationalising work-integrated learning: Creating global citizens to meet the economic crisis and the skills shortage. *Higher Education Research and Development, 29*(5), 535–546. https://doi.org/10.1080/07294360.2010.502287

García, O., & Lin, A. M. (2017). Translanguaging in bilingual education. In O. García, A. M. Lin, & S. May (Eds.), *Bilingual and multilingual education* (pp. 117–130). Springer International Publishing. https://doi.org/10.1007/978-3-319-02258-1_9

García, O. (2009). *Bilingual education in the 21st century: A global perspective*. Wiley/Blackwell.

García, O. (2018). Translanguaging, pedagogy and creativity. In J. Erfurt, E. Carporal, & Weirich (Eds.), *Éducation plurilingue et pratiques langagières: Hommage à Christine Hélot* (pp. 39–56). Peter Lang.

Goebel, Z. (2018). Language diversity and language change in Indonesia. In R. W. Hefner (Ed.), *Routledge handbook of contemporary Indonesia* (pp. 378–389). Routledge. https://doi.org/10.4324/9781315628837-31

Gultom, E. (2016). English language teaching problems in Indonesia. *Proceeding: 7th International Seminar on Regional Education, 3*, 1234–1241. https://isre.prosiding.unri.ac.id/index.php/ISRE/article/download/3235/3147

Hadisantosa, N. (2010). Insights from Indonesia. In R. Johnstone (Ed.), *Learning through english: Policies, challenges and prospects* (pp. 24–46). British Council.

Hendayana, S. (2007). Development of INSET model for improving teacher professionalism in Indonesia. *NUE Journal of International Educational Cooperation, 2*, 97–106.

Kirkpatrick, A. (2017). Language education policy among the Association of Southeast Asian Nations (ASEAN). *European Journal of Language Policy, 9*(1), 7–25. https://doi.org/10.3828/ejlp.2017.2

Kuswandono, P. (2014). Voices of pre-service English teachers: Reflecting motivations during practicum learning. *TEFLIN Journal–A Publication on the Teaching and Learning of English, 25*(2), 185. https://doi.org/10.15639/teflinjournal.v25i2/185-202

Littlewood, W. (2007). Communicative and task-based language teaching in East Asian classrooms. *Language Teaching, 40*(3), 243–249. https://doi.org/10.1017/S0261444807004363

MacDonald, L., Daugherty, M., & Stroupe, R. (2011). Integrating skills in the EFL classroom. In R. Stroupe & K. Kimura (Eds.), *English language teaching practice in Asia* (pp. 86–108). IDP Australia.

Malik, H., Humaira, M. A., Komari, A. N., Fathurrochman, I., & Jayanto, I. (2021). Identification of barriers and challenges to teaching English at an early age in Indonesia: An international publication analysis study. *Linguistics and Culture Review, 5*(1), 217–229. https://doi.org/10.21744/lingcure.v5n1.1485

Mangali, Z., & Hamdan, A. R. B. (2015). Barriers to implementing english school based curriculum in indonesia: Teachers perspective. *International Journal for Innovation Education and Research, 3*(4), 102–110. https://doi.org/10.31686/ijier.vol3.iss4.351

Mattarima, K., & Hamdan, A. R. (2011). The teaching constraints of English as a foreign language in Indonesia: The context of school based curriculum. *Sosiohumanika, 4*(2).

Mudra, H. (2018). Pre-service EFL teachers' experiences in teaching practicum in rural schools in Indonesia. *Qualitative Report, 23*(2). https://doi.org/10.46743/2160-3715/2018.3115

Musgrave, S. (2014). Language shift and language maintenance in Indonesia. In P. Sercombe & R. Tupas (Eds.), *Language, education and nation-building* (pp. 87–105). Palgrave Macmillan.

Nieto, S. (2001). *Language, culture, and teaching: Critical perspectives*. Routledge.

Norton, B. (1997). Language, identity, and the ownership of English. *TESOL Quarterly, 31*(3), 409–429. https://doi.org/10.2307/3587831

OECD/Asian Development Bank (2015) Education in Indonesia: Rising to the challenge. OECD Publishing. https://doi.org/10.1787/9789264230750-en

Palmer, D. K., Martínez, R. A., Mateus, S. G., & Henderson, K. (2014). Reframing the debate on language separation: Toward a vision for translanguaging pedagogies in the dual language classroom. *The Modern Language Journal, 98*, 757–772. https://doi.org/10.1111/modl.12121

Pennycook, A. (1994). *The cultural politics of English as an international language*. Longman.

Pennycook, A. (2007). *Global Englishes and transcultural flows*. Routledge.

Polim, H. (2021). Challenges in the teaching practicum in Indonesia. *The Bulletin of the Graduate School, Soka University, 42*, 439–462.

Raihani. (2008). An Indonesian model of successful school leadership. *Journal of Educational Administration, 46*(4), 481–496. https://doi.org/10.1108/09578230810882018

Rasman, R. (2018). To translanguage or not to translanguage? The multilingual practice in an Indonesian EFL classroom. *Indonesian Journal of Applied Linguistics, 7*(3), 687. https://doi.org/10.17509/ijal.v7i3.9819

Renandya, W. A., Hamied, F. A., & Nurkamto, J. (2018). English language proficiency in Indonesia: Issues and prospects. *Journal of Asia TEFL, 15*(3), 618. https://doi.org/10.18823/asiatefl.2018.15.3.4.618

Retnawati, H., Hadi, S., & Nugraha, A. C. (2016). Vocational high school teachers' difficulties in implementing the assessment in curriculum 2013 in Yogyakarta province of Indonesia. *International Journal of Instruction, 9*(1), 33–48. https://doi.org/10.12973/iji.2016.914a

Riesky, R. (2013). How English student teachers deal with teaching difficulties in their teaching practicum. *Indonesian Journal of Applied Linguistics, 2*(2), 250. https://doi.org/10.17509/ijal.v2i2.169

Riza, H. (2008). Resources report on languages of indonesia. In *Proceedings of the 6th workshop on Asian language resources* (pp. 93–94).

Songbatumis, A. M. (2017). Challenges in teaching English faced by English teachers at MTsN Taliwang, Indonesia. *Journal of Foreign Language Teaching and Learning, 2*(2). https://doi.org/10.18196/ftl.2223

Stroupe, R. (2018). Developing competencies for the "global community": What is the role of English language educators? In Y. N. Leung, J. Katchen, S. Y. Hwang, & Y. L. Chen (Eds.), *Reconceptualizing English language teaching and learning in the 21st century: A special monograph in memory of Professor Kai-Chong Cheung* (pp. 21–32). Crane and ETA.

Stroupe, R., & Maggioli, G. (2018). Maintaining balance: How can ASEAN plus three best preserve diversity and prepare for the globalized world in the 21st century. In S. Zein, & R. Stroupe (Eds.), *English language teacher preparation in Asia: Policy, research and practice* (pp. 281–297). Routledge. https://doi.org/10.4324/9781315105680-15

Stroupe, R., Ardi, P., Delfi, M., Santosa, M. H., & Siregar, M. (2021). *Effective educational leadership in the Indonesian context: Leaders in secondary schools.* Paper presentation at the 67th TEFLIN International Virtual Conference & The 9th ICOELT (online), Padang, Indonesia.
Stroupe, R. (2017). The language educator and globalization: How do we best prepare our learners? In *Asian-focused ELT research and practice: Voices from the far edge* (pp. 33–49). IDP Australia. https://doi.org/10.5746/leia/13/v4/i2/a02/stroupe
Sulistiyo, U. (2016). English language teaching and EFL teacher competence in Indonesia. *Proceedings of ISELT FBS Universitas Negeri Padang, 4*(2), 396–406.
Sulistiyo, U., Mukminin, A., Abdurrahman, K., & Haryanto, E. (2017). Learning to teach: A case study of student teachers' practicum and policy recommendations. *The Qualitative Report.* https://doi.org/10.46743/2160-3715/2017.2671
Tsui, A. B. M, & Tollefson, J. W. (2017). *Language policy, culture, and identity in Asian contexts.* Routledge.
Turnbull, B. (2018). Is there potential for a translanguaging approach to English education in Japan? Perspectives of tertiary learners and teachers. *JALT Journal, 40*(2), 101–134. https://doi.org/10.37546/jaltjj40.2-3
USAid. (2001). *Designing effective pre-service teacher education programs.* USAid.
Zein, S. (2016). Pre-service education for primary school English teachers in Indonesia: Policy implications. *Asia Pacific Journal of Education, 36*(1), 119–134. https://doi.org/10.1080/02188791.2014.961899
Zein, S. (2018a). Preparing Asian English teachers in the global world. In S. Zein & R. Stroupe (Eds.), *English language teacher preparation in Asia: Policy, research and practice* (pp. 1–16). Routledge.
Zein, S. (2018b). Translanguaging in the EYL classroom as a metadiscursive practice: Preparing prospective teachers. In S. Zein & R. Stroupe (Eds.), *English language teacher preparation in Asia: Policy, research and practice* (pp. 47–62). Routledge.
Zein, S., Sukyadi, D., Hamied, F. A., & Lengkanawati, N. (2020). *English language education in Indonesia: A review of current research (2011–2019).* Cambridge University Press.
Zhao, H., & Zhang, X. (2017). The Influence of field teaching practice on pre-service teachers' professional identity: A mixed methods study. *Frontiers in Psychology., 8*, 1264. https://doi.org/10.3389/fpsyg.2017.01264

Richmond Stroupe has worked with university and professional language learners from Asia since 1989. He received a Ph.D. in International Comparative Education from the University of Southern California and has been involved in the development of language learning programs in a number of contexts. He is a professor at Soka University in Tokyo, Japan where he is currently the Chair of the Master's Program in International Language Education: TESOL. He is also an advisor of doctoral students in Applied Linguistics and English Language Teaching Pedagogy in the Graduate School of Letters at Soka University. Richmond has been active in a number of English teaching associations, including TESOL International, and he is the former President of the Japan Association for Language Teaching (JALT). Richmond regularly conducts workshops, publishes and presents on a variety of professional activities and research projects, which include teacher education practices, curriculum and professional development, and developing learners' critical thinking skills. Most recently, his research activities focus on developing frameworks for successful secondary education in limited resource areas, enhancing Global Citizenship Education, and the integration of Artificial Intelligence (AI) into language learning approaches.

Sisilia Setiawati Halimi is a senior lecturer in the Department of Linguistics, Faculty of Humanities, Universitas Indonesia. She earned her B.A. in linguistics from Universitas Indonesia, her M.A. in English Language Teaching (ELT) from the University of Warwick, U.K. and her Ph.D. in ELT from La Trobe University, Australia. Her field of interests includes Language Assessment, English for Specific Purposes, English as a Medium of Instruction, English Language Teaching and Teacher Education, and she has facilitated various teacher training workshops on various ELT topics. She has been an active member of the Association of Teaching English as a Foreign Language in Indonesia (TEFLIN) since 2003.

Open Access This chapter is licensed under the terms of the Creative Commons Attribution 4.0 International License (http://creativecommons.org/licenses/by/4.0/), which permits use, sharing, adaptation, distribution and reproduction in any medium or format, as long as you give appropriate credit to the original author(s) and the source, provide a link to the Creative Commons license and indicate if changes were made.

The images or other third party material in this chapter are included in the chapter's Creative Commons license, unless indicated otherwise in a credit line to the material. If material is not included in the chapter's Creative Commons license and your intended use is not permitted by statutory regulation or exceeds the permitted use, you will need to obtain permission directly from the copyright holder.

Part III
Corpus Linguistics

Chapter 7
Semantic Cognitive Analysis of Chinese Language VO Collocation

Symphony Akelba Christian and Hermina Sutami

Abstract This study used cognitive semantic point of view to find the cognitive semantic elements in play in the formation of Chinese VO collocation. It explains why the object of certain VO collocation cannot be exchange arbitrarily. The focus of this study is the collocation in the transportation domain: the verbs 坐 (zuò), 骑 (qí), and 开 (kāi) as they collocate with their objects. The purpose of the study is to describe the cognitive semantic element embedded in those verbs and nouns. This research was conducted using the Chinese Web 2011 corpus (Sketch Engine). The result of the study on 38,160 collocation indicates that the differences in semantic meaning of verbal and object, differences in categorization of verbal and object, and differences in frames, play a role in the formation of VO collocations of the verbs 坐 (zuò), 骑 (qí), 开 (kāi). The differences in the semantic meanings of the verbs and objects and the differences in the categorization of the verbs and objects form an event frame which then combines in conceptual blending and form VO collocation. These findings also contribute to the field of language learning and teaching since it provides a broader picture and explanation of the formation of Chinese VO Collocation which can be used by teacher, students and textbook/teaching materials designer.

Keywords Verb and object collocation · Semantic · Cognitive

7.1 Introduction

In linguistic terms, a combination of words that has a tendency to occur together is called a collocation (Finch, 2000, p. 152). According to Sinclair (1991, p. 170), this occurrence of two or more words must be within a short space of each other in a text. If Sinclair and Finch see the collocation from the syntactical point of view, Leech (1974) and Kridalaksana (2001) see the collocation from the semantical point of view. Leech explains that the reason why one word can combine with other words and occur together within certain context is because those words have association in

---

S. A. Christian (✉) · H. Sutami
Linguistics Department, Faculty of Humanities, Universitas Indonesia, Depok, Indonesia
e-mail: symphony.akelba@gmail.com

© The Author(s) 2025
R. Stroupe and L. Roosman (eds.), *Applied Linguistics in the Indonesian Context*,
Engaging Indonesia, https://doi.org/10.1007/978-981-97-2336-2_7

meaning, which is called collocative meaning (Leech, 1974, p. 17). In other words, the reason why a word can collocate with other words and form a fixed association of meaning was because those words have meaning relationship (Kridalaksana, 1994, p. 113). So, collocation does not refer to only the words that usually co-occur, but also reveals the important of meaning relationship as a key factor that determine the way one word can collocate with other words.

However, is meaning-based relationship the only thing that determines the way one word collocates with others? Are there no other factors that influence the forming of collocation? In Mandarin the phrase "driving a car" is expressed through the collocation of VO 开汽车 kāi qìchē (kāi: to open; qìchē: car), but the meaning of verb 开 (kāi) itself is not related to drive, the meaning of verb 开 (kāi) means 'to open a thing so that thing is opened'. In this example, the verb 开 (kāi) can collocate with object 汽车 (qìchē: car) although they do not seem to be related in meaning. There must be another element than relations in meaning which contributes to the forming of collocation.

In another example, if the object VO 开汽车 kāi qìchē (the car as an object) is changed into a bicycle (自行车 or zìxíngchē), then, the verb also changes into 骑 (qí) thus forming a phrase 骑自行车 (qí zìxíngchē). The meaning of verb 骑 (qí) is 'to sit on an animal'. The common collocation for verb 骑 (qí) is 骑马 (qí mǎ: ride a horse), because the meaning component of verb 骑 qí fits the meaning component of object 马 (mǎ: horse). This shows that the verb 骑 (qí) can also collocate with object 自行车 (zìxíngchē: bicycle). However, the object 自行车 (zìxíngchē: bicycle) cannot collocate with verb 开 (kāi: to open). This phenomenon leads to the question of what are exactly the elements which causes one verb 开/骑 to collocate with the object 汽车/自行车 and why this collocation is not interchangeable? The authors suspect that cognitive semantic elements play an important role in the forming of collocation.

There is plenty of research on collocation in the field of language teaching and learning. Xiao and Chen (2008) examined the VO collocation competence from the field of language learning. Jin (2012a, 2012b), and Chu (2013) examined the VO collocation error types from Korean leaners and Mongol learners. Research on collocation from the field of linguistics, especially in the context of Mandarin, is still relatively rare. Xiao and McEnery (2006) compares Chinese and English collocation to find the differences of collocation behavior from both languages. Peiyen et al. (2011) examined the collocation of two synonymous words 帮忙 (bāngmáng: help) and 帮助 (bāngzhù: aid) from the view of semantic prosody. Another important study of collocation in context of English is the study conducted by Liu (2010). Although Liu (2010) conducted research on collocation from the point of view of lexicography, but the research proves that not all collocation are arbitrary and collocations can be analyzed from the view of semantic and linguistic cognitive. From the above studies, it can be seen that the study of Chinese language collocation is only limited to the field of language learning and semantics. Therefore, the authors will conduct a study on collocation of VO in Mandarin at the phrase level from the view of cognitive semantic to find what cognitive semantic elements are in play in the formation of Chinese VO collocation. This study is expected to strengthen the coverage of research on Chinese language collocation.

7 Semantic Cognitive Analysis of Chinese Language VO Collocation 119

The focus of this section is Chinese VO collocation in the transportation domain, which includes the verbs 坐 (zuò), 骑 (qí), and 开 (kāi) and the objects which collocate with these three verbs. In addition, this research observes the cognitive semantics point of view of the collocation formation. The reason for the selection of these three verbs is because the inherent meaning of this three verbs are not related to transportation, but when collocate with an object in the domain of transportation, the meaning of the verbs turns into one which can be included into a transportation domain, such as 'to take (a vehicle)', 'to ride' and 'to drive'. It is in these pairings that the cognitive semantic element of the verbs and nouns play a role in the formation of VO collocation of 坐车, 骑车, 开车. The purpose of this study is to describe the cognitive semantic element embedded in the verbs and nouns in the three previously stated examples.

7.2 Methodology

This research was conducted using the Chinese Web 2011 corpus taken from Sketch Engine. There are approximately 38,250 VO collocation observed in this research. The analysis was done on verb 坐 (zuò), 骑 (qí), and 开 (kāi) as well as on nouns that collocate with these three verbs. The analysis on the verbs 坐 (zuò), 骑 (qí), and 开 (kāi) implements the componential analysis suggested by Nida (1975). In addition, the meaning shown from the original characters of these three verbs also play the important role on describing the meaning of the verbs. The analysis on nouns which collocate with these three verbs was conducted with a classification of those nouns based on similarities of meaning and attribute. The categorization of nouns is also considered when doing the componential analysis of the verbs 坐 (zuò), 骑 (qí), and 开 (kāi). The analysis on verbs and nouns forms the semantic network which shows the frames of VO collocations. The frame of verbs and of the nouns will then build the mental space for conceptual blending of VO collocations. The conceptual blending explained in this chapter will reveal the reason why VO collocations in Mandarin, especially in transportation domain, are formed in such a way.

7.3 Ancient Chinese Characters of 坐 (zuò), 骑 (qí), 开 (kāi)

The meaning of verb 坐 (zuò), 骑 (qí), and 开 (kāi) can be first traced back from its Chinese characters. The ancient character of 坐 (zuò) is 坐, which is a picture of someone who sits on the ground, with the feet folded back and pressed against the buttocks. This ancient character then evolved into the character 坐 which is a combination of three characters: the two characters of 人 (rén: human) and one character of 土 (tǔ: land). The character 土 (tǔ: land) is in the bottom and in the middle of two characters of 人 (rén: human). Those characters' combination show the picture of two people sitting face to face on the ground with the sitting position is also with the feet folded back and pressed against the buttocks. The modern character of 坐 (zuò) also represents the same element (of two people and ground) and the same concept (sit).

The ancient character of 骑 (qí) is 𠃋 which pictures someone sitting astride on the back of a horse, which represents the meaning of someone riding a horse. This ancient character then evolved into phonetic compound character of 騎 which is a combination of two characters; the character 马 (mǎ) and the character 奇 (qí). The character 马 (mǎ) represents the meaning, and the character 奇 (qí) represents the phonetic, but the whole meaning is still the same. The modern character today of 骑 is a simplified form of the character 騎, which is still a phonetic compound character, and still represents the same meaning.

The ancient character of 开 (kāi) is 開. It is a picture of a door with two hands and one line between the door and the hands. The line represents the latch on the door. The origin of meaning of this characters is the using of two hands to open the door. This ancient character is then evolved into the character 開 kāi, which still keeps the strokes that represent the door and the latch, but the strokes that represent the hands was simplified, while the meaning is still the same. Nowadays, the character is even more simple; only the strokes that represent the latch and the hands are left, but the meaning is still the same.

According to description above, we can see that the meaning of verb 坐 (zuò: sit) and 开 (kāi: to open) is not related to transportation domain. Only the meaning of verb 骑 qí (ride) seems related to transportation domain if we see the horse as one of form of transportation. Although the meaning represented from ancient characters seems to be unrelated to transportation domain, but the form of the ancient characters will contribute into the forming of VO collocation 坐车, 骑车, 开车 through imagic mapping, as mentioned by Hiraga (2005, p. 203) in his research on Japanese poems. The imagic mapping from the visual form of Chinese characters will be shown in the conceptual blending diagrams at the other part of this paper.

7.4 The Meaning Component/s of the Verbs 坐 (zuò), 骑 (qí), 开 (kāi)

The ancient Chinese characters of 坐 (zuò), 骑 (qí), 开 (kāi) show the meaning of those verbs, but we also have to take a look to the corpus data from present day to get the deeper layers of their meanings and to make the abstract elements of the meanings visible (Philip, 2011, p. 12). As mentioned above, the corpus data was from Chinese Web 2011, and 38,250 VO collocations are observed. We use componential analysis suggested by Nida (1975) to make the meaning of the verbs 坐, 骑, 开 more visible and understood as shown on Table 7.1.

In accordance to Croft's (2012, p. 44) revisions and extensions to Vendler's verbs classification, we try to analyze the inherent aspectual types of the verbs 坐, 骑, 开. The result is these three verbs are categorically different. The verb 坐 (zuò: sit) is a

7 Semantic Cognitive Analysis of Chinese Language VO Collocation

Table 7.1 The matrix of the components of meaning of the verbs 坐, 骑, 开

	坐 (zuò: sit)	骑 (qí: ride)	开 (kāi: to open)
Category of verbs	Transitory states	Undirected activity	Reversible achievement
Agent commits an active action	−	+	+
Need hands to perform an action	−	+	+
Need feet to perform an action	+	+	−
Astride feet position	−	+	−
Reversible	−	−	+
Cause change in condition of an object	−	−	+
The characteristics of object:			
− Concrete	+	+	+
− Not living things (inanimate)	+	±	+
− Can be opened and closed or turned on/off, e.g.: door, lamp	−	−	+
− Part of human body, e.g.: shoulder, back, neck	−	+	−
− Land transportation	+	+	+
− Sea transportation	+	−	−
− Air transportation	+	−	−

transitory state verb because the action of 'sitting' allows alternative construal as a state and an activity; someone is not inherently sitting and these states and processes come and go in the lifetime of an entity. The verb 骑 (qí: ride) is an undirected activity verb because "ride" is a repeated motion of steering reins and legs. The verb 开 (kāi: to open) is a reversible achievement verb because the achievement of opening or closing a door can be reversed and therefore repeated.

From the aspectual types of the verbs, the verb 坐 (zuò: sit) represents the state of the agent who is in a sitting position, and does not represent the agent's actions, while the verb 骑 (qí: ride) and 开 (kāi: to open) requires an active action of an agent. The verb 骑 (qí: ride) needs both agent's hand and feet to perform action (he feet must be in astride position), while the verb 开 (kāi: to open) just need one of the agent's hand to perform action. Another important difference between these three verbs is the fact that the verb 开 (kāi: to open) is a reversible achievement since it causes the change in the states of the object, in the sense that the object can be opened or closed, while the verbs 坐 (zuò: sit) and 骑 (qí: ride) don't cause the change of condition of the objects.

From the objects point of view, the objects collocated with verb 坐, 骑, 开 are all concrete and inanimate object. However, the objects of the verb 骑 qí can be animate and part of human body. The inanimate objects that can be collocated with verb 开 (kāi) must be the objects which can be opened or closed or turned on/off. If we look closely at the domain of the transportation, the form of transportation collocated with verb 坐 (zuò) can be land, sea, and air transportation, while the form of transportation which collocates with the verb 骑 (qí) and 开 (kāi) is limited to only land transportation.

According to the componential analysis of verbs 坐, 骑, 开 described above, we can see at least two important aspects. First, there is a relationship in meaning between the verbs 坐, 骑, 开 and the objects that can be collocated with these three verbs. The meaning components of the verbs fit the certain characteristic of objects and form the VO collocation. In the example of the verb 骑 (qí) and the object 自行车 (zixingche: bicycle), the meaning components of the verb 骑 (qí) needs hands and feet to perform action, and the feet must be in astride position. With the object 自行车 (zìxíngchē: bicycle), which is one of form of transportation, the agent needs both hands and feet to operate, and the position of feet when riding must be in astride position, so it fits each other and forms VO collocation 骑自行车 (qí zìxíngchē: riding bicycle).

The second important aspect is the categorization of the objects. The categorization of objects also plays a part in forming VO collocation. The verb 坐 (zuò) can collocate with land, sea, and air transportation, while the verbs 骑 (qí) and 开 (kāi) can only collocate with land transportation. What are the differences between land transportation that can be collocated with the verb 骑 (qí) and land transportation that can be collocated with the verb 开 (kāi)? To answer this question, we must know more in detail the categorization of land transportation first, and then see which categories of land transportation can be collocated with the verbs 骑 (qí) and 开 (kāi), and analyze the connection between them. On the next section of this paper, we will focus on describing in a more detailed manner the categorization of land transportation.

7.5 The Categorization of Land Transportation in Chinese

The earliest modes of land transportation in ancient Chinese is 车 (chē: cart), and 橇 (qiāo: sledge) (Zheng, 2012, p. 4). In the present day, only 车 (chē: cart) is still referred to as land transportation, but its meaning has extended to vehicle. Ancient character of 车 (chē: cart) is 車, which is a picture of a cart seen from above with an axle on either side. This character is then evolved into a character 車 which still keep the picture of axle (wheel) albeit in more simple strokes. So, the main concept of transportation in Chinese are things with axle (wheel) and use to transport things, people and animal. Today, this character becomes more simple but the meaning has extended into vehicle.

The data we gathered to analyze the categorization of 车 (chē: vehicle) in present day was also from Chinese Web 2011 corpus taken from Sketch Engine. We found a

7 Semantic Cognitive Analysis of Chinese Language VO Collocation

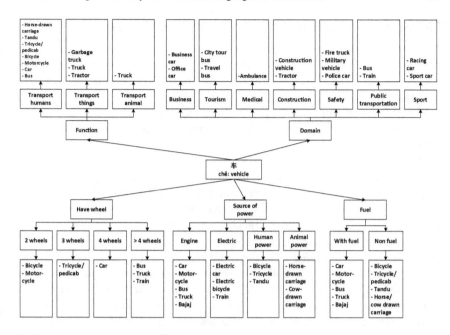

Fig. 7.1 Categorization of noun 车 chē (vehicle)

total of 122 words with 车 (chē) character and the categorization analysis of all this words is shown in Fig. 7.1.

We classified 122 words with 车 (chē) character based on five criteria: number of wheels, source of power, with/non fuel, function, and domain. Each criteria will be further divided into 2–4 groups as shown in Fig. 7.1. After knowing the categorization of the vehicles in Mandarin, we will now glance at the category of vehicle which can collocate with the verbs 骑 (qí) and 开 (kāi). According to the corpus data of Chinese Web 2011, the types of vehicle which can collocate with the verb 骑 (qí) are one, two, or three-wheeled vehicles; vehicle driven by human power; vehicle driven by engine and with fuel; electricity-driven vehicle; and the vehicles which function is to transport human. The vehicles which collocate with the verb 开 (kāi) are vehicles with two or four wheels and must be driven by engine with fuel or by electricity. What we can see from this categorization is the main attribute of the vehicles that can be collocated with the verb 骑 (qí) are the number of wheels it has and vehicles driven by human power. On the other hand, the main attribute of the vehicles which collocate with the verb 开 (kāi) are those not driven by human power. What is causing these differences? The answer will be in the next part of this paper.

7.6 Semantic Network of 坐 (zuò), 骑 (qí), 开 (kāi)

Before we explain more detail about the forming of VO collocation, we must look at the semantic network of the verbs 坐 (zuò), 骑 (qí), 开 (kāi) and the semantic network of the noun 车. This will provide an overall image for the meaning of the verbs 坐, 骑, 开, and the noun 车, and represents the change in meaning and concept of the verbs 坐, 骑, 开, and the noun 车 which play an important role in forming VO collocations.

Through semantic network of the verbs 坐, 骑, 开 as shown in Figs. 7.2, 7.3, and 7.4, we can see the meaning of the verbs 坐 (zuò) and 开 (kāi) are changed when these two verbs collocate with vehicle as an object. The inherent meaning derived from the ancient character and the present day's character of verb 坐 (zuò) is 'to sit with feet folded back and pressed against the buttocks, or with both legs folded towards the body and crossing each other at the ankle/calf, or with buttocks attached to seat or something while the feet dangling or touching the ground/floor'. However, when verb 坐 (zuò) collocates with modes of transportation as the object, the meaning of the verb 坐 changes into 'to take (a vehicle)' and the concept also changes into 'someone taking a transportation to go to somewhere, the condition of which involves not only the action of sitting, but also that of standing'. The modes of transportation collocated with verb 坐 (zuò) can be land, sea, or air transportation.

The meaning and concept changing of verb 开 (kāi) also can be seen in Fig. 7.3. The inherent meaning derived from ancient character and the present day's character of verb 开 (kāi) is 'to use hands to open an object so the objects become opened'. So, the object must be something that can be opened or closed like doors, windows, or boxes. However, when the verb 开 (kāi) collocates with modes of transportation as the objects, the meaning of the verb 开 (kāi) changes into 'to drive (a vehicle)' and the concept also changes into 'someone using both hands holding the steering

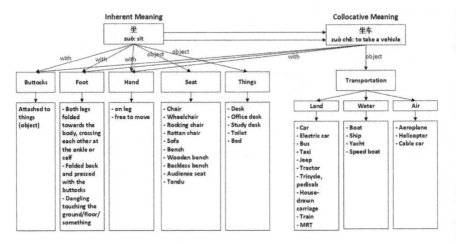

Fig. 7.2 Semantic network of verb 坐

7 Semantic Cognitive Analysis of Chinese Language VO Collocation

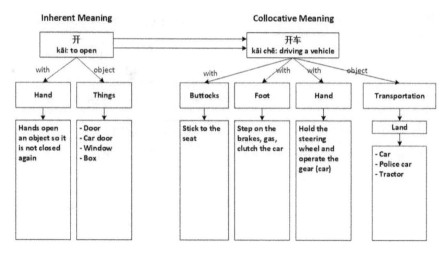

Fig. 7.3 Semantic network of verb 开

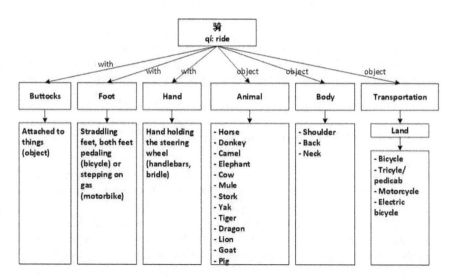

Fig. 7.4 Semantic network of verb 骑

wheel and using his/her feet to step on the brakes, gas and clutch in order to operate a vehicle'. The condition of the agent which performs the action of driving is in sitting position with his/her buttocks on the seat. The mode of transportation which collocates with the verb 开 (kāi) is limited to land transportation which is driven by engine with fuel or by electricity, and it need human involvement in its operation.

For the case of verb 骑 (qí), although the meaning of the verb 骑 (qí) does not change when collocates with modes of transportation as object, due to the development of transportation, the objects collocate with the verb 骑 (qí) also experience an

Fig. 7.5 Semantic network of verb 车

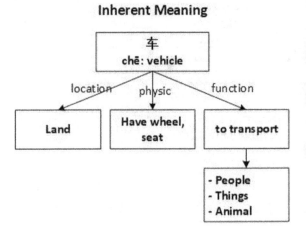

extension in meaning. The objects now are the transportation that can be ridden like a horse, such as bicycle and motorcycle.

The concept of transportation shown in ancient character of noun 车 (chē) is things with an axle (wheel) and is used to transport things, people and animal (Fig. 7.5). To the present day, the concept has not experienced a change, but the type of land transportation was extended due to the development of technology.

7.7 Frames of VO Colocation 坐车, 骑车, 开车

Fillmore (1985, p. 223) says that event frames are 'specific unified frameworks of knowledge or coherence schematization of experience'. It represents the connection between elements associated with events embedded in culture that originate from human experience. Event frames represent the cognitive structure of certain concept that comes from human experience through words. So words do not just show us about the meanings, but they also show us the cognitive structure of concept. Through frames analysis, we can understand the cognitive structure of a concept or an event, and in turns lead to the easy understanding and production of the language (Urgerer & Schmid, 2006, p. 213). Therefore, it is important to understand the frame of an event in order to know the differences between words.

From the semantic network of the verbs 坐车, 骑车, 开车, we also can see the frames of VO collocation that is formed. The elements shown in frame [坐车], [骑车], [开车] are the same; it involves passenger, vehicle, driver, and purpose, but the relation formed between the elements was difference. The frame of [坐车] as shown in Fig. 7.6 represents the relation between passenger and vehicle, while the frame of [骑车] and [开车] represents the relation between driver and vehicle. The differences between the verbs 坐 (zuò), 骑 (qí), and 开 (kāi) is simply a change of perspective within the same frame. Understanding the perspective differences shown from [坐

Fig. 7.6 a The [坐车] frame. b The [骑车] frame. c The [开车] frame

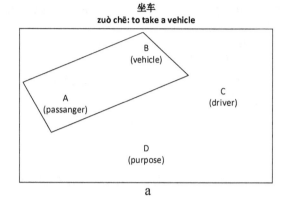

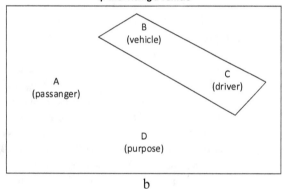

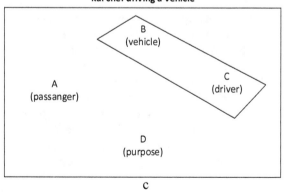

车], [骑车], [开车] frames enable us to understand the forming of VO collocations and produce the correct VO collocations.

Frames are also connected to mental spaces which are the small conceptual packets constructed as we think and talk, and frames structured the elements of mental spaces (Fauconnier & Turner, 2002, p. 40). Understanding these frames help us to understand the mental spaces which build the VO collocations. In the next part, we will try to reveal the forming of VO collocation of 坐车 (zuòchē), 骑车 (qíchē), and 开车 (kāichē) through conceptual blending.

7.8 Conceptual Blending on VO Colocation 坐车, 骑车, 开车

According to Fauconnier and Turner (2002, p. 47), conceptual blending is the integration or blending of two mental spaces into a new blended space which contains information projected from the two mental spaces. Mental spaces are built up from frames, real-world experiences, linguistic input, our personal emotional and bodily states, our personal life experiences and history, and the surrounding culture.

Conceptual blending is built from at least four mental spaces: two input spaces, one generic space, and one blended space. Generic space is an abstract space that is formed from what the input space have in common (Fauconnier & Turner, 2002, p. 41). Between input space one and input space two, there is a partial cross-space mapping that connects the elements in the two input spaces. Blended space is a projection from elements or structures from two input spaces, but not all elements form two input spaces was projected into a blended space. In other words, the projection is a selective one.

Conceptual blending can be found in some of the phenomena in the domain of language and grammar: words formation, compound words, phrase, event structure, and intercategorical polysemy (Fauconnier & Turner, 2002; Zawada, 2007). Although we have not yet discovered the application of conceptual blending in the collocation of verbs and objects, we believe that the conceptual integration theory can also be used in explaining the collocation of verbs and objects. Therefore we will try to describe our findings below.

First, we will explain the conceptual blending of VO collocation 坐车 (zuòchē: to get into a vehicle) as shown on Fig. 7.7. In the case of the verb 坐 (zuò: sit), the 坐 character that is formed from two characters of 人 (ren: human) and another character of 土 (tu: land) which represents two people sitting on their knees on the ground projected to input space 1 坐. The character of 人 (ren: human) is projected into the agent (human), sitting with feet folded back and pressed against the buttocks, which is projected into action of the buttocks attached on things with both legs folded/dangling, and both hands are free to move), and the character 土 (ground) is projected onto the patient (or objects which can be seated). The imagic mapping also occurs from the character 车 which is land transportation with two wheels and is made of

7 Semantic Cognitive Analysis of Chinese Language VO Collocation

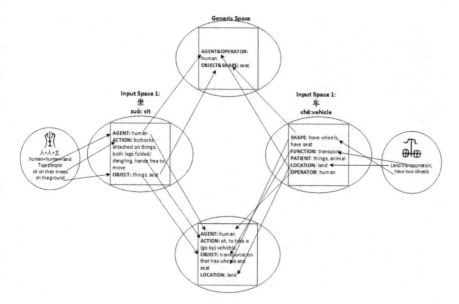

Fig. 7.7 Blended space 坐车 (zuoche: to go by vehicle)

wood put into the input space 2 车. The land transportation from the character is projected to the function 车 (chē) as a mode of transportation and also projected to the location 车 (chē) that is on the land. The visual form of the character 车 that has two wheels is projected into the shape of 车 (chē) which also has wheels. However, in input space 2 车 there is one element, namely the operator (human, animal, item) which is not a visual form projection of the character 车.

What input space 1 坐 and input space 2 车 have in common was shown in the generic space in Fig. 7.7, which are humans and objects that can be seated. One of the objects that can be seated by humans is a seat inside a mode of transportation. The elements of input space 1 坐 and input space 2 车 are then projected into blended space 坐车 (zuòchē: to take a vehicle). The agent of input space 1 坐 and the operator of input space 2 车 are projected into the agent (human) in blended space. The action of input space 1 坐 is projected into the action in blended space (sit, to take a, or to go by a vehicle). The objects (things which can be seated) from input space 1 坐 with the functions (to transport) and shape (has wheels and seats) of input space 2 车 are projected into the objects (transportation that has wheels and seats) in blended space. The location of input space 2 is projected into location (land) in blended space. The projections occur from input spaces 1 坐 and input space 2 车 into blended space 坐车 makes the verb 坐 zuò no longer has the meaning to sit, but it now has the meaning of 'to take a vehicle or to go by a vehicle' (although in certain situations one can sit on a seat or stand up in a transportation vehicle), and also limit the scope of 车 (chē: vehicle) which can collocate with the verb 坐 zuò, which is a land, sea or air transportation that has wheels and a seat.

In the case of the verb 骑 (qí: ride), the 奇 character, which is a picture of someone sitting astride on the back of a horse which represent the meaning of someone riding a horse, is projected to input space 1 骑. The picture of human is projected into the agent (human). The action of sitting astride is projected into action (buttocks attached to things with feet straddling, both pedaling/stepping on gas, and hand/s holding the steering wheel). The picture of horse's back is projected into the object (animal, human body, land transportation). The same imagic mapping from the character 车 as described previously is also visible in the case of VO collocation of 骑车 (qíchē), so we will not describe it anymore.

What input space 1 骑 and input space 2 车 have in common was shown in the generic space in Fig. 7.8, which is a human and the objects that can be seated. One of the objects that can be seated by humans is a seat that is on a mode of transportation. The elements of input space 1 骑 and input space 2 车 are then projected into blended space 骑车 (qíchē; riding a vehicle). The agent of input space 1 骑 and the operator of input space 2 车 are projected into the agent (human) in blended space. The action of input space 1 骑 is projected into the action (of riding) in blended space. The objects (land transportation) from input space 1 骑, and the functions (to transport) and shape (has wheels and seats) of input space 2 车 are projected into the objects (transportation that has wheels and driven by riding with feet straddling) in blended space. The location of input space 2 is projected into location (land) in blended space. The projections occur from input spaces 1 骑 and input space 2 车 into blended space 骑车 still has the meaning and concept of verb 骑 (qí: riding with both feet straddling). At the same time, this also limits the objects or vehicles that can be collocated with verb 骑 (qí). The vehicles that can be collocated with the verb 骑 (qí) are just land transportations which have wheels, have seat, and can be ridden like a horse (with feet dangling).

In the case of verb 开 (kāi: to open), the 開 character which represent the action of someone using two hands to open the door, is projected into input space 1 开. The picture of two hands of human is projected into agent (human) and the action 'open' is projected into an action (which involves the opening of a closed object with both hands). The picture of door and latch is projected into the object (things that can be opened and closed). The same imagic mapping from the character 车 as described above also occur in the case of VO collocation of 开车 (kāichē), but the element of input space 车 is a little bit different from the two cases before. In the case of input space 车 which build the blended space 开车, one element that is 'tools' (hands and feet) used to operate the vehicle is added. We add the element 'tools' because this is one of the common elements between two input spaces (input space 开 and input space 车), besides the element of human. So, what input space 1 开 and input space 2 车 have in common as shown in the generic space in Fig. 7.9 is human and actions which require hands.

The elements of input space 1 开 and input space 2 车 are then projected into blended space 开车 (kāichē: driving a vehicle). The agent of input space 1 开 and the operator of input space 2 车 are projected into the agent (human) in blended space. The action of input space 1 开 and the tools in input space 2 车 is projected into action (to drive with hands and feet) in blended space. The objects (things that can be

7 Semantic Cognitive Analysis of Chinese Language VO Collocation

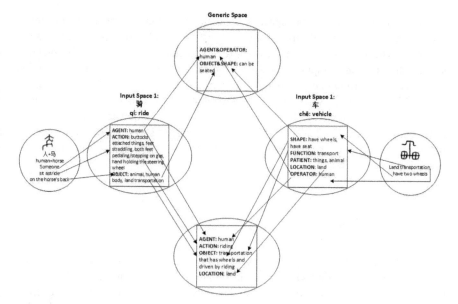

Fig. 7.8 Blended space 骑车 (qi che: riding a vehicle with feet straddling)

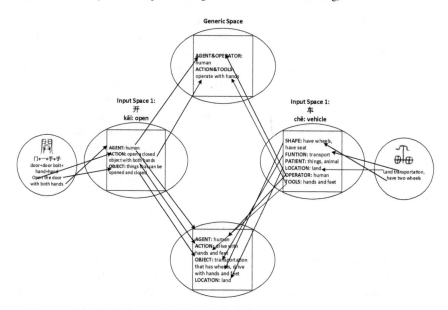

Fig. 7.9 Blended space 开车 (kai che: driving a vehicle)

opened and closed) from input space 1 开 and the functions (to transport) and shape (have wheels and seats) of input space 2 车 are projected to objects (transportation that have wheels, driven with hands and feet, and can be turned on/off) in blended space. The location of input space 2 车 is projected into location (land) in blended space. The projections occur from input spaces 1 开 and input space 2 车 into blended space 开车. This makes verbs 开 (kāi) no longer means to open, but to drive a vehicle, and also limit the scope of 车 (chē: vehicle) which can collocate with the verb 开 (kāi), which is only land transportations that have wheels and seats, can be turned on/off (meaning it is engine operated) or driven by electricity (which can also be turned on/off).

7.9 Conclusion

Many linguists and language educators contend that collocations are arbitrary. Benson (1989, p. 3) believes that collocations are "arbitrary recurrent word combinations". Smadja and McKeown (1991, p. 230) believe that "collocation is an arbitrary recurrent word combinations". Lewis (2008, p. 26) also argues collocation is arbitrary, as can be seen in his statement: "Collocation is, as we have already seen, arbitrary: *high/tall building, tall boy* but not *high boy."

The view or arbitrariness of collocations also affects the language teaching and learning. Most of Chinese language textbooks only provide examples of collocation but not a detail explanation why the collocations are formed in such a way. For example, the collocation part of the textbook "Bridge: A Practical Intermediate Chinese Course" by Chen (2012) just show the list of collocations of each word, such as the objects that can collocate with verb 请示 (qǐngshì: to request/ask) as described on the book. The objects in this case are ~上级 (shàngjí: superior), ~有关部门 (yǒuguān bùmén: related department), ~经理 (jīnglǐ: manager), and ~领导 (lǐngdǎo: leader or boss) (p. 23). There are no further explanations of the collocations in that book. Some textbooks briefly describe the collocations, compare it with the other collocations, and show the domain of collocation. As one of the examples, on the textbook "Road to Success: Advanced Vol. 2" by Li (2008, p.71), the explanation about synonymy 描写 (miǎoxiě: describe) and 描绘 (miǎohuì: describe, depict) do give the scope of objects that can be collocated with each verbs. Such objects that can be collocated with the verb 描写 (miǎoxiě) are 人 (rén: human), 景物 (jǐngwù: scenery), 场面 (chǎngmiàn: scene, situation). The objects that can be collocated with verb 描绘 miǎohuì is 人 (rén: human), 景物 (jǐngwù: scenery), 场面 (chǎngmiàn: scene, situation), and 美丽的景色 (měilìde jǐngsè: beautiful scenery). The differences, however, are not significance, and the author of this book just added a little explanation in objects of 描绘 "使用范围比描写宽" (the range of use much wider than 描写), which is not helpful at all.

Although the information about collocation provided on the textbooks is not very helpful, students also can get the related information from teachers. However, what will happen if the teachers also cannot give a satisfying explanation? What we have done is to solve these problems and to give the explanation about the forming of collocation from the view of semantic cognitive that can be used by teachers when teaching about collocations and can be used by learners in self-study.

First, the Chinese characters do play an important role in VO collocation formation. Every stroke of Chinese characters has its meaning and represents the inherent meaning of Chinese words. Therefore, as we can see in the explanation about conceptual blending, visual form from Chinese character was projected into input space of each verb and object, this is what Hiraga (2005) means by imagic mapping. The imagic mapping plays an important role in meaning component and concept of a word.

Second, the meaning of the verbs and objects and the categorization of objects, also play role in the forming of VO collocation. The meaning components of the verbs fit with the meaning components of the objects and establish the collocative meaning. The collocative meaning and the categorization of objects limit the scope of objects that can be collocated with the verbs. We prove this through the componential analysis of verb 骑 (qí) and objects that can be collocated with this verb. The meaning components of verb 骑 (qí) are that it needs hands and feet to perform action, and the feet must be in astride position. Moreover, the objects must be one of the modes of transportation that need both hands and feet to operate, and the position of feet when riding must be in astride position. An example of this is the object 自行车 (zìxíngchē: bicycle). So, the meaning of verb and categorization of object fits each other and forms a VO collocation 骑自行车 (qí zìxíngchē: riding bicycle).

Third, through semantic network displayed on Figs. 7.2 and 7.3, we can see that there is a change in meaning and concept of verb 坐 (zuò) and verb 开 (kāi) when they collocate with the objects in the modes of transportation domain. This change is caused by the nature of the object. Figures 7.3 and 7.4 show us that the development of technology has an impact on the categorization of objects (especially with vehicles), and extends the objects that can be collocated with the verb 骑 (qí).

Fourth, the semantic network of VO collocation represents the event frames of 坐车, 骑车, 开车, and those frames clearly show us the differences between those collocations, which were simply a change of perspective. We can use frames when explaining the VO collocations or to make a comparison between synonymy. Frames also play a part in building mental space for conceptual blending of VO collocations.

The last of our findings is the fact that conceptual blending can be used as a tool to describe and explain the forming of VO collocations. Through conceptual blending, we can see the visual form of Chinese characters projected into input space and build the components of input space verb and object. Through conceptual blending we can see what input space verb and object have in common, in other words, what elements of those two input spaces fit each other's. Through conceptual blending, we can see which elements of each input spaces projected into blended space forming the VO collocation. The differences of VO collocations in the same domain also can be seen through conceptual blending.

Finally, we realize that our description about VO collocations might be rather complex, but it can be simplified according to certain conditions and be made much easier to be understood by learners. Chinese language teachers can make illustrations (e.g. animated videos) that are very visual to explain the forming of collocations from cognitive semantic perspective. In addition, further research that the author can suggest is the research on the collocation teaching design that considers the principles of collocation formation in terms of semantic cognitive as described in this paper, and also an experimental research to measure how effective the collocation teaching based on semantic cognitive principles.

Acknowledgements This work was supported by Directorate of Research and Community Service of Universitas Indonesia (DRPM UI).

References

Benson, M. (1989). The structure of the collocational dictionary. *International Journal of Lexicography, 2*, 1–14.
Chen, Z. (2012). *Bridge: A practical intermediate Chinese course*. BLCU Press.
Chu, J. (2013). *A research of intermediate Chinese words collocation errors analysis of Mongolia international student as a L2 and countermeasures*. Inner Mongolia Normal University.
Croft, W. (2012). *Verbs: Aspect and causal structure*. Oxford University Press.
Fauconnier, G., & Turner, M. (2002). *The way we think: Conceptual blending and the mind's hidden complexities*. Basic Books.
Fillmore, C. (1985). Frames and the semantics of understanding. *Quaderni di Semantica, VI*, 222–254.
Finch, G. (2000). *Linguistic terms and concepts*. Palgrave.
Hiraga, M. (2005). *Metaphor and iconicity: A cognitive approach to analysing texts*. Palgrave Macmillan.
Jin, K. (2012a). *The error analysis in Chinese V+O structure using of Korean students*. Jilin University.
Jin, X. (2012b). *Hanguo Liuxuesheng Hanyu Dongbin Dapei Xide Qingkuang Fenxi ji Jiaoxue Duice – Yi Zhonggaoji Shuiping de Hanguo Xuesheng Weizhu*. Shandong Normal University.
Kridalaksana, H. (1994). *Pembentukan Kelas Kata dalam Bahasa Indonesia*. Gramedia Pustaka Utama.
Kridalaksana, H. (2001). *Kamus Linguistik*. Gramedia Pustaka Utama.
Leech, G. N. (1974). *Semantics: The study of meaning*. Penguin Books.
Lewis, M. (2008). *Implementing the lexical approach: Putting theory into practice*. Heinle Cencage Learning.
Li, X. (2008). *Road to success: Advanced* (Vol. 2). BLCU Press.
Liu, D. (2010). Going beyond patterns: Involving cognitive analysis in the learning of collocation. *TESOL Quarterly, 44*, 4–30.
Nida, E. A. (1975). *Componential analysis of meaning: An introduction to semantic structures*. Mouton Publishers.
Peiyen, W., Poheng, C., & Shuping, G. (2011). Collocation, semantic prosody and near synonymy: Verbs of 'help' and 'aid' in Mandarin Chinese. In *The 12th Chinese Lexical Semantic Workshop*. National Taiwan University.
Philip, G. (2011). *Colouring meaning: Collocation and connotation in figurative language*. John Benjamins Publishing.
Sinclair, J. (1991). *Corpus, concordance*. Oxford University Press.
Smadja, F., & McKeown, K. (1991). Using collocations for language generation. *Computational Intelligence, 7*, 229–323.

Urgerer, F., & Schmid, H. (2006). *An introduction to cognitive linguistics*. Person Education Limited.
Xiao, R., & McEnery, T. (2006). Collocation, semantic prosody, and near synonymy: A cross-linguistic perspective. *Applied Linguistics, 27*(1), 103–129.
Xiao, X., & Chen, M. (2008). On the acquisition of the Chinese V.+O. Construction of foreign students. *Hanyu Xuebao, 21*, 70–78.
Zawada, B. (2007). Conceptual integration and intercategorical polysemy. *Language Matters: Studies in the Language of Africa, 38*(1), 150–175.
Zheng, R. (2012). *A brief history of vehicles in China*. Social Science.

Symphony Akelba Christian is a doctoral student of Linguistics of Faculty of Humanities, Universitas Indonesia. Her research interests include linguistics, language learning and teaching, especially Chinese linguistics, Chinese language learning and teaching.

Hermina Sutami is a faculty member of Faculty of Humanities, Universitas Indonesia. She earned her doctorate degree from Faculty of Humanities UI in 1999. Her research interests include linguistics, language learning and teaching, especially Chinese linguistics, curriculum design, and lexicography.

Open Access This chapter is licensed under the terms of the Creative Commons Attribution 4.0 International License (http://creativecommons.org/licenses/by/4.0/), which permits use, sharing, adaptation, distribution and reproduction in any medium or format, as long as you give appropriate credit to the original author(s) and the source, provide a link to the Creative Commons license and indicate if changes were made.

The images or other third party material in this chapter are included in the chapter's Creative Commons license, unless indicated otherwise in a credit line to the material. If material is not included in the chapter's Creative Commons license and your intended use is not permitted by statutory regulation or exceeds the permitted use, you will need to obtain permission directly from the copyright holder.

Chapter 8
Collocation of Preposition *Terhadap* in Indonesian Language: A Corpus-Based Analysis

Raya Jayawati Ratnawilis Amanah Notonegoro and Totok Suhardijanto

Abstract As preposition, *terhadap* is polysemous since it has different meanings according to its context. The authors suspect that the context which causes that is collocation or the frequent co-occurrence of words on either side of *terhadap*. The research question of this research is how collocation affects the meaning of *terhadap* in a sentence. This research aims to explain what causes *terhadap* to be polysemous. The method used in this research is a mixed method. This research is corpus-based and uses 6.578 tokens from Korpus Universitas Indonesia. The analysis is carried out by examining the collocate of *terhadap* and pointing the characteristics of *terhadap* in a sentence. As a result, (1) preposition *terhadap* is polysemous because it is flanked by a different combination of collocates. (2) preposition *terhadap* has three different meanings in a sentence, '*pada*' (*T*1), '*kepada*' (*T*2), and '*untuk*' (*T*3). (3) *T*1 is flanked by an abstract noun, adjective, and verb (left), and an abstract noun and non-living concrete noun (right). (4) *T*2 is flanked by an abstract noun (left) and persona noun (right). (5) Lastly, *T*3 is flanked by abstract nouns on its left and right. This research will not only benefit linguistic community but also the field of language teaching.

Keywords Collocation · Corpus · Preposition · *Terhadap*

R. J. R. A. Notonegoro (✉)
Indonesian Language and Literature Department, Faculty of Humanities, Universitas Indonesia, Depok, Indonesia
e-mail: raya.jayawati@ui.ac.id

T. Suhardijanto
Linguistics Department, Faculty of Humanities, Universitas Indonesia, Depok, Indonesia
e-mail: totok.suhardijanto@ui.ac.id

8.1 Introduction

In every language in the world, lexical units, or generally called as words, can be divided into two large groups. First, it is a word which has an inherent meaning. This meaning may be looked up in a dictionary. The second class consists of function words. These words exist to explain or create grammatical or structural relationships into which the content words may fit. The study of word meaning is called semantics, especially lexical semantics. According to Cruse (2004, 88), lexical semantics is the study of the meaning of content words, such as nouns, verbs, adjectives, and adverbs, and they mainly focus on the form of an open framework (open-set items). Semantics is a part of the language studies or linguistics. Semantics examines the relationship between concepts and language signs. Through semantics, linguists can find out the perspective of a language society.

In Indonesian language, there are several words that do not have a lexical meaning, such as preposition *terhadap*. In the previous edition of the Great Dictionary of Indonesian Language or *KBBI* there was no entry of the word *terhadap*, but lexicographers have added an entry of the word *terhadap* in the latest edition of *KBBI*. *KBBI* defines preposition *terhadap* as 'a preposition to mark direction'. This definition refers more to its function in a sentence than to its lexical meaning. Thus, this definition is considered incomplete and needs more addition to it to make it easier for teachers to explain and for students to comprehend.

According to Atkins and Rundell, there are three ways to define a word in a dictionary. One of them is defining the word by using its synonyms (Atkins & Rundel, 2008). However, defining using this method will be more effective if accompanied by information that provides an explanation of certain limitations in the synonyms of the word (Atkins & Rundel, 2008). As a preposition, *terhadap* is polysemous since it has different meanings according to its context. Hence, its meaning can be different in every sentence. Therefore, this method of defining is somewhat suitable to vividly define preposition *terhadap* as a word. To provide in-depth information about the synonyms and their limitations, one must know first what causes preposition *terhadap* to be polysemous in the first place. The authors suspect that the context which causes that is the collocation or the frequent co-occurrence of words on either side of *terhadap*.

8.2 Research Method

This research uses a mixed method. According to Creswell, a mixed method is a research approach that involves quantitative and qualitative data collection, combines two forms of data, and uses different designs, which can involve philosophical assumptions (Creswell, 2016, 5). This research is corpus-based research. According to Sinclair (2005), corpus is 'a collection of pieces of language text in electronic form, selected according to external criteria to represent, as far as possible, a language or language variety as a source of data for linguistic research'. Corpus serves as data in this study because it is considered to be able to provide evidence from function and use of words and community expressions (Leech, 1994). The corpus used in this study was obtained from Universitas Indonesia's Corpus website (Suhardijanto & Dinakaramani, 2018). Universitas Indonesia's Corpus website was chosen as the source of the corpus in this study because it contains many types of categories. Some of them are natural science, applied science, social, international relations, trade and finance, art, beliefs and thoughts, global affairs, and lifestyle.

Based on the problem of this research, there are two analyses that become the focus of this study, the collocation analysis and the meaning analysis of the preposition *terhadap*. The collocation analysis consists of four stages: (1) collecting several theories that can support the research, especially theories about collocation; (2) collecting the corpus from Universitas Indonesia's Corpus website. Based on the website, there are 598 tokens of preposition *terhadap* found in books, textbooks, newspapers, and magazines; (3) conducting the collocation analysis; and (4) determining the location of the collocate that determines the meaning of preposition *terhadap*. Meanwhile, there are five stages in analyzing the meaning of preposition *terhadap*: (1) collecting several theories about prepositions in Indonesian language; (2) matching the preposition function proposed by Ramlan with the existing data; (3) describing the different characteristics of preposition *terhadap*; (4) describing the characteristics of some of the meanings that the word has towards; (5) drawing conclusions from both analyses.

8.3 Collocation

Collocation is the expectancy relations between lexical items. Moon uses the term collocation to refer to the syntagmatic and paradigmatic relationships that words have (Moon, 1998). Meanwhile, through a different approach Carter argues that "collocation is the frequent co-occurrence of words within a specified distance to be four words to either side of the specified focal word or node (Carter, 1998, 51). Collocation consists of two parts, node and collocate (Sinclair, 1991). Node is a word that is being studied. Meanwhile, the collocates are the words that appear in the node environment. Preposition *terhadap* is the node in this study. According to Kjellmer and Smadja, collocates are the words which have the occurrence frequency of more than 2 times in the node environment. This can be seen through the collocation window (Lehecka, 2015, 3).

There have been a number of studies that discuss collocation and its role in language. There are several studies on collocation that have been done in Indonesia (Christianto, 2013; Salsabila, 2014; Sirima, 2014). There are also several studies on collocation that have been done outside Indonesia (Buakaew, 2015; Jafarpour et al., 2013; Wu, 2010). Those studies discuss the function of lexical collocation in the area of teaching and learning. Moreover, the rest discuss lexical collocation in different types of discourses. However, there is not much research that addresses collocation on words that do not have lexical meaning, such as preposition (Kamakura, 2011;

Rahestrie, 2018). Those two studies focus on analyzing collocation on English preposition and there has not been any research which discusses this topic on Indonesian preposition. Therefore, the main focus of this research is to analyze collocation in Indonesian preposition, especially the polysemous one like preposition *terhadap*.

8.4 Collocation of Preposition *Terhadap*

Based on Universitas Indonesia's corpus page, there are 598 tokens of preposition *terhadap*. The 598 tokens consist of 501 words used in various books, i.e. general books and textbooks. The remaining 97 words are used in journalistic texts, such as newspapers and magazines. Before conducting a collocation analysis, the researcher first determines which nodes or words are the focus in this research. The node or word being studied is the preposition *terhadap*. Collocates in this study are the words that appear more than 2 times in frequency in the environment of the preposition *terhadap* (Kjellmer, 1984 and Smadja, 1993 in Lehecka, 2015, 4). In this study, researchers used a collocation window according to Lehecka, which is a window of L5-R5 collocation. That means, researchers have to list 5 words found on the left and 5 words located on the right side of the preposition *terhadap*.

There are several considerations in choosing L5-R5 as the collocation window in this study. First, L5-R5 was chosen so that researchers could see certain words often appear together with preposition *terhadap* within a large range. Second, based on the corpus, the use of preposition *terhadap* often appears in long and complex sentences. Thus, L5-R5 is considered appropriate to be used as a collocation window in this study. After looking at the collocation window of 598 tokens, several words were found on the left and right side of the preposition *terhadap*, and they are suspected as the collocates of the preposition *terhadap*. There are 84 words on the left side of the node that are suspected as collocates or as much as 14% of the total tokens. On the other hand, there are 96 words on the right side of the node that are suspected as the collocates from the preposition *terhadap* or as much as 16% of the total number of tokens.

Each of these words has a different frequency of occurrence in the corpus. To facilitate the process of searching the collocates, the researchers divided the words mentioned into three different groups based on the frequency of their appearance in the corpus. First is words that appear only once in the corpus (=1). Second is words that have the frequency of occurrence of equal to two in the corpus (=2). Third is words which have the frequency of occurrence to equal or more than three (≥ 3) in the corpus. The division can be seen through Table 8.1.

There are 31 words on the left side of the node that appear only once in a frequency corpus. In other words, 37% of the total corpus has a frequency of occurrence one time. These words are *penolakan, serangan, perlakuan, peringatan, rekayasa, pemisah, pembatas, aksesibilitas, percobaan, kereaktifan, analisis, kekeliruan,*

Table 8.1 Frequency of appearance of words on the left side of preposition *Terhadap*

Occurrence frequency	Number of words	Percentage (%)
=1	31	37
=2	17	20
≥3	36	43
Total ($\sum$)	84	100

jawaban, garapan, kebanggaan, perekaman, pengetahuan, perasaan, penghormatan, observasi, perhatian, penyempurnaan, penawaran, peningkatan, pengujian, efek, pendekatan, solusi, pengukuran, intervensi, agresi, kecaman, konsumsi, orbit, gaya, perburuan, kekuatan, penghayatan, pertumbuhan, pencemaran, blokade, memberontak, beraliasi, berpangku tangan, tersinggung, meninggi, miring, kedap, asertif, and *hati-hati*.

There are 17 words on the left side of the node that appear only twice in a frequency corpus. These words are *simpati, penangkapan, kekuasaan, ketidakpuasan, dikenakan, perlindungan, sensitif, jarak, gerakan, heran, reaksi, penelitian, resisten, relatif, pemahaman, berjasa,* and *penyimpangan*. Based on the percentage, 20% of the total words have twice the frequency of appearance in the corpus. In addition, on the left side there are 37 words with the frequency of occurrence equal to or more than three times in the corpus. In other words, 43% of the total number of words have the frequency of occurrence equal to or more than three times. Each of these words has a different frequency of appearance in the corpus. This division can be seen through Table 8.2.

Meanwhile, on the right side of the preposition *terhadap*, the frequency of occurrence of words is also divided into three groups. First is words that appear only once in the corpus (=1). Second is words that have the frequency of occurrence of equal to two in the corpus (=2). Third is words which have the frequency of occurrence to equal or more than three (≥3) in the corpus. The division can be seen through Table 8.3.

There are 62 words on the right side of the node that appear only once in the corpus. These words are *daerah, besaran, Malaka, VOC, ancaman, proklamasi, sekutu, Republik indonesia, Tokoh-tokoh, program, kebijakan, Tuhan, negara, bangsa, struktur, pemerintah, Anggaran Pembangunan Desa (APD), keputusan, kekuatan, dasardasar, piagam, pesan, konflik, sila, urusan, negara, penyerangan, keragaman, produksi, minyak tanah, biji, musim, dehidrasi, sinar, pertumbuhan, peningkatan, perumahan, puisi, posko, kelompok, laporan, uraian, rintangan, keduaduanya, Sulam (nama orang), kandungan, ekonomi, hemoglobin, hutan, oksigen, gangguan, virus, tekanan, toksin, benda, hasil, masalah, hal, daerah,* and *hama*. Based on the percentage, 62% of the total number of words have the occurrence frequency of equal to one in the corpus.

On the right side there are 18 words that appear only twice in the corpus. These words are *penjelasan, pembaca, bacaan, sumber, belanda, keutuhan, rumusan, wilayah, jenis, sumbu, penampilan, pendapat, kenaikan, lapisan, terjadi, rasa, cipta,* and *bidang*. Based on the data, 18% of the total corpus has the appearance frequency

Table 8.2 Words with frequency of occurrence of ≥3

Occurrence frequency	Number of words	Word
3 times	11 words	perlawanan, posisi, gangguan, tekanan, kepedulian, kritik, pengawasan, daya, berubah, kesadaran, and tindakan
4 times	7 words	ancaman, penghargaan, setuju, penyelidikan, keberatan, pengamatan, and sumbangan
6 times	5 words	pemecahan, tanggung jawab, selera, kontribusi, and pelanggaran
7 times	2 words	pemecahan, tanggung jawab, selera, kontribusi, and pelanggaran
8 times	2 words	dampak and pandangan
10 times	1 word	Adaptasi
12 times	1 word	kebutuhan
13 times	1 word	penyesuaian
14 times	2 words	tanggapan and penilaian
16 times	1 word	Peka
24 times	1 word	permintaan
27 times	1 word	Sikap
56 times	1 word	pengaruh

Table 8.3 Frequency of appearance of words on the right side of preposition *Terhadap*

Occurrence frequency	Number of words	Percentage (%)
=1	62	62
=2	18	18
≥3	19	19
Total ($\sum$)	99	100

of two. In addition, there are 19 words on the right side of the node which have appeared equal to or more than three times in the corpus. Meanwhile, 19% of the total corpus has the frequency of occurrence equal to or more than three times in the corpus. Every word has a different frequency of appearance in the corpus. The division can be seen through Table 8.4.

Next, the researchers tested the data using the chi-square testing method with IBM SPSS software. The chi-square testing method is used to test the independence of two or more variables. This test produces a coefficient value correlation that will show the relation between the observed variables. In this chapter the authors analyzed whether there are significant relations between the locations of collocations found in the corpus and the occurrence frequency of preposition *terhadap* using the chi-square testing method. The chi-square testing cross-tabulation data can be seen through Table 8.5.

8 Collocation of Preposition *Terhadap* in Indonesian Language ...

Table 8.4 Words with frequency of occurrence of ≥ 3

Occurrence frequency	Number of words	Word
3 times	7 words	*tempat, persoalan, perjuangan, peristiwa, hewan, rangsang,* and *anak*
4 times	2 words	*masalah* and *cerita*
5 times	1 word	*orang*
6 times	3 words	*air, permasalahan,* and *keadaan*
7 times	1 word	*matahari*
8 times	1 word	*perubahan*
9 times	2 words	*kehidupan* dan *bumi*
18 times	1 word	*lingkungan*

Table 8.5 Chi-square testing cross-tabulation data

		Occurrence frequency			
		=1	=2	≥ 3	Total
Left	Count	31	17	36	84
	Expected count	42.7	16.1	25.2	84.0
	% within location (%)	36.9	20.2	42.9	100.0
	% within the word frequency (%)	33.3	48.6	65.5	45.9
Right	Count	62	18	19	99
	Expected count	50.3	18.9	29.8	99.0
	% within location (%)	62.6	18.2	19.2	100.0
	% within the word frequency (%)	66.7	51.4	34.5	54.1
Total	Count	93	35	55	183
	Expected count	93.0	35.0	55.0	183.0
	% within location (%)	50.8	19.1	30.1	100.0
	% within the word frequency (%)	100.0	100.0	100.0	100.0

In Table 8.5 we can see the actual count value of each variable component. The actual count value of the variable component is the value that is actually observed when the data are being collected, while the expected count value is a value that is expected to occur if there is no relationship between the two variables analyzed, which are namely the location of the word and the occurrence frequency of preposition *terhadap*. The initial hypothesis [null hypothesis (H_0)] of the chi-square test in this study is that the location of the collocate does not affect the frequency of occurrence of the preposition *terhadap*, whereas the alternative hypothesis (H_i) of this test is that the location of words affects occurrence frequency of the preposition *terhadap*. The standard level of significance used in the chi-square test (α) is 5% (0.05). To prove the truth of the hypothesis the researcher must compare Pearson chi-square (P) values obtained from chi-square analysis with value of α. If the P value obtained is smaller than α (P < α), it can be said that H_0 is not acceptable and the accepted hypothesis is H_i.

In Table 8.6, the P value from the chi-square test is 0.001. This value is much smaller than value of α. Therefore, it can be concluded that statistically the location of words affects the frequency of occurrence of preposition *terhadap*. However, Chi-square testing cannot provide information about the significance of the relationship between the two variables analyzed. Therefore, the authors also calculate the value of the correlation coefficient of the variables analyzed using the value of Phi and Crammer's V (see Table 8.7).

The value of Phi and Crammer's V obtained from the analysis is 0.281 (28%). That value indicates that the influence of the location is at low to medium or weak–moderate (Rea & Parker, 1992, 203). Based on that test, the impact of the location of the word to the frequency of occurrence of preposition *terhadap* cannot be clearly seen. Thus, to see the tendency the researchers must dissect the existing data.

Kjellmer defines collocates as words that have a frequency of occurrence more than two times in the environment of words against (Kjellmer, 1984 and Smadja, 1993 in Lehecka, 2015, 4). Thus, it can be concluded that the words in the corpus which belong in the group of occurrence frequency of ≥3 are the collocates of the preposition *terhadap*. The effect of word location on the occurrence of the preposition *terhadap* can be seen in Table 8.8. Table 8.8 shows that 66% of the group are words located to the left of the preposition *terhadap*, whereas only 34% are words located to the right of the preposition *terhadap*. Therefore, it can be concluded that the words located to the left side of the preposition *terhadap* have a high tendency to be the collocates of the preposition *terhadap* that determine the meaning of the preposition.

Meanwhile, groups of words that have a frequency of occurrence =1 are less likely to be words that determine the meaning of preposition *terhadap*. Based on the data, 67% of the words which belong in this group are words that are located on the right of the preposition *terhadap*. Meanwhile, 33% of the words are located on the left side of the preposition *terhadap* (Table 8.8). Thus, it can be concluded that the

Table 8.6 Result of chi-square test

	Value	df	Asymp. sig. (2 sided)
Pearson chi-square	14.484a	2	0.001
Likelihood ratio	14.673	2	0.001
Linear-by-linear association	14.398	1	0.000
N of valid cases	183		

Table 8.7 Phi and Crammer's V

		Value	Approx. sig.
Nominal by nominal	Phi	0.281	0.001
	Cramer's V	0.281	0.001
N of valid cases		183	

Table 8.8 Frequency of occurrences of words with preposition *Terhadap*

Location of the words	Frequency of occurrences of words with preposition *Terhadap*		
	=1 (%)	=2 (%)	≥3 (%)
Left	33	49	66
Right	67	51	34

words which are located on the right side of the preposition *terhadap* do not have a high tendency to be the collocates of the preposition *terhadap* that determine the meaning the preposition. Therefore, collocates that are found on the right side of *terhadap* are considered to be free combination collocates of preposition *terhadap*. According to Benson, Benson, and Ilson, the free combination is a form consisting of elements which can be freely replaced at any time (Bahns, 1993, 57). This matter causes the tendency for these groups of words to appear one time at a time with the preposition *terhadap* in the corpus.

The researchers also examined more deeply about groups of words that have frequency occurrence with the preposition *terhadap* = 2, because the researchers want to find out more about the reasons why Kjellmer and Smadja determine the number 2 as the limit of the collocate criteria. In this chapter the researchers found that only 20 and 18% of the words which are located in the left and right side of preposition *terhadap* belong to this group of words. The percentage indicates that these groups of words are classified into groups that have special cases. There are two possibilities that can be identified by the authors for these words:

- Unidentified collocates are words that are actually collocates of words against, but its appearance does not appear much in the corpus.
- False collocates are words that are not actually collocates of words against, but they are often found in the corpus.

As stated before, according to Ramlan and Kridalaksana, the word *terhadap* belongs to the preposition word class. Therefore, the appearance of the preposition *terhadap* in a sentence has a function as a link or connector between the word to the left of the preposition *terhadap* (C1) and the word to the right the preposition *terhadap* (C2). In other words, the preposition *terhadap* appears in a sentence because C1 requires a grammatical form that can connect it to C2. This causes the preposition *terhadap* to be determined by C1. Meanwhile, C2 is a free combination collocate or free combination of C1 + preposition *terhadap*. Other than that, the appearance of C2 is also determined by the context or topic being discussed in the sentence. Thus, in a different context or topic C2 can be replaced by other words that have a paradigmatic relation to the word (Stubbs, 2001, 30). This can be seen through the two example sentences contained in corpora 8 and 164 below.

- (8) <u>Sikap</u> penyair terhadap $\begin{Bmatrix} \text{C1} & \text{C2} \\ \text{persoalan} \\ \text{pembaca} \end{Bmatrix}$

- (164) <u>Permintaan</u> terhadap $\begin{Bmatrix} \text{C1} & \text{C2} \\ \text{barang} \\ \text{makanan} \\ \text{pakaian} \\ \text{sembako} \end{Bmatrix}$

8.5 Characteristics of Preposition *Terhadap*

Based on the corpus, there are three types of meanings possessed by the preposition "against". First, the preposition *terhadap* has a similar meaning to '*pada*' or 'to' (*T*1). For example is (264) *Pelanggaran terhadap norma hukum akan dikenai denda*. Second, the preposition *terhadap* has a similar meaning to '*kepada*' or 'towards' (*T*2). For example is (30) *Keputusan bersama dapat dipertanggungjawabkan terhadap Tuhan*. Third, the preposition *terhadap* has a similar meaning to '*untuk*' or 'for' (*T*3). For example is (228) *Sumbangan terbesar Lavoisier terhadap pengembangan ilmu kimia membuatnya dijuluki bapak kimia modern*. This chapter will explain some characteristics possessed by the three meanings of preposition *terhadap*.

First, the preposition *terhadap* has a similar meaning to '*pada*' (*T*1). According to Ramlan, there are several grammatical functions possessed by the preposition *pada* (Ramlan, 1980, 91–95). First, the preposition *pada* has a function of being an 'existence' marker. For example is *Saya sudah bekerja pada dinas perkreditan desa di Kebumen*. The preposition *pada* in that sentence shows the place where the person or *saya* works, which is *dinas perkreditan* or 'credit service'. Second, the preposition *pada* can also function as a marker of the meaning of the intended direction. For example is *aku mencoba mengonsentrasikan diri pada pelajaran*. In the sentence, the word *pelajaran* or 'lesson' is the direction that *aku* or that person is headed. The preposition *pada* is also used as a marker of sufferers. In this case, the proposition *pada* is in line with the function of the preposition *akan*. For example is *dia merasa malu pada dirinya*. Finally, the preposition "on" also functions to mark the meaning of "recipient". For example is *laporan ini disampaikan pada Direktorat PTS*. In that sentence, *pada* functions as to and the recipient is *Direktorat PTS*.

The preposition *terhadap* which has a similar meaning to *pada* has a high number of occurrences in the corpus. This is probably because the preposition *pada* is the main meaning of the preposition *terhadap*. Based on the corpus, the preposition *terhadap* which has a meaning similar to '*pada*' (*T*1) can form two types of phrases. First is nominal phrases. For example is *gangguan terhadap sebagian wilayah negara dan penyesuaian terhadap nilai*. Second is prepositional phrases. For example is *terhadap rangsangan* dan *terhadap matahari*. Prepositions *terhadap* which form nominal phrases can occupy three types of gatra in sentences: the subject, object, and complement of gatra. Meanwhile, the proposition *terhadap* that forms a prepositional phrase occupies only one gatra, i.e. the description of gatra. Based on the example sentences contained in Table 8.9, it appears that the preposition *pada* in these sentences has similar meanings to the preposition *pada*. In other words, T1 has the same function as *pada* stated by Ramlan. In the sentence, T1 functions as a marker of meaning "the direction to go" by C1. Meanwhile, C2 is the direction where C1 is headed.

The appearance of $T1$ in sentences is caused by two factors. The first factor is that collocate of preposition *terhadap* or the words to the left of the preposition *terhadap* (C1). Based on the corpus, C1 connected by $T1$ is in the form of basic abstract nouns and has affixes and verbs with *ber-* affix. Some basic abstract nouns found by the researchers are *selera, dampak, peka, tanggung jawab, pengaruh,* and *revolusi*. In addition, the researchers also found abstract nouns that have special meaning. First, the abstract nouns mark the meaning of 'result of a deed', such as *gangguan, ancaman, tekanan,* and *tanggapan*. Second, the abstract nouns have the meaning of 'ownership', such as *kepedulian, kesadaran, keberatan,* and *kebutuhan*. Third, the abstract nouns have the meaning of 'process', such as *pengawasan, penghargaan, pelanggaran, penyesuaian, adaptasi, pengamatan, pemecahan,* and *penilaian*. Finally, the abstract nouns have the meaning of 'things', like *perlawanan*

Table 8.9 $T1$

	Phrase form	Sentence
1	Noun phrases that occupy the subject of gatra	(31) *Gangguan terhadap sebagian wilayah negara berarti...* (96) *Kepedulian masyarakat terhadap peningkatan kualitas lingkungan memaksa para pengembang untuk makin...* (118) *Pengawasan terhadap batas minimal kandungan fosfat dalam detergen atau bahan...*
2	Noun phrases that occupy the object of gatra	(137) *Kita harus meningkatkan pengawasan yang melibatkan semua pihak terhadap penggunaan hutan* (50) *...tidak melakukan tekanan terhadap negara lain* (240) *Suatu masyarakat memiliki kesadaran terhadap masa lalunya*
3	Noun phrases that occupy the complementary of gatra	(29) *Hal itu merupakan gangguan terhadap keutuhan Negara Kesatuan Republik Indonesia* (432) *Salah satu kategorinya adalah penghargaan terhadap inovasi yang dilakukan oleh karyawan* (64) *Bentuk daun tersebut merupakan bentuk adaptasi teratai terhadap tempat hidupnya*
4	Prepositional phrases which occupy the description of gatra	(483) *Kepala ULP bertanggung jawab terhadap pengadaan barang* (80) *Bumi berevolusi satu kali terhadap matahari* (15) *Peristiwa alam selalu berdampak terhadap kehidupan*

and *permintaan*. The verbs with *ber-* affix found by the researchers are *berevolusi, berdampak, beradaptasi,* and *berpengaruh*.

The second factor is the free combination collocate of preposition *terhadap* or the words found on the right side of preposition *terhadap* (C2). Based on the corpus, C2 to which C1 is headed is an abstract and concrete non-living nouns. Abstract nouns found in corpus are in the form of basic and affixed abstract nouns. Some basic abstract nouns that were discovered by the researchers are *kandungan, nilai, norma,* and *kualitas*. In addition, the researchers also found abstract nouns that mark the meaning of 'fields' (*ekonomi* and *sosiologi*) and 'time markers' (*masa lalu*). Another special meaningful abstract noun found by the researchers in the corpus is abstract nouns that mark the meaning of 'ownership' (*keadaan* and *kehidupan*), 'process' (*pementasan* and *penggunaan*), and 'things' (*pertumbuhan*). Meanwhile, there are two types of concrete animate nouns that the researchers found in the corpus. First is tangible non-living concrete nouns, such as *Piagam Jakarta, barang,* and *air*. Second is non-living concrete nouns that mark the meaning of 'the name of a place', such as *sebagian wilayah negara, bumi manusia,* and *posko penampungan korban banjir*.

Based on the corpus, the researchers found several sentences that use the preposition *terhadap* whose meaning is similar to '*kepada*' or 'towards'. According to Ramlan, there are several functions possessed by the preposition *kepada* (Ramlan, 1980, 77–78). First, the preposition *kepada* functions to mark the receiver. For example is *Onasis memberikan hadiah kepada Lee*. Second, preposition *kepada* functions as a marker of the meaning of something or someone to whom it is intended. For example is *Lampu-lamu sudah diarahkan kepada kita*. In addition, preposition *kepada* also marks "the patient" in a sentence. For example is *Orang tua itu sayang kepada anak-anaknya*. *Orang tua* or 'parent' is the patient in that sentence. Preposition *terhadap* which has a similar meaning to '*kepada*' has a low number of occurrence in the corpus. Based on the corpus, only three examples of sentences were found using the preposition *terhadap* which has a meaning similar to '*kepada*' (see Table 8.10).

Based on the corpus, the preposition *terhadap* which has a similar meaning to *kepada* (*T*2) can form one type of phrase, which is the nominal phrase. For example is *perlawanan terhadap Belanda*. Based on the corpus, *T*2 that forms a nominal phrase can occupy three types of gatra in sentences, i.e. gatra subject, object, and

Table 8.10 *T*2

	Phrase form	Sentence
1	Noun phrases that occupy the subject of gatra	(411) *Program CSR dalam mewujudkan rasa kepedulian yang tinggi terhadap masyarakat*
2	Noun phrases that occupy the object of gatra	(18) *Sultan Hasanuddin memimpin perlawanan terhadap Belanda*
3	Noun phrases that occupy the complementary of gatra	(363) *Hal tersebut merupakan konsekuensi dari pelanggaran yang dilakukan pemain terhadap pemain lawan*

complement. Based on the corpus, it appears that $T2$ has a similar syntactic structure with $T1$. In addition, C1 in the nominal phrase of $T2$ does not differ from C1 in the nominal phrase of $T1$. Based on the corpus, C1 connected by T2 is in the form of an affixed abstract noun. There are two types of affixed abstract nouns found by the researchers. First, the affixed abstract nouns mark the meaning of 'ownership', such as *kepedulian*. Second, the affixed abstract nouns mark the meaning of process, such as *pelanggaran*. The context that causes preposition *terhadap* to have a meaning similar to '*kepada*' is caused by C2. Based on the corpus, free variation collocates or C2 from $T2$ is in the form of living persona nouns, such as *masyarakat, Belanda,* and *pemain lawan*. According to Kridalaksana, there are five types of persona noun (Kridalaksana, 1999): (1) a person's name; (2) kinship; (3) person or a thing that is treated like a person; (4) group name; (5) non-living things. Based on these explanations, it is evident that $T2$ has a meaning similar to '*kepada*'. Preposition *terhadap* which has a similar meaning to '*kepada*' has a low number of occurrence in the corpus. The researchers suspect that this happens because people use *kepada* more often to refer to someone.

Based on the corpus, the researchers found several sentences that use the preposition *terhadap* which has a similar meaning to '*untuk*' or 'for'. According to Ramlan, there are several grammatical functions possessed by the preposition for (Ramlan, 1980, 116). One of its functions is to mark the meaning of 'designation'. In this case, the proposition *untuk* has the same function as the preposition *bagi*. For example is *dia tidak pernah lupa membawa oleh-oleh* <u>untuk</u> *ibu dan adik-adiknya* and *dia tidak pernah lupa membawa oleh-oleh* <u>bagi</u> *ibu dan adik-adiknya*. Through these two sentences, it appears that *untuk* and *bagi* have the same function which is to explain the designation. The preposition *terhadap* which has a similar meaning to '*untuk*' has a low number of occurrence in the corpus.

Based on the corpus, only nine sentences were found, and those use the preposition *terhadap* which has a similar meaning to '*untuk*'. Based on the corpus, preposition *terhadap* which has a similar meaning to '*untuk*' ($T3$) can form one type of phrase, which is the nominal phrase. Based on the corpus, $T3$ forms nominal phrases that can occupy two types of gatra in sentences, which are the subject and object of gatra. Based on the example sentences contained in Table 8.11, it appears that the preposition *terhadap* in those sentences has a similar meaning to the preposition '*untuk*'. In other words, $T3$ has the same function as the preposition *untuk* proposed by Ramlan. In the sentence, $T3$ functions as a marker to link C1 and C2. Meanwhile, C2 is the direction intended by C1. Based on the corpus, it appears that $T3$ has a similar syntactic structure with $T1$ and $T2$. However, the researchers found the context that led to the emergence of $T3$ in a sentence. Based on the corpus, $T3$ appears together with C1 in the form of abstract nouns to mark 'giving something to other people', such as *sumbangan* and *kontribusi* or donations and contributions. Meanwhile, based on the corpus, the free variation collocates or C2 that is intended by C1 is in the form of abstract nouns. Abstract nouns found in the corpus are in the form of basic and affixed abstract nouns. Some of them are abstract nouns to mark the meaning of 'fields' (economics and sociology) and abstract nouns to mark results, such as income.

Table 8.11 T3

Form	Sentence
1 Noun phrases that occupy the subject of gatra	(271) *Beberapa sumbangan penting Comte terhadap sosiologi sebagai berikut* (424) *Kontribusi layanan data terhadap pendapatan XL Axiata sudah mencapai 68 persen*
2 Noun phrases that occupy the object of gatra	(269) *Comte memberi sumbangan yang begitu penting terhadap sosiologi* (186) *Peternakan dan kehutanan yang memberikan kontribusi cukup besar terhadap pendapatan nasional* (229) *Lavoisier memberikan banyak kontribusi terhadap sains dan ekonomi*

8.6 Discussion

Based on the research that has been done, there are several things that were discovered by the researchers from the collocation analysis of the preposition *terhadap*. First, the chi square test shows that the location of words has a significant effect on the frequency of occurrence of preposition *terhadap*. The Phi and Cramer's V test is used to measure the significant value between two variables. Phi and Cramer's V value obtained from the analysis is 0.281 (28%). This value indicates that the effect of the location is at the low to medium level or weak to moderate. Therefore, the effect of the location to the frequency of occurrence of preposition *terhadap* cannot be seen clearly and directly. Thus, to see this tendency, the researchers must dissect the existing data.

The majority of words that have a frequency of occurrence along with *terhadap* ≥ 3 are found on the left side of the node. Based on Kjellmer's theory, the "real" collocates are the words found on the left side of preposition *terhadap*. Therefore, collocates that are found on the right side of preposition *terhadap* have more chance to be the collocates that determine the meaning of preposition *terhadap*. Meanwhile, the majority of collocates that have a frequency of occurrence along with *terhadap* $=1$ are found on the right side of the node. Therefore, collocates that are found on the right side of *terhadap* are considered as a free combination collocate. Therefore, the authors concluded that the notion mentioned being stated before is considered valid, and collocation does determine the meaning of *terhadap* in a sentence.

Second, preposition *terhadap* is polysemous because it is flanked by a different combination of collocates. Second, preposition *terhadap* has three different meanings in a sentence, '*pada*' or 'to' ($T1$), '*kepada*' or 'towards' ($T2$), and '*untuk*' or 'for' ($T3$). Based on the corpus, preposition *terhadap* which has a similar meaning to '*pada*' ($T1$) has a high rate of occurrence in the corpus. Meanwhile, preposition *terhadap* which has a similar meaning to "towards" ($T2$) and "against" ($T3$) has a low rate of appearance in the corpus. Therefore, the researchers conclude that $T1$ is the main meaning of the preposition *terhadap*. Meanwhile, *T*2 and *T*3 are the other meanings that the preposition *terhadap* has.

Based on the corpus, preposition *terhadap* which has a similar meaning to '*pada*' or 'to' (*T*1) has a locative function in a sentence. *T*1 is flanked by abstract noun (*gangguan, keberatan, penyesuaian*), adjective, verb (*berevolusi, berdampak, beradaptasi*) on its left and abstract noun (*Piagam Jakarta, barang, air*) and non-living concrete noun (*sebagian wilayah negara, bumi manusia, posko penampungan korban banjir*) on its right. Preposition *terhadap* which has a similar meaning to '*kepada*' or 'towards' (*T*2) has a function as a person indicator in a sentence. *T*2 is flanked by abstract noun (*kepedulian, pelanggaran*) on its left and persona noun (*masyarakat, Belanda, pemain lawan*) on its right. Preposition *terhadap* which has a similar meaning to '*untuk*' or 'for' (*T*3) has a benefactive function in a sentence. *T*3 is flanked by abstract noun (*sumbangan, kontribusi*) on its left and abstract noun (*ekonomi, sosiologi, pendapatan*) on its right.

The researchers also found groups of words that have a frequency of occurrence along with *terhadap* =2. The researchers consider these words as words that have special cases. Based on observations made by the researchers of existing data, these words can be classified into two types. First, unidentified collocates or words are actually the collocate of preposition *terhadap* but not widely used in the corpus under study. Second, false collocates or words are actually not a collocate of the preposition *terhadap*, but by chance many are used with preposition *terhadap* in the same text in the corpus under study.

8.7 Conclusion

This research will benefit not only linguistic community but also the field of language teaching in Indonesia. The findings of this research can help the field of lexicography to support some details on words that do not have lexical meanings (e.g., *terhadap*). This research can also boost the efficiency of Indonesian language teaching by making it easier for teachers to explain and for students of Indonesian language for foreign speakers (BIPA) to comprehend the use of this particular preposition in a discourse. Based on the research that has been done, here are some things that can still be developed from this research. First, further research could increase the number of corpus being the research data. In this way, researchers will find it easier to find the meanings of the preposition *terhadap* and the causes of the emergence of those meanings. Second, further research could identify other prepositions in Indonesian and generate a rule that can help L2 learners to understand these prepositions. Therefore, this research can still be refined by further research.

References

Atkins, B. S., & Rundell, M. (2008). *The Oxford guide to practical lexicography*. Oxford University Press.
Bahns. (1993).
Buakaew, R. (2015, May–August). A study of collocation usage in food and beverage advertisements. *Panyapiwat Journal, 7*(2).
Carter. (1998).
Christianto, L. (2013). *Wacana Status Akun Twitter Liputan9: Telaah Konteks, Kolokasi, dan Makna Satire*. Fakultas Ilmu Pengetahuan Budaya Universitas Indonesia.
Creswell, J. W. (2016). *Research design: Pendekatan Metode Kualitatif, Kuantitatif, dan Campuran Edisi Keempat*. Pustaka Pelajar.
Cruse, D. A. (2004). *Meaning in language: An introduction to semantics and pragmatics*. Oxford University Press.
Jafarpour, A. A., Hashemian, M., & Alipour, S. (2013, January). A corpus-based approach toward teaching collocation of synonyms. *Theory and Practice in Language Studies, 3*(1), 51–60. Academy Publisher.
Kamakura, Y. (2011). *Collocation and preposition sense: A phraseological approach to the cognition of polysemy*. University of Birmingham. http://etheses.bham.ac.uk/id/eprint/1592/1/Kamakura_11_PhD.pdf
Kridalaksana. (1999).
Leech, G. (1994). Text corpora in education: The grand design. In *Conference Handbook of the 1st International Conference on Teaching and Language Corpora (TALC94)* (pp. 24–25). Lancaster University.
Lehecka, T. (2015). Collocation and colligation. In J.-O. Östman (Ed.), *Handbook of pragmatics*. John Benjamins.
Moon. (1998).
Rahestrie, T. (2018). *Makna Orientasi Ruang pada Preposisi Bahasa Inggris yang Digunakan oleh Penutur Bahasa Indonesia*. Fakultas Ilmu Pengetahuan Budaya Universitas Indonesia.
Ramlan. (1980).
Rea & Parker. (1992).
Salsabila, N. S. (2014). *Kolokasi Kata Sakura dalam Lirik Lagu Bahasa Jepang*. Fakultas Ilmu Pengetahuan Budaya Universitas Indonesia.
Sinclair, J. (1991). *Corpus, concordance, collocation*. Oxford University Press.
Sinclair, J. (2005). Corpus and text—Basic principles. In M. Wynne (Ed.), *Developing linguistic corpora: A guide to good practice* (pp. 1–16). Oxbow. http://ota.ox.ac.uk/documents/creating/dlc/. Diakses pada Oktober 2018
Sirima, A. T. (2014). *Hubungan Antara Kolokasi dengan Penguasaan Kosakata sebagai Salah Satu Kompetensi Dasar Berbahasa Mandarin*. Fakultas Ilmu Pengetahuan Budaya Universitas Indonesia.
Smadja, F. (1993). Retrieving collocation from text: Xtract. *Computational Linguistics, 19*(1), 143–177.
Stubbs. (2001).
Suhardijanto, T., & Dinakaramani, A. (2018). *Korpus Beranotasi: Ke Arah Pengembangan Korpus Bahasa-Bahasa di Indonesia*. Kongres Bahasa Indonesia XI 28–31 Oktober 2018.
Wu, S. (2010). *Supporting collocation learning*. The University of Waikato.

Raya Jayawati Ratnawilis Amanah Notonegoro was born in Jakarta, 18 December 1997. After graduating from high school, she continued her education at the undergraduate level at the Indonesian Language and Literature Study, the Faculty of Humanities, Universitas Indonesia. For 3.5 years pursuing the field of language, she took a specialization in linguistics and philology.

In 2017, she was awarded as a student with the highest GPA from the Indonesian Language and Literature Study, the Faculty of Humanities, Universitas Indonesia. She has also been a member of the education bureau of the Indonesian Language and Literature Study called Kedisina. As a member of Kedisina, she is in charge of managing the social media and helping other students who have questions and difficulties in the academic field.

Totok Suhardijanto obtained a bachelor degree in the Indonesian Studies from Universitas Indonesia in 1993. He received a Master's degree in linguistics from Universitas Indonesia in 2000 and a PhD in Media and Governance from Keio University in 2012. He was a visiting lecturer at the Faculty of Policy Management, Keio University, Japan from 2002 to 2008. During his studies at the graduate school in Keio University, he was also working for Tokyo University of Foreign Studies, Japan as a part-time lecturer and at the Faculty of Bioresources, Nihon University, Japan from 2008 to 2012. In 2012, after graduation, he returned to home university in Indonesia. He is now working for the Department of Linguistics, Universitas Indonesia, Jakarta as a senior lecturer. From 2013 to 2015, he was also working for Google APAC, as a project manager and led the Indonesian speech team in voice search development in Indonesian language. His research interests are in the area of computational linguistics, natural language processing, and digital humanities, as well as many areas of linguistics including morphosyntax, phonetics, and historical linguistics. Currently he is working with the Language Development and Fostering Agency, the Ministry of National Education in a national-scale project of language mapping and language database building.

Open Access This chapter is licensed under the terms of the Creative Commons Attribution 4.0 International License (http://creativecommons.org/licenses/by/4.0/), which permits use, sharing, adaptation, distribution and reproduction in any medium or format, as long as you give appropriate credit to the original author(s) and the source, provide a link to the Creative Commons license and indicate if changes were made.

The images or other third party material in this chapter are included in the chapter's Creative Commons license, unless indicated otherwise in a credit line to the material. If material is not included in the chapter's Creative Commons license and your intended use is not permitted by statutory regulation or exceeds the permitted use, you will need to obtain permission directly from the copyright holder.

Chapter 9
Claiming Importance of Research: A Corpus Linguistics Analysis on Indonesian Students' Research Papers

Risa Rumentha Simanjuntak

Abstract Research in universities has been deemed as a key aspect in showing rigor and accountability as well as the gatekeeper for academic quality. Research writing and publication, including those composed by students, are expected to provide strong and compelling applications of knowledge in their field. This present research investigated strategies used by students in claiming importance by way of presenting stance and arguments in their research writings. Corpus for this study was 1,178 student research abstracts from undergraduate student final papers in Indonesia. Two sub-corpora were built from this corpus, consisting of English version abstracts and Indonesian original abstracts. Corpus analysis was conducted to identify the lexical use and the context of the use of rhetorical markers by analyzing frequency, clusters, concordance, and collocations in the corpus. Using AntConc 4.2.4 as the tool for corpus analysis, the investigation was focused on the strategies in using hedges and boosters to present stance and arguments. Results of this study showed students used distinctive rhetorical markers in their abstracts, including the frequent recurrence of passive verbs (7 passive verbs out of 20 verbs). Results also showed the word "*metode*" (method) was frequently used (occurring 1,079 times in the Indonesian sub-corpus) in comparison to the word "*hasil*" (result) (occurring 588 times in the sub-corpus). Students also used more hedges (24 types) than boosters (17 types), contrary to common understanding. The findings of this study indicated the strategies students used to claim importance of their research. Students were also clearly aware of the value of writing as evidence of academic achievements and adherence. The conclusion for this study demonstrated the importance of providing students with alternative routes to show rigor and quality in writing. Implications for further research and for data-driven applications in writing courses were also discussed.

Keywords Corpus analysis · Indonesian students · Hedges · Boosters · Research

R. R. Simanjuntak (✉)
Research Interest Group Digital Language and Behavior, Bina Nusantara University, Kebon Jeruk, Indonesia
e-mail: risarsimanjuntak@binus.edu

English Department, Faculty of Humanities, Bina Nusantara University, Jakarta, Indonesia

© The Author(s) 2025
R. Stroupe and L. Roosman (eds.), *Applied Linguistics in the Indonesian Context*, Engaging Indonesia, https://doi.org/10.1007/978-981-97-2336-2_9

9.1 Introduction

Research in higher education has been considered as an integral part of learning (Koltay, 2017; O'Connor, 2009). The nature of research, centralized in the inquisitive and methodical process for finding answers, is empowered by presenting plausible arguments. In the proposition of arguments, the authors' job is to convince readers of the importance of their research (Habibie & Hyland, 2019). Having successfully completed the stages in research, presenting the importance of the research is an equally important goal in the success of research writing (Flowerdew, 2008).

Following the notion of research writing, publishing research papers has been strongly supported and imposed as a requirement by many governments, including the Indonesian government (Arsyad & Arono, 2018; Pertiwi, 2020; Safnil, 2006). The narrative of having more accountability for learning outcomes is viewed as international acceptance of the quality education in Indonesia (Pertiwi, 2020). The increasing amount of research publications in universities also denotes the standing of universities. Many national universities are now embarking on open competition with universities across the globe. Scholars in universities all over the world produced as many respected publications and volumes of publications regularly as possible as evidence of quality (O'Connor, 2009).

Subsequently, there is a sense of urgency for research writing in academic writing courses (Swales & Feak, 1994, 2009). Both lecturers and students in many universities are expected to be familiar with research writing structure and language (Flowerdew, 2012, 2013). However, writing in academic discourse, and more specifically in specific genres, could be a great challenge for students (Flowerdew, 2013). Students in universities often feel inadequate when dealing with research and writing their research papers (Lestari, 2020; Pertiwi, 2020; Safitri et al., 2021; Sitompul & Anditasari, 2022). Students may also feel an additional burden since producing research writing, such as undergraduate final papers, was considered as partial fulfillment for a degree in many universities.

Many courses have been designed to help students in writing research papers (Swales & Feak, 1994, 2009). Universities also provide guidelines for research writing for their students and lecturers (Swales & Feak, 1994, 2009). Supervised sessions have also been dedicated to developing the students into becoming good writers. Despite the importance of guidelines and assessment criteria, there is limited time to assist students with the process of writing. Students are usually expected to follow the models of research writing, and examples are used to illustrate the steps in writing. Students rarely have the chance to communicate their writing plans, and their understanding of the guidelines may be incomplete. Therefore, many students often refer to research writing as difficult and demotivating (Lestari, 2020; Pertiwi, 2020; Safitri et al., 2021; Sitompul & Anditasari, 2022). Additionally, students are often still left with questions on how to find their real voice in presenting opinions through writing.

Reflecting on the situation, the gap between theories on how to write research papers and the actual writing process conducted by students needs to be eliminated.

There is a necessity to create a workable writing environment for students to write on research in their field. To create such an environment, students need to be exposed to contextual and applicable models of research papers. These models provide information on the structure and language features which students can use. The models could be created using corpus, which refers to the body of information on real use of language (Hyland, 2012a, 2012b; Reppen, 2010; Römer, 2004, 2009). Using corpus in teaching writing means exposing students to authentic samples of research writing, including the use of specific academic English (Klimova, 2015), and vocabularies (O'Keeffe et al., 2007). As a result of being exposed to corpus in the specific field, students could have more confidence and more accessible linguistic repositories during the writing process (Simanjuntak, 2017).

Students from non-English native language backgrounds find writing in English challenging (Davies, 2003; Flowerdew, 2001; Lestari, 2020; Mauranen, 2012; Pertiwi, 2020; Swales & Feak, 1994; Tribble, 2019). Non-native English writers generally refer to writing difficulties as escalated due to a lack of vocabulary. Limited vocabulary and traditions in presenting ideas through writing are notable in many students' experiences (Akbarian et al., 2017; Apple, 2014; Nation, 2001, 2009; Wei, 2021; Marhamah et al., 2023). Realistically, these hurdles need to be addressed so that students would have better avenues in writing in the future.

9.1.1 Previous Studies in Research Writing

Studies in students writing research papers have shown that there is a language-comprehension factor related to the problems in students' writing (Cahyono, 2001; Arsyad, 2014; Arsyad et al., 2019; Habibie & Hyland, 2019). Studies on Indonesian student writers showed the reluctance to do research resulting from a lack of information (Lestari, 2020; Pertiwi, 2020; Sitompul & Anditasari, 2022; Marhamah et al., 2023). These studies revealed that students were struggling to do research in two large areas: in conducting the steps of research, and in reporting the research through writing. One notable challenge is in understanding theory. When students conduct research, they need to comprehend the theoretical framework on which to base their arguments. Reading theories in their first language can be challenging, let alone reading about them in a foreign language. When students struggle in understanding what they read, they most likely would have difficulties in rephrasing them.

Another issue found in these studies was the difficulties in explaining some facts in the research results and in reaching some conclusions. It was reported that "Although I knew how to compare my results with other studies, I still get [sic.] difficulties in identifying and elaborating the results to reach their implications" (Sitompul & Anditasari, 2022, p. 140). Providing implications is very important for researchers in order to indicate the importance of their own present research. Presenting strong arguments to show the contributions and significance of the study is not easy for any researcher. Students as novice researchers and writers would feel a compelling need to demonstrate clearly and to convince readers of the importance of their research.

A study carried out by Lestari (2020) investigated students in the final year of their study. These students are from the English Language Teacher Education (ELTE) degree programs in Indonesia, and they needed to write their undergraduate thesis in English as part of the requirement to earn their degree. The researcher found several factors leading to students' difficulties in research writing. These factors were vocabulary limitations, difficulties in understanding theories, and limited knowledge on how to write sections in research papers. These sections, which were based on previous research and the methodology sections, were shown to be the most difficult for the students. Low motivation was also identified as a hindrance in writing amongst the students.

The study by Pertiwi (2020) showed how final year students struggled when writing their research papers. In order to graduate from the course, students need to conduct research and submit a research report. While writing this research report, students faced difficulties using technical words and specific terms. These vocabulary items were difficult to understand, and the students struggled to use them in their writing.

While some studies draw conclusions related to incomprehensibility, some issues remain unexplained. More studies are needed to investigate students' writing beyond the identification of errors and incomprehensibility. More investigations are needed to further understand the process in students' writing, including what strategies students' use to get the meaning across in the form of writing.

9.1.2 Genre Studies and the Importance of Corpus Linguistics

Swales (1990) defines genre as comprising "a class of communicative events, the members of which share some set of communicative purposes" (p. 58), which differentiates in general a genre from register. In his view a genre is developed because of active participation between interlocutors of the language and by these active interactions which exhibit a certain pattern for interaction. This patterned interaction is what Sales refers to as an "event" and in essence is very dynamic in nature. Swales' definition puts a high emphasis on communicative purposes, which suggests that the classification of a genre is carried out based on two aspects: linguistic and socio-cultural/sociological. Swales' definition, however, does not provide a model for carrying out the investigation of genre and therefore is instrumentally limited.

Considering the socio-cultural/sociological aspect in Swales' (1990) definition of genre, a genre is context-bound. In an academic field, the context, or an "event" (Swales, 1990, p. 56) in the academic community is specific and disciplinary-oriented. This event may be frequently held, and its communication bears a noticeable pattern by the members of this community (Swales, 1990, 2004). Naturally, writers as members of this community may use expressions to transfer information and knowledge in their fields and therefore structure the expressions in certain ways (Swales, 2004). Such expressions may be seen in recurring events of writing, including memos, scribbles, short conversations, which may contain abbreviations, terms, or lexical constructions well known to the field (Swales, 2004).

Swales' (1990, 2004) description of genre as a social event could be contrasted with students as novice writers. Students may not have similar experiences and exposure to events in the community as a field of knowledge which they are researching and writing on. Students may not understand the context of the written genre and therefore may produce variations in writing which were intentional to serve specific functions (Bhatia et al., 2008; Holtz, 2011; Hyland, 2000). Therefore, analyzing genre would also focus on identifying patterns or any occurrence of "functional variation" (Bhatia et al., 2008, p. 10) across disciplines. Genre-based studies have also looked at variations in socio-cultural backgrounds (Connor, 2008; Dudley-Evans & St John, 1998), which is important to the study of genre. These variations have become the central issues in genre analysis.

Halliday and Hasan (1989, 2013) define genre as a "type of discourse" (Halliday & Hasan, 1989, p. 62), which is identified by the cohesiveness of its context. The importance of contextual value to identify a text as belonging to a particular genre, in which a text that is familiar to the members of its community, was underlined in this definition (Halliday & Hasan, 1989). For a text to be classified as a particular genre, obligatory move(s) should be apparent to its readers. Moves are parts of a text, which provide different information and serve different functions (Swales, 1990). In an abstract, for example, parts could be identified as the purpose of research, method, results, and conclusion. A typical abstract would then consist of these moves.

The fundamental perspective of genre is that genre is social in nature. Halliday described a genre as "a system of meanings that constitutes the 'reality' of the culture" (1978, p. 196). Halliday believes that when acquiring English, a learner will remember in what situation a particular expression, words, or phrases were being used. In the context of the written genre, this valuable memory helps a student to write her ideas and meaning based on what she has read or learned earlier.

Miller (1984) coined the phrase "social action" (p. 155) in her article and explained the evolving nature of genre. First considered as oral traditions, genre had moved forward to the documentation of this tradition in writing. She further argued that genre was not only "a particular type of discourse classification" (Miller, 1984, p. 155). On the contrary, genre was strategic and active as it "consequently open rather than closed and organized around situated actions" (Miller, 1984, p. 155). In essence, a genre was believed to be the social recognitions that guide future rhetorical action (personal communication, September 14, 2019). Investigating a genre, therefore, provides important information on how an author presents their opinion to the readers and at the same time reveals information regarding the authors' strategies and identity.

Bazerman et al. (2009) recognizes this social action as "patterned variation in cognition around the literate practices of disciplines and professions" (Bazerman et al., 2009, p. 289). He also argues that "the emergence of differentiated written genres within differentiated activity systems have shaped the practices of knowledge, thought" (p. 290) to show the tradition of genre as integral to literacy since the beginning of time. His ideas highlight the sociological nature of Applied Linguistics, allowing studies on genre to expand from language forms to the authors as members of academic society.

The tradition of genre, in general, has been mostly categorized by two traditions, namely the Systemic Functional Linguistic (SFL) tradition and Corpus Linguistics. The SFL tradition or the Sydney School tradition is discussed by Halliday (2004), Halliday and Hasan (2013) regarding the two important aspects of genre analysis. The first aspect of genre is the systemic aspect, which refers to "systems of choices" (Bawarshi & Reiff, 2010, p. 30), made available to students to realize meaning. The second aspect is the functional aspect, referring to "the work that language does within particular contexts" (Bawarshi & Reiff, 2010, p. 29). Having been influenced by the general perspective of being contextual, genre becomes deeply rooted in the context of the language use.

Corpus linguistics as the second tradition in genre analysis is vital in its heuristic nature. Corpus linguistics uses an inductive approach by moving away from previously available categories or typologies in grammar (e.g., the use of modality in Introduction genre) and yields itself to the available data before making any classifications. Biber (1988, 1996) presented a model for corpus-based study for genre, focusing on the variations in writing. In his study Biber (1996) classifies some linguistic features (called dimensions), such as "narrative vs. non-narrative," and "non-impersonal versus impersonal style" (Biber, 1996, p. 72), and identified the occurrence of these features/dimensions over 23 genres. His study resulted in multidimensional analysis of genre beyond the limited construction of whether a particular genre uses more modals compared to other genres.

9.1.3 Analyzing Variations in Students' Writing as Socio-ideational Construction

Composition pedagogy moved forward to a genre approach in the 1990s, with Swales' definition, and later by Bhatia (2017) when he proposed a comprehensive model for genre analysis. With a genre approach, a composition is taught beyond the importance of composition as a product. Rather, composition is seen as a social system, in which a certain community of knowledge communicates its conventions and strategies through written form. An example of such communication can be found in the multimodal approach, in which considerations were not only focused on traditional/conventional compositions performed in words (Granger et al., 2002; Gilquin et al., 2007). In a multimodal approach attention is also cast on learners' written productions, such as doodles, short messages, and symbols as different arrays of texts encountered by the learners in all aspects of life.

Language acquisition is seen as socio-ideationally constructed (Connor, 1996, 2008). Students writing in English would then make use of the models available to them when writing in their first language. From the socio-ideational perspective, the experience of writing in the second language would be assisted with the use of structure and linguistic devices in the first language models. Students would then compose writings following the constructs of their texts previously composed in their first language (Connor & Lauer, 1988; Purves, 1988a, 1988b). Writing with these familiar forms, students would then use information from the available interaction with texts and information that they could comprehend, and through examples made by other writers (Bondi, 2006, 2014; Hyland, 2012a, 2012b).

Developments in second language learning have reached the stage where focus on learners has also included the awareness of students' multi-faceted and evolving self (Byram and Grundy, 2003; Connor et al., 2008). Pioneered by the work of Halliday in the 60s, second language learning has put more focus on the ecological conditions of the learners (Halliday, 1978). This contextual importance brings forth the necessary knowledge of the surroundings of learners. Halliday asserts that such an environment will then be influential to the language needed and used by the learners to function sufficiently.

Socio-ideational construction comes as a response to previously dichotomized junctures of English competence of non-native speakers and native speakers. The widely accepted norm would include native likeness, being the ideal model for successful language learning. The socio-ideational concept considers Halliday's notion on "ecological and social environment of language function" (Halliday & Matthiessen, 2004, p. 28). Both Halliday and Matthiessen (2004) suggested that amongst the basic functions of language are making sense of one's experience and acting out one's social experience. Because of these functions, language dedicates its realizations to expressing what one has in mind. When someone's intention is being realized using language, her expressions require language sufficient to construe what she means. Ideational function, alongside Halliday and Matthiessen's (2004) interpersonal and textual functions, becomes the essence of communication.

As a response to the error correction approach, variations in the genre would not be seen as incidental. Rather, a recurrence of patterns made available by students is a system accessed by students in utilizing the language (Orasan, 2001). This notion on the importance of looking at errors as reflections of language learners' interaction with the language learnt is one of systematic construction. As Corder (1967) has mentioned earlier, one who is learning a language must have in her an "available syllabus" (p. 76), which she constantly consults. Referring to what Chomsky (1965) called as the "innate" (p. 23) or internal capacity of language processing in humans, this executive functioning is enhanced by the language realities experienced by the student writers.

9.1.4 Analyzing Research Abstract as Important Information on Learning

Koltay (2010) categorized abstracts into two types; one that is written in conjunction with the full report (article) written by the same author(s), and one that is written apart from the full report (article) and written by different authors. The latter kind of abstract requires "abstractors" (p. 21) or people who write abstracts for or based on other people's articles/research. The activity of writing abstracts for or based on other people's articles/research is called "abstracting" (p. 3). In most cases, abstractors would write abstracts for referencing purposes, providing information in journals or similar databases (which provides readers with the gist of the articles/research).

Abstracting has received particular attention, especially in the information era and since the rise of the Internet and technology-based information provisions in the 1960s. Abstracting is important because it allows information to be delivered in an economical way (Werlich, 1988 as cited in Koltay, 2010, p. 3). In the interest of second language acquisition, the activity of abstracting has been recognized to be important for composition pedagogy, especially for novice or beginner students of writing (Stotesbury, 2003). The importance of this activity is recollected by Stotesbury (2003), an Adjunct Professor from the University of Eastern Finland, when assisting her students with research paper writing assignments. As a writing instructor herself, she argued that the activity of abstracting for her students is fundamental for two reasons. First, students were exposed to real language situations. Second, the abstracts written by the students become the source of information on how the students use the language in writing (Stotesbury, 2003). She further revealed the importance of abstracting as a means to gain understanding of how her students plan their writings and use their language repositories (both in English and Finnish) when writing in English.

In Indonesian universities, English composition is taught as one of the key skills in the curriculum. English in general is taught in every university in Indonesia and eventually is used in writing the abstract section of students' graduating papers. English skills in universities are also considered as supplement or support in improving the skills for international communication (Aziz et al., 2003). In effect, many of the materials included in the syllabus are focused on social interactions and communications and not necessarily on communicating the core competence/knowledge of the students' majors/disciplines. Students did not typically learn English from their own field of study. The general English textbooks did not provide information on the English in the specific academic context.

Abstract and abstracting are consequently perceived as both practical and interdisciplinary (Koltay, 2010). Students are required to have contact with the texts and are exposed to the content through reading the full article before being involved in an intensive composition process. Abstract and abstracting are even considered as a distinct genre and one of the skills for the twenty-first century (Koltay, 2010). This positive sentiment is further displayed by noting the fact that abstracting has been included in UNESCO nomenclature for Science and Technology (a system for classifying research papers and doctoral dissertations), in which Abstracting has received a specific code of 5701.01 (under the generic code of 57 for Linguistics as broader concept and under 5701 for Applied Linguistics as narrower concept) (https://skos.um.es/unesco6/5701/html). Abstracting evidently becomes "one of the higher-level activities of information literacy" (Koltay, 2010, p. 10).

9.1.5 Claiming Importance of Research Using Stance and Arguments

Stance deals with how writers can be seen as having the authority to present an argument, being in the authoritative position of presenting ideas of arguments. Using an authorial stance requires writers to have genuine opinions, or positions, while maintaining the ethos valued by the knowledge society or by maintaining an objective perspective. Hyland (2005a, 2005b) explains the features of authorial stance in writing as such:

> Stance can be seen as an attitudinal dimension and includes features which refer to the ways writers present themselves and convey their judgements, opinions, and commitments. It is the ways that writers intrude to stamp their personal authority onto their arguments or step back and disguise their involvement (Hyland, 2005a, 2005b, p. 176).

These characteristics of stance may depend on the conventions of the discipline. In the social sciences or humanities, for example, the writers are more involved and apparent to the readers. Inherently, authors use expressions such as, "I argue that…". Meanwhile, such expressions are least favorable in the science and engineering fields. Third person point of view or passive voice would be used to present facts and arguments to the readers (Hyland and Jiang, 2017a, b, Jiang, 2017).

There has been a general misconception on how to create an effective stance. One study noted that effective stance-taking is done by making "proclamations" (Chang, 2012, p. 223) and by "simplistic interplay" between assertion and factual statement. This combination of facts and personal or subjective promoting efforts resulted in a forced tone rather than a naturally convincing argument. Previous research has also shown the typical authorial stance markers depended on the discipline (Hyland, 2005a, 2005b). In the hard sciences, for example, the use of a highly formalized reporting system is applied to minimize the authors' presence in their texts (Hyland, 2005a, 2005b); one way of doing this is by using passive voice.

Stance, therefore, has focused on the author's proposition (Pho, 2008; Hyland and Guinda, 2012). Stance is also known by other names, such as evidentials (Chafe, 1986), evaluation (Stotesbury, 2003), and authorial stance (Almeida, 2012; Chang 2012; Kafes, 2009). Authorial stance, also known as writer stance, focuses on the author's way of presenting their voice, their opinion, while using the facts to support the descriptions and arguments. In short, stance is the way writers use language to explain themselves to their readers.

While considered to be discipline-related, in general, authorial stance can be further seen as comprising four main elements or markers, namely "hedges, boosters, attitude markers, and self-mentions" (Hyland, 2005a, 2005b, p. 178). Hedges are words or expressions used to "indicate the writer's decision to withhold complete commitment to a proposition" (Hyland, 2005a, 2005b, p. 178) because asserting claims needs to be done carefully in academic compositions (Hyland, 1998a, 1998b). By using hedges, writers present the ideas as opinions and not facts, implying that "a statement is based on plausible reasoning rather than certain knowledge" (Hyland, 2005a, 2005b, p. 178). Examples of hedges are possible, might, and perhaps. Boosters are words used by writers to "express their certainty in what they say" (Hyland, 2005a, 2005b, p. 179). Writers also use boosters to highlight shared information, group membership, and engagement with readers (Hyland, 1999). By using boosters, writers want to position themselves well within the argument. Typical examples of boosters are the adverbs clearly, obviously, and the verb demonstrate.

This paper discusses the importance of using students' writings to reveal the variations in writing as ideological construction cues. The socio-ideological markers are believed to also appear in academic genre, in how the students present arguments. Using corpus of students' writing would also validate the identification of patterns and markers in writing. The use of corpus is of vital importance since authentic texts from students would offer genuine and most compelling evidence of students' efforts in presenting importance in writing.

The goal of this paper is to answer the following questions: (1) what strategies are used by students in presenting their arguments in research by looking at the use of hedges and boosters, and (2) what possible factors are affecting the use and influencing the ideological construction of students' writing.

9.2 Method

9.2.1 Corpus

The corpus of this present study consists of abstracts from students' final papers. Indonesian students are expected to write a bilingual abstract, in Indonesian and in English. The total number of abstracts used in this present study was 1,178, with two sub-corpora of Indonesian abstracts and English abstracts. Details are provided in Fig. 9.1 for the Indonesian abstracts, containing 539 abstracts, 6,054 entries, and 76,665 tokens.

Meanwhile, the English abstracts included 539 abstracts, 5,713 entries, and 84,765 tokens as seen in Fig. 9.2.

In total there were 161,430 tokens in the corpus. A small corpus required for generalization conventionally consists of 30,000 tokens or words (Reppen, 2010).

9.2.2 Keyword List

The keyword lists used in this study consisted of two lists: boosters and hedges. Keyword lists of boosters and hedges are compiled from Holmes (1990), Hyland (1998a, 1998b), Hyland and Milton (1997), and Varttala (2001) with Hyland's list of hedges and boosters used as main reference for data analysis. The lists of markers for hedges (148 markers) and boosters (84 markers) can be seen in Table 9.1.

9 Claiming Importance of Research: A Corpus Linguistics Analysis … 165

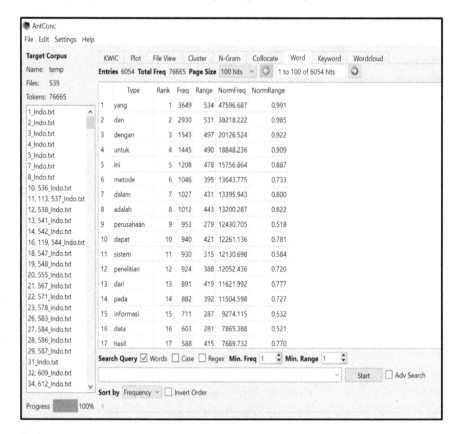

Fig. 9.1 Indonesian abstract sub-corpus (539 abstracts)

Eighty-four markers for boosters were used as keywords for sieving the use of the markers from the students' corpus. The list of the boosters can be seen in Table 9.2.

9.2.3 Tool for Analysis

Data collected from the corpus using Word, Keyword, and KWIC features in the AntConc corpus tool. AntConc was created by Lawrence Anthony from University of Waseda and it is a free corpus application for corpus building and analysis. The tool was downloaded from the website, https://www.laurenceanthony.net/software/antconc/ for Windows and the newest version of AntConc 4.2.4 (Anthony, 2023) was used in data analysis, including Collocate and Wordcloud (see Fig. 9.3).

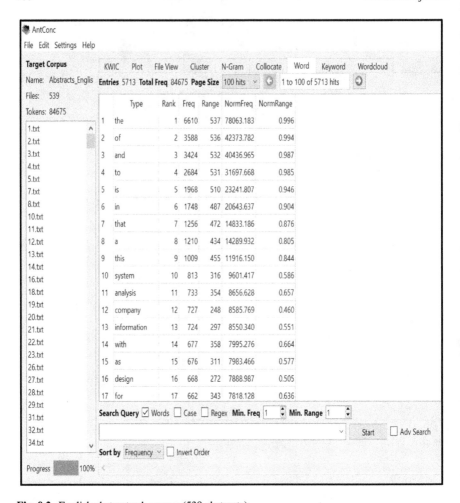

Fig. 9.2 English abstract sub-corpus (539 abstracts)

9.3 Analysis

Results from this present study showed the use of language as the strategies students used in writing their research. Analysis of the results revealed the ideological constructions of students in handling the task of writing their research. Most importantly, students used these strategies to claim importance for the success of their research endeavors. Possible factors affecting the use and influencing the ideological construction of students' writing led to the use of writing guidelines and the influence of Indonesian as the students' first language. The following sections presented the use of language, structures to reveal the strategies, and ideological constructions in students' writing.

9 Claiming Importance of Research: A Corpus Linguistics Analysis ...

Table 9.1 List of hedges (148 markers)

Can	Doubtless	Relatively	Indicative
Could	Fairly	Reportedly	Large
May	Frequently	Roughly	Likely
Might	Generally	Seemingly	Little
Should	Given that	Seldom	Main
Will	Greatly	Significantly	Major
Would	Highly	Slightly	Modest
Observe	Hypothetically	Sometimes	Noticeable
Perceive	Largely	Somewhat	Plausible
Presume	Likely	Strongly	Possible
Propose	Mainly	Substantially	Probable
Prove	Markedly	Supposedly	Rare
Report	Maybe	Tentatively	Relative
Seem	Modestly	Theoretically	Remarkable
(Can be) seen	Mostly	Typically	Rough
Speculate	Nearly	Unlikely	Significant
Suggest	Normally	Usually	Slight
Suppose	Occasionally	Vastly	Small
Suspect	Often	Virtually	Substantial
About	Partially	Widely	Theoretical
Allegedly	Partly	Apparent	Typical
Almost	Perhaps	Approximate	Uncommon
Apparently	Possibly	Common	Unlikely
Approximately	Potentially	Conceivable	Usual
Around	Practically	Considerable	Well-known
Arguably	Presumably	Consistent with	Alternative
Barely	Primarily	Frequent	Approximation
Commonly	Probably	General	Assertion
Conceivably	Provided (that)	Hypothetical	Assessment
Considerably	Quite	Improbable	Assumption
Allegedly	Partly	Apparent	Typical
Almost	Perhaps	Approximate	Uncommon
Belief	Estimate	Idea	Opinion
Chance	Estimation	Implication	Possibility
Claim	Evaluation	Indication	Proposal
Conclusion	Expectation	Interpretation	Suggestion
Doubt	Hope	Likelihood	Tendency

Table 9.2 List of boosters (84 markers)

Can't	Always	Intensively	Clear	Confidence
Couldn't	Assuredly	Necessarily	Complete	Evidence
Have to	Basically	Never	Confident	Fact
Must	Certainly	No doubt	Definite	Precision
Will	Clearly	Obviously	Essential	
Won't	Completely	Of course	Evident	
Would	Definitely	Patently	Exact	
Assure	Entirely	Plainly	Extreme	
Confirm	Essentially	Precisely	Impossible	
Demonstrate	Evidently	Really	Inevitable	
Do	Exactly	Surely	Obvious	
Establish	Explicitly	Truly	Perfect	
Find	Extremely	Totally	Plain	
Indicate	Factually	Thoroughly	Really	
Know	Fully	Unarguably	Real	
Predict	Fundamentally	Undeniably	Sure	
Reinforce	Indeed	Undoubtedly	Thorough	
Show	Indisputably	Unquestionably	Total	
Absolutely	Inevitably	Absolute	True	
Actually	In fact	Certain	Certainty	

Fig. 9.3 Wordcloud from the Indonesian abstract sub-corpus

9.3.1 The Use of Language and the Structure of Information in Student' Writing

Students used language and structure in writing their research abstracts. The corpus contained two sub-corpora of abstracts, one for those abstracts written in Indonesian and subsequently followed with the English translation. In the corpus, it was noted that students followed the genre structure of an abstract, with introduction followed by the purpose move, then method, results, and conclusion moves. All abstracts contained purpose and method rhetorical moves. Results showed students used recurring lexical items, as shown in Table 9.3.

The most frequently used word in Indonesian abstracts was the word *yang* (3,784 times). The word *yang* was a conjunction or subordinating conjunction. The most frequently used NP (Noun Phrase) was *metode* (method) (1,079 times), and the most frequently used VP (Verb Phrase) was the word "*menggunakan*" (use) (560 times). In the Indonesian sub-corpus, the most recurring lemma was "*guna*", which occurred in "*menggunakan*" (to use), and "*digunakan*" (was used, is used, are used, to be used). Another lemma was "*laku*", which formed the words "*dilakukan*" (was done, is done, were done, was done, has been done, to be done), and "*melakukan*" (to do), do, does). The student abstracts contained a high frequency of occurrence for the headword use. The words derived from the lemma "use" were the past form used (occurred 897 times), progressive form using (occurred 796 times), and the present

Table 9.3 Frequency of words (Indonesian abstracts), top 50

Type	Freq	Type	Freq	Type	Freq
yang	3784	hasil	615	lebih	306
dan	3031	analisis	564	teknologi	278
dengan	1614	proses	564	teknologi	278
untuk	1513	menggunakan	560	oleh	262
ini	1258	digunakan	519	membantu	258
metode	1079	di	506	tersebut	244
dalam	1068	pt	482	yaitu	244
dalam	1068	perancangan	475	terhadap	242
adalah	1066	bisnis	462	studi	229
perusahaan	990	serta	438	sehingga	226
dapat	969	tujuan	432	secara	225
sistem	967	strategi	409	meningkatkan	223
penelitian	947	e-	399	website	221
dari	931	dilakukan	380	dicapai	216
pada	910	aplikasi	348	sebagai	214
informasi	733	melakukan	340	pelanggan	210
data	629	akan	339		

form (to) use (occurred 287 times). Out of 418 occurrences of the headword use, 131 occurrences were in the NP category.

From Table 9.4, the most frequently used word was "system," which was categorized as a NP. The most frequently used VP was the word "use" (318 times) followed by "research" (305 times). The words "use" and "research" were also used as NPs (100 and 733 times consecutively).

In the Indonesian and English abstracts, the use of each part of speech could be seen in Table 9.5.

Table 9.4 Frequency of words (English abstracts), top 50

Type	Freq	Type	Freq	Type	Freq
System	1426	Study	537	Development	302
Information	1068	Technology	495	Performance	287
Research	994	Results	472	More	284
Company	988	Result	471	Project	282
Analysis	985	Use	418	New	278
Application	951	Web	403	Order	277
Design	921	Website	398	Analyze	273
Used	897	Methods	389	Conclusion	268
Method	880	User	381	Database	268
Data	812	Strategy	378	Time	258
Using	796	Purpose	368	Problems	256
Business	748	Management	353	There	249
Thesis	686	Support	341	One	245
Process	657	Support	341	Online	244
Based	582	Learning	339	Provide	243
Marketing	576	Help	329	Through	242
e	561	Systems	305		

Table 9.5 Frequency of words (Indonesian abstracts), top 50

POS (Indonesian)	Types	POS (English)	Type
Ajektiva	4	AdjP	4
Adverbia	6	AP	6
Partikel	21	Conj	16
		Prep	5
Nomina	44	NP	44
Verba	25	VP	25
Pronomina	1	Pro	1
Numeralia	1	Num	1
Total	102	Total	102

In Table 9.5, data showed the most frequently used words were from NP type (44 times), followed by VP (25 different words or types), whilst other types in the reference words were strikingly underused. The use of Adjectives were 4 types, Adverb 6 types, which indicates students used mostly Nouns and Verbs in their presentation of ideas. The limited use of adjectives could be interpreted as being from an academic genre: research abstracts were focusing on presentation of facts and research actions. There was not enough room for subjective or qualitative description, which was apparent in the data. It could be remarked from this finding that research abstracts were conventionally a presentation of facts and exposition of methods. It was then sensible to say that presenting claims in abstracts would be more challenging due to the nature of the genre.

9.3.2 Strategies Used by Students in Presenting Their Arguments in Research

Data from corpus was processed using AntConc and Keyword list was used to map the appearance of hedges and boosters. Using the list of keywords in hedges, data showed that students used 67 types of hedges (out of 140 in the list) and 40 types of boosters (out of 84 markers in the keyword list). This indicates that the use of hedges was 47.86% out of the markers available. Interestingly, students used 47.62% of the boosters from the available markers. The limited use of hedges and boosters could mean students were not using enough stance to claim importance for their paper. It could also imply that students overuse similar hedges and boosters due to limited exposure to other available metadiscourse markers. Metadiscourse is defined as the way writers interact with their readers (Ädel, 2006). Metadiscourse markers could show students' strategies in presenting the interactions (Hyland 2004, 2006, 2007, 2010, 2017a)

The use of hedges and boosters is presented in Tables 9.6 and 9.7. In Table 9.6 data of hedges used in the abstracts showed the use of the markers to present stance and arguments in writing the abstracts.

There were sixty-seven types of hedges used in the corpus. Data from Table 9.6 showed the most frequently used hedge was should (appeared in 21 abstracts) followed by proposed (appeared in 20 texts). Several hedges (14 types) appeared in 10–21 abstracts, while most hedges only appeared scarcely in any abstract. Data on recurring patterns on the use of boosters can be seen in Table 9.7.

There are a total of forty types of boosters as shown in Table 9.4. From the data, students used more types of hedges (67 types) as compared to the use of boosters (40 types). The results provide important notions to patterns of students' writing. Data showed students used hedges more than boosters. Finding from this study suggests that the practice of using hedges is very apparent in students' writings.

This finding is in line with previous study, in which students overuse hedges when compared to professional writers (Hyland & Tse, 2004, 2005a, b, 2007). Students of

Table 9.6 The use of hedges to present stance and arguments in writing

Hedges	F	Hedges	F	Hedges	F	Hedges	F
Should	21	Usually	8	Assumption	2	Implication	1
Propose	20	Generally	7	Chance	2	Likelihood	1
Would	19	Hope	7	Estimate	2	Likely	1
May	18	Proposal	6	Highly	2	Might	1
Assessment	15	Widely	6	Mostly	2	Opinion	1
Large	15	Relatively	5	Nearly	2	Partially	1
Small	15	Around	4	Normally	2	Partly	1
Estimation	14	Common	4	Possibility	2	Potentially	1
Often	14	Commonly	4	Possibly	2	Primarily	1
Alternative	12	Fairly	4	Roughly	2	Seldom	1
General	11	Little	4	Sometimes	2	Strongly	1
Idea	10	Prove	4	Typically	2	Typical	1
Possible	10	Theoretical	4	Allegedly	1	Uncommon	1
Significantly	10	Approximately	3	Approximate	1		
Major	8	Frequent	3	Considerable	1		
Quite	8	Mainly	3	Expectation	1		
Suggest	8	Observe	3	Frequently	1		
Suggestion	8	Almost	2	Greatly	1		

Table 9.7 The use of boosters to present stance and arguments in writing

Type	F	Type	F	Type	F	Type	F
Do	52	Always	7	Exact	3	Clearly	1
Total	30	Clear	7	Perfect	3	Completely	1
Must	26	Establish	7	Precisely	3	Confident	1
Know	24	Precision	7	Intensively	2	Entirely	1
Show	23	Indicate	5	Predict	2	Extreme	1
Complete	20	Actually	4	Really	2	Necessarily	1
Fact	16	Confidence	4	True	2	Never	1
Real	14	Basically	3	Absolutely	1	Obviously	1
Fully	10	Certainly	3	Assure	1	Surely	1
Certain	9	Evidence	3	Certainty	1	Thorough	1

this present study also used less boosters. This result is in line with previous study where students underuse boosters when compared to authors of published articles (Hyland & Tse, 2004; Kafes, 2009). The overuse of hedges and underuse of boosters may be interpreted as students being careful in asserting strong achievements of their research.

The use of "do" as a booster may seem to overlap with the more generic meaning of doing a generic action. Nonetheless, this finding suggests students use the strategy of using a safer and more generic verb when they could not access a more technical term or word. Another interesting finding was in the use of the words "must" (appeared in 26 abstracts) and "certain" (9 abstracts), which were categorized as bold or strong statements. Students were accessing these markers to make their points and to draw attention on the importance of their research. Overall, the use of hedges and boosters in students' abstracts showed clear strategies on claiming importance for their research.

9.3.3 Ideological Construction in Students Writing

Results also showed an interesting use of the words *ialah* and *adalah*. In English, both of these words were translated as "was," functioning as functional lexis. However, in Indonesian, both words have slightly different functions. Figure 4 showed the entries of the word "*ialah*" and "*adalah*" in Indonesian Main Dictionary (Kamus Besar Bahasa Indonesia). In the entry, the word "*ialah*" is a particle which functions as a connector between two clauses of a sentence. The main purpose for the use of "*ialah*" is to provide more details for the first preceding clause.

As defined in the dictionary, the use of "*ialah*" refers to detailed steps, ways, or items as mentioned in the first clause of the sentence. Meanwhile, the entry for the word "*adalah*" in the Indonesian dictionary indicates the word "*adalah*" acts as a verb to present a similar quality with the preceding word or clause. The word also acts as a verb to indicate the first clause as belonging or becoming a part of the second clause.

> a.da.lah
> *v* identik dengan:
> *Pancasila -- falsafah bangsa Indonesia*
> *v* sama maknanya
> dengan: *Desember -- bulan kedua belas*
> *v* termasuk dalam kelompok atau golongan: *saya -- pengagum Ki Hajar Dewantara*

When an author used *ialah*, the intention was to further detail the information related to the preceding clause. Data in the corpus showed the use of the word "*ialah*" was to specify the purpose of the study. The full sentence can be seen in the quotation:

> Tujuan penelitian ini ialah membantu masyarakat umum dalam menghitung premi kredibilitas dan dibuat kedalam suatu aplikasi web yang interaktif dan menarik.
>
> (Hanafi, 2013, p. ii)

The English version of the abstract can be seen below:

> The purpose of this thesis, is to design and create a system of reservation that were previously manual application of a mobile-based sales system with the android platform.

(Hanafi, 2013, p. ii)

From the English version, the author detailed the purpose of the thesis into two parts. There is a clear decision made by the author on the use of the word "*ialah*", which helped him to list the actions conducted in the research. Therefore, the author was able to construct the ideas following the correct use of words. Findings from this study clearly show the active efforts students made in writing their thesis. Indonesian students use language resources to express adherence and commitment to the research process. They apply Indonesian lexical and syntactical structures in composing English abstracts.

9.4 Conclusion

The present study has drawn attention to the importance of understanding how students write their research. Using abstracts as genre in discussion, students have clearly shown the avenues they chose to claim importance of their research. The recurring use of the passive form and several lexical items were consistent in the students' abstracts. The results also indicated limitations students had in presenting objective points of view and contribution to research. Students also used more types of hedges compared to types of boosters to show stance and arguments, typical to more expert writers. However, the frequency for both categories were still under 50% of the available marker types which indicates students need more exposure to the metadiscourse. Pivoting on the findings, using corpus while assisting students in writing research is of utmost importance. This could be done in two ways. First, students could be introduced to the corpus of the same genre to provide reference when writing. Students would benefit from being exposed to corpus, especially in their own field of study or projected industry. The specific academic language students found in the corpus would leverage their knowledge on the issues as well as how experts write in this area of research. Second, language instructors need to give additional time and assistance when students write abstracts because writing abstracts would function as a guide for students to write the next sections of their research papers. At the same time, instructors could use abstracts as evidence of students' language repository.

Recommendations to language institutions and curriculum designers would also include introducing students to real cases and project proposals in smaller scale research. When universities expect students to write research, it is best not to teach English for social or general purposes. Focusing on English for specific purposes would include creating supplementary materials from corpus in the intended field of study or industry. Computer Science students for example would benefit from reading comprehension activities from computer science journals. Additionally, access to such materials also needs to be supported by the university library. Universities also could open opportunities for students to be engaged with lecturers' or researchers' projects in the university, as enrichment opportunities in doing research. The initiatives could be managed in a similar manner to apprenticeship or internship activities, which are very common in the fields of professions and industry. Having students be involved in real research projects, grants, and industry internships would provide an excellent natural environment to expose them to the needed lexical items.

Research in the future could include investigation on various majors or courses, to compare the variations on claiming importance of research in different fields. Results from such research on social studies may show different or similar strategies as compared to strategies used in the writing in pure science research. Longer observations and experimental studies could also be conducted to incorporate immersion and longer exposure of language items leading to research and writing skills. With more systemic endeavors, results from these studies would present wider horizons to students' writing. At the same time, studies in learner corpora could reveal the dynamics and multidimensional aspects of learning, especially in academic writing.

References

Ädel, A. (2006). *Metadiscourse in L1 and L2 English*. John Benjamins.
Akbarian, I., Ghanbarzadeh, Z., & Shahri, M. A. (2017). Profiling vocabulary in psychology journal abstracts: A comparison between Iranian and Anglo-American journals. *Iranian Journal of Language Teaching Research, 5*(1), 51–69.
Almeida, F. A. (2012). Sentential evidential adverbs and authorial stance in a corpus of English computing articles. *Volumen Monografico*, 15–31.
Apple, M. T. (2014). The vocabulary and style of engineering research abstract writing. *OnCUE Journal, 7*(2), 86–102.
Arsyad, S. (2014). The discourse structure and linguistic features of research article abstracts in English by Indonesian academics. *The Asian ESP Journal, 10*(2), 191–224.
Arsyad, S., & Arono. (2018). *Memahami dan menulis abtrak artikel jurnal*. Halaman Moeka Publishing.
Arsyad, S., Purwo, B. K., Sukamto, K. E., & Adnan, Z. (2019). Factors hindering Indonesian lecturers from publishing articles in reputable international journals. *Journal on English as a Foreign Language, 9*(1), 42–70. https://doi.org/10.23971/jefl.v9i1.982
ASEAN University Network (AUN). https://www.aunsec.org/
Aziz, E. A., Sudana, D., & Norman, S. (2003). *Culture-based English for college students*. Grasindo.
Bawarshi, A., & Reiff, M. J. (2010). *Genre: An introduction to history, theory, research, and pedagogy*. Parlor Press.
Bazerman, C., Bonini, A., & Figueiredo, D. (Eds.). (2009). *Genre in a changing world*. Parlor Press.
Bhatia, V. (Ed.). (2017). *Critical genre analysis: Investigating interdiscursive performance in professional practice*. Routledge.
Bhatia, V. K., Flowerdew, J., & Jones, R. H. (Eds.). (2008). *Advances in discourse studies*. Routledge.
Biber, D. (1988). *Variation across speech and writing*. Cambridge University Press.
Biber, D. (1996). *University language: A corpus-based study of spoken and written registers*. John Benjamins North America.
Bondi, M. (2006). Emphatics in academic discourse: Integrating corpus and discourse tools in the study of cross-disciplinary variation. In A. Ädel & R. Reppen (Eds.), *Corpora and discourse: The challenges of different settings* (pp. 31–55). John Benjamins.

Bondi, M. (2014). Changing voice: Authorial voice in abstracts. In M. Bondi & L. S. Sanz (Eds.), *Abstracts in academic discourse: Variation and change* (pp. 243–270). Peter Lang AG.
Bondi, M., & Sanz, L. S. (Eds.). (2014). *Abstracts in academic discourse: Variation and change.* Peter Lang AG
Byram, M. & Grundy, P. (2003). Introduction: Context and culture in language teaching and learning. (pp. 1–3). Multilingual Matters. https://doi.org/10.21832/9781853596728-001
Cahyono, B. Y. (2001). Research studies in second language writing and in contrastive rhetoric. *Kata, 3*(1), 39–52.
Chafe, W. 1986. Evidentiality in english conversation and academic writing. In W.L. Chafe & J. Nichols (Eds.), *Evidentiality: The linguistic coding of epistemology. Advances in discourse processes* (pp. 261–72). Ablex Publishing.
Chang, P. (2012). Using a stance corpus to learn about effective authorial stance-taking: A textlinguistic approach. *ReCALL, 24*, 209–236. https://doi.org/10.1017/S0958344012000079
Chomsky, N. (1965). *Aspects of the theory of syntax.* M.I.T. Press.
Connor, U. (1996). *Contrastive rhetoric: Cross-cultural aspects of second-language writing.* Cambridge University Press.
Connor, U. (2008). Mapping multidimensional aspects of research: Reaching to intercultural rhetoric. In U. Connor, E. Nagelhout, & W. V. Rozycki (Eds.), *Contrastive rhetoric reaching to intercultural rhetoric* (pp. 299–315). John Benjamins.
Connor, U. & Lauer, J. (1988). Writing across languages and cultures. In A.C. Purves (Ed.), *Cross-cultural variation in persuasive student writing* (pp. 138–159). Sage.
Connor, U., Nagelhout, E., & Rozycki, W. V. (2008). *Contrastive rhetoric reaching to intercultural rhetoric.* John Benjamins.
Corder, S. P. (1967). The significance of learner's errors IRAL. *International Review of Applied Linguistics in Language Teaching, 5,* (1–4). https://doi.org/10.1515/iral.1967.5.1-4.161
Davies, A. (2003). *The native speaker: Myth and reality.* Multilingual Matters.
Dudley-Evans, T., & St John, M. J. (1998). *Developments in English for specific purposes: A multi-disciplinary approach.* CUP.
Flowerdew, J. (2001). Attitudes of journal editors to nonnative speaker contributions. *TESOL Quarterly, 35*(1), 121–150.
Flowerdew, L. (2008). Corpora and context in professional writing. In V. K. Bhatia, J. Flowerdew, & R. H. Jones (Eds.), *Advances in discourse studies* (pp. 115–127). Routledge.
Flowerdew, L. (2012). Corpora in the classroom: An applied linguistic perspective. In K. Hyland, C. M. Huat, & M. Handford (Eds.), *Corpus applications in applied linguistics* (pp. 208–224). Continuum.
Flowerdew, L. (2013). Corpus-based research and pedagogy in EAP: From lexis to genre. *Language Teaching, 26,* pp. 1–18. https://doi.org/10.1017/S0261444813000037
Gilquin, G., Granger, S., & Paquot, M. (2007). Learner corpora: The missing link in EAP pedagogy. *Journal of English for Academic Purposes, 6*(1), 319–335. https://doi.org/10.1075/lic.3.1.05gil
Granger, S., Hung, J., & Petch-Tyson, S. (Eds.). (2002). *Computer learner corpora, second language acquisition and foreign language teaching.* John Benjamins B.V.
Habibie, P., & Hyland, K. (Eds.). (2019). *Novice writers and scholarly publication.* Palgrave Macmillan.
Halliday, M. A. K. (1978). *Language as social semiotic: The social interpretation of language and meaning.* Edward Arnold.
Halliday, M. A. K., & Hasan, R. (1989). *Language, context, and text: Aspects of language in a social-semiotic perspective.* Oxford University Press.
Halliday, M. A. K., & Hasan, R. (2013). *Cohesion in English.* Routledge.
Halliday, M. A. K., & Matthiessen, C. M. I. M. (2004). *An introduction to functional grammar* (3rd ed.). Hodder Arnold.
Hanafi. (2013). *Analysis and design credibility premium using the biggest accuracy method on car insurance based on web (Case study: PT. Asuransi Adira Dinamika Jakarta).*

Holmes, J. (1990). Hedges and boosters in women's and men's speech. *Language & Communication, 10*(3), 185–205.
Holtz, M. (2011). *Lexico-grammatical properties of abstracts and research articles. A corpus-based study of scientific discourse from multiple disciplines*. Unpublished doctoral dissertation, Technical University of Darmstadt. http://tuprints.ulb.tu-darmstadt.de/2638/
Hyland. (1998a). Boosting, hedging and the negotiation of academic knowledge. *Text & Talk, 18*(3), 349–382. https://doi.org/10.1515/text.1.1998.18.3.349
Hyland, K. (1998b). *Hedging in scientific research articles*. John Benjamins.
Hyland, K. (1999). Disciplinary discourses: Writer stance in research articles. In C. Candlin & K. Hyland (Eds.), *Writing: Texts: Processes and practices* (pp. 99–121). Longman.
Hyland, K. (2000). *Disciplinary discourses: Social interactions in academic writing*. Longman.
Hyland, K. (2004). *Genre and second language writing*. University of Michigan Press.
Hyland, K. (2005a). *Metadiscourse*. Continuum.
Hyland, K. (2005b). Stance and engagement: A model of interaction in academic discourse. *Discourse Studies, 7*(2), 173–192. https://doi.org/10.1177/1461445605050365
Hyland, K. (2006). The 'other' English: Thoughts on EAP and academic writing. *The European English Messenger, 15*(2), 34–57.
Hyland, K. (2007). Genre pedagogy: Language, literacy and L2 writing instruction. *Journal of Second Language Writing, 16*, 148–164. https://doi.org/10.1016/j.jslw.2007.07.005
Hyland, K. (2010). Metadiscourse: Mapping interactions in academic writing. *Nordic Journal of English Studies, 9*(2), 125–143.
Hyland, K. (2012a). Bundles in academic discourse. *Annual Review of Applied Linguistics, 32*, 150–169. https://doi.org/10.1017/S0267190512000037
Hyland, K. (2012b). Corpora and academic discourse. In K. Hyland, C. M. Huat, & M. Handford (Eds.), *Corpus applications in applied linguistics* (pp. 30–46). Continuum.
Hyland, K. (2017a). Metadiscourse: What is it and where is it going? *Journal of Pragmatics, 11*(3), 16–29. https://doi.org/10.1016/j.pragma.2017.03.007
Hyland, K. (2017b). English in the disciplines: Arguments for specificity. *ESP Today: Journal of English for Specific Purposes at Tertiary Level, 1*, 5–23. https://doi.org/10.18485/esptoday.2017.5.1.1
Hyland, K., & Guinda, C. S. (2012). *Stance and voice in written academic genres*. Palgrave-Macmillan.
Hyland, K., Huat, C. M., & Handford, M. (Eds.). (2012). *Corpus applications in applied linguistics*. Continuum.
Hyland, K., & Jiang, F. (2017a). 'We believe that...': Changes in an academic stance marker. *Australian Journal of Linguistics*, 1–22. https://doi.org/10.1080/07268602.2018.1400498
Hyland, K., & Jiang, F. K. (2017b). Is academic writing becoming more informal? *English for Specific Purposes, 45*, 40–51. https://doi.org/10.1016/j.esp.2016.09.001
Hyland, K. & Milton, J. (1997). Qualification and certainty in L1 and L2 students' writing. *Journal of Second Language Writing, 6*(2), 183–205. https://doi.org/10.1016/S1060-3743(97)90033-3
Hyland, K., & Tse, P. (2004). Metadiscourse in academic writing: A reappraisal. *Applied Linguistics, 25*, 156–177. https://doi.org/10.1016/j.esp.2004.02.002
Hyland, K., & Tse, P. (2005a). Evaluative-that constructions: Signaling stance in research abstracts. *Functions of Language, 12*(1), 39–64. https://doi.org/10.1075/fol.12.1.03hyl
Hyland, K., & Tse, P. (2005b). Hooking the reader: A corpus study of evaluative that in abstracts. *English for Specific Purposes, 24*, 123–139. https://doi.org/10.1016/j.esp.2004.02.002
Hyland, K., & Tse, P. (2007). Is there an "academic vocabulary"? *TESOL Quarterly, 41*(2), 235–253. https://doi.org/10.1016/j.jslw.2007.07.005
Jiang, F. (2017). Stance and voice in academic writing: The "noun + that" construction and disciplinary variation. *International Journal of Corpus Linguistics, 22*(1), 85–106. https://doi.org/10.1075/ijcl.22.1.04jia

Kafes, H. (2009). *Authorial stance in academic English: Native and non-native academic speaker writers' use of stance devices (modal verbs) in research articles.* Unpublished doctoral dissertation, Anadolu University. https://earsiv.anadolu.edu.tr/xmlui/bitstream/handle/11421/4214/190 131.pdf?sequence=1

Klimova, B. F. (2015). Teaching English abstract writing effectively. *Procedia—Social and Behavioral Sciences, 186*, 908–912. https://doi.org/10.1016/j.sbspro.2015.04.113

Koltay, T. (2010). *Abstracts and abstracting: A genre and set of skills for the twenty-first century.* Chandos.

Lawrence, A. (2023). *AntConc Version 4.2.4.* https://www.laurenceanthony.net/software/antconc/

Lestari, D. M. (2020). An analysis of students' difficulties in writing undergraduate thesis at English education program of Muhammadiyah University of Bengkulu. *Premise Journal, 9*(1) April, 17–29.

Marhamah, M., Yulianto, & Afrizal, J. (2023). Students' academic vocabulary mastery: A descriptive study at English language education of FKIP-UIR. *International Journal of Language Pedagogy, 2*(2), 34–40. https://doi.org/10.24036/ijolp.v2i1.31

Mauranen, A. (2012). *Exploring ELF: Academic English shaped by non-native speakers.* Cambridge University Press.

Miller, C. (1984). Genre as social action. *Quarterly Journal of Speech, 70,* 151–167. https://doi.org/10.1080/00335638409383686

Nation, I. S. P. (2001). *Learning vocabulary in another language.* Cambridge University Press.

Nation, I. S. P. (2009). *Teaching ESL/EFL reading and writing.* Routledge.

O'Connor, R. (2009). *Writing scientific research articles: Strategy and steps.* Wiley-Blackwell.

O'Keeffe, A., McCarthy, M., & Carter, R. (2007). *From corpus to classroom: Language use and language teaching.* CUP.

Orasan, C. (2001). Patterns in scientific abstracts. In P. Rayson, A. Wilson, T. McEnery, A. Hardie, & S. Khoja (Eds.), *Proceedings of the Corpus Linguistics 2001 Conference* (pp. 433–443). Lancaster University (UK). http://ucrel.lancs.ac.uk/publications/CL2003/CL2001%20conference/contents.htm

Pertiwi, W. H. S. (2020). *Teaching research in undergraduate English language teacher education degree programs in Indonesia: A case study.* Unpublished doctoral dissertation, Charles Darwin University. https://ris.cdu.edu.au/ws/portalfiles/portal/35231915/Thesis_CDU_34727926_Pertiwi_W.pdf

Pho, P. D. (2008). Research article abstracts in applied linguistics and educational technology: A study of linguistic realizations of rhetorical structure and authorial stance. *Discourse Studies, 10*(2), 231–250. https://doi.org/10.1177/1461445607087010

Purves, A. C. (Ed.). (1988a). *Writing across languages and cultures. Issues in contrastive rhetoric.* SAGE.

Purves, A. C. (Ed.). (1988b). *Cross-cultural variation in persuasive student writing.* SAGE.

Reppen, R. (2010). *Using corpora in the language classroom.* Cambridge University Press.

Römer, U. (2004). Comparing real and ideal language learner input: The use of an EFL textbook corpus in corpus linguistics and language teaching. In G. Aston, S. Bernardini, & D. Stewart (Eds.), *Corpora and language learners* (pp. 151–168). John Benjamins.

Römer, U. (2009). The inseparability of lexis and grammar: Corpus linguistic perspectives. *Annual Review of Cognitive Linguistics, i,* 140–162. https://doi.org/10.1075/arcl.7.06rom

Safitri, C. D., Azizah, S., & Annur, M. J. (2021). The analysis of students' challenges to thesis writing at UIN Alauddin Makasssar. *English Language Teaching for EFL Learners, 3*(2), 41–53. https://doi.org/10.24252/elties.v3i2.21013

Safnil. (2006). *Rhetorical structure analysis of the Indonesian research articles.* Unpublished Doctoral Dissertation, Australian National University. https://openresearch-repository.anu.edu.au/handle/1885/48183

Simanjuntak, R. R. (2017). Students' strategies: Insights for teaching lexical cohesion. *Advanced Science Letters, 23*(2), 958–960. https://doi.org/10.1166/asl.2017.7455

Sitompul, S. K., & Anditasari, A. W. (2022). Challenges in writing academic research: An exploration of master's students' experiences. *Getsempena English Education Journal, 9*(2), 136–148. https://doi.org/10.46244/geej.v9i2.1805

SKOS, (1988). UNESCO nomenclature for fields of science and technology. https://skos.um.es/unesco6/5701/html

Stotesbury, H. (2003). Evaluation in research article abstracts in the narrative and hard sciences. *Journal of English for Academic Purposes, 2*, 327–341. https://doi.org/10.1016/S1475-1585(03)00049-3

Swales, J. M. (1990). *Genre analysis: English in academic and research settings*. Cambridge University Press.

Swales, J. (2004). *Research genres: Explorations and application*. Cambridge University Press.

Swales, J. M., & Feak, C. B. (1994). *Academic writing for graduate students-essential tasks and skills: A course for nonnative speakers of English*. The University of Michigan Press.

Swales, J. M., & Feak, C. B. (2009). *Abstracts and the writing of abstracts*. The University of Michigan Press.

Swales, J. M., Jakobsen, H., Kejser, C., Koch, L., Lynch, J., & Mølbæk, L. (2000). A new link in a chain of genres? *Hermes: Journal of Linguistics, 25*, 133–141. https://doi.org/10.7146/hjlcb.v13i25.25589

Tribble, C. (2019). Expert, native or lingua franca? Paradigm choices in novice academic writer support. In P. Habibie & K. Hyland (Eds.), *Novice writers and scholarly publication* (pp. 53–78). Palgrave Macmillan.

Varttala, T. (2001). *Hedging in scientifically oriented discourse: Exploring variation according to discipline and intended audience*. Electronic dissertatio. Acta Electronica Universitatis Tamperensis 138. https://acta.uta.fi, https://trepo.tuni.fi/bitstream/handle/10024/67148/951-44-5195-3.pdf?sequence=1&isAllowed=y

Wei, L. (2021). Teaching academic vocabulary to English Language Learners (ELLs). *Theory and Practice in Language Studies, 11*(12), 1507–1514. https://doi.org/10.17507/tpls.1112.01

Dr. Risa Rumentha Simanjuntak obtained her degree in Applied Linguistics from Atma Jaya University, Indonesia. She received her master's degree in Applied Linguistics from the University of Melbourne and she also received a master degree in Education Management from University of Leeds. Her research interests are corpus linguistics, academic writing, and technology in language learning. Dr. Simanjuntak has published in reputable journals and is currently the Research Interest Group Leader for Digital Language and Behavior (RIG D-LAB) at Bina Nusantara University, Indonesia.

Open Access This chapter is licensed under the terms of the Creative Commons Attribution 4.0 International License (http://creativecommons.org/licenses/by/4.0/), which permits use, sharing, adaptation, distribution and reproduction in any medium or format, as long as you give appropriate credit to the original author(s) and the source, provide a link to the Creative Commons license and indicate if changes were made.

The images or other third party material in this chapter are included in the chapter's Creative Commons license, unless indicated otherwise in a credit line to the material. If material is not included in the chapter's Creative Commons license and your intended use is not permitted by statutory regulation or exceeds the permitted use, you will need to obtain permission directly from the copyright holder.

Chapter 10
N-gram Based Authorship Analysis in Indonesian Text: Evidence Case Study in Authorship Dispute Cases

Devi Ambarwati Puspitasari, Adi Sutrisno, and Hanif Fakhrurroja

Abstract Threats through anonymous letters continue to be reported in Indonesia. Threatening letters are being sent via SMS, e-mail, and private messaging apps such as WhatsApp. Authorship analysis is commonly used to determine the author of an anonymous text. The study uses N-gram tracing to determine the author of an anonymous letter by analyzing three sets of texts from three unique authors. The data was analyzed by determining, tracing, and computing N-grams in each set of texts being compared, both at the character and word levels. Statistical tests were also performed during the data analysis stage, utilizing the similarity comparison method and the Jaccard Coefficient calculation to assess the accuracy of N-gram tracing in identifying authors. Character analysis of N-grams reveals that, as the smallest N-unit, characters play an essential role in authorship attribution. Data analysis at the word level reveals that, lexically, word choice is the most dominating and influential linguistic element of authorship attribution in defining the author's profile and accurately distinguishing one author from another.

Keywords Authorship analysis · Authorship attribution · Corpus linguistics · Digital text · Forensic linguistics · Indonesian text

---

D. A. Puspitasari (✉) · H. Fakhrurroja
Research Center for Language, Literature, and Community, National Research and Innovation Agency of Republic Indonesia, Jalan Gatot Subroto No.10, Jakarta Selatan, Jakarta 12710, Indonesia
e-mail: devi018@brin.go.id

H. Fakhrurroja
e-mail: hani010@brin.go.id

A. Sutrisno
Faculty of Cultural Sciences, Universitas Gadjah Mada, Jalan Nusantara No.1, Bulaksumur, Yogyakarta 55281, Indonesia
e-mail: adisutrisno@ugm.ac.id

10.1 Introduction

In Indonesia, proving electronic text evidence in judicial matters is frequently problematic. Digital forensic searches can only give proof of origin and traces of electronic text transmission (Akcapinar Sezer et al., 2020). Based on the contents of the text, digital forensics has been unable to identify the author (Coulthard, 2004; MacLeod & Grant, 2012). Denial of text authorship and claims to text authorship are common obstacles to demonstrating electronic writings in Indonesia (Puspitasari et al., 2023). Denial of electronic text authorship occurs when electronic text evidence is proven through digital traces or electronic transmissions from someone's device, but the author denies authorship owing to piracy or social media account hacking (Grant, 2022; MacLeod & Grant, 2012). On the other hand, a claim of authorship of an electronic text occurs when a text or digital document is acknowledged to have been written by someone, but its authenticity is doubted. These obstacles to proving electronic texts from a linguistic perspective are what encourage linguists to carry out authorship analysis.

Authorship analysis is an approach to identifying text profiles that is often used in the realm of forensic linguistic studies. Forensic authorship analysis is the process of determining the original author of an anonymous text using factors included within the text itself (Yang et al., 2017). Attribution to anonymous text is not based on factors external to the text, such as paper, ink, type, or document of origin. The main idea is that each author has a writing style that is different from each other (Akimushkin et al., 2017). This is because each person's writing behavior and style are different and have been proven by various authorship attribution research projects that have been carried out from time to time.

Authorship analysis emphasizes the consideration of writing style as a basis for identification (Grieve et al., 2019). Authorship analysis determines the author of documents whose authorship is disputed, as in attributing crime texts to authors from a list of potential authors as well as profiling unknown authors based on linguistic characteristics (Coulthard, 2004).

Grant and Coulthard (2005) describe the stages for determining a case's authorship using the forensic stylistic method, beginning with determining a comparison text (known text/KT) as a reference for the text of the current evidence. This begins with determining the subject or owner of the text based on the circumstances of the current case or references to the results of the police investigation. For example, if the text in question (QT) is a short message (SMS), then the closest references are short messages, emails, and supporting personal texts from the same owner. The Q-text is then compared to two or more other references. If it is discovered that K-text 1 is a short message produced at a different time, then K-text 2 can be a different sort of text, such as an email or social media upload.

Determining n-units can start with the smallest attribution, namely characters, letters, and punctuation marks. To quantify similarities and detect differences, some experts employ the Jaccard Coefficient (Coulthard, 2013; Larner, 2014). Researchers use computing technologies to obtain rapid and accurate statistical test findings as technology advances. These findings serve as the foundation for a qualitative study of the text's writing style.

In Indonesian language texts, the writing style of Indonesian people has a high potential for uniqueness. Apart from the use of characters, other linguistic units such as words and phrases will create a very personal writing style. Personal texts in Indonesia have the potential to be influenced by regional languages (Ramadhani, 2018; Rustono, 2016) and term trends in cyberspace (Sukma et al., 2021; Tur, 2019). Digital forensic searches cannot provide accurate evidence regarding claims of ownership of a text. Authorship cannot be proven based on the location and ownership of the device alone. In proving cases of authorship disputes in Indonesia, forensic linguistic analysis is needed to claim accurate ownership of a text. However, it cannot be denied that forensic linguistics has not been able to present evidence that is absolute and has minimal relativity in the judicial process, as digital forensics has.

Due to the demand for the presence of absolute scientific evidence in forensic linguistic analysis and proof in the legal process, this research analyzes a collection of personal texts in Indonesian from a legal case involving anonymous letters with the aim of threatening the victim. Authorship analysis is carried out with the aim of identifying ownership of a text (authorship) and the author's profile based on N-gram tracing, as well as identifying authorship attribution in Indonesian language texts. The research questions formulated are as follows:

1. What linguistic patterns and features are revealed by N-gram tracing that are typical markers of authorship attribution in Indonesian digital texts?
2. How do linguistic features extracted through N-gram tracing contribute to accurate author identification in the context of authorship analysis of Indonesian texts?

Authorship analysis occupies a unique position in Indonesia's diversified language landscape, delving into the complexities of linguistic nuances inherent to Bahasa Indonesia, regional dialects, and cross-cultural influences. As this research progresses, it will reveal the rich tapestry of language use and diverse writing styles that make authorship analysis in Indonesian text such an intriguing subject of study. Through this study, we engage on a journey to identify the hidden linguistic signatures left in digital works by authors, revealing light on their distinct digital identities.

10.2 Method

Authorship analysis involves several important stages in the process. This research adopts the authorship analysis research concept of Belvisi et al. (2020), Grieve et al. (2019), and Nini (2018), which uses N-gram tracing to identify certain authorship attribution patterns produced by an author. N-gram tracing is carried out on each text set, and the search results are compared using statistical tests to identify author attributes or characteristics and make authorship claims on each set tested (text set). The N-gram tracing and text set comparison methods in this research adopt the concepts of comparative authorship analysis (CAA) belonging to Tom Grant (2022) and the similarity comparison method (SCM), which refers to the forensic stylistic concept proposed by McMenamin (2019).

This study uses N-gram tracing to determine the author of an anonymous letter by analyzing three sets of texts from three unique authors (Tables 10.1 and 10.2). To identify authorship attribution markers for each text, N-gram tracing is performed at both the character and word levels. Tracing N-grams at the character level prioritizes detailed character usage. The characters in question are alphabetic and non-alphabetic characters, which consists of numbers, punctuation, emoji, spaces, enter (↵), and other characters found on the keyboard on the device. N-gram tracing also includes counting the number of characters and their usage patterns. Additionally, at the word level, N-gram tracing is used to determine the number of words and patterns of word use, such as frequency of word use (token), word type (entry), word distribution, word order, phrase length, and sentence length, that are indicators of a writer's authorship attribution. Tokens and entries are initial attributions that facilitate tracking and analysis. Tokens are individual words or units of text that act as linguistic fingerprints, whereas entries are the quantity of word types that demonstrate an author's preference for words. As seen in the table below, these two data items serve as an initial starting point for N-gram tracing.

This research initiated the work of developing a profile for the author of the anonymous letter by comparing data from threatening situations, specifically the anonymous letter (questioned text/Q-text) as shown in Table 10.1, with three text files from potential authors (know text/K-text) as shown in Table 10.2. This profile-creation process is based on language analysis, and N-gram tracing is an effective method for revealing the distinct linguistic fingerprints that authors leave behind. This procedure allows us to identify distinct linguistic traits such as vocabulary, sentence patterns, and expressions that may be useful in determining authorship.

N-gram tracing is also used to find linguistic features that represent authorship markers/attributes (authorship attribution). To quantify the accuracy of N-gram tracing in identifying authors, the patterns discovered using N-gram tracing are weighted in a series of statistical tests using the similarity comparison approach and the Jaccard Coefficient formula, seen in Fig. 10.1.

In the context of the Jaccard coefficient or other similarity metrics, there is no globally established or standard threshold for similarity. The calculation of a similarity threshold is frequently problem-specific and depends on a variety of criteria, including the nature of the data, the application, and the analysis's aims.

The Jaccard coefficient measures the similarity of two sets by dividing their intersection size by their union size. Jaccard similarity values are frequently normalized to a scale of 0–1 in settings such as text analysis or information retrieval. A value of 1 (one) indicates that the sets are identical, whereas a value of 0 (zero) indicates that there is no overlap. In the context of authorship analysis, with a result of 0 (zero) indicating that the two texts are completely different and a result greater than 0 (zero) or close to 1 (one) indicating that they are identical. The difference between these is shown by the decimal result between zero and one. As a result, if the findings of the N-gram analysis and the computation of the Jaccard coefficient for two texts are

10 N-gram Based Authorship Analysis in Indonesian Text: Evidence Case ...

Table 10.1 Data of the anonymous letter

Author	Text	Tokens	Entries
Anonymous author	**Q-text 1:** *Hati-hati, maut akan mengintai anda, pelan tapi pasti, jaga baik-baik anak dan istrimu* [Be careful, death will stalk you, slowly but surely, take good care of your children and wife] **Q-text 2:** *Hati-hati, perbuatan semua ini akan ada balasnya, jaga dirimu baik-baik* [Be careful, there will be retribution for all these actions, take good care of yourself] **Q-text 3:** *Hati-hati, perbuatan semua ini akan ada balasnya, jaga dirimu baik-baik* [Be careful, there will be retribution for all these actions, take good care of yourself] **Q-text 4:** JAGA DIRIMU BAIK-BAIK, ANAK ISTERIMU JAGA BAIK-BAIK, PELAN TAPI PASTI, MAUT AKAN MENUNGGUMU [TAKE CARE OF YOURSELF, CHILD TAKE CARE OF YOUR WIFE, SLOWLY BUT SURELY, DEATH WILL AWAIT YOU] **Q-text 5:** PERMAINANMU DGN SDR AJIS AKAN DAPAT GANJARANNYA, NYAWATARUHANNYA [YOUR GAME WITH AJIS WILL REWARD THE REWARDS, LIVE THE BETS] **Q-text 6:** HATI-HATI SAJA JAGA DIRIMU BAIK-BAIK, KITA LIHAT NASIBMU SELANJUTNYA [JUST BE CAREFUL, TAKE CARE OF YOURSELF, WE'LL SEE YOUR NEXT FATE] **Q-text 7:** PERMAINANMU BUSUK AKAN DAPAT GANJARANNYA, NYAWA TARUHANNYA [YOUR POINTY GAME WILL BE REWARDED, YOUR LIFE IS AT BET]	80	36

Table 10.2 Data of potential author of the anonymous letter

Author	Total text	Total tokens	Total entries
Potential author 1	6 K-texts	245	68
Potential author 2	9 K-texts	197	59
Potential author 3	10 K-texts	203	65

Fig. 10.1 Jaccard coefficient

$$J(A, B) = \frac{|A \cap B|}{|A \cup B|}$$

Information:
A: Jaccard index
A: coefficient A
B: B coefficient
∪: union
∩: intersection
A ∩ B: number of intersections of coefficients A and B
A ∪ B: sum of coefficients A and B

1 (one) or close to 1 (one), the results will be classified as identical or considered to be authored by the same author. However, if the result is less than one and even closer to zero, the two electronic writings are deemed to have been authored by two different authors.

10.3 Analysis

10.3.1 Jaccard Index as a Basis for Determining Authorship Claims

N-gram tracing is a method that is widely used and proven to be accurate in authorship analysis (Frye & Wilson, 2018; Ragel et al., 2013). N-grams have been proven to be able to identify patterns in a writer's writing style (Belvisi et al., 2020; Grieve, 2023; Markov et al., 2017). Through this method, the frequency with which words and characters appear in the text being analyzed or are known in predetermined N-units. This process generally starts with an N-gram search at the word level with N-unit values starting with $N = 1$. Through this process, lexical preferences, language style, and the use of special words are obtained, which can indicate similarities or differentiate the authors of the two sets of texts tested. The calculation of word frequencies in this study was carried out using statistical tests using the Jaccard Coefficient formula (Grieve et al., 2019; McMenamin, 2019). Statistical tests for N-gram searches and Jaccard index calculations in this research have been packaged in an application. This application is designed to automatically calculate word frequencies and measure the index of the extent to which two sets of texts are similar or different based on predetermined N-units.

The results of calculating the Jaccard coefficient from two sets of texts, referred to as the Jaccard index in this study, will be in the range 0–1. A value of 0 indicates that there are no words (N-units) that are identical between the two authors, whereas a value of 1 indicates that all words are identical between the two authors. The higher

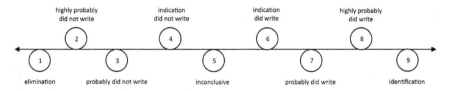

Fig. 10.2 Authorship scale (McMenamin, 2019)

the Jaccard Coefficient value, the more similar the writing styles of the two authors are (Ding et al., 2019; Grieve et al., 2019). To make it easier to draw conclusions, namely in the form of claims for ownership of a text and identification of the author, this research converts the Jaccard index obtained from statistical test results to the authorship claim scale (McMenamin, 2019), as seen in Fig. 10.2.

To analyze similarities and similarities in writing patterns, this study compared evidence (labeled with code E) data with three potential authors who were labeled with codes (author 1 = A.1, author 2 = A.2, and author 3 = A.3). The following Table 10.3 presents the results of statistical tests for calculating word frequencies for tracing similarities from three sets of Q-text and K-text data documents in this study.

In general, statistical tests demonstrate differences in the similarity of writing style between the two sets of texts evaluated, which are based on searching for similarities in word occurrences and calculating their frequencies. Based on the findings of statistical tests, there are two sets of texts that can clearly claim authorship of the three sets of texts evaluated, namely the sets of texts with high scores, namely data 2 and data 3. Both statistics obviously point to strengthening and rejection. A high (10) authorship scale and a very low (0.1) authorship scale reflect a strong claim. These statistical findings make it easy to form conclusions, such as a high authorship scale indicating that the text was written by the same author, and a low scale indicating that the material was produced by a different author. This convenience is derived from statistical test results that are at the extremes of the statistical range (very high or extreme low). However, index results that were equivocal or exhibited less strong indicators, such as in data 1, were also discovered. These three results demonstrate differences in the level of author identification and elimination across the texts studied.

Table 10.3 Statistical test results for authorship claims using the Jaccard coefficient

Data	Compared text-sets	Index Jaccard results	Authorship claim scale	Authorship claim status
1	E and A.1	0.48	5	Inconclusive
2	E and A.2	0.91	10	Identification
3	E and A.3	0.08	1	Elimination

10.3.2 Patterns of Lexical and Character Choices Indicate Authorship Attribution

Following the findings of the $N = 1$ statistical test, data analysis continued with an investigation of writing style and the construction of an author's profile. This process involves a more in-depth analysis of the author's writing style, which includes exploring the use of words, phrases, language style, and unique sentence structures. The analysis of writing style in this research still uses the N-gram tracing method, which has been packaged in an application to facilitate automatic tracing. The difference between this second process and the first process is the level and N-unit value used. In the first step, N-units are used only at the word level, with a value of $N = 1$. In this second stage, the N-gram search is carried out at the character level (char-level) and word level with N-units greater than $N = 1$. Searching N-grams at two levels and different N-unit values makes it easy to identify the author's writing style through its patterns in the text. This process also aims to recognize typical patterns in word choice and sentence structure that can differentiate writers.

Text processing in N-gram searches in this research was carried out without removing punctuation marks or special characters and without changing all words to lowercase (writing in capital letters was left as is) so that the authenticity of the text in the analysis was maintained. Each text is processed at two levels, namely character level (char-level) and word level. These two levels are applied with the aim of seeing the author's uniqueness in as much detail as possible as a marker of authorship attribution.

The N value used in this research is $N = 1$ to $N = 5$ at the character level. Meanwhile, at the word level, the N values used are $N = 1$ to $N = 3$. At the character level, each character usage in the text is traced to see patterns that emerge as markers of author attribution, such as whether the author tends to use upper- or lower-case letters; how often they use punctuation marks or symbols, and what punctuation marks are often used; do you often use special characters such as numbers or certain symbols; and others. Meanwhile, at the word level, each word and phrase structure is traced for pattern tendencies, such as the intensity of words and phrases that often appear, what the writing pattern is, and its consistency. Table 10.4 shows the results of the N-gram search analysis to detect the uniqueness of the author's language style.

Based on N-gram tracing on each set of texts in Table 10.4, the attribution of a writer or text owner can be detected from the N-gram patterns visible in the text they wrote. At the word level, generally, two text sets are identified as having the same pattern at $N = 1$ and $N = 2$. In authorship analysis, determining $N = 1$ is an

Table 10.4 N-unit search results at the word level

Data	$N = 1$	$N = 2$	$N = 3$
1	18/385	1/596	1/621
2	19/140	3/192	0/194
3	1/119	0/167	0/179

important benchmark considering diction significantly affects a writer's attribution markers. A word can be very personal for a writer, especially the choice of personal pronouns. Personal pronouns are an important attribution that is closely related to the author's background, such as regional characteristics, linguistic characteristics, age, and even personality.

In the evidence text (data E), the dominant personal pronoun that appears is the second-person pronoun. The N-gram search results show that the author uses the word "*kamu/mu* [you/your]" which is very general. Meanwhile, in data 3, the personal pronouns that appear are the words "*gw* [I]" and "*lu* [you]" which are firm regional characteristics for those who live in Jakarta and the surrounding areas, because it is the Betawi language. However, the word "*gue*" in Betawi language also has several variants. In research related to word trends on social media (Puspitasari, 2022; Sukma et al., 2021), the word "*gue*" which means I/my/me in Indonesian is written by cyberspace users in six variants, namely "*gw*", "*gua*", "*gue*", "*guwa*", "*guwe*", and "*guweh*". Even though the meaning is the same, an author who uses the word "*gw*" is certainly different from an author who chooses the word "*gue*" or other variants. The comparison results among the writers are shown in Table 10.5.

Word choice is very personal, and in authorship analysis, this is a characteristic that profiles the author quite strongly. Therefore, it is not surprising that the author in data 3 generated a low Jaccard index and shows a claim of authorship as a different author (see Table 10.4). Search results on larger N-units also increasingly show that the same language patterns and characteristics are not found between case evidence data and authors in data 3.

An examination of the character level also shows that there is a writer's habit of never using periods and other punctuation marks at the end of sentences in both sets

Table 10.5 Results of comparison of the use of personal pronouns

Author	Text
Anonymous author	JAGA DIRI**MU** BAIK-BAIK, ANAK ISTERI**MU** JAGA BAIK-BAIK, PELAN TAPI PASTI, MAUT AKAN MENUNGGU**MU** [TAKE CARE OF YOURSELF, CHILD TAKE CARE OF YOUR WIFE, SLOWLY BUT SURELY, DEATH WILL AWAIT YOU]
Potential author 1	Baik **pak**, sudah saya kirim dgn faktur pajaknya Maaf **pak**, apa tidak apa-apa **saya** lampirkan satu dulu? [OK sir, I've sent it with the tax invoice. Sorry sir, is it okay if I attach one first?]
Potential author 2	penawaran dari subcon tadi **aku** ada titip di yono, trus katanya ditaruh di meja**mu** [I left the offer from Subcon at Yono and he said that he put it on your table]
Potential author 3	ya ntar kl **gw** ud dikirimin **gw** kabari **lu** tunggu aj pe urusan tender kelar, fokus situ aj [Yes, when I've sent it, I'll let you know Just wait for the tender to finish, just focus on that]

of texts. The anonymous author in the data tends to choose simple sentence structures and use the enter feature or move to the bottom line to separate one sentence from another. In other words, the author uses the enter feature as a replacement for the dot (.) in both sets, and it works consistently. The similarity of the writing style and the pattern tendencies that emerge in both sets (data E and 2) indicate the same author attribution. This is confirmed by the Jaccard data 2 index of 10, which is the highest value on the authorship scale, which leads to the conclusion of the authorship claim: both sets were written by the same author. The results of this analysis are strengthened by several studies (Ding et al., 2019; Posadas-Durán et al., 2017) demonstrating that N-gram searches at the character level were found to be consistent in K-text and Q-text show similarities in authorship attribution, therefore claiming that the two sets of texts were written by the same author and vice versa.

Word choice (lexical choice) in an author's profile is an important marker for identifying a writer's authorship attribution (Belvisi et al., 2020). In word choice, there are several linguistic features that appear simultaneously, such as morphological, semantic, pragmatic, and sociolinguistic features. In semantics, word choice is related to the meaning of words and how words are chosen to express certain concepts that are the author's aim. Authorship analysis in the semantic domain identifies how words interact and contribute to the meaning of sentences and texts (Deng et al., 2021; Giraud & Artières, 2012; Rodrigues & Sousa Silva, 2022). From a pragmatic perspective, word selection features can be related to how text writers (speakers) use words in real communication contexts to achieve certain communicative goals (Fobbe, 2020). In a sociolinguistic context, word choice can influence how an author is identified within a particular social group or how the language used by the author of a text expresses social, cultural, or regional identity (Perkins, 2021; Rodrigues & Sousa Silva, 2022).

The way a writer chooses words in a text is also closely related to the writer's choice of method or use of characters (Belvisi et al., 2020). In digital communication, the arrangement of characters in a word is a form of orthographic selection by a writer and has a great influence on the morphology of the words in the writer's "world". Morphological features in this context are usually manifested in the form of writing words that are different from the proper Indonesian morphological concept. In choosing orthography, a writer of personal texts generally prefers choosing and writing words that are arbitrary and free from rules. Writers make decisions about how to spell certain words. This selection includes the use of upper- or lower-case letters, the choice of special letters, the use of punctuation, and other writing styles that can affect the way words are written. Consequently, all the words identified as part of the writer's "world" can be a clue to how he expresses himself in writing.

10.3.3 The Challenge of N-gram Tracing in Exploring the Meaning of Text and the Communication Goals of an Author

Based on previous research and the results of this research analysis, N-gram tracing can identify a writer's authorship attribution pattern. But the challenge is to look deeper into the level of meaning. N-gram tracing identifies lexical and grammatical patterns that appear in text. Furthermore, through this research it was found that the choice of certain words and characters in a text can also influence pragmatic communication and how messages are conveyed. The anonymous letter data in this study has quite strong pragmatic feature markers through the word choice made by the author, as shown in Table 10.6.

All Q-texts in data E involve pragmatic features in understanding the message contained beyond the literal meaning of the words. Understanding this message depends on the communicative context and the implicatures that arise. This attribution is marked by the striking choice of the word *caution*. The word is chosen by the author and used with high frequency, repeated distribution, and directly dominates the tokens that appear in the text set. These findings indicate that high word frequency can be an attribution of authorship because the distribution and frequency of a word will become a pattern of author identity.

Table 10.6 Pragmatic features in the anonymous letter data (data E)

Q-text	Text	Implicature	Communicative context (message conveyed)
Q-teks 1	Hati-hati, maut akan mengintai anda, pelan tapi pasti, jaga baik-baik anak dan istrimu [Be careful, death will stalk you, slowly but surely, take good care of your children and wife]	There is a threat or danger lurking if someone (the message recipient) is not careful	Aku akan membunuhmu dan keluargamu (anak dan istrimu) [I will kill you and your family (your children and wife).]
Q-teks-2	Hati-hati, perbuatan semua ini akan ada balasnya, jaga dirimu baik-baik [Be careful, there will be retribution for all these actions, take good care of yourself]	If someone is not careful or commits bad deeds, they will face certain consequences or retribution	Aku akan membalas dendam atas perbuatan buruk yang kamu lakukan kepadaku [I will take revenge for the bad deeds you did to me.]
Q-teks 7	PERMAINANMU BUSUK AKAN DAPAT GANJARANNYA, NYAWA TARUHANNYA [YOUR POINTY GAME WILL BE REWARDED, YOUR LIFE IS AT BET]	A person who commits evil deeds will face the consequences of death	Aku akan membunuhmu [I will kill you.]

Pragmatic features in authorship analysis can help to understand the communicative context of the text created by an author, including understanding who the target audience is, what the author's communication goals are, and situations or social contexts that may influence writing style. This feature can help identify specific writing style characteristics for certain authors to strengthen authorship claims. In certain texts, the author may use implicatures to convey messages that are more than just words, such as implied messages that may relate to the author's motivation or intentions.

This feature can be characterized by words related to language actions, namely how words are used to perform certain actions in communication, such as the use of commands, prohibitions, or requests in texts. For example, the use of the word "*hati-hati* [careful]" is found together with the words "*maut* [death]" and "*nyawa* [life]" in one text. The selection and use of these words will direct the investigation to understand the author's implicature or intention regarding hidden meanings that are relevant in the investigation, namely death threats. However, this feature is not necessarily also found in the comparison text (K-Text) because it is related to thematic differences in the two sets of texts being compared. Therefore, it is likely that pragmatic features will only be found in one set of texts.

Through advanced qualitative analysis of statistical test results, N-grams can be used to discover pragmatic features that have an important role in understanding the communicative context, intentions, implicatures, and language actions in texts that can identify the characteristics of an author's writing style. Identifying the purpose of this communication is also a key component in efforts to identify or eliminate authors in forensic linguistics research. This effort cannot yet be replaced by machines, and this is where the role of a language expert is really needed. With the results of statistical tests using N-gram tracing and in-depth qualitative analysis, authorship analysis will be more accurate and in-depth.

10.3.4 Claim of Authorship

At the statistical test stage that has been completed, the author's profile can be identified, and authorship claims can be made. However, there are certain conditions, such as court demands, where the need for authorship analysis still requires additional steps before making a claim. The results of this research show that there is data that is in the middle of the scale (data 1). If deeper supporting variables are required to perceive the skew in the direction of the authorship claim scale, data such as data 1 can be explored using more qualitative analysis that is performed manually, such as pragmatic analysis. A digital forensic test can also be performed if required to reinforce the results.

Forensic digital analysis includes examining metadata, time traces, IP addresses, source devices, and other digital traces that can identify the author. This field is not a linguist's area since it entirely involves the role of computing technology, which has been designed to perform digital trace tracking. In addition, from that, the police have the authority to execute this process. The role of the linguist in this process is to provide comparative data, namely the results of linguistic analysis of the identity of the claimed author.

In practice, digital forensic analysis is used as the main benchmark for identifying author profiles and claiming ownership of a text based on digital trace analysis. However, the case of Jenny Nichol proves that digital forensic analysis is not entirely correct (Coulthard, 2004; Grant & Baker, 2001; McMenamin, 2019). Nicholl, a student in Richmond, North Yorkshire, England, was kidnapped and murdered by her boyfriend. Nicholl's parents reported her missing on July 4, 2005, after losing communication with her for three days. Following the interrogation of multiple prospective witnesses, his family received messages sent from Nicholl's cell phone, leading his family and police to assume he was alive and well. However, the police are calling these texts into question, and the investigation is continuing. The investigation was converted from a missing person case to a murder investigation in November 2005. The message sent from Nicholl's cell phone was revealed to be fake. The murder was later arrested and confessed to the police during an investigation interview in May 2007. The evidence of this case was then investigated for authorship analysis by many forensic linguistic experts and the case became widely recognized. This case demonstrates how digital traces can be manipulated by criminals, but an author profile is a unique identity for everyone, just like a fingerprint.

This research demonstrates that author identification in personal texts in Indonesian can be done using linguistic analysis, namely authorship analysis. The collaboration of quantitative and qualitative methods itself has often been applied in authorship analysis research for strong claims of accuracy, especially in the realm of forensic linguistics (McMenamin, 2019). Linguistics can be an accurate and reliable test tool for identifying authors in Indonesian texts. Computing technology is an important factor in the rationalization, accuracy, and detail of information on conclusions and authorship claims from the text being tested.

10.4 Conclusion

In the legal process of proving evidence, digital forensic analysis is used as the main benchmark for identifying author profiles and claiming ownership of a text based on digital trace analysis. However, several authorship dispute cases demonstrate that digital forensic analysis is not entirely correct (Coulthard, 2013; Grant & Baker, 2001). Criminals can change digital traces, but an author profile, like a fingerprint, is a unique identity for each author.

Through N-gram searches, linguistic patterns are revealed in the form of (1) the use of keywords; (2) vocabulary preferences; (3) syntactic patterns; and (4) idiosyncratic patterns, such as sentence length, and the use of punctuation marks, which are typical markers of authorship attribution in Indonesian language digital texts. Linguistic features extracted through N-gram search contribute significantly to author identification with a relatively high level of accuracy in the context of authorship analysis of Indonesian texts. These features help in recognizing signs of each author's unique and distinctive writing style, enabling author attribution with a high degree of confidence. The research demonstrates that linguistic analysis can be used to identify the author of personal texts in Indonesian. Linguistics can be an accurate and reliable test tool for identifying authors in Indonesian texts. In addition, computing technology is an important factor in the rationalization, accuracy, and detail of information on conclusions and authorship claims from the texts being tested.

This research is limited to data with tokens under one hundred and limited comparative text (K-text). The accuracy of N-grams must be continued in further research involving larger data and involving more authors. Analyzing large data will be the possibility of a clearer picture to answer the challenge of N-gram tracing in exploring meaning in personal texts which tend to be short with limited tokens.

References

Akcapinar Sezer, E., Sever, H., & Canbay, P. (2020). Deep combination of stylometry features in forensic authorship analysis. *International Journal of Information Security Science, 9*(3), 154–163. https://www.researchgate.net/publication/344408746

Akimushkin, C., Amancio, D. R., & Oliveira, O. N. (2017). Text authorship identified using the dynamics of word co-occurrence networks. *PLoS ONE, 12*(1), e0170527. https://doi.org/10.1371/journal.pone.0170527

Belvisi, N. M. S., Muhammad, N., & Alonso-Fernandez, F. (2020). Forensic authorship analysis of microblogging texts using n-grams and stylometric features. In *8th International Workshop on Biometrics and Forensics, IWBF 2020-Proceeding.* https://doi.org/10.1109/IWBF49977.2020.9107953

Coulthard, M. (2004). Author identification, idiolect, and linguistic uniqueness. *Applied Linguistics, 25*(4), 431–447. https://doi.org/10.1093/applin/25.4.431

Coulthard, M. (2013). On admissible linguistic evidence. *Journal of Law & Policy, 21*(2), 441–466. https://brooklynworks.brooklaw.edu/jlp/vol21/iss2/8

Deng, Y., Wang, Y., Qiu, C., Hu, Z., Sun, W., Gong, Y., Zhao, X., He, W., & Cao, L. (2021). A Chinese conceptual semantic feature dataset (CCFD). *Behavior Research Methods, 53*(4), 1697–1709. https://doi.org/10.3758/s13428-020-01525-x

Ding, S. H. H., Fung, B. C. M., Iqbal, F., & Cheung, W. K. (2019). Learning stylometric representations for authorship analysis. *IEEE Transactions on Cybernetics, 49*(1), 107–121. https://doi.org/10.1109/TCYB.2017.2766189

Fobbe, E. (2020). Text-linguistic analysis in forensic authorship attribution. *Fobbe, Text-Linguistic Analysis in Forensic Authorship Attribution JLL, 9*, 93–114. https://doi.org/10.14762/jll.2020.093

Frye, R., & Wilson, D. C. (2018). Defining forensic authorship attribution for limited samples from social media. In *Proceedings of the 31st International Florida Artificial Intelligence Research Society Conference, FLAIRS 2018.*

Giraud, F., & Artières, T. (2012). Feature bagging for author attribution. *Working Notes Papers of the CLEF 2012 Evaluation Labs.*

Grant, T. (2022). The idea of progress in forensic authorship analysis. *Cambridge University Press.* https://doi.org/10.1017/9781108974714

Grant, T., & Baker, K. (2001). Identifying reliable, valid markers of authorship: A response to Chaski. *International Journal of Speech, Language and the Law, 8*(1), 66–79. https://doi.org/10.1558/sll.2001.8.1.66

Grant, T. D., & Coulthard, P. M. (2005). *Authorship attribution in a forensic context*. The University of Birmingham.

Grieve, J. (2023). Register variation explains stylometric authorship analysis. *Corpus Linguistics and Linguistic Theory, 19*(1), 47–77. https://doi.org/10.1515/cllt-2022-0040

Grieve, J., Clarke, I., Chiang, E., Gideon, H., Heini, A., Nini, A., & Waibel, E. (2019). Attributing the Bixby letter using n-gram tracing. *Digital Scholarship in the Humanities, 34*(3), 493–512. https://doi.org/10.1093/llc/fqy042

Larner, S. (2014). *Forensic authorship analysis and the world wide web*. Palgrave Pivot. https://doi.org/10.1057/9781137413758

Markov, I., Baptista, J., & Pichardo-Lagunas, O. (2017). Authorship attribution in Portuguese using character n-grams. *Acta Polytechnica Hungarica, 14*(3), 59–78. https://doi.org/10.12700/APH.14.3.2017.3.4

Macleod, N., & Grant, T. (2012). Whose tweet? Authorship analysis of micro-blogs and other short-form messages. In S. Tomblin, N. MacLeod, R. Sousa-Silva, & M. Coulthard (Eds.), *Proceedings of the International Association of Forensic Linguists' Tenth Biennial Conference* (pp. 210–224). Aston University.

McMenamin, G. R. (2019). *Forensic linguistics: Advances in forensic stylistics*. CRC Press LLC.

Nini, A. (2018). An authorship analysis of the Jack the ripper letters. *Digital Scholarship in the Humanities, 33*(3), 621–636. https://doi.org/10.1093/llc/fqx065

Perkins, R. C. (2021). The application of forensic linguistics in cybercrime investigations. *Policing (Oxford), 15*(1), 66–78. https://doi.org/10.1093/police/pay097

Posadas-Durán, J. P., Gómez-Adorno, H., Sidorov, G., Batyrshin, I., Pinto, D., & Chanona-Hernández, L. (2017). Application of the distributed document representation in the authorship attribution task for small corpora. *Soft Computing, 21*(3), 627–639. https://doi.org/10.1007/s00500-016-2446-x

Puspitasari, D. A. (2022). Corpus-based speech act analysis on the use of word 'lu' in cyber bullying speech. In *Proceedings of the 1st Konferensi Internasional Berbahasa Indonesia Universitas Indraprasta PGRI, KIBAR 2020, 28 October 2020, Jakarta, Indonesia* (pp. 1–10). https://doi.org/10.4108/eai.28-10-2020.2315314

Puspitasari, D. A., Fakhrurroja, H., & Sutrisno, A. (2023). Identify fake author in Indonesia crime cases: A forensic authorsip analysis using n-gram and stylometric features. In *2023 International Conference on Advancement in Data Science, E-Learning and Information System (ICADEIS)* (pp. 1–6). https://doi.org/10.1109/ICADEIS58666.2023.10271069

Ragel, R., Herath, P., & Senanayake, U. (2013). Authorship detection of SMS messages using unigrams. In *2013 IEEE 8th International Conference on Industrial and Information Systems* (pp. 387–392). https://doi.org/10.1109/ICIInfS.2013.6732015

Ramadhani, A. R. (2018). Lingua franca in the linguistic landscape of Gresik Kota Baru (GKB). *Etnolingual, 2*(2), 125–134. https://doi.org/10.20473/etno.v2i2.10569

Rodrigues, A. S., & Sousa Silva, S. R. (2022). A forensic authorship analysis of threats. *RevSALUS - Revista Científica Da Rede Académica Das Ciências Da Saúde Da Lusofonia, 4*(Sup), 98–99. https://doi.org/10.51126/revsalus.v4isup.324

Rustono, T. C. (2016). Akulturasi budaya dalam pilihan bahasa pedagang etnis tionghoa pada ranah perdagangan di kota salatiga [Cultural acculturation in the language choices of ethnic Chinese traders in the trade realm in Salatiga city]. *Seloka - Jurnal Pendidikan Bahasa Dan Sastra Indonesia, 5*(1). https://journal.unnes.ac.id/sju/index.php/seloka/article/view/12769

Sukma, B. P., Puspitasari, D. A., Afiyani, S. A., Okitasari, I., Palupi, D., Kusumawardani, F., Husnul, K., & Prayoga, R. A. (2021). Cyberbullying speech patterns among Indonesian students. *Jurnal Bahasa, Sastra, Seni Dan Pengajarannya, 49*(2), 205–223. https://doi.org/10.17977/um015v49i22021p205

Tur, A. P. A. (2019). Patterns of linguistics features in private chats of social media account leading someone to be a victim of a cybercrime. *LEKSIKA, 13*(1), 29–38. https://doi.org/10.30595/lks.v13i1.3858

Yang, X., Xu, G., Li, Q., Guo, Y., & Zhang, M. (2017). Authorship attribution of source code by using back propagation neural network based on particle swarm optimization. *PLoS ONE, 12*(11), e0187204. https://doi.org/10.1371/journal.pone.0187204

Devi Ambarwati Puspitasari, M.Pd. *Ph.D. student of Linguistics, Universitas Gadjah Mada. Associate Researcher in National Research and Innovation Agency of Republic Indonesia (BRIN).* A researcher at the Language, Literature and Community Research Center, National Research and Innovation Agency of Republic Indonesia (BRIN) whose research interests revolve around forensic linguistics, corpus linguistics, multilingualism, and DaF (Deutsch als Fremdsprache). She is presently pursuing her studies in the Doctoral Program of Humanities, Faculty of Cultural Science, Universitas Gadjah Mada.

Dr. Adi Sutrisno, M.A. *Assistant Professor of English Department, Faculty of Cultural Sciences, Universitas Gadjah Mada.* A lecturer of the English Department at the Faculty of Cultural Sciences, Universitas Gadjah Mada whose research interests revolve around applied linguistics.

Dr. Hanif Fakhrurroja, S.Si., M.T., *Senior Researcher in National Research and Innovation Agency of Republic Indonesia (BRIN).* A researcher at the Research Center for Smart Mechatronics, National Research and Innovation Agency (BRIN). His areas of expertise include Human–Machine Interaction, Natural Language Processing, Internet of Things (IoT), Big Data and Data Analytics.

Open Access This chapter is licensed under the terms of the Creative Commons Attribution 4.0 International License (http://creativecommons.org/licenses/by/4.0/), which permits use, sharing, adaptation, distribution and reproduction in any medium or format, as long as you give appropriate credit to the original author(s) and the source, provide a link to the Creative Commons license and indicate if changes were made.

The images or other third party material in this chapter are included in the chapter's Creative Commons license, unless indicated otherwise in a credit line to the material. If material is not included in the chapter's Creative Commons license and your intended use is not permitted by statutory regulation or exceeds the permitted use, you will need to obtain permission directly from the copyright holder.

Part IV
Critical Discourse Analysis

Chapter 11
The Persuasive Power of Advertisements: An Analysis of Structure and Context in Javanese in 1935–1953

Diah Mardiningrum Joyowidarbo, Atin Fitriana, and Dwi Puspitorini

Abstract An advertisement is not only aimed to promote the content, but also shows the existence of other functions related to socioculture. The language of advertisement that is constantly heard will settle in the minds of the community. The research on advertisements has been conducted on many advertisements and in other languages as done by Wibisono, Mulyawan, Lubecka, Purwa, and Riani. Wibisono and Purwa conducted a research on advertisements under pragmatic analysis. On the other hand, Mulyawan and Riani explained the research on advertisements using discourse analysis, and Lubecka explained a research about national identity in advertisements. Purwa's and Mulyawan's research focused on the structure to find the persuasive aspects, yet did not referr to the contextual aspects. Based on these previous studies, research on discourse analysis regarding the persuasive power of past advertisements hasn't been studied. Also, the research on the discourse of Javanese-language advertisements published in the period before and the beginning of independence has never been done. Unlike today's advertisements, the advertisements in the past show a different structure. This research focuses on the analysis of superstructures, readers' attention propositions, and sociocultural contexts to explain the persuasive power of advertisement through the languages used in *Panjebar Semangat* magazine published in 1935–1953; the period before and after independence. In the analysis, this research uses the discourse analysis approach; precisely on the theory of discourse of advertisement formulated by Leech and Bolen's, and Fairclough's theory is used to analyze the context in advertising. The results show that the persuasive power of advertisement present in the superstructure (headlines, signature lines, and illustrations) and microstructure of advertisement (the use of imperative and interrogative sentences). The advertisement also succeeds in reflecting the sociocultural state of the nation during the period before and after

---

D. M. Joyowidarbo · A. Fitriana · D. Puspitorini (✉)
Faculty of Humanities, Javanese Literature, Universitas Indonesia, Jakarta, Indonesia
e-mail: dwi.puspitorini@ui.ac.id

D. M. Joyowidarbo
e-mail: diah.mardiningrum@ui.ac.id

A. Fitriana
e-mail: atinfitriana@ui.ac.id

independence. Contextually, the advertisement managed to convey the sociocultural function which showed the Dutch influence was still highly attached to the period before independence. As for the period after independence, there was a national idea contained in the advertisement, which was seen from the elements of discourse in the advertisement. This study contributes to understanding the persuasive functions of utterances in Javanese-language advertisements and how the persuasive power of Javanese used in advertisements gets its perlocutionary effect, as well as to explain how the Javanese culture reflects on the elements of the advertisements.

Keywords Contextual · Structural · Persuasive power · Javanese advertisement · Javanese culture

11.1 Introduction

Advertisements, available in the community, are basically used to convey information and draw public attention to the object advertised. Therefore, advertisement is a communication method to change the role of a reader into a consumer (Wrihatni, 2018). There are several things that need to be considered to achieve that aim, namely the ad-style presentation and the language used that may change over time.

The language used is one of the important aspects of a successful advertisement. Language plays an important role in the delivery of the intended message to the communities; to influence the public and make them interested in the product. This important role of language in advertisement is the manifestation of one of the language functions, namely, the persuasive function. In regard to that function, Goddard (1998) explained that "advertisement" was derived from the Latin verb "*advertere*" means "to divert", it means, the ad has a persuasive function to divert the reader and make them interested in it. In Mulyana and Yahya (2005), it is stated that the persuasive function is highlighted to achieve the perlocutionary effect of a speech. To achieve this perlocutionary effect, the landscape gauge used must have persuasive power. In Brierley (1995), it is stated that successful ads are those that can move the mind and heart and touch the emotion. Therefore, advertisement requires persuasive force as a power to achieve that aim.

Besides influencing (persuasion), advertisements also has other functions: to accelerate decision-making (precipitation), to reinforce a decision that has been taken by the community (reinforcement), and to provide a constant reminder of the product (reminder) (Shimp, 2003). In relation to these functions, the language of advertisement, as a form of social reality, also influences the community in determining their ideas and behavior. The language of advertisement that is constantly being heard will settle in people's minds. In time, the ideas constructed in the language of advertisement have a big influence on people's lives.

Panjebar Semangat, the Javanese-language weekly magazine published in Surabaya in the period before independence (1933), contains advertisements that are quite interesting to study, especially on how advertisements and its language use in the period before and the beginning of independence demonstrated their sociocultural function. The advertisement published in 1939 (1) and 1940 (2) shows that the Dutch were quite influential power holders in Surabaya at that time.

1) **WANITA KANG PINTER**

Arepa olah-olah lan masak apa waé sak-gen.dhingé, bakal bisa kaleksanan Arep gawé kenthang ongklok, hutspot kroket, cornedbeaf, l.s p nganti 139 warna? Arep gawé dhaharan tjara Eropah podheng roepa-roepa, pannekoek, proffertjes, tulband, l.s.p Ys mocca l.s p nganti 64 warna? Toer dipitoetoeri bab

(p-1/30/12/39)

Arepa olah-olah lan masak apa waé sak-gendhingé, bakal bisa kaleksanan, arep gawé kenthang ongklok, hutspot kroket, cornedbeaf l.s.p nganti 139 warna? Arep gawé dhaharan tjara Eropah podheng roepa-roepa, pannekoek, proffertjes, tulband, l.s.p Ys mocca l.s.p nganti 64 warna?

"You want to cook anything you wish; it can be done, you want to make *ongklok* potatoes, croquette, corned beef, etc. up to 139 types? Do you want to make a variety of European dishes such as pudding, pancake, *proffertjes, tulband*, l.s.p Ys mocca and others up to 64 types?"

Example (1) is a food recipe book advertisement. The publication of Dutch snacks recipe book reveals that at that time, Javanese also consumed Dutch snacks. The influence of Dutch culinary is mentioned in Anggreini (2015); it started from the introduction of food ingredients, cooking technology, and teaching in *Sekoelah Roemah Tangga* to learn the culinary habits of Dutch society.

2)

KALENDER 1941.
WONTEN WARNI TIGA.
I. MAANDKALENDER 1941, oekoeran 35 × 44 cm, ngewrat pananggalan Walandi, Djawi lan Tionghoa, oegi bab dinten ageng tigang bangsa, sarta bab dinten ing Karaton Soerakarta lan Ngajogjakarta, katerangaken djangkep, oegi mratélakaken bab garhana. Regi f 0.35 + porto f 0.06.
II. JAV. WANDKALENDER 1941 (almanak dinding), mawi gambar Dalem S. D. I. S. K. Soesoehoenan P. B. XI, sakaiijan Prameswari Dalem G. K. Ratoe Pakoeboewana, oegi ngewrat pananggalan djangkep kados pratélan ing nginggil, sarta oegi ngewrat bab grahana. Regi dalah porto f 0.05. Prajegi moendhoet kalih pisan regi dalah porto f 0.41.

(p.2-/27/12/41)

MAANDKALENDER, JAV. WANDKALENDER
'MONTHLY CALENDAR, JAV. WALL CALENDAR'

Example (2) above is an advertisement for a monthly calendar and wall calendar written in the Dutch language.

The strong influence of the Dutch language and culture on Javanese-language advertisements in the period before independence is certainly not surprising. The situational and cultural context of the two advertisements is evidently depicted in the name of a typical Dutch snack and Dutch calendar. However, the use of national heroes, such as Dr. Soetomo and Ir. Sukarno as well as R. A. Kartini, is found in several advertisements. The following is an example of the use of a figure's name in a pin ad (3).

3)

(p.1-/7/12/40)

Soepaja kita teroes éling marang semangaté pemimpin kita. Saiki kita wis bisa gawé peniti-insigne saka metal (perak-alpacca). Portrété Dr. Soetomo, Ir. Soekarno, R. A. Kartini.

In order for us to keep remembering the spirit of our leaders. Now we can make *insigne* pins from metal (alpaca silver). The pictures of Dr. Soetomo, Ir. Soekarno, R. A. Kartini.'

Advertisement (3) was published during the Dutch colonial period in 1940. However, the external context of the advertisement discourse depicts and illustrates the national movement. The product advertised, a pin, is decorated with a picture of national heroes, though the Indonesian state has not yet existed. Meanwhile, based on its superstructure, the book advertisements published in *Panjebar Semangat* in 1935 and 1938 portrayed the same case, the images of the independence movement figure.

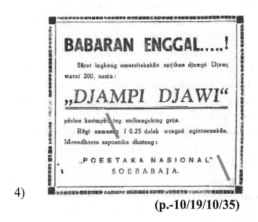

4)

(p.-10/19/10/35)

Rĕgi namoeng f 0.25 dalah wragad ngintoenakĕn. Moendhoeta sapoenika dhateng:„POESTAKA NASIONAL" SOERABAJA

"The price is only f 0.25 .... Buy now at, POESTAKA NASIONAL (National Library)" SURABAYA'

The signature lines of the book advertisement above indicate the existence of a publisher named POESTAKA NASIONAL SOERABAJA. The word NASIONAL is interesting because the Indonesian state has not yet existed. It reflects the advertiser's spirit of nationalism and promotes her/his hope of independence. Based on the explanation above, Javanese-language advertisements in the period before independence showed a sociocultural influence from the Dutch seen from the use of the Dutch language and products. This phenomenon is due to the powerful influence of the Dutch at that time. Therefore, this research attempts to analyze advertisements through discourse analysis. The research aims to find out the presence of persuasive power through its structure and function, and also the sociocultural aspects of the advertisement.

Research on the discourse of advertisements has been conducted on many printed advertisements, both Javanese and other languages. However, the research on the discourse of Javanese advertisements published in the period before or the beginning of independence has never been done so far. The research on the persuasive power of advertisement has been conducted descriptively based on the type of implicature and rhetorical language used on billboards (Purwa, 2015). The results of the study show that the persuasive technique appearing in the ad implicature is used to: (a) glorify the product's excellence, (b) direct order of product usage, and (c) affirm the product's name. This implicature arises from conclusions based on the background knowledge of the product advertised. However, Purwa's research (2015) only focused on the persuasive techniques used in advertisements, so that the persuasive power has not been found in the data. There are many studies on advertisements using discourse analysis. One of them is conducted by Mulyawan (2010). A research, entitled "Discourse Structure of Print Media Advertising Study of Van Djik Structure," was carried out using the theory on the structure of advertisement discourse by Van Dijk (Mulyawan, 2010). The data used is a shampoo product ad: *Lifebuoy Hydro-Protein Shampoo*. The results reveal that the superstructure, especially the body copy, shows persuasive power. The microstructure level, underutilized with grammatical analysis, shows the use of ellipsis, substitution, and references. However, in Mulyawan's research (2010) the persuasive power is seen based on the superstructure elements contained in the advertisements without enclosing the contextual meaning implied in the elements of the advertisement. The fundamental difference between this research and Purwa (2015) and Mulyawan (2010) lies in the results, and the period/range of time of the advertisement publication. Meanwhile, Purwa (2015) and Mulyawan (2010) focused on the structure of discourse and the data used were published from 2000, this research explains the persuasive force used in advertisements in terms of structure and contextual ads published from 1935 to 1950, which contributes to the understanding of the speech persuasive function used in Javanese-language advertisements and how it gets its perlocutionary effect.

In this research, the persuasive power is analyzed in its manifestation to attract readers' attention. Discourse analysis is employed through two main supporting elements, namely internal and external elements (Mulyana & Yahya, 2005). The internal element analysis of advertisement discourse is conducted through superstructures (Leech, 1966) and the propositions structure (Bolen, 1984). The analysis of the external elements is conducted through social and cultural context analysis (Fairclough, 1998). This research focuses on superstructure analysis, attention-attractor proposition, and sociocultural context was which compiwled to explain the persuasive power of advertisement through the presentation and its language use in *Panjebar Semangat* magazine published in 1935–1953. The research on the persuasive power of advertisement has been conducted descriptively based on the type of implicature and rhetorical language used on billboards (Purwa, 2015). The results of the study show that the persuasive technique appearing in the ad implicature is used to: (a) glorify the product's excellence, (b) direct order of product usage, and (c) affirm the product's name. This implicature arises from conclusions based on the background knowledge of the product advertised. If compared with this similar research by Purwa (2015), this research focuses on the structure of advertisement, while the research conducted by Purwa (2015) focuses on the persuasive techniques used in advertising. The purpose of this research is to analyze the structure and the contextual meaning of Javanese advertisements. This is done because the data used in this research were produced in different periods, whereas the data used by Purwa (2015) and Mulyawan (2010) are published from 2000.

11.2 Methodology

The data used in this research are Javanese-language advertisements published in *Panjebar Semangat* magazine. They are divided into two: the pre-independence edition 1935–1942 and the post-independence edition 1951–1953 (both are stored in the National Library of Indonesia). For the purpose of this research, there are 130 advertisements collected. This research is conducted qualitatively because the determinant tool is derived from the language itself (Sudaryanto, 2015). In Sudaryanto (2015), it is stated that the determinant tool in the framework of qualitative method is and always was part of the language of the research object, such as words (rejection, prepositions, adverbial, etc.), syntactic functions (subject, object, predicate, etc.), clause, syllable, and intonation. After the data are collected, the data are classified based on the distribution of the advertisement superstructure (Leech, 1966), namely, headline, signature line, standing details, and illustrations. The classification is also carried out based on its intrinsic element, namely, the type of sentence (imperative, declarative, and interrogative) and the advertisement type which includes the name of the figures, national ideas, and national vocabulary. The data is coded in the order of page number/date/month/year. For example, the advertisement data published on June 5, 1951, page 11, then the code is p.11–5/ 6/51.

The analysis in this research uses a discourse analysis approach to advertisement, namely the superstructure (Leech, 1966). According to Leech (1966), advertisements consist of the headline, signature line, body copy, standing detail, and illustration and the approach to the structure of advertising discourse in terms of propositions. In regard to standing detail, Mardjadikara (2004) referred to it as the baseline or information that included logos, slogans, company names, etc., and later, the illustration is referred to as part of visual elements. According to Bolen (1984) (Rani et al., 2004), the structure of advertisement discourse in terms of its proposition consists of the main headlines to attract attention, ad body to communicate, and closing to change behavior. In this research, the analysis of discourse structure focuses on the headline to explain how propositions as attention–attractor serve as the persuasive power of advertisements. Proposition, in this respect, is the sentence used in the headline as the persuasive power of advertisements. In addition, the contextual meaning of the discourse on advertisement is analyzed using social–cultural practices analysis by Fairclough (Eriyanto, 2001) In this level, the analysis is carried out on sociocultural practices. Fairclough (2011) divides the analysis of sociocultural practices into three levels of analysis: situational, institutional, and social level. These three levels of analysis do not constitute a level of analysis that must be taken through each, rather it can be chosen at one level, because each level is served to reveal designated results. This research employs social analysis to see the effect of changes in society at the social and cultural levels toward the discourse contained in the media. According to Fairclough, the discourse that appears in the media is determined by changes in society.

11.3 Analysis

As a form of discourse, the advertisement language has distinct characteristics, so that in advertisement, the language used is one of the important aspects of successful advertisement (Mulyana. & Yahya, 2005). Mulyana (2005), states that advertisement language must become the manifestation or presentation of the advertisers' desire to the public. Regarding the statement, the advertisements posted can affect the community or the other way around. That influence can be reflected in the way the advertisement is delivered. In general, the persuasive power of this research lies in the superstructure elements, propositions, and contextual aspects. Therefore, in this research, the explanation/discussion of the delivery of Javanese-language advertisements in 1935–1953 is divided into three sections: superstructure analysis, proposition analysis, and contextual analysis.

11.3.1 Superstructure Analysis

In *Panjebar Semangat* magazine edition of 1935–1953, the ad superstructure looks different from today's advertisement. The analysis shows that the ad superstructure at that time tended to be in the form of a long narrative (around 85–230 words) and was often found using headlines, signature lines, and only a few advertisements that used illustrations (pictures) as a persuasive power.

11.3.1.1 Headline

According to Book and Schick (1997a), the headline form serves in conveying a message, claim, or order, arousing curiosity, offering, and introducing products through words, sentences, or slogans and there is no such necessity for its presence in an advertisement. In the data, headlines that show persuasive power are found in the form of big-size fonts, the use of bold fonts, imperatives, and introducing products through sentences, the names of national heroes, and slogans. In addition, the data also show that not all advertisements consist of one headline, but there are also those that consist of two headlines because they meet the characteristics of the headline form mentioned above. Here are examples of advertisements with persuasive powers that lie in the headlines; almanac book advertisement (1) that shows persuasive power on the slogan and price which are printed in bold with larger size compared to other letters on the ad and *kethoprak* advertisement (2) with the persuasive power implemented on the imperative headlines which were published in a magazine in 1935, *book advertisement from 1940* (3) where persuasive power formed on the bold printed slogan using capital letters, and with the distinct sentence placement compared to other sentences in the ad, and *In the horoscope book ad* (4) published in 1953, the headlines were presented in Indonesian, though the contents of the ad were in Javanese which will trigger the audience's attention along with the use of capital letters and large font size.

(1)

(p. -8/7/12/35)

In the advertisement of the almanac book above, there are two forms of headlines providing price information and slogans which then cause readers' curiosity. Headline (1) offering the price of product "F 3000" is a form that causes curiosity because it is published in a bold and larger size which is much larger than the letters on the body copy so that it attracts the reader's attention to read it. In the advertisement, the slogan headline *Larise kaja Roedjak Lotis* 'The best-seller one like Roedjak Lotis' is printed differently than other letters on the ad; the largest size, printed in bold, different type of font, underlined, and located on the top of the section of the advertisement. Besides the attractive visuals, the persuasive power of advertisement also lies in the image of *"Roedjak Lotis"* as one of the most popular foods of the community at that time. The use of the word "bestseller" shows that the book is as favored as *Roedjak Lotis*. In other words, the advertisement conveys the message that books are popular in the community. Based on that explanation, the slogan and price are highlighted and serve as the persuasive power of the advertisement so that consumers will be interested in reading advertisements and buying the products. Below is an example of a *kethoprak* ad in 1935 which consists of three headlines,

(2)
(p.-16/26/10/35)

The two headlines were constructed in the imperative form, namely, *ADJA LALI, AJO ENGGAL NONTON* "Don't Forget, Let's Watch" and *Ajo, loer, rame-rame, ngiras njokong Gedhong kita* 'Come on, brothers, come together, support our House." Both headlines contain instructions so that readers are willing to come to watch the kethoprak event as well as to support the continuity of the building where it takes place. Meanwhile, the headline "Tjak Doerasim......!" is the name of a famous East Javanese Ludruk figure and is well-liked by the public, so that the presence of that character in Kethoprak who will be performing will attract readers to watch.

(3)
> BOEKOE-BOEKOE.
> Keterangan Pedoman Batin, dening: Soeardiman Ranoewidjojo, saka Oesaha Boekoe Kepandaian, Batavia C.
> Boekoe iki isiné katoedjokaké marang panggoelawenthah toemrap para pandoe, rinengga ing gambar-gambar saperloené.

(p.-2/27/1/40)

In the book advertisement (3) published in 1940, the headline, in the form of sentences, is employed to introduce the product along with the author and publisher information. The headline sentence is BOEKOE-BOEKOE. *Keterangan Pedoman Batin, dening: Soeardiman Ranoewidjojo, saka Oesaha Boekoe Kepandaian, Batavia C.* "The Inner Guidlines, by: Soerdiman Ranoewidjojo, from the Oesaha Boekoe Kepandaian, Batavia C." The Headline sentence is bold-printed, and the word BOEKOE-BOEKOE is capitalized so that readers are interested in reading it.

(4)

(p.-5/30/5/53)

In the horoscope book ad (4) published in 1953, the headlines were presented in Indonesian, though the contents of the ad were in Javanese. The word "PENTING" in the ad is seen as a form of headlines that stimulate readers' curiosity. Because lexically, it is important that the headlines are presented using capital letters with the largest font size of all words in the ad, thus it can trigger readers to read the contents of the ad further.

11.3.1.2 Signature Line (Identity)

Leech (1966) states that the signature line contains the name of the product and may be in the form of a slogan. According to Gieszinger (2001), signature lines consist of three forms, namely independent signature lines, marked signature lines, and unmarked signature lines. From the data published in 1935–1951, there are independent signature lines, which are syntactically and graphically separated from body copy and marked signature lines that are syntactically integrated with body copy, but graphically are marked by the use of bold or capital letters, which represents the persuasive power of the advertisement itself.

a. Independent Signature Lines

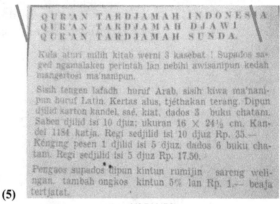

(5)

(p.-4/25/4/53)

The Holy Qur'an advertisement displayed in 1953 above is an example of an ad using Independent Signature Lines. In the Qur'an advertisement above, the identity of the product being advertised stands alone, and is located separately from the paragraph and syntactically different. *QUR'AN TARDJAMAH INDONESIA, QUR'AN TARDJAMAH DJAWI, QUR'AN TARDJAMAH SUNDA.* 'QUR'AN INDONESIAN TRANSLATION, QUR'AN JAVANESE TRANSLATION, QUR'AN SUNDANESE TRANSLATION'. Based on the signature line, it shows that the advertised product is the holy Al-Qur'an in three languages (Javanese, Sundanese, and Indonesian). The signature line in the ad, besides introducing the product, is also an attraction because its font size is larger than the other and boldly printed so that they stand out more and shows the persuasive power.

b. Marked Signature Lines

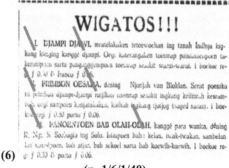

(6)

(p.-1/6/1/40)

The ad above is a book advertisement published in 1940. In this advertisement, there are three marked signature lines. They are located in paragraphs and are not syntactically separated from other words in sentences. Those three signature lines are the titles of the advertised book products, namely DJAMPI DJAWI, PRIMBON OESADA, and PANOENTOEN BAB OLAH-OLAH. The three signature lines are presented using a larger font size and capital letters. It indicates that the signature lines in the ad also function as ad attractions to persuade the readers.

11.3.1.3 Standing Details

In the advertisement superstructure, the *standing details* are found to convey information in the form of coupons or additional information related to products that are usually written in small font sizes (Leech, 1966). In the data analysis, it is found that *Standing details* are not found in all advertisements. If there are, the standing details found are written inconsistently; small letters, some are as large as the signature line, and are bigger than the headline. The following are examples of balm ads (6),

(5)

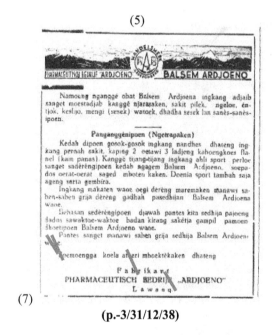

(7)

(p.-3/31/12/38)

Balm advertisement (7) is an example of an advertisement that its standing details are bigger than the signature line and body copy which indicates the persuasive power. Standing details in the advertisement (7) are presented in two styles: a lowercase letter in the sentence *Soemoegga koela atoeri mboektèkaken dhateng* and capital letters in the sentence *Fabrikant PHARMACEUTISCH BEDRIJF,,ARDJOENO" L a w a n g.* "I invite to prove to the FACTORY OF PHARMACEUTICAL COMPANY,

ARDJOENO L a w a n g." In this matter, lowercase means the same size as the body copy whereas the uppercase letters are larger than the body copy and even the same as the signature line. The product name BALSEM ARDJOENO is positioned at the top of the ad. The sentence contains additional information about the name of the company and the city where the product is produced.

11.3.1.4 Illustration

Illustrations are pictures or photos of products, models, or scenes to attract people's attention. In the data from 1935 to 1938, illustrations were rarely found in advertisements, only in kethoprak, pins, and dentists' advertisements. The use of illustrations popularly began from 1939 to 1953 in various types of advertisements, such as *kethoprak*, book, ice cream, radio technician, almanac, identity plate, drug, herb, and calendar advertisements. Based on the data, the advertisements that use illustrations most are *kethoprak* (displays photos of actors) and books (display front cover images). The observation reveals that the illustrations used in the advertisement show persuasive functions, because the images of the product and unrelated images yet drawing public attention. The following are examples of advertisements in *Panjebar Semangat* magazine that employ persuasive power illustrations.

(8)

(p.-9/21/10/50)

The Calendar ad (8) in 1950 above displays an example of decorative pictures as illustrations to support the physical description of the calendar. It is written in the sentence *Iki gambaré rerengganè kalender (penanggalan) kita tahun 1951. Wujudé, bakal luwih gedé saka gambar ing nduwur sarta nganggo kleur warna: abang, idjo, soklat lan putih.* "This is the design of our calendar in 1951. It is bigger than the picture above and it uses various colors: red, green, brown, and white." The sentence elaborates on the size, decoration, and color that are used on the calendar product, and states that the image in the advertisement is the physical example of that elaboration to attract readers' attention as a persuasion.

(8)

(18/4/53)

Advertisement (8) is an example of a book advertisement, which uses illustration as an attention drawer. But the illustration doesn't use the product picture. The book product is entitled PERTJAJA DIRI PRIBADI, but the illustration used is not related to the book advertised but to the headline. The illustration contained in the advertisement is a sketch of a person talking using a speaker. Therefore, it is relevant to the sentence in the headline, "Hello, hello, attention, attention …!" and it aims to attract the reader's attention, hence containing the persuasive function.

11.3.2 Proposition Analysis

From the aspect of a proposition of advertisement, the headline is one of the crucial elements of the discourse (Bolen, 1984). If related to its objectives, the headline aims to attract attention (Rani, 2004). Therefore, it is necessary to analyze the types of propositions in the headlines used to see how sentences persuade readers in 1935–1953. Based on the analysis, to attract the reader's attention, the advertisement sentence is constructed in the imperative and interrogative sentences.

11.3.2.1 The Imperative Proposition

In the ad sentences, imperative sentences use the suffix *a-* and *-na* affixed to verbs. The imperative words are *ajo, sumangga, mangga* and the request words are *perlu, kedah, projogi, betjik, dan pantes*. Verbs in the advertisement are often found with the suffix *a-* as in the verbs *moendhoet* and *toekoe*. Besides using suffixes, advertisements also use imperative sentences with imperative words which are pragmatically meaningful signs of politeness and are often found written in the speech level *krama*. Meanwhile, it is also often found in imperative sentences that are pragmatically meaningful as a request (appeal), that aims to encourage the reader to use and hand the product. Based on that elaboration, the imperative sentence used in the advertisement (1) serves as a description (baseline) to persuade the reader to buy the product. The following is an example of an imperative sentence,

(9) **Moendhoeta** *sapoenika dhateng:"POESTAKA NASIONAL" SOERABAJA* (hlm.-7/19/10/35).
'Buy now at: „POESTAKA NASIONAL" SOERABAJA'
(10) **Toekoewa** *saiki sing tjap-tjapan ka III. a f 0.15"* (p.-5/18/11/39).
'Buy the 3rd edition now. A f 0.15'

The verbs *moendhoet* and *toekoe* in the sentences (9) and (10) mean transactions of exchanging money for goods marked with the suffix *-a*. The presence of the verb "buy" makes up the imperative sentence. Based on this, the verb *moendhoet* and *toekoe* which makes the imperative sentence functions to persuade readers to buy the product (book).

(11) *Para maos,* **soemangga** *sami ngĕrsakakĕn moendhoet Sĕpatoe – Selop Sandhal, tas, bal, pakean kapal.* (p.-1/20/6/35).
'Everyone, please buy shoes - slipper, sandal, bag, ball, clothes for sailing'

The sentence (11) uses imperative mood *soemangga* as a means of politeness or social courtesy. In sentence (11), the imperative mood serves to invite the reader to buy shoes, sandals, bags, and clothing products. In other words, it makes the sentence function imperatively but in a polite manner.

11.3.2.2 Interrogative Proposition

If compared with the imperative proposition, the interrogative proposition is rarely found. Interrogative prepositions often attract greater attention if the questions cope with the problems experienced by consumers (Rani 2004: 69). Based on the data, interrogative sentences present in the ad serve to convey the excellence of the product to the reader. This example is a recipe book advertisement:

(12) *Arepa olah-olah lan masak apa waé sak-gendhingé, bakal bisa kaleksanan, arep gawé kenthang ongklok, hutspot kroket, cornedbeaf l.s.p nganti 139 warna? Arep gawé dhaharan tjara Eropah podheng roepa-roepa, pannekoek, proffertjes, tulband, l.s.p Ys mocca l.s.p nganti 64 warna? Toer dipitoetoeri bab mrènata mèdja dhahar lan oerot-oerotané wetoening dahahar, kabèh maoe bisa tinemoe ing BOEKOE OLAH-OLAH tjilid II.* (p.-1/30/12/39)

"Want to cook anything you wish, it can be done, want to make *ongklok* potatoes, croquette, corned beef l.s.p up to 139 kinds? Want to make various European dishes such as pudding, pancake, *poffertjes, tulband*, l.s.p Ys mocca l.s.p up to 64 kinds? As well as being told how to set the dining table and the manner, all of that can be found in BOEKOE OLAH-OLAH II."

In the interrogative sentence (12), the excellence of the product is mentioned such as the useful contents of the book about cooking. That sentence implies that if the reader has a BOEKOE OF OLAH-OLAH II, the reader can find out information about how to cook European foods, how to set the table, and the table manners. Based on this, interrogative sentences, besides conveying information about product excellence, are also indirectly serving to attract the attention of readers to own the product.

11.3.3 Contextual Analysis

Basically, a discourse consists of a context. According to Sumarlam in Andriyani (2013) the context of discourse is the internal aspects of discourse and everything that externally covers a discourse. The analysis of social–cultural practices by Fairclough consists of three levels of analysis, namely situational, institutional, and social (Eriyanto, 2001). This research employs social-level analysis to see the effect of community changing from the macro aspect, that is the political system and the cultural system of society comprehensively. In the data, sentences with a strong situational and cultural context are found that depict the condition of the nation before and after independence. The results of the analysis show that changes in society in the period pre-independence and post-independence influenced the products advertisement style. It can be observed through dictions, names of national figures, national language use, and words related to nationality. Here is the elaboration.

11.3.3.1 The Independence Movement Figures

In the advertisement of book (1) and pin (2), several names of national figures are presented as the product excellence. In addition, those names are also presented in the contents. The following is an example of a book advertisement (1) and pin (2).

(13) *Jaikoe boekoe kang gedhe banget, oekoeran 23 X 30 c.m. kandele 76 katja, toer rinengga ing gambar-gambare para pemimpin, Dr. Tjiptomangoenkoesoemo, Ir. Soekarno, nganti Mr. Latuharhary sarta isi pitoetoer lan wedjangan kang paedah, kang ora bakal mamboe (wadhang) disimpen lawas.* (p.-8/27/11/37)

'It's a very large book, dimension 23 X 30 c.m. 76 pages, and decorated with the pictures of leaders, Dr. Tjiptomangoenkoesoemo, Ir. Soekarno, and Mr. Latuharhary, also completed with useful advice that will last forever.'

The sentences in the advertisement above were published in 1937; in the period before Indonesia's independence. The sentence tells the product excellence decorated with images of leaders. Those leaders are Dr. Tjiptomangoenkoesoemo, Ir. Soekarno, and Mr. Latuharhary. Dr. Tjiptomangoenkoesoemo is one of the founders of Boedi Oetomo—a modern organization in Indonesia in 1908, and he's one of the founders of the first political party in the colonial era named Indische Partij in 1912. Ir. Soekarno at that time was known for his struggle as an activist from Jong Java of Surabaya, and also the founder of the Algemeene Club 1926 as the embryo of the Indonesian National Party which was founded later in 1927. Mr. Latuharhary was the chairman of *Serikat Ambon* (Ambon Union) in 1928. By referring to the year of publication and the name of the figures in the advertisement, it shows that there was a spirit of nationalism in the society before independence. Indonesian nationalism initially emerged as an answer to colonialism. The experience of suffering as a colonized resulted in the spirit of solidarity as a community that must rise up and live to become an independent nation (Abidin, 2017). It also relates to the Javanese culture of *gotong royong* "mutual cooperation." The following is an example of a pins product advertisement that mentions the names of independence movement figures,

> (14) <u>Soepaja kita teroes éling marang semangaté pemimpin kita</u>. *Saiki kita wis bisa gawé peniti-insigne saka metal (perak-alpacca). Portrété Dr. Soetomo, Ir. Soekarno, R.A. Kartini.* (p.-1/7/12/40)
>
> 'In order for us to keep remembering to the spirit of our leaders. Now we can make *insigne* pins from metal (alpaca silver). The pictures of <u>Dr. Soetomo, Ir. Soekarno, R.A. Kartini</u>.

Advertisement (14) is a pin product ad, which was published in 1940; the period before independence. The names of the nation's leaders are mentioned in the sentence *Portrété Dr. Soetomo, Ir. Soekarno, R.A. Kartini* compiled with their photo and the product. Dr. Soetomo was the founding father of Boedi Utomo—the first movement organization in Indonesia in 1908. Ir. Sukarno was also a national movement figure too. While R.A. Kartini is a figure in the national movement of Indonesian women who have raised the position of women. Beside the name of national figures, the product excellence is also published in *Soepaja kita teroes éling marang semangaté pemimpin kita*, which means that the product can make consumers remember the spirit of the leader. Semantically, a leader means a person who leads. In the sentence, the leader refers to Dr. Soetomo, Ir. Soekarno, R.A. Kartini. The presence of those names as the product excellence in the period before independence shows the efforts of the community in promoting the spirit of nationalism.

11.3.3.2 National Language

In advertisements, the presence of words that indicate the use of national languages such as "Indonesian" and "basa kita dhewe" on book products is used as the advantage. It shows that the use of national language is something that the community is proud of. Indonesian language has become the national language after it was declared in the Youth Oath in 1928, particularly in the sentence 'We are the Sons and Daughters of Indonesia, respect the language of unity, Indonesian language.' Here are the examples of ad sentences that represent the national language,

> (15) <u>Basané Indonésia,</u> *ning iya runtut, ija gampang, dimangertèni, mentes, pepak lan maremakè.* (p.-7/20/6/53)
>
> '<u>The language is Indonesian,</u> it's coherent, easy to understand, brief and insightful, complete, and satisfying.'

> (16) *Boekoe pèngetan nalika conferentle Badan Perlindoengan Perempoean Indonesia dalam Perkawinan ing 22–23 Juli 1939 ing Mataram. Basanè Indonesia, karengga gambar-gambar sawatara, dloewangè aloes.* (p.-2/27/1/40)
>
> The handbook at the conference of Indonesia's Women Protection Agency in Marriage on July 22–23, 1939 in Mataram. The language is Indonesian, decorated with pictures.

In advertisements (15) and (16), the product excellence is shown through the use of the Indonesian language. It is written in the sentence *Basané Indonésia* "Indonesian Language." The suffix *-né* in the word *Basa* refers to the book advertised, that is the handbook in the conference program of Indonesia's Women's Protection Agency in Marriage. The sentence of book advertisement (16) was published in 1953; a period after the declaration of Indonesia's independence. The use of the Indonesian language in advertisements after independence shows that advertisement is also a medium to promote the sense of pride of Indonesian as the national language. The same thing is also found in the book advertisement (16), which also uses the national language as a product excellence. The use of national language is also found in the sentence *Basané Indonésia*. The difference with advertisement number (15) is that advertisement (16) was published in 1940; the period before independence. This is interesting because even though it was still in the colonial period, the Indonesians dared to present the nationality elements in advertisements.

11.3.3.3 National Vocabulary

In the sentences in advertisements published in the period before independence, the use of the words *bangsa* "nation," *nasional* "national," *Indonesia* "Indonesia," *nusa* "homeland," and *negara* "country." The vocabularies are related to nationality and show the importance of supporting and advancing the nation. In the sentences, some of the vocabularies are constructed in the form of invitation, and the description of product excellence. The products that present these vocabularies are *kethoprak* art show and book. The following are examples of advertisements in 1935, 1936, and 1937,

(17) *Ajo, loer, rame-rame, ngiras njokong Gedhong kita...kĕtoprak,,SRIWOELAN" kang main ing Pendhapa Gedong Nasional.* (p.-11/26/10/35)
"Come on, brothers, come together, support our House. Ketoprak, SRIWOELAN "which will be performed at the hall of National Building."

The sentence above (5) was published in 1935 in *kethoprak* art advertisement. The word *Gedhong* refers to the building where *kethoprak* performance is held. The name of the building is mentioned in the advertisement as *Pendhapa Gedhong Nasional* "the hall of National Building." By using the verb *njokong* "to help, it can be inferred that the ads sentence appeals to the readers to support the existence of the building. This is because the high number of audiences of *Kethoprak* event held in the building means that the existence of the building is also saved. The use of the word 'National' in the name of the building shows the nationality characteristics and socialized through the ad. In addition, the national ideas also present in the word *Gedhong kita* "Our Building." The word *kita* refers to the people of Indonesia which also refers to the word *Nasional*. The following is an example of a book product advertisement that uses the words "nusa" and "bangsa,"

(18) *Boekoe poenika para poetri prajogi simpĕn, sagĕda dados panggoerandaning penggalih toemrap poetri ingkang anggajoeh santosaning tekad, kangge ngoehorakĕn bangsa toewin noesa.* (p.-3/4/1/36)
'This book should be kept by women, so that it becomes a guide for women who want to achieve good determination to unite the country and nation.'

The sentence (6) was published in 1936; the period before the declaration of independence, yet it contained the words *nusa* "homeland" and *bangsa* "nation." The word "nusa," which semantically means an island shows the geographical characteristics of Indonesia which consist of islands. While the word "bangsa," which semantically means a group of people from various ancestors, customs, languages, and histories, strongly resembles the characteristics of various ethnicities in Indonesia. The advertisement calls on young women to handbooks because the book is useful as a guide for young women to realize the national vision; to unite the homeland and the nation. Referring to the year of the publication of advertisements, its nationalism aspect is taken as the product superiority, which later shows the importance of the spirit of nationalism in society.

(19) *Para maos kang bisa golek mitra abonne anjar sidjie wae, kedjaba ategesmeloe-meloe asoeng kemadjoewan toemrap bangsa kita, dene woewoeh sidji bangsane kang seneng matja Koran kabangsan kang maedahi, oega bakal nampa tandha, trima kasih: saka ita, awoejoed barang kang gedhe adjine, kang paedah toemrap batinne, jaikoe boekoe CONGRES INDONESIA RAJA.* (p.-3/27/11/37)

'Readers who can look for just one new customer, who participates in the progress of our nation, and one who likes to read useful *Koran kebangsaan* (national papers) will also receive a token of gratitude from us in a form of high-value goods, that are useful for the mind, namely CONGRES INDONESIA RAYA book.'

The sentence (7) above was published in 1937; a period before independence. In the advertisement, the superiority of book products is conveyed, which includes the quality of the contents and physical form of the book. Furthermore, the elements of nationalism and the superiority of the product are conveyed through the phrase *Kabangsan* newspaper which means "our national product." The words *asoeng kemadjoewan toemrap bangsa kita* shows enthusiasm for the development of the nation. The title of the book CONGRES INDONESIA RAJA represents the name of the Indonesian nation, because the content of the book discusses the Indonesian nation. Based on the year of the ad publication, the advertisement depicted that there was a nationalism, and the advertisement was a means to channel the spirit of unity as the nation.

Based on the analysis that has been done on the data of the Javanese-language magazine *Panjebar Semangat* in 1935–1953, it was found that the persuasive power of the advertisement lies in the structure of the ad presentation and the proposition. In addition, advertisements reflect the social and cultural background of the community at that time. The basic difference between today's advertisement and advertising in the past lies in its the presentation. Based on that, an advertisement must have its own characteristics in order to attract the public attention and make it memorable by using model, song, visual, and catchy slogans in accordance with trends as the persuasive power.

In *Panjebar Semangat* magazine, the advertisements tend to be descriptively presented and contain detailed information about the product or service advertised. Moreover, ad persuasive power stands out in the imperative and interrogative sentences. Another finding that was discovered in the advertisements was that we could trace the condition of the Indonesian socially and culturally before and after independence. In the advertisements, there are also sentences that reflect Javanese culture like *unggah-ungguh* (social courtesy). This can be seen in the advertisement sentences using *krama* speaking manner in promoting products. In addition, through advertisements also we can know the community's need that was popular at that time. In the period before independence, the influence of Western culture, especially the Netherlands, looked strong on the products advertised. Nevertheless, the idea of nationality in advertisements is still present in the Javanese-language advertisements. The idea of nationality comes through the product advertised, the use of the name of the independence movement figures, and the use of the Indonesian language.

11.4 Conclusion

This research reveals that Javanese advertisements circulated in the period before independence had the same elements as advertisements today. Likewise, its persuasive power was also presented through the same elements, though few differences in promotion methods were found. In general, advertisements are made by articulating the advantages of a product. However, based on the analysis of the data in this research, it is found that advertisements promoting their products were not presented through the articulation of the product's superiority. This study also reveals that the persuasive power of advertisement reflects the social and cultural background of the community at that time.

This research shows that advertisements can be used as research data to observe social and cultural aspects of society at a designated time. Furthermore, this research also provides a new approach to the understanding of the sociocultural conditions of the Javanese people before and after the independence through the analysis of advertisement. The results assert that advertisements published in the 1930s did not show the spirit of nationalism. However, the advertisements published in the 1940s clearly presented the spirit of nationalism through images of national figures such as Soekarno and Kartini.

Linguistically, this research offers a comprehensive understanding of the influence of Indonesian and foreign languages on Javanese that has occurred since pre-independence period. Due to the Dutch control, the foreign language that influenced the advertisement was Dutch. The unique finding in this research is the absence of *Krama* language of Javanese in the advertisements today that was commonly used in advertisements in the 1930s and 1940s. Javanese *Krama* language is used in the advertisements targeting the segmented market (social stratum), usually the educated one. This proves that social factors determine the use of *Krama* language more than kinship and age factors. The findings of this research strengthen Rizky and Puspitorini's (2019) research which examined the use of Javanese speech levels in a Javanese film entitled Kartini. Moreover, Poedjosoedarmo (1979) and Harjawiyana (2001) did not mention the factors that determine the use of Krama speech level of Javanese in their book on the etiquette of Javanese language.

Acknowledgements This work was supported by Universitas Indonesia's Research Grant (PITMA B 2019) managed by DRPM UI/Indonesian Ministry of Research, Technology, and Higher Education's Research Grant (PTUPT 2019) managed by DRPM UI / DRPM UI

References

Abidin, Z. (2017). Representasi Nasionalisme dalam Film Nagabonar Jadi 2 Analisis Semiotika Roland Barthes Mengenai Representasi Nilai-Nilai Nasionalisme Dalam Film Nagabonar Jadi 2, 2(1), 42–61.
Andriyani, F. (2013). Analisis Tekstual Dan Kontekstual Dalam Novel Traju Mas, 03(02), 12–18.
Anggraeni, P. (2015). Menu Populer Hindia Belanda (1901–1942): Kajian Pengaruh Budaya Eropa Terhadap Kuliner Indo. Jurnal Sejarah Dan Budaya, 9(1), 88–95.
Bolen, W. H. (1984). Advertising. Wiley.
Book, A. C., & Schick, C. D. (1997). Fundamentals of copy & layout. Lincolnwood: National Textbook Company.
Brierley, S. (1995). The advertising handbook.
Eriyanto. (2001). Analisis Wacana: Pengantar Analisis Teks Media. Yogyakarta: Lkis Yogyakarta.
Fairclough, N. (1998). Political discourse in the media: An analytical framework. In Approaches to media discourse (pp. 142–162). Oxford: Blackwell.
Fairclough, N., & Publishing., B. (2011). Media discourse. London; New York: Bloomsbury Academic.
Gieszinger, S. (2001). The history of advertising language: The advertisements in the times from 1788 To 1996. Peter Lang.
Goddard, A. (1998). The language of advertising: Written texts. Routledge.
Harjawiyana, H., & Supriya, T. (2001). Marsudi unggah-ungguh basa Jawa. Penerbit Kanisius. https://books.google.co.id/books?id=nylaupbAwEwC.
Leech, G. (1966). English in advertising: A linguistic study of advertising in Great Britain. London: Longman.
Lubecka, A. (2013). National identities on display. The Role of Advertisements in the Management of Polish National Identity. https://doi.org/10.7592/EP.2.lubecka.
Mulyana., & Yahya, M. (2005). Kajian Wacana: Teori, Metode & Aplikasi Prinsip-Prinsip Analisis Wacana. Yogyakarta: Tiara Wacana.
Mulyawan, I. W. (2010). Makna dan Pesan Iklan Media Cetak Kajian Hipersemiotika I Wayan Mulyawan, 15(28).
Poedjosoedarmo, S., & dan Pengembangan Bahasa, P. P. (1979). Tingkat tutur bahasa Jawa. Pusat Pembinaan dan Pengembangan Bahasa, Departemen Pendidikan dan Kebudayaan.
Purwa, I. M. (2015). Implikatur Dan Retorika Pemakaian Bahasa Pada Iklan Papan Nama, 27(1), 13–24.
Rizky & Puspitorini. (2019). Tingkat Tutur Bahasa Jawa dalam Film Kartini. Journal of Language Education, Literature, and Local Culture, 1(2).
Rani, A., Arifin, B., & Martutik. (2004). Analisis Wacana: Sebuah Kajian Bahasa Dalam Pemakaian. Malang: Bayumedia.
Riani. (2015). Kajian Wacana Iklan pada Pesan Singkat (SMS). Jurnal Kajian Bahasa, 4(1), 47–60.
Shimp, T. A. (2003). Periklanan Promosi & Aspek Tambahan Komunikasi Pemasaran Terpadu, Jilid I (Edisi 5). Jakarta: Erlangga.
Sudaryanto. (2015). Metode dan Aneka Teknik Analisis Bahasa: Pengantar Penelitian Wahana Kebudayaan Secara Linguistik. Duta Wacana University Press.
Wibisono. (2008). Representasi Nasionalisme Dalam Iklan Korporat Pt. Gudang Garam Tbk. Jurnal Ilmiah SCRIPTURA, 2(1), 38–47.

Wrihatni, N. S. (2018). *Utilizing local content: strategy to get closer to the consumers through suprastructure and positioning analysis.* https://doi.org/10.4108/eai.21-12-2018.2282738.

Diah Mardiningrum Joyowidarbo was born in Jakarta, 5 June 1997. She is the second child of three siblings. She graduated from Elementary School in 2010 (SD Seruni Don Bosco), and Junior High School in 2013 (SMP Pangudi Luhur Jakarta), and Senior High School in 2015 (SMA Tarakanita 1 Jakarta). She is currently a student (batch 2015) at Javanese Literature Study Program at Faculty of Humanities, Universitas Indonesia.

Atin Fitriana is a lecturer of Javanese literature at Universitas Indonesia. She was born in 1990. Atin Fitriana holds a bachelor's degree from Javanese Literature in Universitas Indonesia and a master's degree from Linguistics Program in Universitas Indonesia. Her thesis in bachelor's and master's degree is about linguistics in Old Javanese. Now, she takes doctoral degree at the Linguistics Department, Universitas Indonesia.

Dwi Puspitorin was born in Magelang, 11 October 1964. Currently, she is teaching Javanese, Old Javanese, Javanese Morphology and Syntax at the Faculty of Humanities, Universitas Indonesia. She conducted many studies on Javanese morphology and syntax; both modern and old Javanese. She also teaches Indonesian for Foreign Speakers. She has published several books, among them are Wiwara: pengantar bahasa dan kebudayaan Jawa (Gramedia 2001), Untaian Bahasa (LBI FIB UI, 2010), Everyday Indonesian (Kesaint Blanc, 2013), Jalan Bahasa Pelajaran Praktis Tata Bahasa Bahasa Indonesia (Penaku, 2014), Bahasa Jawa Dasar (Penaku, 2015). She also has published some scientific articles: Bismaprawa: An Old Javanese Text from the Merapi-Merbabu Tradition Derived from Adiparwa (co-author); Utarasabda in Java and Bali (co-author), Particle pwa and ta in the Old Javanese Language; Passive Diathesis in Javanese (bersama Atin Fitriana); Kajian Linguistik Bahasa Jawa Kuno dalam Sastra Gocara Journal of Old Javanese Studies Volume II No. 2 October 2017.

Open Access This chapter is licensed under the terms of the Creative Commons Attribution 4.0 International License (http://creativecommons.org/licenses/by/4.0/), which permits use, sharing, adaptation, distribution and reproduction in any medium or format, as long as you give appropriate credit to the original author(s) and the source, provide a link to the Creative Commons license and indicate if changes were made.

The images or other third party material in this chapter are included in the chapter's Creative Commons license, unless indicated otherwise in a credit line to the material. If material is not included in the chapter's Creative Commons license and your intended use is not permitted by statutory regulation or exceeds the permitted use, you will need to obtain permission directly from the copyright holder.

Chapter 12
Understanding Promises from the Perspective of Argumentation: The Cases from Presidential Debates

Dwi Purwanto and Filia

Abstract Promises in political context, especially through the notion of commitment and intention, have captivated researchers in the field of linguistics and philosophy of language and mind in recent times. In a political context, promises may have other purposes, for gaining supports, besides declaring the sincere intention to do a future action. The notion would potentially flout Austin's felicity conditions and Gricean maxim of quality, hence, proposing more challenges in identifying promises through the concept of intentionalism. This article aims to address the challenges by proposing a theoretical model of argumentative commitment. 161 utterances from the speeches of the presidential and vice-presidential candidates who participated in the first to third rounds of the 2019 presidential election debates were used as data for further investigation. By using the 8 hypothetical conditions adapted from Searle's 9 criteria of non-defective promise, a total of 50 argumentative commitments were extracted. Further analysis that was conducted confirmed that as a perlocutionary effect, the intention to commit in argumentative commitments is negotiable through the presence of other speech acts such as assertions, which were later called backings. Our findings then confirmed the presence of four kinds of backings, namely, assumptive, apprehensive, circumstantive, and resultative backings. From the findings, we argued that in a political context, promises, which are in the form of argumentative commitments, may consist of two elements, the commitment indicator and backings.

Keywords Argumentative commitments · Presidential debates · Conditions

D. Purwanto · Filia (✉)
Universitas Indonesia, Jakarta, Indonesia
e-mail: filia@ui.ac.id

D. Purwanto
e-mail: dwi.purwanto81@alumni.ui.ac.id

12.1 Introduction

The need for affirmation and mutual trust is fundamental to human life. Therefore, in every interaction, humans will try to convince each other to be trusted and accepted. Language as a communication tool is generally used to achieve this goal. Examples can be found in various aspects of everyday life, such as traders who use language to convince buyers that the goods being sold are of acceptable quality.

In political discourse, political actors use language to gain public support to vote for them in general elections. One way is to say utterances containing commitments such as promises. In this case, commitment is defined as an intention to tie oneself to an obligation to do certain actions in the future. In contrast to everyday discourses, utterances containing commitment in political discourse, such as in campaign promises, have a crucial role to provide certainty and generate trust, which later, will form social coordination (Habib, 2021). In other words, the campaign promises are mostly persuasive. This phenomenon presents another layer of complexity to the concept of sincerity proposed by Austin (1962) and Searle (1969), as well as the Gricean maxim of quality.

Several studies have been conducted for the last decade to discuss the concept of commitments in campaign promises further. Generally, they were analyzed in normative and deconstructive manners. Normative studies on campaign promises mainly addressed the issue of promising costs and consequences, such as from (Aragonès et al., 2007; Thomson et al., 2017). The previous normative studies of commitments and promises agree that both speakers and hearers were aware that a promise would tie the speaker to an obligation, which then would also affect the speaker's credibility as the cost.

On the other hand, the deconstructive studies of promises and commitments tried to address the issue of possible deceptions and insincerities. Studies, such as from Marsili (2014, 2016, 2017, 2020), tried to explain which conditions that may indicate that a promise is insincere. For the study, he indicated that an insincere promise may happen if the speaker either has no intention to do the action he promised, or has no belief that he/she could do the action proposed, or both.

In the field of linguistics, promises in political contexts were analyzed using the perspective of intentionalism, such as through the theory of commissive speech act proposed by Austin (1962) and Searle (1969). The primary purpose of the analysis is to identify patterns that could explain various characteristics of the speech act. Previous studies such as from Hashim (2015), Dylgjeri (2017), Azizah (2020), Alemi et al. (2018), Istikoma and Wijayanti (2019), Herfani and Manaf (2020), and Rizki and Golubović (2020) have contributed in finding several of the characteristics, such as the presence of various Illocutionary Force Indicating Device (IFID) of promising. One intriguing finding from the previous studies mentioned in the different view of the future modal marker, "will", as the IFID of promising. While some consider the presence of the modal marker as the IFID of promising, others do not. The phenomenon raises a question of why the different views emerged and how it affects the way we identify promises. This article aimed to discuss the problem.

In the first part of this article, we illustrate the challenges to identify promises using the perspective of intentionalism on utterances from the speeches of the presidential and vice-presidential candidates, who participated in the 2019 presidential election debates. In the second part of the article, we proposed to look at promises as perlocutionary effects, rather than illocutionary acts, in an attempt to address the problem. In the third part of this article, we conducted an investigation to identify promises and outline some of the characteristics using our theoretical model of argumentative commitment. The primary purpose of the investigation was to provide more textual evidences that an utterance could be considered as a promise.

12.2 Problems in Identifying a Promise

We begin our discussion by defining what a promise is, how promises can be identified and problems regarding the identification process. Perhaps we first need to go back on how the concept of promise was defined in linguistics and how it creates confusion. Popularly, the notion of promises has been discussed within the theory of speech acts as commissives. Austin (1962) defined promises as an undertaking, that is, an act of committing or declaring an intention to get involved in something. However, Austin did not specifically put intention and commitment into a box called commissives. Instead, he introduced the two concepts as inherent in other types of speech acts. Hence, in cases like the following example:

I agree with your idea to reform the economy.

On one side, the example could be identified as an expositive speech act as the above example shows the speaker's attempt to clarify his/her position on a topic (indicated by the verb, agree). On the other side, the example may also be considered as a commissive speech act as it shows the speaker's intention and commitment to support a certain topic. Through the example, rather than giving clear boundaries between commissives and other types of speech acts, Austin highlights the possibility for one speech act to overlap with the others. Then a question arose, how could promises be identified and be sorted out from other types of speech acts?

In an attempt to answer the question, Searle (1969) proposed his theory of non-defective promises. He argues that for an utterance to be identified as a successful (non-defective) promise, the utterance claimed to be a promise should fulfill nine conditions. However, these conditions may not serve as a handy practical concept. Consider the utterance of CP 1 and CP 2 on Excerpt 1, taken from the 2019 Indonesia's presidential debate:

Excerpt 1

Moderator: *Kepastian hukum sangat penting bagi warga, pelaku usaha, dan jalannya pemerintahan. Namun ternyata, banyak peraturan perundang-undangan yang tumpang tindih serta tidak harmonisnya peraturan di tingkat pusat serta daerah. Apa strategi Anda untuk menyelesaikan masalah tersebut? Akan dimulai ketika Anda menjawab. Waktunya adalah 2 menit, silakan.* >> 'Legal certainty is very important for citizens, business actors, and the running of the government. However, it turns out that there are many overlapping laws and regulations and inharmony of regulations at the central and regional levels. What is your strategy to solve this problem? The time, 2 minutes, will start when you answer, please.'

CP 1: *Kami akan melakukan perundingan dengan DPR.* >> 'We will hold a negotiation with the House of Representatives.'

CP 2: *Kami akan memberdayakan badan pembinaan hukum nasional. Kami akan perkuat dengan pakar-pakar hukum yang terbaik untuk melakukan sinkronisasi dan penyelarasan. Dengan begitu, undang-undang peraturan di pusat tidak bertabrakan dengan peraturan-peraturan di daerah. Ini sulit, ini pekerjaan besar, tapi harus kita lakukan, supaya ada kepastian hukum, supaya semuanya tahu sistem hukum di Indonesia, dan hukum itu bekerja untuk semuanya.* >> 'We will empower the national legal development agency. We will strengthen with the best legal experts to synchronize and harmonize. In this way, the laws and regulations at the center do not collide with regional regulations. This is difficult, this is a big job, but we have to do it, so that there is legal certainty, so that everyone knows the legal system in Indonesia, and the law works for all.'

At face value, both the utterance of CP1 and CP2 could be identified as promises. However, according to Searle, to certainly confirm that an utterance is a successful/ non-defective promise, normal output and input conditions should be achieved. In other words, both the speaker and the hearer are aware of what they did, are able to understand the language used, and are in a situation where neither of them does a role playing. In Excerpt 1, let us consider normal and healthy Indonesian audiences as the hearers. Both CP1 and CP2 utterances would easily fulfill the first condition as the audiences are aware of their positions in the debate, are able to understand what the speaker said and are not in a situation where they are pretending or playing a role-play. In his next condition, Searle stated that in a non-defective promise, the speaker expresses his/ her proposition of promising in the utterance. It means, the speaker should clearly express his intention to promise, for example, by using IFID (Illocutionary Force Indicating Device) of promising such as "I promise". In the case of Excerpt 1, both the utterance of CP1 and CP2 fail to fulfil the condition. Hence, both utterances could be identified as some kind of speech act other than promises.

The problem with Searle's condition is that in the case of Excerpt 1, the modal auxiliary "will" could show the speaker's intention and commitment to his/her propositions, but as the modal auxiliary, "will" can also have various functions in sentences, thus, it requires more evidence to consider the modal auxiliary exclusively as the IFID of promising. This notion created confusions amongst linguists in recent decades. Some researches, such as Mohammed Hashim (2015), Dylgjeri

(2017), Azizah (2020), Alemi et al. (2018), Istikoma and Wijayanti (2019), Herfani and Manaf (2020), and Rizki and Golubović (2020) considered the use of modal auxiliary "will" as an indicator to identify promises, while others did not.

Other confusion comes from the use of the expression *berkomitmen* (committed) and *bertekad* (determined) in the utterance of the 2019 Indonesia's presidential debates. On the surface, both expressions may indicate the speaker's commitment to a certain extent, which could be considered as the IFID of promising. However, attempts to separate the speech act of promising from guaranteeing, declaring oath, and committing, such as in Husain et al. (2020), have made the words difficult to be exclusively considered as the IFID of promising. The difficulties illustrated by the above expositions may explain why, despite the similar use of speech act theory, different studies may look at the notion of promises and the IFID of promising differently, creating confusions.

Hence, how should a promise be identified without creating more confusion? Geurts (2019a, b) suggested that intentions in commitments, such as promises, are self-referential. He infers that that the speaker will try his/her best to ensure that the hearer recognizes the speaker's intention in the proposition as a promise. The phenomena of self-referential were also illustrated in the recent studies which found out that certain epistemic and evidential modalities may indicate more information that could confirm the presence of commitments (Cornillie, 2018; Greco, 2018; Mazzarella et al., 2018; and Silk, 2018). Other studies suggested to look at the concept of promises as a scalar phenomenon (Marsili, 2014, 2016, 2020). Thus, rather than a matter of sincere-insincere, promises could also be seen as a scalar phenomenon through the scale of weak-strong.

From the above exposition of problems related to the attempts of identifying promises, we would like to look at promises from another perspective. We tried to support the notion of self-referential and acknowledge the abstract concept of intention. In the next section, we would like to adjust our position in the current theories of promises and provide our reasonings for choosing the position.

12.3 Argumentative Commitments: A Methodology to Analyze Commitments

Following previous studies, we identified that there is a need to define promises in ways to minimize confusions and allow more textual evidences to analyze. Taking into account problems that emerged when identifying promises, we tried to do two things. First, to avoid further confusion regarding different types of commissive speech acts, such as promising, pledging, committing, guaranteeing, etc., we treated them as commitments (as they will commit the speaker to do something). Then, by referring to Geurts (2019a, b), we divide commitments into two kinds, assertion-based commitment and intention-based commitment. While assertion-based commitment implies that the speaker is committed to the present truth-value of his/her proposition, intention-based commitment refers to an act in which the speaker is committed to have an intention and to tie him/herself with the obligation of doing something. In the case of this paper, we limit the interpretation of commitment as an intention-based commitment.

Next, as suggested by the studies, such as from Cornillie (2018), Greco (2018) Mazzarella et al. (2018), and Silk (2018) that modal markers could indicate a degree of commitment, we tried to treat commitment as a perlocutionary effect instead of an illocutionary act. In other words, we view the concept of commitment as the hearer's inference, communicated by the speaker, hence the term non-natural meaning proposed by Grice (Moeschler, 2013) or an attributed commitment as said by Boulat and Maillat (2017). Then, by referring to Walton (2008) we also consider commitment as a kind of concession, thus, we would highlight the correlation between commitments in promises and commitments in argumentations. By doing so, we revisited Searle's nine conditions of non-defective promises (in this case, commitments) and investigated how this change of perspective affects the conditions. Consider the utterance of CP1 and CP2 in Excerpt 1.

The first condition talks about the normal input and output condition, which infers that both speakers and hearers could understand each other. However, in the case of Excerpt 1, there are three instances involved, the speaker (S), the moderator (M), and the hearer (H). M's primary role is to mediate communication between the S and H. In other words, S will talk in accordance with what was being asked by M, and H will act as an observer, with no chance to interfere with the communication. Let us consider S as CP 1 and 2, and L as the audience and the researcher. In such situation, one way we could know the fulfilment of the condition is by identifying whether S gives a relevant response (T) to M's question. This could be done by identifying any keyword reduplication. Assumed that there are three keywords from M's questions; law and regulation, the government, central and regional level; reduplication can take form explicitly and inferentially. In the case of CP1's utterance, the reduplication is inferential, indicated by the use of the term DPR (the House of Representatives) which is relevant to all keywords as DPR represents the government of a nation, the policymakers that act both in central and regional level. Meanwhile, CP2 took things explicitly by restating the keywords in the utterance. Thus, the utterance of CP1 and CP2 could be assumed to fulfilled the first condition.

The second condition of Searle's non-defective promise demanded that S expresses his/her proposition of promise (p) in T. In brief, both CP1 and 2 could be assumed to fulfill the condition if IFIDs of p (in this case, p refers to commitments) are present. The presence of verbs such as *berkomitmen* (committed), *berjanji* (promise), and *bertekad* (determined) would be sufficient to prove the fulfillment. In this case, only the utterance of CP2 fulfilled the condition. However, as we treat the concept of commitment as a scalar phenomenon (Marsili, 2014, 2016, 2017) of likely-unlikely, this does not mean the utterance of CP1 conveys no commitment. Further investigation is needed.

The third condition of Searle's non-defective commitment require S to explicate his/her future action (A) on the T. This could be identified by parts of the utterance such as *Kami akan melakukan* (We will hold) and *Kami akan memberdayakan* (We will empower). To identify A in T, we could identify any self-claim of actions modified by the future modal marker *akan* (will) or any adverbs indicating future time. The self-claim can be inferred by first person pronoun *saya* (I) or *kami* and *kita* (we). With the method, we could assume CP1 and 2's utterances fulfilled the condition.

The next condition Searle's non-defective commitment describes that H would prefer S doing A to his not doing A, and S believes H would prefer his doing A to his not doing A. To simplify, H will get benefits from A, and both S and H expect A to happen. We saw the need to clarify this condition as beliefs, preferences, and expectations are subjective, thus hard to measure. This is where we rely on the view of argumentation. By seeing commitments as an act of persuading or convincing H, there will be parts in S' utterance that would provide details highlighting points that A will benefit H based on several observations conducted by S. Thus, there are some ways to fulfill the conditions, by explicating epistemic and evidential modal markers, by explicating numerical data in T, and by referencing. The presence of causal-assumptive epistemic modal marker *agar* (so that) on the utterance of CP2 would indicate that the utterance fulfills the condition.

On the next condition, Searle stated the importance of a non-defective commitment to show that it is not obvious to both S and H that S will do A in the normal course of events. This condition can be contextually proven by taking into account regarding CP1 and CP2 profiles. Assuming that both CP1 and CP2 have ever worked as a policymaker and have access to do A, both fail to fulfill the condition, as there is no reason for them to declare their commitment since both can do what they are committing immediately.

The next condition, Searle's non-defective commitment requires S to sincerely intend to do A. Using the perspective of attributed commitment, concepts such as intention can only be assumed, and cannot be proven unless H has access to S' mind. That said, we look at this condition as prima facie, rendering both CP1 and CP2 fulfill the condition, unless proven otherwise.

The seventh and eighth conditions of Searle's non-defective commitment describe the need for S to sincerely intend to put him/herself under the obligation to do A and S intend to produce the knowledge (K) of the obligation and expect H to recognize it. Under the perspective of attributed commitment and argumentation, a modification to this commitment is required. We propose to look at the obligation as the process of negotiation (Kim, 2021), bargaining, and agreement (Stoljar, 1988), modifying the condition so that a non-defective commitment requires S to negotiate his/her obligation to do A with H. The presence of various epistemic and evidential modalities, as well as deontic and dynamic modalities (Alwi, 1992; Palmer, 2001). The presence of the term *harus* (must) as a deontic-obligative modality could provide supporting evidence that CP2 has fulfilled the condition.

The last condition of Searle's non-defective commitment requires S and H to agree that the T is semantically and dialectically relevant and recognized to be used for *p*. This could be contextually proven by identifying the profile of S, H, and M. In the case of Excerpt 1, S, H, and M are the natives of the same country, sharing the same language and culture. The contextual evidence could function as evidence that the utterances of CP1 and 2 fulfill the condition.

From the above method, we then tried to modify Searle's conditions to propose hypothetical conditions to identify commitments as follows. To differentiate the hypothetical model of commitment from Searlean commitment, we proposed the term Argumentative Commitment. By referring to our view of commitment and the definition of argumentation from (Sinnott-Armstrong & Fogelin, 2015), we define an argumentative commitment as an act of convincing or persuading hearers to believe that the speaker committed to do something in the future.

After proposing the hypothetical condition, we found out that there is a need to group the conditions into two categories, a primary condition and the secondary condition. While the secondary conditions will determine whether a commitment could be considered strong or weak, a primary condition will determine whether an utterance can be assumed to contain a commitment or not. By reflecting on the conditions, condition C3 could function as the primary condition, as without proposing future action, there will be no clear indication of what is being committed. By setting condition C3 as the primary condition, the utterance of CP1 fulfills 4 out of 9 (8 if conditions 7 and 8 are combined), while the utterance of CP2 fulfills 8 out of 9 conditions. Therefore, we can conclude that the utterance of CP2 will more likely to contain stronger argumentative commitment than the utterance of CP1.

However, the conclusion does not mean that the utterance of CP2 will convince hearers more than the utterance of CP1. Further experiment is needed to test whether the utterance such as CP2 would produce a perlocutionary effect of a more convincing argumentative commitment. Regardless, at the moment, we try to focus more on how to identify argumentative commitments, proving the method's validity and reliability, as well as analyzing some characteristics that argumentative commitments may have. Hence, we leave the question open for further research.

12.4 Investigating Argumentative Commitments in the 2019 Indonesia's Presidential Debates

To prove the validity of our hypothetical conditions (Table 12.1), we designed a simple investigation by applying the conditions to 161 utterances that C1 and C2 made during all three rounds of the 2019 Indonesia's presidential debates. Before conducting the investigations, we first ignore condition C15 as the condition will always be true in the context of the debate. Next, we converted the conditions into 14 indicators. Each utterance will be analyzed using the indicators. Then, we adopted the procedure for the test of validity and reliability from Kang et al. (2015). The test includes *Cronbach tests of consistency* dan *Guttman split-half coefficient test*. From the test, the average *Cronbach alpha* score of 0.712, and *Guttman split-half coefficient* of 0.78 were obtained. To interpret the score, we referred to the table proposed by Taber (2018) (See Appendix 2). By using the table, the 14 indicators seemed to do an acceptable job in determining which utterances contain commitments and which do not. From the indicators, we successfully identified as many as 50 commitments.

12 Understanding Promises from the Perspective of Argumentation: The ...

Table 12.1 Hypothetical conditions to identify commitments

Code	Conditions
C1	Normal input & output conditions
C2	The speaker (S) expresses his/her proposition of promise (p) in utterance (T)
C3	S explicates his/her future action (A) on the T
C4	S proposed p to H to convince H to believe that S would do A for the benefit of H, and H would prefer S to do A, than to his not doing A
C5	It is not obvious to both S and H that S will do A in the normal course of events
C6	S intended to do A
C7	S negotiates his/her obligation to do A with H and wants H to recognize the obligation
C8	S and H agree that the T is semantically and dialectically relevant and recognized to be used for p

Following the result of the investigation, further analysis to identify patterns of argumentative commitments was done. Through the analysis, we learned that argumentative commitments may contain two elements, the commitment indicator (CI) which is the part indicating the fulfillment of condition C3, and backings, which are parts providing information supporting the commitment indicator. The backing might be assumptive, apprehensive, circumstantive, and resultative. The distribution of the backings can be seen in Table 12.2.

Assumptive backing provides information about the speaker's attempt to make sense of his/her world and create a needs to propose his argumentative commitment. The example is illustrated in the following Excerpt 2. The underlined part is the backing.

Excerpt 2: *Dalam sistem bernegara, seorang kepala negara disebut chief executive, kepala eksekutif. Berarti, seorang kepala negara yakni presiden adalah chief law enforcement officer. Dia adalah petugas penegak hukum tertinggi di negara ini.*

Table 12.2 The distribution of different types of backing in argumentative commitments of the 2019 Indonesia's presidential debates

Types of backing	N	n1	n2	n3	Percentage (%)
Resultative backing	25	13	5	8	35.7
Circumstantive backing	17	9	5	18	24.3
Assumptive backing	14	7	4	3	20
Apprehensive backing	14	7	4	3	20

Notes
N: Total occurrences
n1: Occurrences in the first debate
n2: Occurrences in the second debate
n3: Occurrences in the third debate

Karena itu, saya akan menatar seluruh aparat penegak hukum. Saya akan instruksikan dan tegaskan bahwa tidak boleh diskriminasi terhadap suku, agama dan etnis apa pun. ... >> 'In the state system, the head of state is called the chief executive. This means that the head of state, namely the president, is the chief law enforcement officer. The president holds the highest power in the law enforcement of the country. Because of that, I will empower all law enforcement officers. I will instruct and emphasize that there must not discrimination against any ethnicity, religion or ethnicity. ....'.

In Excerpt 2, the speaker's commitment to do actions, presented with verbs such as *menatar* (empower), *instruksikan* (instruct), and *tegaskan* (emphasize), is preceded by parts which provide additional information in the form of the speaker's knowledge of the role of a head of state. This information is further embellished with deductive epistemic modal markers such as *berarti* (this means) that indicates the speaker's attempt to make an inference from an observable phenomenon. The linguistic evidence had provided adequate support to assume that Excerpt 2 is an argumentative commitment, which one of the parts functions as assumptive backing.

Other kinds of backing that were identified from the argumentative commitments are apprehensive backing and resultative backing. Both backings highlight the outcome of the actions proposed by the speaker on his/her argumentative commitment. The main difference between them is that apprehensive backing was born out of negative situation, something that the speaker would like to avoid, which then became his/her motivation to propose an argumentative commitment. In the following Excerpt 3, the negative situation is introduced by the use of expressions such as *salah kita semua* (it's all of our fault).

Excerpt 3: *Kita akan mengamankan semua sumber-sumber ekonomi bangsa Indonesia. Kita akan menjaga pundi-pundi bangsa Indonesia supaya kekayaan kita tidak mengalir ke luar negeri. Masalah pokok bangsa kita adalah bahwa kekayaan kita tidak tinggal di republik kita. Ini bukan salah siapa pun,* **ini salah kita semua sebagai bangsa.** >> We will secure all the economic resources of the Indonesian nation. We will keep the coffers of the Indonesian people so that our wealth does not flow abroad. The main problem of our nation is that our wealth does not stay in our republic. This is not anyone's fault, it is ours, as a nation.'

Meanwhile, resultative backing highlights a positive situation that the speaker expects to happen out of his/her argumentative commitment. The example is reflected from the following Excerpt 4. The use of desiderative modal marker, such as *ingin* (want) indicates the speaker's future expectation, which made Excerpt 4 an example to address the presence of resultative backing in an argumentative commitment.

Excerpt 4: *Kami akan memulai program promotif preventif dua puluh dua menit per hari berolahraga.* **Kita ingin** *masyarakat badan yang sehat dan jiwanya juga sehat.* >> We will start a preventive promotive program if twenty-two minutes per day of exercise. We want people to have a healthy body and a healthy soul.'

The last kind of backing that was identified from the argumentative commitments is circumstantive backing. This type of backing highlights the contextual application, or conditions, of the actions proposed by the speaker in his/her argumentative commitment. In a conventional sense, this type of argumentative commitment could also be categorized as a conditional promise. In Excerpt 5, for example, the backing is illustrated by the use of the conditional modal marker *manakala* (whenever).

Excerpt 5: *Untuk itu Prabowo-Sandi, manakala kita yang memimpin pemerintahan, kita akan benar-benar investasi besar-besaran dalam pendidikan dan kesehatan, untuk membantu rakyat yang paling bawah, rakyat (yang) paling miskin.* >> 'For that Prabowo-Sandi, when we lead the government, we will really invest heavily in education and health, to help the people at the bottom, the people (the) poorest.'

Through the test of reliability and validity of the indicators, as well as the analysis conducted, we provided support to our argument that argumentative commitments (such as campaign promises) are self-referential. Through the analysis, we provided some explanation on how the speaker's intention can be negotiated and justified through the presence of backings. We also identified several kinds of backings, which could reflect the speaker's motive to propose his/her argumentative commitments. However, we should note that our findings may not be applicable in other contexts. Further investigation in various contexts should be done to identify any possibilities of new characteristics of argumentative commitments.

12.5 Conclusion

From the investigation we conducted, we confirmed the presence of two components that make up a promise, under our model of argumentative commitment, namely, commitment indicator and backings. While the commitment indicator shows the future actions that the speaker will do, the backings function as the tool of negotiation to convince hearers to believe that an utterance is indeed a promise. Based on the data, the negotiation can happen by adding information to show the speaker's attempt to make sense of the reality (assumptive backings), highlighting particular outcomes that potentially happen when the action proposed is successfully done (apprehensive and resultative backings), or emphasizing the contextual application, or conditions, of the actions proposed by the speaker (circumstantive backings).

Through our investigation and findings, we confirm that although the notion of intention in promises could be seen as abstract, and should be accepted as *prima facie*, it is possible for the intention to be textually represented through the language choices made by the speakers. The presence of backings in the argumentative commitments of the 2019 Indonesia's presidential debates confirmed the previous studies that the notion of intention is self-referential. Additionally, our findings suggested that besides looking at the concept of promises only from the perspective such as the presence of IFID of promising, such as "I will" or "I promise," through the model of argumentative commitment, promises, especially in political context, could also be integrative. Argumentative commitment proposes a perspective to look at promises as a combination of more than one speech acts, in an attempt to negotiate and justify the speaker's attempt to convince the hearer that his/her proposition is indeed a promise.

Acknowledgements This work was supported by Universitas Indonesia's Research Grant (PITMA B 2019) managed by DRPM UI/Indonesian Ministry of Research, Technology, and Higher Education's Research Grant (PDUPT 2019) managed by DRPM UI.

Appendix 1: Indicators to Identify Argumentative Commitments

Code	Indicators
i1	Reduplication of keywords in the moderator's speech aisfound in the candidate's utterance
i2	Parts containing clauses with IFID of commitments with first-person pronouns, such as I promise, I swear, I am committed to, etc., can be found in the candidate's utterance
i3	Parts containing future tense clauses with verbs that are collocated with first-person pronouns can be found in the candidate's utterance
i4	Parts containing clauses with epistemic modal markers can be found in the candidate's utterance
i5	Parts containing clauses with sensory evidential modal markers can be found in the candidate's utterance
i6	Parts containing clauses with reported evidential modal markers can be found on the candidate's utterance
i7	Parts containing clauses with cardinal numbers indicating data can be found in the utterance
i8	Clauses containing actions that the speaker will do are in line with the duties, authorities, and responsibilities of a president/vice president, in accordance with the 1945 Constitution
i9	The speaker does not have the physical and psychological capacity and ability to start performing the actions committed before the actions were proposed through the utterance
i10	Parts containing clauses preceded by causal conjunctions, such as thus, therefore, and so on, which relate to the speaker's future actions in the observed speech can be found in the utterance
i11	Parts containing clauses with deontic-permissive modal markers can be found in the candidate's utterance
i12	Parts containing clauses with deontic-obligative modal markers can be found in the candidate's utterance
i13	Parts containing clauses with dynamic-desiderative modal markers can be found in the candidate's utterance
i14	Parts containing clauses with dynamic-abilitive modal markers can be found in the candidate's utterance
i15	All participants involved in the debates have the same cultural background, and have the ability to understand each other's language

Appendix 2: Taber's Cronbach Alpha Score Interpretation

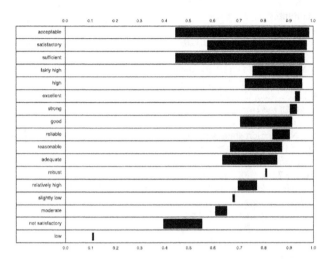

References

Alemi, M., Latifi, A., & Nematzadeh, A. (2018). Persuasion in political discourse: Barak Obama's presidential speeches against ISIS. *Russian Journal of Linguistics, 22*(2), 278–291. https://doi.org/10.22363/2312-9182-2018-22-2-278-291.
Alwi, H. (1992). *Modalitas dalam Bahasa Indonesia* (1st ed.). Kanisius.
Aragonès, E., Palfrey, T., & Postlewaite, A. (2007). Political reputations and campaign promises. *Journal of the European Economic Association, 5*(4), 846–884. https://doi.org/10.1162/JEEA.2007.5.4.846.
Austin, J. L. (1962). *How to do things with words*. Oxford University Press. https://doi.org/10.1093/acprof:oso/9780198245537.001.0001.
Azizah, N. F. (2020). Tindak tutur ekspresif dan komisif dalam debat calon presiden Republik Indonesia 2019 (analisis pragmatik). *Jurnal Penelitian, Pendidikan, dan Pembelajaran, 15*(20).
Boulat, K., & Maillat, D. (2017). She said you said i saw it with my own eyes: A pragmatic account of commitment. In J. Blochowiak, C. Grisot, S. Durrleman, & C. Laenzlinger (Eds), *Formal Models in the Study of Language: Applications in Interdisciplinary Contexts* (pp. 261–279). Springer. https://doi.org/10.1007/978-3-319-48832-5_14.
Cornillie, B. (2018). On speaker commitment and speaker involvement. Evidence from evidentials in Spanish talk-in-interaction. *Journal of Pragmatics, 128*, 161–170. https://doi.org/10.1016/j.pragma.2017.11.014.
Dylgjeri, A. (2017). Analysis of speech acts in political speeches. *European Journal of Social Sciences Studies, 2*(2), 19–26. https://doi.org/10.46827/ejsss.v0i0.66.
Geurts, B. (2019a). Commitments continued. *Theoretical Linguistics, 45*(1–2), 111–125. https://doi.org/10.1515/tl-2019-0009.
Geurts, B. (2019b). What's wrong with Gricean pragmatics. *ExLing 2019: Proceedings of 10th International Conference of Experimental Linguistics*. ExLing Society.
Greco, P. (2018). Evidentiality and epistemic modality in witness testimony in the context of Italian criminal trials. *Journal of Pragmatics, 128*, 128–136. https://doi.org/10.1016/j.pragma.2017.10.005.

Habib, A. (2021). "Promises". In E. N. Zalta (Ed.). *The Stanford Encyclopedia of Philosophy*. (Fall 2021 Edition). https://plato.stanford.edu/archives/fall2021/entries/promises/.

Herfani, F. K., & Manaf, N. A. (2020). Tindak tutur komisif dan ekspresif dalam debat capres-cawapres pada Pilpres 2019. *Jurnal Bahasa dan Sastra, 8*(1), 36–51. http://ejournal.unp.ac.id/index.php/ibs/article/view/108871.

Husain, A., Hamamah, H., & Nurhayani, I. (2020). Commissive speech act in Indonesian presidential debate. *OKARA: Jurnal Bahasa dan Sastra, 14*(1), 81. https://doi.org/10.19105/ojbs.v14i1.3141.

Istikoma, N. A., & Wijayanti, D. (2019). Bentuk tindak tutur ekspresif dan komisif dalam debat cawapres pilpres 2019 putaran ke-3. *Seminar Nasional SAGA#2*, 23–28.

Kang, Y., Tan, A. H., & Miao, C. (2015). An adaptive computational model for personalized persuasion. *Proceedings of the Twenty-Fourth International Joint Conference on Artificial Intelligence (IJCAI)*, pp. 61–67.

Kim, J. Y. (2021). Negotiation statements with promise and threat. *Review of Economic Design*. https://doi.org/10.1007/s10058-021-00261-8.

Marsili, N. (2016). Lying by promising. *International Review of Pragmatics, 8*(2), 271–313. https://doi.org/10.1163/18773109-00802005.

Marsili, N. (2017). Lying and Certainty. In J. Meibauer (Ed.), *The oxford handbook of lying* (pp. 170–182). Oxford University Press.

Marsili, N. (2020). Lying, speech acts, and commitment. *Synthese, 199*, 3245–3269. https://doi.org/10.1007/s11229-020-02933-4.

Marsili, N. (2014). Lying as a scalar phenomenon. In S. Cantarini, W. Abraham & E. Leiss (Eds.), *Certainty-Uncertainty – and the Attitudinal Space In Between*, pp. 153–173. John Benjamins Publishing. https://doi.org/10.1075/slcs.165.09mar [Studies in Language Companion Series 165].

Mazzarella, D., Reinecke, R., Noveck, I., & Mercier, H. (2018). Saying, presupposing and implicating: How pragmatics modulates commitment. *Journal of Pragmatics, 133*, 15–27. https://doi.org/10.1016/j.pragma.2018.05.009.

Moeschler, J. (2013). Is a speaker-based pragmatics possible? Or how can a hearer infer a speaker's commitment? *Journal of Pragmatics, 48*(1), 84–97. https://doi.org/10.1016/j.pragma.2012.11.019.

Mohammed Hashim, S. S. (2015). Speech acts in political speeches. *Journal of Modern Education Review, 5*(7), 699–706. https://doi.org/10.15341/jmer(2155-7993)/07.05.2015/008.

Palmer, F. R. (2001). Mood and modality. *Cambridge University Press*. https://doi.org/10.1017/CBO9781139167178.

Rizki, S., & Golubović, J. (2020). An analysis of speech act of Omar Mukhtar's utterances in *Lion of the desert* movie. *Englisia: Journal of Language, Education, and Humanities, 7*(2), 210. https://doi.org/10.22373/ej.v7i2.6358.

Searle, J. R. (1969). Speech acts: An essay in the philosophy of language. *Cambridge University Press*. https://doi.org/10.1017/CBO9781139173438.

Silk, A. (2018). Commitment and states of mind with mood and modality. *Natural Language Semantics, 26*(2), 125–166. https://doi.org/10.1007/s11050-018-9144-4.

Sinnott-Armstrong, W. & Fogelin, R. J. (2015). *Understanding arguments: An introduction to informal logic* (9th Edition). Cengage Learning. [Cengage advantage books.]

Stoljar, S. (1988). Promise, expectation, and agreement. *The Cambridge Law Journal, 47*(2), 193–212. https://doi.org/10.1017/S0008197300117994.

Taber, K. S. (2018). The use of Cronbach's Alpha when developing and reporting research instruments in science education. *Research in Science Education, 48*, 1273–1296. https://doi.org/10.1007/s11165-016-9602-2.

Thomson, R., Royed, T., Naurin, E., Artés, J., Costello, R., Ennser-Jedenastik, L., Ferguson, M., Kostadinova, P., Moury, C., Pétry, F., & Praprotnik, K. (2017). The fulfillment of parties' election pledges: A comparative study on the impact of power sharing. *American Journal of Political Science, 61*(3), 527–542. https://doi.org/10.1111/ajps.12313.

Walton, D. (2008). Informal logic. *Cambridge University Press.* https://doi.org/10.1017/CBO978 0511808630.

Dwi Purwanto is an M. Hum graduate from the Dept. of linguistics at the Faculty of Humanities, Universitas Indonesia. His research interests include TEFL/TESOL, pragmatics and discourse analysis. His previous publication was The Lucrative Language: A Linguistic Landscape Study of Restaurant Advertisements in Pontianak City was published in *Literatus Journal*, 2(2), 123–132 (2020).

Open Access This chapter is licensed under the terms of the Creative Commons Attribution 4.0 International License (http://creativecommons.org/licenses/by/4.0/), which permits use, sharing, adaptation, distribution and reproduction in any medium or format, as long as you give appropriate credit to the original author(s) and the source, provide a link to the Creative Commons license and indicate if changes were made.

The images or other third party material in this chapter are included in the chapter's Creative Commons license, unless indicated otherwise in a credit line to the material. If material is not included in the chapter's Creative Commons license and your intended use is not permitted by statutory regulation or exceeds the permitted use, you will need to obtain permission directly from the copyright holder.

Chapter 13
The Development of the Uses of the Word *dengan* from Indonesian Newspaper Period 1910–2010

Gita Ayodhiya Sanarta and Dien Rovita

Abstract As a word, *dengan* will always develop as long as it is used by its speakers. The aim of this study is to explain the development of the uses of the word *dengan* in bahasa Indonesia based on its function as a conjunction or a preposition in a clause from the year 1910 to 2010. The data sources used in this chapter are Indonesian newspapers from the year 1910 to 2010. The methodology used in this chapter is mixed research of quantitative and qualitative approaches. The quantitative approach is used to see the frequency of the uses of *dengan*. On the other hand, the qualitative approach is used to classify the word *dengan* into conjunction or preposition; to determine the meaning of the preposition *dengan*, and to determine the collocation between the verb and the preposition *dengan*. As a result, (1) *dengan* as conjunction could function as a subordinate and coordinative conjunction, (2) *dengan* as a preposition has eleven meanings, (3) the use of the word *dengan* between 1910 and 2010 as conjunction has been decreasing while the use as a preposition has been increasing, (4) *dengan* as a preposition could only collocate with certain verbs.

Keywords Language development · Dengan · Newspaper · Collocate · Verb

13.1 Introduction

The dynamic nature of language makes languages continuously experience development or changes as long as they are used by the speakers. This is in line with Chaer's opinion that language cannot be separated from human activities and movements (2014). To understand the development of language, the comparison of language uses from different periods needs to be conducted.

G. A. Sanarta
Indonesian Studies, Faculty of Humanities, University of Indonesia, Jakarta, Indonesia
e-mail: gita.ayodhiya@ui.ac.id

D. Rovita (✉)
Department of Linguistics, Faculty of Humanities, University of Indonesia, Jakarta, Indonesia
e-mail: rovita@ui.ac.id

This research uses written data sources in the form of newspapers as research data. According to Romli (2017), newspapers function as mass communication media that contain various news. This study uses several newspapers as research data, such as *Pantjaran Warta* (1910) or PW-1910, *Merdeka* (1960) or M-1960, and *Kompas* (2010) or K-2010. The data is collected from different sources to observe the different uses of language among speakers not only from one newspaper. Moreover, the different periods can also exhibit the language characteristics used in certain periods.

It is interesting to study grammatical words as an element of language development, particularly the word *dengan*. The word *dengan* can be classified into two word classes, conjunction and preposition. *Dengan* as a conjunction can combine two or more clauses into one sentence. For the example, in *Seorang Belanda **dengan** seorang njonjanja berkendaraan fiets/* 'A Dutchman **and** his lady rode a fiets' sentence, the word *dengan* functions to combine two clauses into one sentence. The first clause is *Seorang Belanda berkendaraan fiets/* 'A Dutchmand rode a fiets' and the second clause is *seorang njonja Belanda berkendaraan fiets/* 'a Dutchman's lady rode a fiets'.

The word *dengan* as a preposition has several meanings, such as accompaniment, instrument, manner, et cetera. The preposition *dengan* as an accompaniment has a similar meaning to the use of the word *bersama* 'together' or 'with'. The preposition *dengan* as an instrument is to state an instrument or a device used in an event. Meanwhile, the preposition *dengan* as a manner is to illustrate the condition or the situation when an event is occurring.

Accompaniment	*kata Agassa dalam wawancara **dengan** radio Perancis* 'said Agassa in an interview **with** a France radio'
Instrument	*… soedah di beli oleh seorang Europa **dengan harga mahal*** '… it has already been bought by a European **at an expensive price**'
Manner	*Boemipoetra **dengen moeda** bisa mentjari kehidoepan sedikit…(PW-1910)* 'Boemipoetra can **easily** find a bit of life…'

Based on the example, *dengan* as a preposition has several meanings, which are interesting to examine. By knowing the differences of each preposition meaning, speakers can better understand the meaning of the clause. Furthermore, the study analysis of verbs that can collocate with preposition *dengan* can provide the structure that will simplify the meaning classification of the preposition *dengan*.

13.2 Literature Review

Previous studies have researched the development of grammatical words, such as Lapoliwa (1992), Mahardika (2017), Sabila (2018), and Mudhongafah (2018). Lapoliwa studied the meaning of preposition *dengan* in newspapers, magazines, and proses. In the research, Lapoliwa identified a new meaning of preposition *dengan* that has not been found by previous researchers. Mahardika studies verb + preposition collocation *tentang* 'about' in BIPA (Indonesian Language for Foreign Speakers) textbooks. The study aims to understand the verb behavior as a left collocate and a unit meaning that follows *tentang* as a right collocate. Sabila studied the development of the use and the meaning of preposition *daripada* 'than' from the seventeenth to twenty-first century in proses. The study aims to trace the differences in functions and meaning of preposition *daripada* from different periods. Meanwhile, Mudhongafah studied the development of the conjunction *maka* 'so' from the seventeenth to twenty-first century. The results of the study show that there are differences in the functions of conjunction in each period.

The differences between this study and the previous study are in the data used and the research purpose. Previous studies have not studied the link between the meaning of verbs and prepositions. Therefore, the research can fill the research gap in the study of grammatical words, particularly in the study of the word *dengan* in bahasa Indonesia. This study discusses the development of the word *dengan* as a conjunction and a preposition, and the meaning of verbs that collocate with the preposition *dengan* as left collocate in the newspapers in the period 1910–2010. With regard to the problem, this research aims to explain the development of the uses of the word *dengan* based on its function as a conjunction or a preposition in a clause. Besides that, this research also aims to identify the meaning of the preposition *dengan* and the meaning of verbs that collocate with the preposition *dengan* as left collocate in the newspapers in the period 1910–2010.

13.3 Method

This study uses mixed methods. According to Creswell (2013), the mixed methods adopt both qualitative and quantitative approaches. Quantitative approach is used to see the frequency in the development of the use of the word *dengan* in the newspaper in the period 1910–2010. Qualitative approach is used to determine the word class of the word *dengan*, the meaning of the preposition *dengan*, and the meaning of the verbs that collocate with the preposition *dengan* according to the context of the clause.

This study uses a corpus linguistics approach. According to Budiwiyanto (2014), the corpus is a collection of texts from both spoken and written languages that are arranged systematically. Therefore, the corpus of this study is the data source from the newspapers. This study uses digital corpus in.*txt* format.

The data source of this study is newspapers published in 1910, 1960, and 2010. According to the data references from PNRI, there are several newspapers published in 1910, 1960, and 2010. After conducting an observation, the author decided to use *Pantjaran Warta* newspaper published in 1910, *Merdeka* newspaper published in 1960, and *Kompas* newspaper published in 2010 as the data of the study. These newspapers are chosen because these three newspapers were published in the center of the Indonesian government, DKI Jakarta.

Although the time interval for the publication of the newspapers does not reach one hundred years each period, the three newspapers are able to exhibit the development in the uses of the word *dengan*. There is a difference in the use of language between the first source and the other sources. The first source uses Malay language while the second and third sources use bahasa Indonesia. In addition, the time interval of 50 years between the second source and the third source demonstrates the development in the use of the word *dengan*.

13.4 The Development of the Uses of the Word *Dengan*

Conjunctions and prepositions have their own functions although they are classified in the same category, grammatical words. Ramlan (1980) argued that prepositions are always in exocentric phrases while conjunctions are in endocentric phrases. Therefore, the function of prepositions is to show unit relationships at the word or phrase level. On the other hand, the function of conjunctions is to connect words, phrases, and clauses.

The word *dengan* studied in this research is the single word *dengan*. Therefore, the use of combined words such as *sesuai dengan* and *sampai dengan* is not discussed in this research. In the data, the writing of the *word* dengan in the newspapers is various. In PW-1910, the word *dengan* is written as *dengan* and *dengen*. In M-1960, the word *dengan* is written as *dengan* and *dgn*. Meanwhile, in K-2010, the word *dengan* is merely written as *dengan*. Table 13.1 illustrates the frequency of the word *dengan* appears in the newspapers.

Based on Table 13.1, the word *dengan* most frequently appears in M-1960, followed by PW-1910 and K-2010. Meanwhile, the use of *dengan* as a conjunction most frequently appears in PW-1910, and it appears the least in K-2010. Therefore, it can be concluded that the use of conjunction *dengan* decreases in each period.

The preposition *dengan* most frequently appears in M-1960. Meanwhile, the preposition *dengan* appears more frequently in K-2010 compared to PW-1910. This is because in 1910 the uses of the word *dengan* as a conjunction were used quite frequently, while in 2010 the word *dengan* as a conjunction was rarely used.

A. **The Behavior of the Word *dengan* as a Conjunction and a Preposition**

Table 13.1 The frequency of appearance of the word *dengan* in the newspapers

Source	Number of tokens	Appearance	Frequency of the word *dengan* (%)	Conjunction *dengan* (%)	Preposition *dengan* (%)
PW-1910	14.992	103	0,69	0,13	0,56
M-1960	16.068	153	0,95	0,11	0,85
K-2010	14.582	95	0,65	0,03	0,62

Table 13.2 The frequency of appearance of the conjunction and preposition *dengan*

Source	Conjunction (%)	Preposition (%)
PW-1910	18,4	81,6
M-1960	11,1	88,9
K-2010	4,2	95,8

The word *dengan* can be classified as a conjunction and preposition. In the data, the word *dengan* as a conjunction and a preposition is used in every newspaper period. Table 13.2 shows the uses of *dengan* as a conjunction and a preposition in the newspaper in each period.

1. **The Word *dengan* as a Conjunction**

Alwi et al. (2003) categorizes conjunctions into two, coordinating conjunctions and subordinating conjunctions. Moreover, Alwi classified subordinating conjunctions into thirteen groups: time, condition, hypothetical, purpose, concession, equation, cause, effect, instrument, manner, complement, attributive, and comparison. The word *dengan* is classified into two conjunctions, instrument and manner. According to the data, the word *dengan* as a conjunction is found in each newspaper. In the data, there are two types of conjunction, namely subordinating conjunction and coordinating conjunction. The following example is the discussion of the conjunction *dengan* in the data.

1) The Word *dengan* as a Coordinating Conjunction

The word *dengan* as a coordinating conjunction can be replaced by the conjunction *dan* 'and'. In PW-1910, the coordinating conjunction is used once. The following example is the use of *dengan* as a coordinating conjunction in PW-1910.

(1) *Seorang Belanda **dengan** seorang njonjanja berkendaraan fiets dari Kidoel akan Mengalor.*
   'A Dutchman **with** his lady rode a fiets from Kidoel to Mengalor.'

Example (1) shows that the function of the conjunction *dengan* is to connect independent clauses. The two subjects in the sentence carry out the same action. It can be observed from the clauses in the sentence,

a) *seorang Belanda berkendaraan fiets dari Kidoel akan mengalor;*
   'A Dutchman rode a fiets from Kidoel to Mengalor;'
b) *seorang nyonya berkendaraan fiets dari Kidoel akan mengalor.*
   A Dutchman's lady rode a fiets from Kidoel to Mengalor.

Besides being used in PW-1910, coordinating conjunction *dengan* is also used in M-1960. Coordinating conjunction is used once in M-1960. The following example is the use of coordinating conjunction in M-1960.

(2) *upatjara itu berlangsung dilapangan* ___ *Polisi dibelakang Kantor Komisariat Polisi Djakarta* **dengan** *dihadiri oleh kurang lebih 1 Batalion anggota kepolisian...*

'the ceremony took place in the field ___ The Police behind the Djakarta Police Commiserate Office attended **by** approximately 1 Battalion of police officers...'

Based on example (2), two different information are obtained. The first information is that the ceremony took place at the field behind the Police Commiserate Office. Meanwhile, the second information is that the ceremony was attended by approximately one battalion of police officers.

2) The Word *dengan* as a Subordinating Conjunction

Based on expert opinion, the subordinating conjunction *dengan* functions as an instrument and manner conjunctions. However, based on the data, the conjunction *dengan* can also function as purpose, complement, and attributive conjunctions. The function of instrument conjunction is to connect independent clauses and dependent clauses that state the instrument used. In PW-1910, instrument conjunction appeared four times and six times in M-1960. Meanwhile, there is no use of instrument conjunction in K-2010.

(3) *Istrinja pergi senangken diri* **dengan** *pegang kartu (PW-1910)*

'The wife goes making herself happy **by** holding cards'

(4) *...akan mengadakan sooting besar-besaran dipantai Baron* **dengan** *menggunakan lk. 6000 orang penduduk... (M-1960)*

'...will hold a massive shooting in Baron's Beach **with** 6000 residents'

Based on examples (3) and (4), the function of dependent clause *dengan* is to connect the action and the instrument used by the actor. In example (3), *memegang kartu* 'holding cards' is the instrument used by the actor. Meanwhile, in example (4), the instrument used to support the action is six thousand citizens.

The function of manner conjunction is to state the manner relationship used to do the action in the independent clause. Manner conjunction is used 12 times in PW-1910, 4 times in M-1960, and 1 time in K-2010. The examples of *dengan* as manner conjunction are as follows.

(5) *Kita pikiri hal gerakannja bangsa Tionghoa,* **dengan** *memandang kaadaan di ini masa (PW-1910)*

'We think about the movements of Chinese people, **by** looking at the situation in this era'

(6) *Tentu hal ini akan meluas kedaerah2* **dengan** *mendirikan tjabang2nja (M-1960)*

'This will certainly extend to the regions **by** establishing branches'

(7) *Dia lalu meminta Ayman Thawahiri membentuk milisi bersenjata* **dengan** *memanggil kembali para pemuda... (K-2010)*

'He then asked Ayman Thawahiri to form an armed militia by recalling the youths...'

Three examples above show that the function of the word *dengan* is to explain the actions that need to be taken to reach the main action. For example, in example (7), *dia* 'he/she' undertakes two actions. The first action or the main action of *dia* is to ask Ayman Thawari to form an armed militia. To reach the action, the second action or the manner in which the main action is reached by *dia* is to call the youth back.

Besides functioning as an instrument and manner conjunctions, *dengan* also serves to convey purpose. In PW-1910 and M-1960, purpose conjunction is used once. Meanwhile, purpose conjunction is not used in K-2010. The following example is the use of purpose conjunction in the data.

> (8) ...*ada gerakan Tiong Hoa Hwe Koan, jang pertama kali digeraken di Betawi,* **dengan** *bermaksoed aken memadjoeken atoeran dan adat-istiadat sedjati dari bangsa Tionghoa (PW-1910)*
>
> '...there was the movement Tiong Hoa Hwe Koan, which was first started in Batavia, **meaning to** improve the true rules and customs of Chinese people'
>
> (9) ...*mengobarkan revolusi nasional* **dengan** *bertudjuan guna melepaskan diri dari belenggu pendjadjahan dan memperoleh kemerdekaan atas dasar kedaulatan rakjat (M-1960)*
>
> '...initiate a national revolution **with** the aim of escaping from the shackles of colonialism and gaining independence on the basis of people's sovereignty'

Based on the data, the use of purpose conjunction is followed by the word *bermaksud* 'mean to' and *bertujuan* 'intend to'. Both verbs also convey purpose. Therefore, it can be concluded that the dependent clause in purpose conjunction is to convey purposes or results that the independent clause wants to reach.

Another subordinating conjunction used in PW-1910 and M-1960 is the complement conjunction. The function of complement conjunction is to connect the supplementary clause and the independent clause. Complement conjunction is used once in PW-1910 and twice in M-1960. The following are examples of the use of complement conjunction.

> (10) *tentoelah saja djawab* **dengan:** *„Boekan patoet lagi, tetapi wadjib, misti perloe ditiroe" (PW-1910)*
>
> 'of course I was answered **by:** "not only it is a must, but it is an obligation, it needs to be imitated"'
>
> (11) *KASAD mengachiri pidato sambutannja itu* **dengan** *mengatakan: "mudah-mudahan" (M-1960)*
>
> 'KASAD ended his welcoming speech **by** saying: "hopefully"' (M-1960)

According to the data, the word *dengan* as a complement conjunction is always followed by direct quotes. The conjunction *dengan* is used as an utterance marker said by the subject in the independent clause. In example (10), the subject *saya* 'I' reveals the answer that he mentioned using the word *dengan* and a direct quote of the answer. Meanwhile, in example (11), the word *mengatakan* 'saying' that follows *dengan* functions as an affirmation of KASAD's speech marker.

Meanwhile, attributive conjunction is also used in the data. However, attributive conjunction only appeared in *Kompas* - two times and did not appear in other newspapers. The following example is the use of attributive conjunction in the data.

> (12) *Defisit anggaran Indonesia diperkirakan 1,6 persen* **dengan** *kemungkinan naik menjadi 2 persen dari produk domestik bruto...* (K-2010)

'Indonesia's budget deficit is estimated at 1.6 percent **with** the possibility of rising to 2 percent from the gross domestic product...'

The conjunction *dengan* in the example above functions as an additional explanation of the main clause. The main clause in example (12) is *defisit anggaran Indonesia diperkirakan 1,6%*, while the dependent clause is *kemungkinan naik menjadi 2 persen dari produk domestik bruto*. In example (12), *dengan* functions as additional information that the state's deficit was approximately about 1,6% to 2% of Indonesia's GDP.

Based on the data, the conjunction *dengan* appeared 19 times (18.4%) in PW-1910, 17 times (11.1%) in M-1960, and 4 times (4.2%) in K-2010. The conjunction *dengan* in the data can function as coordinating and subordinating conjunction in the newspapers. Table 13.3 illustrates the appearance of conjunction *dengan* in each period.

Based on the data in the table, the use of the conjunction *dengan* in the newspaper witnesses an increase in each period. Meanwhile, different from the expert's opinion, in its uses, subordinating conjunction *dengan* can function as instrument, manner, purpose, complement, and attributive conjunctions, not only instrument and manner. In PW-1910 and M-2010, the conjunctions used in the data have similar appearances. It is different from the use of conjunction *dengan* in K-2010 that uses manner and attributive conjunctions.

1. The Word *Dengan* as a Preposition

Van Wijk (1909) stated that preposition *dengan* has several meanings: accompaniment, instrument, manner, time, absence, and connectors of two adjectives. Slamet Muljana (1957) added that the preposition *dengan* has a bipartite meaning. Moreover, Lapoliwa (1992) completes the meaning of the preposition *dengan*, namely objective or receiver, agentive or subject, and possession. Meanwhile, the meaning of *dengan* stated by Alwi et al. (2003) underwent a narrowing, namely accompaniment, manner, and instrument.

Based on the explanation of the experts, the preposition *dengan* has eleven meanings, namely accompaniment, instrument, manner or adverbial, time, absence, equation, connector of two adjectives, bipartite, agentive, objective, and possession. The 11 meanings of preposition *dengan* are the basis for analyzing the meaning of the preposition *dengan*.

Based on the data, the preposition is used 84 times in PW-1910, 136 times in M-1960, and 91 times in K-2010. From eleven meanings of the preposition *dengan*,

Table 13.3 The Appearance of Coordinating and Subordinating Conjunction

Period	Coordinating conjunction	Subordinating conjunction
1910	Yes	Instrument, manner, purpose, and complement
1960	Yes	Instrument, manner, purpose, and complement
2010	No	Manner and attributive

there are ten meanings of the preposition *dengan* found in the data namely accompaniment, instrument, manner, bipartite, equation, objective, agentive, absence, time, and possession. The following are the explanations of the meanings of the preposition *dengan*.

1) *Dengan* as a Preposition of Accompaniment

The function of *dengan* as a preposition of accompaniment is to convey an accompaniment relationship. The use of preposition *dengan* with accompaniment has a similar meaning to the use of the word *bersama* 'together' or 'with'. Based on the data, *dengan* as a preposition of accompaniment is used 12 times (14.3%) in PW-1910, 41 times (30.1%) in M-1960, and 14 times (15.4%) in K-2010. The following examples are the uses of *dengan* as a preposition of accompaniment.

(13) ...*ia [Pek Liong Sek] di Tangerang ada perkara* **dengan polisie** *(PW-1910)*

'...he/ she [Pek Liong Sek] in Tangerang has some cases **with the police**'

(14) *Setelah mengadakan pembitjaraan* **dengan beberapa instansi pendidikan di Washington**... *(M-1960)*

'After holding talks **with several educational establishments in Washington**...'

(15) ...*kata Agassa dalam wawancara* **dengan radio Perancis**... *(K-2010)*

'said Agassa in an interview **with** a France radio...'

Based on the acquired data, *dengan* as a preposition of accompaniment is followed by animate noun (AN) and noun phrase (NP) as right collocate in each newspaper period. Example (13) shows the use of *dengan* as a preposition of accompaniment followed by AN. Meanwhile, examples (14) and (15) show the use of *dengan* followed by NP. Therefore, the structure of *dengan* as a preposition of accompaniment is *dengan* + AN/NP.

Although the preposition *dengan* states an accompaniment relationship, there are several clauses that contain other accompaniment affirmation elements. This can be observed from the use of certain words that function as an affirmation of the accompaniment's meaning. The use of affirmation words can be found in M-1960 and K-2010. The following example is the use of affirmation words that accompany the preposition *dengan* to state accompaniment meaning.

(16) *Menteri produksi Brigdjen Soeprajogi* **dengan disertai** *Pangdam V-Djaya Kol. Umar Wirahadikusumah hari Kamis jang akan datang ini akan mengadakan*... *(M-1960)*

'The Minister of Production Brigdjen Soeprajogi **accompanied by** Pangdam V-Djaya Kol. Umar Wirahadikusumah on Tuesday next week will hold...'

(17) ...*upaya untuk merekayasa kasus terhadap pimpinan KPK dilakukan* **bersama-sama dengan pihak lain** *(K-2010)*

'...attempts to fabricate cases against KPK leaders are carried out together **with other parties**'

Based on the three examples, it is proven that the use of the word *bersama-sama* 'together with' and *disertai* 'accompanied with' functions as an affirmation to the word *dengan* as a preposition of accompaniment. If the use of the preposition *dengan* or the affirmation is omitted in a clause, the clause still shows accompaniment meaning. The use of *dengan* as a preposition of accompaniment in the three newspapers has several structures, namely, (1) *dengan* + AN/NP, (2) affirmation + *dengan* + AN/NP, and (3) *dengan* + affirmation + AN/ NP.

2) *Dengan* as a Preposition of Instrument

The function of *dengan* as a preposition of an instrument is to state an instrument or a device used in an event. *dengan* as a preposition of an instrument is used 37 times (44%) in PW-1910, 33 times (24.3%) in M-1960, and 41 times (45.1%) in K-2010. The following examples are the uses of *dengan* as a preposition for an instrument.

(18) ...*soedah di beli oleh seorang Europa* **dengan harga mahal** *(PW-1910)*

'... it has already been bought by a European **at an expensive price**'

(19) *rakjat bernjanji2 dan berlari2an di djalan2 raja ibukota jg dihiasi* **dgn bendera** *(M-1960)*

'the people sing and run in the streets of the capital, which are decorated **with flags**'

(20) *Lalu Lintas Polda Metro Jaya dilakukan* **dengan pemindai** *(K-2010)*

'Polda Metro Jaya's traffic is done **by a scanner**'

Based on the examples, *dengan* as a preposition of the instrument generally has the right to collocate with inanimate noun (IN) or noun phrase (NP) that form the structure *dengan* + IN/ NP. Moreover, the instrument used can be abstract or concrete. The use of abstract instruments is in example (18). The phrase *harga mahal* 'expensive price' does not have a physical form, so *harga mahal* can be considered abstract. Meanwhile, concrete instruments are used in examples (19) and (20), namely *bendera* 'flag' and *pemindai* 'scanner'.

Although generally followed by IN or NP, there are several uses of *dengan* that are followed by an animate noun (AN). The use of AN only appears in PW-1910. The following example is the use of *dengan* + AN.

(21) ...*disini djoega akoe aken menoeker namakoe* **dengan,,Witte Tijger"** *(PW-1910)*

'... here also I will switch my name **to "Witte Tijger"**'

Dengan as a preposition of instrument that right-collocates with NB in PW-1910 is used three times. From the three appearances, the AN used is only a personal name similar to the example (21). The use of AN is to state the change of the subject name.

Although the function of *dengan* as a preposition of instrument is to state the instrument used in an action, affirmation words conveying instrument are also used in the clause. Affirmation word is used in K-2010. The following is an example.

(22) *Uji coba SAR yang baru ini* **dengan menggunakan pesawat tanpa awak** *akan dilakukan... (K-2010)*

'This new SAR test **by using unmanned aircraft** will be conducted...'

In example (22), the preposition *dengan* and the word *menggunakan* 'use' have the same function. Therefore, the word *menggunakan* is an affirmation of *dengan* as a preposition of an instrument in a clause. The use of affirmation forms a construction *dengan* + *affirmation* + *NP* that only appears in K-2010.

The use of *dengan* as a preposition of an instrument is generally followed by IN and NP. However, in PW-1910, there is a use of *dengan* followed by AN in the form of a personal name. Besides, in K-2010, there is an affirmation word that is used together with the preposition *dengan*. Therefore, *dengan* + *IN/NP* is the structure of *dengan* as a preposition of an instrument that appears in all newspapers. In PW-1910, there is a different structure, namely *dengan* + *AN* (personal name). Meanwhile, in K-2010, there is a structure *dengan* + *affirmation* + *NP*.

3) *Dengan* as a Preposition of Manner

The function of *dengan* as a preposition of manner is to illustrate the condition or the situation when an event is occurring. *Dengan* as a preposition of manner is used 19 times (22.6%) in PW-1910, 32 times (23.5%) in M-1960, and 4 times (4.4%) in K-2010. The following examples are the use of *dengan* as a preposition of manner.

(23) *Boemipoetra **dengen moeda** bisa mentjari kehidoepan sedikit...(PW-1910)*

'Boemipoetra can **easily** find a bit of life...'

(24) *...pembesar2 keamanan Djepang **dengan tidak ragu2 lagi** menjatakan dimuka umum umum... (M-1960)*

'...Japan's security authorities **without hesitation** made a public statement...'

(25) *Kalau politiknya oke, saya optimis **dengan hati-hati** ekonomi akan membaik (K-2010)*

'If the political (situation) is okay, I'm optimistic that the economy will **carefully** get better'

From the three examples, *dengan* as a preposition of manner is generally followed by an adjective (Adj) and an adjective phrase (AP) as right collocate. In PW-1910 and M-1960, *dengan* as a preposition of manner collocates the most with Adj. However, collocation with AP is not widely used in the newspaper. Furthermore, in K-2010, *dengan* as a preposition of manner is only followed by Adj. Based on the data, the structure of *dengan* as a preposition of manner is *dengan* + *Adj/AP*.

4) *Dengan* as a Preposition of Bipartite

The function of *dengan* as a preposition of bipartite is to state the event occurring between the first and second parties. *Dengan* as a preposition of bipartite is used 4 times (4.8%) in PW-1910, 5 times (3.7%) in M-1960, and 13 times (14.3%) in K-2010. The following examples are the uses of preposition *dengan* as a preposition of bipartite in the data.

(26) *Kaloe adjam djantan bertemoe **dengen ajam djantan jang lain**... (PW-1910)*

'When a rooster meets **[with] other roosters**..'

(27) *Kita ingin bersahabat **dengan segala negara** (M-1960)*

'We want to be friends **with all countries**'

(28) *Sylviana Murni sempat meninjau layanan baru itu dan berbincang **dengan warga** (K-2010)*

'Sylviana Murni had time to review the new service and chat **with residents**'

Based on the example in the data, *dengan* as a preposition of bipartite is always preceded by reciprocal verbs. Moreover, *dengan* as a preposition of bipartite can be followed by AN and NP. Therefore, the structure of *dengan* as a preposition of bipartite is *dengan* + AN/NP.

5) *Dengan* as a Preposition of Agentive

The function of *dengan* as a preposition of agentive is to state the subject or the causes of the action. The use of *dengan* as a preposition of agentive can be replaced with the preposition *oleh*. Based on the data, *dengan* as a preposition of agentive is used 3 times (3.6%) in PW-1910, 6 times (4.4%) in M-1960, and 3 times (3.3%) in K-2010. The following examples are the uses of *dengan* as a preposition of agentive in the data.

    (29) ...*tida heran lagi djikaloe sesaorang correspondent sring sekali kena di aboein **dengan kabar, jang bagitoe roepa** (PW-1910)*

    '...no wonder if a correspondent is frequently reported **with a news, that is so much**...'

    (30) *Penetapan tsb. disesuaikan **dengan perubahan koers rupiah** (M-1960)*

    'The determination is adjusted **to changes in the rupiah exchange rate**'

    (31) *pengembangan kreativitas sepatutnya didukung **dengan langkah nyata pemerintah** (K-2010)*

    'the development of creativity should be supported **by concrete steps of the government**'

The three examples illustrate that *dengan* as a preposition of agentive is always preceded by passive verbs with the affix *di-*. Moreover, *dengan* as a preposition of agentive in the data is followed by NP. Based on the data, the structure of *dengan* as a preposition of agentive is *dengan* + NP.

6) *Dengan* as a Preposition of Objective

Dengan as a preposition of objective is found in all newspapers in this study. *Dengan* as a preposition of objective is used two times (2.4%) in PW-1910, three times (2.2%) in M-1960, and five times (5.5%) in K-2010. *Dengan* as a preposition of objective can be replaced by the prepositions *akan, terhadap,* or *pada*. The following examples are the uses of *dengan* as a preposition of objective in the data.

    (32) *Bagaimanakah **dengan pensioenan wedana ini**?* (PW-1910)

    'How **about this retired regent's aide**?'

    (33) *Saja kira sdr2 sekalijan sependapat **dengan saja*** (M-1960)

    'I think you all agree **with me**'

    (34) *Penonton televisi ternyata juga suka **dengan "reality show" Pansus*** (K-2010)

    'Television viewers also like **with the Special Committees "reality show"**'

Based on the data, *dengan* as a preposition of an object can be followed by NP and Pronouns (Pro). In examples (32) and (34), *dengan* is followed by an NP. However, in example (33), the preposition *dengan* is followed by a Pro. The structures of *dengan* as a preposition of an object in the newspapers are (1) *dengan* + *NP* and (2) *dengan* + *Pro*.

7) *Dengan* as a Preposition of Time

The function of *dengan* as a preposition of time is to state the period of time needed to finish an event. *Dengan* as a preposition of time is used two times (2.4%) in PW-1910. The following example is the use of *dengan* as a preposition of time.

(35) ***Dengan sigera*** *ia paranin boeat menoeloeng* (PW-1910)
'He/ she **immediately** came to help'

Based on the data, *dengan* as a preposition of time can be followed by Adj, as in the example (35). The use of the word *sigera* in the sentence refers to the time needed by *ia* to help the object. Therefore, the use of *dengan* as a preposition of time in PW-1910 follows the structure *dengan* + *Adj*.

8) *Dengan* as a Preposition of Absence

The use of *dengan* as a preposition of absence with the word *tidak* 'not' or *tiada* 'no' means without. The preposition *dengan* conveying absence is used 5 times (6%) in PW-1910 and 1 time (0.7%) in M-1960. The following examples are the uses of the preposition *dengan* conveying absence.

(36) ...*kita nanti menoelis sasoewatoe perkara **dengan tida memandang** kanan dan kiri...* (PW-1910)
'...we will write about something **by not looking right and left**...'

(37) ...*maka penerbangan itu dilakukan mungkin **tidak dengan sengadja*** (M-1960)
'...then the flight may not be done **intentionally**'

In PW-1910, there are two uses of *dengan* as a preposition of absence, namely *tidak* + *dengan* and *dengan* + *tidak*. The two forms can be followed by a verb as right collocate that forms the structure *tidak* + *dengan* + *V* and *dengan* + *tidak* + *V*. Meanwhile, the structure used in M-1960 is *tidak* + *dengan* + *Adj*.

9) *Dengan* as a Preposition of Equation

The function of *dengan* as a preposition of the equation is to express the event that occurs in the clause. *Dengan* as a preposition of equation is used 5 times (3.7%) in M-1960 and 2 times (2.2%) in K-2010. The following examples are the use of *dengan* as a preposition of equation.

(38) ...*Djamhur dan Nani kabarnja dilarang oleh Persidja seperti halnja **dengan pemain2 BBSA*** (M-1960)
'...Djamhur and Nani were reportedly banned by Persidja **as well as the BBSA players**'

(39) ... *pengujian sensor CP-SAR dengan wahana satelit dapat dilakukan pada 2014 sejalan dengan program Lembaga Penerbangan dan Antariksa Nasional (Lapan)...* (K-2010)
'...the testing of the CP-SAR sensor with a satellite vehicle can be carried out in 2014 **in line with the National Institute of Aeronautics and Space (Lapan) program**'

In M-1960, words or phrases used to precede the use of the preposition *dengan* as a preposition of similarity are *sama* 'same', *serupa* 'similar', *seperti halnja* 'as well as', and *sebagaimana halnja* 'as in the case'. Based on example (38), the use of *seperti halnja* + *dengan* conveys a similarity connection between one party and other parties. The clause expresses the similarities between Djamhur, Nani, and *pemain-pemain BBSA*.

Meanwhile, in K-2010, the preposition *dengan* conveying meaning is preceded by the word *sejalan* 'in line'. Similar to the use of *dengan* as preposition of similarity in M-1960, preposition *dengan* in K-2010 is also followed by NP as in example (39). Based on the data, the preposition *dengan* conveying similarity is always followed by a companion, such as *seperti halnja* and *sejalan* so that it forms the structure *accompaniment* + *dengan* + *FN*.

10) *Dengan* as a Preposition of Possession

The function of the preposition *dengan* conveying possession expresses the extension of the noun or noun phrase that precedes the preposition *dengan*. The preposition conveying meaning is used 3 times (2.2%) in M-1960 and 5 times (5.5%) in K-2010. The following examples are the use of the preposition *dengan* conveying possession.

(40) ...*Bill Nieder pemegang rekor dunia* **dengan lemparan sedjauh 19,9 meter**... (M-1960)

'...Bill Nieder who holds the world's record **with a throw of 19.9 meter**...'

(41) *Negara-negara maju* **dengan defisit anggaran yang membengkak** *akan mengeluarkan*... (K-2010)

'Developed countries **with bloated budget deficits** will issue...'

In example (40), the phrase *lemparan sedjauh 19.9 m* is an extension of possession owned by a world record-holder, Bill Nieder. Meanwhile, the phrase *defisit anggaran yang membangkak* dalam (41) is the extension of the phrase *negara-negara maju*. Based on the data, the preposition *dengan* conveying possession has the structure *N/ NP dengan* + *NP*.

11) Preposition *Dengan* Conveying Other Meanings

Based on the data, the preposition *dengan* has other meanings that have not been specifically classified by experts. Other meanings are used 2 times (1.5%) in M-1960 and 2 times (2.2%) in K-2010. The following examples are the uses of the word *dengan* conveying other meanings in the data.

(42) *Bank Indonesia dalam minggu ini naik* **dengan 0,11%** (M-1960)

'Bank Indonesia in this week rose **by 0.11%**'

(43) ...*operator bertambah* **dengan 110 buah** (M-1960)

'...operator increased **by 110 pieces**'

(44) *Proses pengurusan KTP ini berbeda* **dengan perpanjangan surat izin mengemudi** (K-2010)

'The process of obtaining an ID card is different **from the renewal of a driving license**'

The use of preposition *dengan* in the three examples cannot be classified in any of the meanings *dengan* that have been classified by the experts. The function of preposition *dengan* in example (42) is to express *sebesar* 'in the amount of' or *sebanyak* 'as much as'. In example (43), the function of *dengan* is to state 'becoming'.

Meanwhile, in example (44), the function of *dengan* is to express 'differences' between two parties. The use of the verb *berbeda* 'differs from' shows the differences connected by the preposition *dengan*. The differences involve the *proses pengurusan KTP* and *proses perpanjangan surat izin mengemudi*.

Based on Graph 13.1, there are several meanings of preposition *dengan* found in each newspaper, including accompaniment, instrument, manner, bipartite, agentive, and objective. On the other hand, the uses of other meanings are found in different newspapers. *Dengan* as a preposition of time is only used in PW-1910. D*engan* as a preposition absence is only found in PW-1910 and M-1960. Moreover, the preposition *dengan* conveying similarity and possession is found in M-1960 and K-2010. Meanwhile, there are also preposition *dengan* with special meanings, referred to as other meanings in M-1960 and K-2010.

B. **The Structure of Verb-Preposition *dengan***

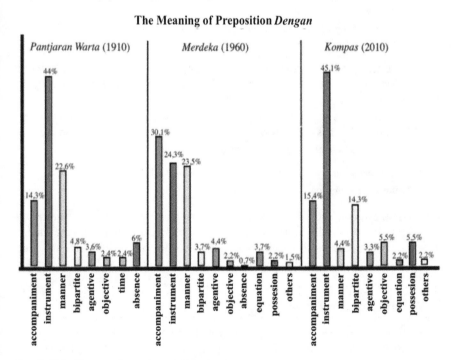

Graph 13.1 The meanings of preposition *dengan*

The appearance of a verb in a clause can cause the preposition *dengan* to appear. Cook (1989), in Soeb (1955: 33) classified the meanings of verbs into twelve categories: state verbs (SV), state experiential verbs (SEV), state benefactive verbs (SBV), state locative verbs (SLV), process verbs (PV), process experiential verbs (PEV), process benefactive verbs (PBV), process locative verbs (PLV), action verbs (AV), action experiential verbs (AEV), action benefactive verb (ABV), and action locative verbs (ALV). Based on the 10 meanings of the preposition *dengan* found in the data, there are 5 meanings of the preposition *dengan* that have a connection to verbs, such as accompaniment, bipartite, instrument, agent, and manner. Meanwhile, there are 5 types of verb meanings based on 12 Cook's verb types, including AV, AEV, ALV, ABV, and PEV.

1. **Verb-Preposition of Accompaniment**

Based on the data, the preposition *dengan* conveying accompaniment has the most collocations with AV. The verbs classified into AV in the data is *ditukar* 'be switched', *membakar* 'to burn', and *mengatur* 'to set'. The following example is the use of *verb + dengan*.

(45) *orang2 polisi rahasia AS telah tiba di Tokio guna **mengatur** tindakan2 keamanan dengan kepolisian Djepang* (M-1960)

'US secret police officers have arrived in Tokio to **arrange** security measures with Japanese police'

The verb *mengatur* in the example requires subject and object. The subject in the example is *orang2 polisi rahasia AS*. Meanwhile, *tindakan2 keamanan* is the object, and *dengan kepolisian Djepang* refers to the companion of the object.

Besides AV, the preposition *dengan* conveying accompaniment can also collocate with ALV although it has only a few numbers. The example of ALV used in the data is the verb *pergi*. The following is an example of a clause in the data.

(46) *ia telah **pergi** pada prampoean hina, dengan bini moeda* (PW-1910)

'he **has gone** with a lowly woman, with a mistress'

Based on example (46), the subject *ia* performs locative action in the verb *pergi* 'go'. In the clause, *ia* is the subject = object, *pada prampoean hina* states the change of location of *ia* before he/she carries out the action of going. Therefore, the structure of verb-preposition *dengan* conveying accompaniment can be: AV/ ALV + *dengan* + AN/NP.

2. **Verb-Preposition of Bipartite**

The verb that refers to biparty/reciprocity meaning based on the data is the reciprocal verb *ber-*. The verb *ber-* found in the data is classified into AV and AEV. The following examples are the uses of verbs that collocate with the preposition *dengan* conveying bipartite.

(47) *adjam djantan* **bertemoe** *dengen ajam djantan jang lain* (PW-1910)
'a rooster **meets** [with] other roosters'

(48) ...*yang akan saya lakukan adalah* **berbicara** *dengan banyak pemain* (K-2010)
'...what I will do is **talk** to a lot of players'

The verb *bertemu* 'to meet' is classified into AV. In its use, *bertemu* requires two cases, subject and object. The action of *bertemu* in the clause shows the action done by the two parties. In AV structure, the subject and object have to be an animate entity.

Different from the verb *bertemu*, *berbicara* 'to talk' is classified into AEV. It is because the action done by *saya* can affect the psychological changes of the object *banyak pemain*. Based on the data, the structure of verb-preposition *dengan* conveying biparty can be: *AV/ AEV (ber-) + dengan + AN/NP*.

3. Verb-Preposition of Instrument

Based on the data, *dengan* as a preposition of accompaniment can collocate with AV, AEV, and ALV. Meanwhile, the preposition *dengan* conveying instrument can also collocate with PEV. The following examples are the uses of verbs found in the data.

(49) *djimat terboeatt dari kertas jang* **ditoelis** *dengan hoeroef Arab* (PW-1910)
'the amulet is made of paper **written** in Arabic letters'

(50) ...*menjatakan* **telah melihat** *dengan mata-kepalanja sendiri majat Hitler*... (M-1960)
'...claims to **have seen** with his own eyes the corpse of Hitler...'

(51) *Secretaris residensie Bandoeng nanti* **pegi** *ka Europa dengan verlof satoe tahoen* (PW-1910)
'Bandung's secretary residensie will **go** to Europe with one year permission'

(52) *Partai Golkar yang mendapat kesempatan pertama bertanya langsung* **mencecar** *Marsillam dengan pertanyaan seputar statusnya*...(K-2010)
'The Golkar Party, which got the first opportunity to ask questions, immediately **attacked** Marsillam with questions about her status...'

Example (49) is the use of AV that collocates with *dengan* as a preposition of instrument in the clause. In the uses, *ditulis* 'be written' requires subject and object. Object in the clause is *djimat* 'amulet', while the subject that carries out the action undergoes omission in the clause. However, based on the example, information is required that the subject writes *djimat* using Arabic letters.

The verb *melihat* 'to see' is classified into PEV. In example (50), *melihat* requires one experiencer and one object. Based on the clause, *seorang bekas serdadu Uni Sovjet* is an experiencer. On the other hand, the object in the clause is *mayat Hitler.* The action of seeing is experienced by the experiencer using his/ her eyes.

In example (51), the verb *pegi* or *pergi* 'go' contains locative meaning. This is proven by the subject *secretaris residensie Bandoeng* 'Bandung residence secretary' carries out the locative action *go* to Europe. Meanwhile, the function of preposition *dengan* in the clause is to state abstract instrument used by the subject, *verlof satoe tahoen* 'taking leave for a year'.

The verb *mencecar* 'to harshly ask' is classified into AEV. It is because the object experiences psychological changes after the action is carried out. In example (52), *Partai Golkar* as the subject carries out the action of *mencecar* that can affect the condition of the object *Marsillam*. The instrument used to do the action of *mencecar* is the *pertanyaan seputar status Marsillam dalam sejumlah rapat KSSK* 'the questions about Marsillam's status in several KSSK meetings'. Based on the data, the structure of *dengan as* a verb-preposition of the instrument is: *AV/ AEV/ ALV/ PEV* + *dengan* + *N/NP*.

4. **Verb-Preposition of Manner**

Based on the data, *dengan* as a preposition of manner collocates the most with AV. However, there are the uses of ABV in the clause. The following example is the use of a verb with *dengan* as a preposition of manner.

(53) *sebab Atjim maski landraad bebrapa kali soedah kasih ingat padanja aken* **membri** *ketrangan dengan sebenar-benarnja* (PW-1910)

'because Atjim although has been on district court several times has reminded him to **provide** truthful information'

(54) *Proklamasi kemerdekaan tsb.* **disambut** *dengan gegap gempita* (M-1960)

'The Declaration of Independence **greeted** with great enthusiasm'

The verb *memberi* 'to give' is an example of the use of ABV that collocates with *dengan* as a preposition of manner. In example (53), the action of *memberi* causes the benefactor to lose something. Here, the missing object is *keterangan* 'information'.

Meanwhile, the verb *disambut* 'be greeted' is an example of the use of AV in a clause. The verb *disambut* requires a subject and an object. In the clause, the subject is omitted. Meanwhile, the object in the clause is *proklamasi kemerdekaan tersebut* 'that independence proclamation'. Based on the data, the structure of the verb-preposition *dengan* is: *AV/ ABV* + *dengan* + *Adj/ FA*.

5. **Verb-Preposition of Agent**

Based on the data, *dengan* as a preposition of agent can only collocate with AV. Verb classified into this group is the passive verb *di-*. The following example is the use of verb in the data.

(55) *pengembangan kreativitas sepatutnya* **didukung** *dengan langkah nyata* (K-2010)

'the development of creativity should be **supported** by concrete steps'

In the data, the verbs *di-* that are classified into the group of verb-preposition of agent are *didukung* 'be supported', *dibuka* 'be opened', and *dimulai* 'be started'. In example (55), *langkah nyata* 'concrete step; is the subject. Meanwhile, *pengembangan kreativitas* 'creativity development' is the receiver in the clause. Therefore, the structure of verb-preposition *dengan* is *AV* + *dengan* + *NP*.

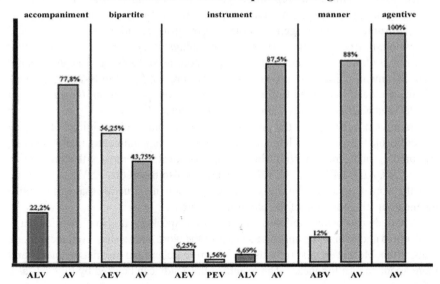

Graph 13.2 The structure of verb-preposition *dengan*

Based on the data, there are five meanings of verb that collocates with the preposition *dengan* as a right collocate, such as AV, ALV, AEV, ABV, and PEV. The meaning of the verb collocates with five meanings of the preposition *dengan*, such as accompaniment, biparty/ reciprocity, instrument, manner, and agent. *Dengan* as a preposition of accompaniment can collocate with AV and ALV. The preposition *dengan* conveying biparty can collocate with AV and AEV. *Dengan* as a preposition of instrument can collocate with AV, AEV, ALV, and PEV. *Dengan* as a preposition of manner can collocate with AV and AEV. Meanwhile, *dengan* as a preposition of agent can only collocate with AV. Graph 13.2 illustrates the structure of verb-preposition *dengan*.

13.5 Conclusion

The word *dengan* serves as a conjunction and a preposition in the newspapers published in Indonesia. Based on the research, the use of the word *dengan* from 1910 to 2010 as a conjunction has been decreasing while the use as a preposition has been increasing. Moreover, according to the data, *dengan* functions as coordinating and subordinating conjunctions. The experts argued that the word *dengan* as a subordinating conjunction can only be instrument and manner conjunctions. However, this study found that *dengan* as a subordinating conjunction can be instrument, manner, purpose, complement, and attribute conjunctions.

The word *dengan* as a preposition has eleven meanings. However, the data in this study only presents ten meanings of preposition *dengan,* namely, accompaniment, instrument, manner, agentive, objective, bipartite, equation, time, absence, and possession. In PW-1910, there are several meanings of the preposition *dengan* that were not used, including equation and possession. In M-1960, time meaning is not used. Meanwhile, time and absence meanings were not found in K-2010. Besides, this research also identified different meanings of the preposition *dengan* used in M-1960 and K-2010, namely, *sebesar, menjadi* and *perbedaan.*

Among ten meanings of the preposition *dengan,* only five meanings of *dengan* that collocate with a verb as left collocate, such as accompaniment, biparty, manner, instrument, and agent. The preposition *dengan* collocates the most with action verbs, such as AV, ALV, AEV, and ABV. Moreover, it is also found that PEV can collocate with the word *dengan.* The analysis of verbs can result in a structure that will simplify the meaning classification of the preposition *dengan.*

This study can benefit Indonesian and foreign speakers. It also allows language speakers to understand the appropriate uses of the word *dengan* as a conjunction or a preposition. Moreover, this study also benefits researchers and linguists to understand more about bahasa Indonesia. The results of this study can be used by linguists as a reference to classify *dengan* as a conjunction and a preposition as well as the meaning of the preposition *dengan* from the year 1910 to 2010.

Acknowledgements This paper is part of Hibah Riset Awal FIB UI Tahun 2018 titled 'Perkembangan Struktur Kalimat Pasif dalam Bahasa Indonesia', which was supported by the Faculty of Humanities, University of Indonesia to Dien Rovita, Priscila Fitriasih Limbong, and Gita Ayodhiya Sanarta.

References

Alwi, H., dkk. (2003). *Tata Bahasa Baku Bahasa Indonesia.* Edisi Ketiga. Jakarta: Balai Pustaka.
Budiwiyanto, A. (2014). Korpus dalam Penyusunan Kamus. http://badanbahasa.kemdikbud.go.id/lamanbahasa/content/korpus-dalam-penyusunan-kamus, diakses pada 1 Februari 2019.
Chaer, A. (2014). *Linguistik Umum.* Edisi Revisi. Jakarta: Rineka Cipta.
Creswell, J. W. (2013). *Research design; Qualittaive, quantitative, and mixed methods approaches.* SAGE Publications Inc.
Lapoliwa, H. (1992). *Frasa Preposisi dalam Bahasa Indonesia.* Jakarta: Pusat Pembinaan dan Pengembangan Bahasa.
Mahardika, N. (2017). Ranah Semantis Kolokat Kanan Verba Berafiks + Preposisi *Tentang* dalam Korpus Pemelajar Bahasa Indonesia untuk Penutur Asing (Bipa): Kajian Linguistik Korpus. Makalah Jurnal Program Studi Indonesia Universitas Indonesia; tidak dipublikasikan.
Mudhongafah, S. U. (2018). "Perkembangan Konjungsi Maka dari Abad ke-17 sampai Abad ke-21". Skripsi Sarjana Program Studi Indonesia Universitas Indonesia; tidak dipublikasikan.
Muljana, S. (1957). *Kaidah Bahasa Indonesia II.* Jakarta: Djambatan.
Ramlan, M. (1980). *Kata Depan atau Preposisi dalam Bahasa Indonesia.* Yogyakarta: U.P. Karyono.
Romli, K. (2017). *Komunikasi Massa.* Jakarta: Grasindo.

Sabila, A. A. (2018). "Perkembangan Preposisi *Daripada* dari Abad Ke-17 sampai Abad Ke-21". Skripsi Sarjana Program Studi Indonesia Universitas Indonesia; tidak dipublikasikan.
Soeb, K. G. (1995). *Konstruksi Verba Berderet dalam Bahasa Indonesia: Kajian Semantis.* Universitas Indonesia; tidak dipubliskasikan.
Wijk, D., Gerth van. (1909). *Tata Bahasa Melayu.* Translated by T.W. Kamil from Spraakler der Maleische Taal. Jakarta: Balai Pustaka.

Gita Ayodhiya Sanarta was born in Palembang, 29 November 1996. She graduated from Indonesian Studies, Faculty of Humanities, University of Indonesia in 2019. Her research interest is language development.

Dien Rovita graduated with a Master's Degree in Linguistic, the Faculty of Humanities, University of Indonesia in 2007. Now, she teaches some linguistic classes in Indonesian Studies, the Faculty of Humanities, University of Indonesia. She is interested in doing linguistic researches, specifically on the Indonesian language development and also the lexicology and lexicography field. Some of her works that are related to those fields have been presented on the national and international seminars.

Open Access This chapter is licensed under the terms of the Creative Commons Attribution 4.0 International License (http://creativecommons.org/licenses/by/4.0/), which permits use, sharing, adaptation, distribution and reproduction in any medium or format, as long as you give appropriate credit to the original author(s) and the source, provide a link to the Creative Commons license and indicate if changes were made.

The images or other third party material in this chapter are included in the chapter's Creative Commons license, unless indicated otherwise in a credit line to the material. If material is not included in the chapter's Creative Commons license and your intended use is not permitted by statutory regulation or exceeds the permitted use, you will need to obtain permission directly from the copyright holder.

Chapter 14
Connecting Texts and Thoughts: How Translanguaging and Multilingual Writings Reflect Hybrid Identities in Colonial Times

Afwa Zakia Al Azkaf, Nurenzia Yannuar, Yazid Basthomi, and Yusnita Febrianti

Abstract Indonesian multilingualism has been affected by outside factors including colonialism and globalization. During the Dutch colonial period in the early 1900s, Indonesian intellectuals wrote mainly in Dutch, and occasionally English and other regional languages. A hybrid identity was embraced as these speakers moved from one language to another in their speech. This study seeks to examine the manner in which a multilingual writer constructs his self-identity while expressing his opinions through newspaper columns, as well as the influence of colonialism on the writer's self-identification. Using qualitative analysis of textual data taken from Indonesian newspapers published in the 1930s and 1970s, this study demonstrates that the multilingual writer recognized his hybrid self-identity since he could utilize a different language in different contexts. A hybrid identity was developed by the multilingual writer when he created a meaning-making system, shaped experience, and acquired understanding or knowledge using various languages in his repertoire. Despite the different identities, he remained loyal to one primary identity.

Keywords Bilingualism · Translanguaging · Writings · Self-identity · Hybrid identity

---

A. Z. Al Azkaf · N. Yannuar (✉) · Y. Basthomi · Y. Febrianti
Department of English, Universitas Negeri Malang, Malang, Indonesia
e-mail: nurenzia.yannuar.fs@um.ac.id

A. Z. Al Azkaf
e-mail: afwazakia@gmail.com

Y. Basthomi
e-mail: ybasthomi@um.ac.id

Y. Febrianti
e-mail: yusnita.febrianti.fs@um.ac.id

14.1 Introduction

In the past, many Indonesians did not acquire a high degree of proficiency in the Indonesian language. However, in 1928, a variant of Malay was selected as the language of unity primarily due to its widespread usage as a lingua franca throughout the archipelago (Abas, 1987; Sneddon, 2003). Throughout the history of the nation, there were some factors that influenced how Indonesians use other languages in their spoken or written language, such as colonialism, migration, and globalization. The unconditional surrender of Dutch colonialism to the Japanese had led Indonesia into a new chapter of history (Yasmis, 2007).

The Indonesian language became more prominent during Japanese colonization (Anderson, 1966; Dumadi, 1988). The Japanese prohibited using Dutch in any context and desired to establish Japanese as the official language; however, achieving this objective within a limited timeframe proved unfeasible (Abduh & Rosmaladewi, 2019; Anderson, 1966). As a result, the Indonesian language, viewed as a simple, flexible, and neutral language unrelated to ethnic groupings, gained prominence in government, classrooms, and mass media (Anderson, 1966; Sneddon, 2003). During this time, the Dutch language lost its place and purpose, and the Indonesian language quickly took its place (Abduh & Rosmaladewi, 2019).

The dynamics of language use also influenced the newspapers and journalists. Sin Tit Po (STP) was a nationalist newspaper published in 1929 by a number of Chinese–Indonesian citizens in Surabaya, East Java (Setiono, 2008). According to Hatta (1979), the Chinese–Indonesian Party, which was led by Liem Koen Hian, who was also the founder of Sin Tit Po, fought together with the indigenous people of Indonesia for Indonesian independence. The members of the Party also wished to renounce their Chinese citizenship to become Indonesian citizens after independence. STP was published before Indonesia's independence and mainly discussed Indonesia's movement towards independence.

On the other hand, Indonesia Raya (IR) was published after Indonesia's independence. IR was a national newspaper published in two periods, i.e., during the Old Order government and the New Order era (Djati & Anderson, 2010). Both newspapers represent the authentic legacy of Indonesian history and a closer examination of how languages were used in the newspapers is crucial to understanding language and identity in the multilingual country within those periods.

A well-known journalist who contributed to STP and IR newspapers was Kwee Thiam Tjing (Kwee), known by his pen name, Tjamboek Berdoeri. His writing materials covered all levels of society: friends-foes, male–female, young-old, and others. He began contributing to the STP newspaper throughout the period of 1938–1939, utilizing this platform to express his perspectives on the various events that happened during that era. In addition, Kwee also wrote about the situation in Indonesia during the colonialism era in IR newspaper columns. Djati and Anderson (2010) compiled Kwee's writings in newspaper columns at IR (1971–1973) into a book entitled *Menjadi Tjamboek Berduri: Memoar Kwee Thiam Tjing*. All of Kwee's writings in the book were written from July 22, 1971, to July 28, 1973, which portrayed his recount of the world around him from the Dutch East Indies colonial period and the Japanese era to the early period of Indonesian independence (Djati & Anderson, 2010).

The idiosyncratic orthography employed in these newspaper columns may be a challenge for contemporary Indonesian readers. STP (1938–1939) used the Van Ophuijsen and Soewandi spelling, on the other hand IR (1971–1973) used *Ejaan Yang Disempurnakan (EYD)*. The first standard spelling for Indonesian was referred to as the Van Ophuijsen Spelling System, which was implemented before the establishment of the Republican or Soewandi Spelling System. Van Ophuijsen Spelling System was used from 1901 to 1947, while the Republican Spelling System was used from March 17, 1947 to the establishment of *Ejaan Yang Disempurnakan* (The Perfected Spelling System) in 1972 (Arifin & Tasai, 1995; Montolalu & Suryadinata, 2007).

The literary works published by Kwee during the historical period toward Indonesian independence have been the subject of extensive research. Amelia (2016) argued that Indonesian literature had the potential to contribute significantly to global postcolonial literature despite challenges in translation of them, citing a multilingual book written by Tjamboek Berdoeri, entitled *Indonesia dalem Api dan Bara* 'Indonesia on Fire and Charcoals'. Previous studies such as Dannari et al. (2021), Hapsari (2014), and Streifeneder and Missbach (2008) have also focused on the book, which provides a comprehensive account of the historical context in Indonesia during the 1940s, emphasizing the final stages of Dutch colonization and the subsequent Japanese occupation.

However, there has been limited research conducted on the linguistic components included in Kwee's newspaper columns, despite his intriguing language style. As a polyglot, Kwee combined various linguistic codes and seamlessly transitioned between different languages. Wahyuni et al. (2023) discussed how Kwee's translingual practice functions as a mediational instrument to facilitate the negotiation of identities as he repositioned himself and others within a dominant power structure.

Against this background, the present study will analyze Kwee's writings during the colonial period and investigate the way a multilingual writer articulated his self-identity and conveyed his opinions through the medium of newspaper columns. Additionally, the study aims to examine the influence of colonialism on the writer's process of self-identification.

Translanguaging framework (García & Wei, 2014; Baker, 2011) is employed in this study to examine the language used in the writings. In the following section, we review the concept of translanguaging, and then explore the relationship between writing and identity.

14.2 Translanguaging

Both translanguaging and code-switching studies allow researchers to investigate the complex nature of bilingual and multilingual speech, which includes how speakers mix and switch languages (Balam, 2021). Code-switching represents the outsider point of view of bilinguals; for example, switching from one language to another is recognized as an action involving two different languages (Baker, 2011; Chan, 2021; García, 2009). Code-switching typically involves a language hierarchy, wherein one language assumes a greater level of dominance over the other, commonly known as the matrix language (Myers-Scotton, 2011).

On the other hand, translanguaging is more focused on exploring how bilinguals make meanings of the world around them using different languages in their repertoire (García & Wei, 2014). In this way, translanguaging is different from code-switching, because the former involves the speaker's construction of a meaning-making system. Translanguaging underscores the insider point of view, and is no longer interested in the name or categorization of different languages involved in multilingual speech (García & Wei, 2014). Translanguaging is the use of all the linguistic repertoire without regard to conventional barriers across languages (Otheguy et al., 2015; Wei, 2011). As multilingual speakers transcend language barriers, they create a translanguaging space, wherein they foster creativity and critical thinking in the utilization of several languages (Wei, 2011).

Translanguaging is the process by which speakers shape their experiences, obtain understanding or information in the utterance utilizing two or more languages, and make meaning of the speech (Baker, 2011). This definition was related to multilingual classroom situations where bilingual children were forced to take a test in one language, which hindered them from using the total capacity of their language repertoire (Baker, 2011; García & Wei, 2014). Exploring translanguaging in language classrooms can help teachers see bilinguals from another perspective and support their personal identity. Similarly, this research employs Baker's (2011) definition, which enables the analysis to center on how multilingual speakers use each of the languages in their repertoire to create meaning, shape experiences, and gain understanding or knowledge in printed media.

14.3 Writing and Identity

Writing is affected by life histories and personal backgrounds (Ivanič, 1998). According to Richardson (2000), writing is a way to discover and analyze the world. Writers' personal and cultural backgrounds shape their writing; in this way, writing is a means for authors to reflect and represent their identity. According to Ivanič (1998), identity is commonly understood as individuals' personal understanding of themselves. However, the limitation of this definition lies in its failure to include the notions of social construction and boundaries (Ivanič, 1998).

The cognitive processes and thought patterns of bilingual individuals are influenced by their reflection on the world around them and their understanding of personal identity (Broadbent & Vavilova, 2015). The relationship between cognition and thought is intricately linked to their proficiency in several languages, enabling them to draw upon various linguistic information (Pavlenko, 2014).

Defining one's identity is a complex process, particularly for multilingual speakers who perceive themselves as belonging to many identities. An individual may possess a hybrid identity, which merges aspects of multiple identities. The term can also be defined as the convergence of the categorization of identity within certain boundaries, such as the local and the global, such as Asian and Western identities (Ang, 2003). Hybrid identity assumes no boundary among the different identities (Ang, 2003; Smith & Leavy, 2008). The blend results in a hybrid form that 'signifies the encounter, conflict, and/or blending of two ethnic or cultural categories which, while by no means pure and distinct in nature, tends to be understood and experienced as meaningful identity labels by members of these categories' (Lo, 2002).

14.4 Method

In this paper, the language used in old newspapers such as Sin Tit Po (STP) and Indonesia Raya (IR) is investigated. This study is descriptive and qualitative in nature. The qualitative method is used because the research yield in this method produces descriptive data taken from spoken or written sources (Taylor et al., 2016). The data analysis is focused on examining the translanguaging and hybrid identity in old newspaper columns written by Kwee. The data were collected in several steps. First, we collected the newspapers written by Kwee. The newspapers were divided into two sources, the first one was STP (1938–1939) and the second was IR (1971–1973). The two articles taken from STP newspaper are *Bing Swie 'nSia poenja Verslag* written on March 26th, 1938, and *Gertak Soerabaja* written on October 22nd, 1938. Subsequently, we collected the articles from IR newspapers that were parts of Anderson and Djati's (2010) *Menjadi Tjamboek Berdoeri: Memoar Kwee Thiam Tjing*. Three articles were taken from the aforementioned compilation, namely: *Kaula Belanda Bukan Bangsa Belanda, Ben Jij Een Chinese?* and *Mas Tom*, which were written approximately between 1971 and 1973. Several languages are observed in the writings, including Indonesian, Dutch, Hokkien, and Javanese.

The analysis of the data in this study is aimed at answering the following research questions: (1) how does a multilingual writer self-identify himself when sharing thoughts through newspaper columns? and (2) how does colonialism influence the writer's self-identification?

Using the translanguaging framework proposed by Baker (2011) and García and Wei (2014), we demonstrate that Kwee did not intentionally switch between languages as he displayed a high level of proficiency in all of the languages he had acquired, thus did not recognize the boundaries between them as separate languages. Further, self-identity is investigated by locating the process of 'making meaning, shaping experiences, and gaining understanding or knowledge through using two languages' (Baker, 2011) in the texts. In this light, the framing of self-identity was connected to the social context of the era, showing how social background impacts the writer's identity.

It is important to note that the primary data for the present study comprises texts written by a writer proficient in multiple languages. While direct interviews with the author to uncover the precise motivations behind their multilingual practice were not feasible, our research centers on exploring the themes present in the text and investigating how language choice may be closely linked to these themes (Yannuar, 2022).

14.5 Analysis

14.5.1 Making Meaning

Baker (2011) pointed out that translanguaging is how a bilingual speaker makes meanings out of their various languages. In this section, four examples are provided to show that self-identification could be explained through translanguaging. Using the examples, we describe how the characters in the writing move from one language to another when they express specific emotions, feelings, sarcasm, and make connections to their specific ethnic groups or groups.

(1) *Mendenger itoe pertanja´an, saja kepaksa terangken pada itoe sobat dari Ngoenoet, apa jang Hong Tjiang baroesan bitjaraken semoea memang betoel kedjadian. Tjoema sadja ia loepa terangken diblakangnja itoe sekalian Shanghay, Hankow enz, koedoe ditambahin "straat". Dan halnja Hong Tjiang saben-saben kepaksa moesti pindah, ini meloeloe disebabken kerna Hong Tjiang terkenal sebagi orang jang soesah sekali loenasin toenggakan sewa roemahnja, hingga seringkali kedjadian sampe dioesir oleh jang poenja.*

"Dikrotjok djaran poetéh! Tjah Soerabaia arep njlomoti botjah Ngoenoet!"

Sembari menggrendeng, si sobat dari Ngoenoet kemoedian berlaloe dengen tida brenti golengken kepalanja, jang roepanja dirasaken moemet kerna keterdjang gertak Soerabaja.

'Hearing that question, I had to explain to my friend from Ngunut what Hong Tjiang just said really happened. But he just forgot to explain that behind those Shanghay, Hankow etc., they had to be added "a street". And the reason Hong Tjiang always had to move was because Hong Tjiang was known as a person who was difficult to pay off the arrears on his rent, so it often happened that he was evicted by the owner of the house.

"Bitten by the white horse! Surabaya people lie to Ngunut people!"

While grumbling, the friend from Ngunut then left by not stopping shaking his head, since he felt dizzy because of Surabaya's bluff.'

Excerpt (1) is taken from an article entitled *Gertak Soerabaja* 'Surabaya's bluff', which talks about Hong Tjiang, who came from Surabaya. He was famous for his arrogance because of his big-city character. He fooled another character, named Kwee's friend from Ngunut or *Tjina goenoengan* 'mountain Chinese people or village people'. Hong Tjiang lied about his journey as a nomad who constantly moved from one place to another in China. He told Kwee's friend from Ngunut that he had lived in all parts of China and bragged about his life. The friend from Ngunut was obviously amazed by Hong Tjiang. As a villager who met a big city person, the friend from Ngunut must have felt insecure. That is why in the story, he was shown to be speechless and described as listening quietly because he felt that he was no equal to HT.

Yet, when the friend from Ngunut was told by Kwee about Hong Tjiang and when he already knew that he was fooled by Hong Tjiang in (1), he directly expressed his anger in Javanese. '*Dikrotjok djaran poeteh! Tjah Soerabaja arep tjlomoti botjah Ngoenoet!*' 'Attacked by a white horse! Surabaya people lied to Ngunut people!' the friend from Ngunut said.

The utterance shows that the friend from Ngunut was disappointed and angry at Hong Tjiang because of his bragging. The friend from Ngunut felt so worthless that he lost all the words to describe the great Hong Tjiang. His insecurity drove him to not respect himself for just a story given by a stranger that was actually nonsense. We already knew how the friend from Ngunut felt, and it was shown in the way he spoke. In that specific context which drives spontaneous responses such as anger, a daily used language will appear. In (1), we can assume that his daily language was Javanese.

On different occasions, a friend from Ngunut used Indonesian when talking to Hong Tjiang. This shows that Indonesian is a unitary language that is generally used by Indonesians to communicate when they encounter a stranger. In (1), the meaning-making process is shown by the use of the phrase *Dikrotjok djaran poeteh!* to express personal emotions and anger. The utilization of animal names such as *djaran* 'horse' helps reinforce this assertion. Some animals in Javanese such as dogs, horses, and crickets are employed as objects of verbal derogation during episodes of anger (Sumadyo, 2013).

The meaning-making here is understood in the way bilinguals express their specific emotion using their daily used language and the way they speak the unitary language as the medium to communicate with other people. They are able to use different languages in the repertoire for different specific situations and emotions.

(2) "*Djadi '**nko** ini dateng dari Ngoenoet?*" *tanya Hong Tjiang.*

"***Owee, siansing***," *djawab jang ditanja,*

"'So, are you (Chinese used '*nko* to call other people in the first meeting as the nickname instead of calling 'you') coming from Ngunut?" asked Hong Tjiang.

"Yes, Sir," answered the one asked.'

Example (2) depicts a conversation between Chinese descents, as shown from the nickname used to greet each other. In Hokkien, '*nko*' means brother or a term of address for an unfamiliar person. The term is commonly used to convey deference when people meet others for the first time.

The conversation illustrates how people of Chinese descents were respectful towards each other, especially since they were the minority during the era. In (2), the addressee answered in Hokkien, "*Owee, siansing*". *Owee* means 'I am' and *siansing* means 'Sir', which is normally written in Pinyin as *Xian Sheng*. Kwee, however, chose to write it as *siangsing*, presumably capturing his Javanese pronunciation.

In this conversation, we see that the Hokkien nickname was used as a friendly greeting to start a nice and peaceful conversation filled with respect. The choice to use a Hokkien phrase while speaking Malay shows that the bilinguals in the story were able to choose and use the proper language depending on the addressee. The conscious shift demonstrates that the speakers know how to adapt themselves in a specific situation and blend their ethnic identity.

(3) *Ngrk! Ngrk! Krk-Krk-grok!*

Astaga! Saja poen terperandjat boekan maen! Ternyata 'nSia kita bisa maen moesiek dalem tidoernja! Soenggoeh mati, djika saja lebih doeloe taoe jang si 'nSia ada begitoe **muzikaal**, **goblok** *bener saja moesti adjak ia, biarpoen ia sepoeloeh kali pande* **stenografie**.

'((Snoring sounds))

Oh my! I am very shocked! It turns out that our 'nSia is able to play music (snores loudly) in his sleep! Remarkably dead, if only I had known at the first time that 'nSia produces music in his sleep, I am so stupid why I had to invite him, even though in fact he is ten times as good at stenography.'

Kwee wrote an article entitled *Bing Swie 'nSia poenja Verslag* 'Bing Swie 'nSia's report', in a captivating manner. The article explicates the numerous responsibilities a journalist might be overburdened with.

For example, journalists had to travel to different places in order to gather some news. They had to follow certain rules, because if they did not, their actions might lead to a press offense. In short, the whole article was about journalists' world.

In (3), Kwee wrote about how he was forced to go with 'nSia because 'nSia was the only one who mastered stenography. Unfortunately, 'nSia snored loudly in his sleep and made Kwee uncomfortable. The feeling that Kwee felt triggered an internal emotion within him to say a specific word. The use of the word was not because of a societal external perspective, as it expressed his inconvenience because his roommate was snoring and drooling. He was very tired but he had to deal with a roommate that made loud noises. He defined himself as *goblok* 'stupid' in the sentence *goblok bener saja moesti adjak ia*, 'I am so stupid, why did I have to invite him'. The shift to Javanese in this sentence shows that for Kwee, the use of a rude Javanese word is perceived as the best way to describe the chaotic situation that befell him.

(4) *Mas Tom masuk, minta si* **patient** *buka pakaian, masuk kelain kamar, berikan serupa perintah pada orang lain jang sudah menunggu kedatangannya. Balik pula kekamar pertama, sisakit diperiksa dengan teliti, berikan* **recept** *dan sisakit boleh pergi untuk diganti oleh lain orang yang sudah masuk.*

'Mas Tom entered and asked the patient to open their clothes, enter the room, and give the same order to another patient who had waited for him. Going back to the first room, the patient was carefully checked, gave a receipt and the patient was allowed to leave to be replaced with another patient.'

In (4), the focus of the story is the job of a doctor. Kwee narrated the life of Dr. Soetomo, also known as Mas Tom, who always helped people despite their backgrounds or social status. Kwee personally wrote a eulogy for Dr. Soetomo in a newspaper. Kwee respected Dr. Soetomo and his work by using proper words to describe him and his job, such as *patient* 'patient' and *recept* 'prescription'. In the same article, he used the word 'goodwill' to describe Dr. Soetomo's passion for humanity as a professional who helped people without asking for money in return. For those who wanted to pay, they could pay; yet if they did not have money, they would be exempted. The role of meaning-making in the Dutch language shows the character's identity.

It is worth noting that in his writings, Kwee would shift to Dutch when the topics were related to journalism or other jobs in colonial times. Having a proper job during the Dutch colonial period was not easy. Respectable jobs with specific knowledge or skills were only available to those with a Dutch education. Since education was a luxury, only limited to people who were rich or of Dutch descent, Kwee wanted to underline the discourse that if someone enrolled in a Dutch school, they would have to master the Dutch language. People who were able to speak Dutch were considered intelligent and clever, and so they deserved better jobs and to be involved in the government system.

The Dutch journalist jargon exemplified in (3) are *stenografie, redactie,* and *verslag*. The word *stenografie* 'stenography' refers to the action of quick and concise writing. Journalists during the colonial period needed to learn this skill in formal schools in order to be able to write fast because there were no tools or technology to record the source. In that era, stenographers mostly consisted of educated people who were able to enroll in Dutch schools. The analysis also focuses on the minority groups who seemed to be keeping their pride and dignity when talking to themselves. A person of Chinese ancestry would feel more freedom in articulating their thoughts and emotions using Hokkien, especially when engaging in conversations with fellow Chinese individuals, as shown in (1) and (2).

14.5.2 Shaping Experience

The second point in Baker's (2011) definition of translanguaging is how bilingual speakers shaped their experience. In this section, we provided two examples to discuss the self-identification of the speaker. Using the examples, we can classify what factors are involved in the formation of self-identity from bilingual.

> (5) *Belum tentu diputus salah, masa sudah harus djadi korban dari* "**gerroddel en ge zwets van het publiek**", *(kutukan dari pihak umum), katanja. Tetapi dalam hal saja, saja toch tjuma satu* **Nederlandse onderdaan ne Nederlander** *alias* **Inlander** *sadja. Saja bangga dengan* **Inlanders**, *tetimbang arus djadi* **Belanda Staatsblad** *atau* **Belanda anderhaive pop**.
>
> 'It was not necessarily wrong to be decided, the masses had to become the victims of "the curse of the public side", they said. But in my case, I am just the one who is the Dutch servant but is not the Dutch people as known as only Inlander. I am proud to be Inlanders, rather than having to be a half Dutch puppet.'

Excerpt (5) is derived from an article entitled *Kaula Belanda Bukan Bangsa Belanda* 'Dutch servants but not Dutch people'. The article provides information about the identity of the writer, Kwee, specifically that he was an Indonesian with Chinese ancestry. Kwee's portrayal of himself and of his identity within the community he was affiliated with reflected his Chinese background.

He was a journalist of Sin Tit Po, which was published by a community of Chinese-Indonesian citizens in Surabaya. The Indonesian Chinese also formed a party whose aim was to acquire Indonesian citizenship after independence. They felt that the experience of being Chinese during the colonial period was very painful. This experience was also felt by other minorities, including indigenous Indonesians.

Kwee's writings are first account narratives that provide authentic historical evidence. The phrase *Nederlandse onderdaan ne Nederlander* in (5) refers to someone who was involved in the Dutch government systems but did not have Dutch identity. Kwee shared his experience of being a part of the Dutch government, yet he strongly declared in the newspaper article that he was not Dutch. He shaped his identity and personal framing as a loyal Indonesian who was proud to be a part of the Indonesian community. He already knew that their identity also consisted of Chinese, not only Indonesian, hybrid identity, but during the colonialism era they proudly announced themselves as Indonesians because of the sense of belonging to the nation. This analysis is in line with Shah et al. (2020) who found that bilinguals tend to have unconscious instincts to index their bi-, multilingual, or hybrid identities in social events where they mingle with people from different backgrounds.

In this newspaper column, he exposed the life of a convict. He started by narrating about the life of a journalist which was full of uncertainties. One day a journalist could be invited to a party, but the next day he might be jailed. Kwee told about a time when he was imprisoned for a month after being accused of insulting a government official in his writing. Exposing the injustices he faced in prison was Kwee's way to share his experiences and to remind the readers of the bad memories in prison. Kwee was not worried about his reputation as a convict, rather, he positioned himself as a real journalist who was reporting his real-life experience.

Through the column, Kwee used his experience to also express his sense of belonging. Kwee shared that the convicts who were not Dutch experienced discrimination. He explained the reason he was in prison and how corrupt the prison system was during the Dutch occupation. He openly admitted that he was not a Dutch puppet by saying, *saja bangga dengan* **Inlanders***, tetimbang arus djadi* **Belanda Staatsblad** *atau* **Belanda anderhaive pop**, 'I am proud to be Inlanders, rather than having to be half Dutch puppet'. The sentence shows that he was proud to be an Inlander, or an ordinary Indonesian. During that time, being loyal to the Dutch government offered more advantages, so someone with the Kwee's spirit was rare. By going to jail, Kwee left his identity as a Dutch official, and embraced the identity as a minority.

(6) *Dalam begitu banjak perkelahian jang saja lakukan buat balas hina'an dan pandangan rendah jang ditudjukan pada saja si* **"Tjina loleng buntute digoreng,"** *saja musti akui, si anak totok umumnya lebih fair.*

'In so many fights which I have done to avenge the insult and contempt that aimed to me as a "Chinese *laolang* (pig basket) whose tail is fried," I have to admit that full-blooded children are fairer.'

In his writings, Kwee also focused on the discrimination that he faced during colonialism. The discrimination could either be caused by his identity as of Chinese descent or one that could also happen to Indonesian people. Kwee realized that his identity as an Indo-Chinese must be fought for. Excerpt (6) was taken from Kwee's article entitled *Ben Jij Een Chinees?* 'Are You Chinese?' which was about his life journeys and experiences that had possibly affected his multilingual writings. He was born in a Chinese family, was raised in Chinese culture, and was taught to speak Hokkien. He began to learn Javanese from the community around him, as their family settled in East Java. The assimilation between Javanese and Chinese dialects had created a unique register. The use of Hokkien words and phrases when speaking Javanese or Malay had strengthened the identity of the community. Later on, Kwee moved to *in de kost* 'a boarding house' with his adopted Dutch parents and studied at *Eerste Europese Lagere School* or ELS, a school for the Dutch and other privileged groups.

In (6), he experienced the discrimination of becoming the minority in the school. At that time, when someone was not part of the majority, they would most likely be bullied. The sentence shows the exact phrases used to bully him. He knew that most of his classmates gave him an alienating view, yet, at that important point, he did not give up and fought back. His friends called him *Tjina loleng buntute digoreng* 'Chinese *laolang* (pig basket) whose tail is fried', and then he often got into a fight. The term *Tjina* employed in (6) does not solely denote people who come from China, but rather serves as a pejorative expression to insult and degrade people of Chinese descent. As discussed by Kurnia et al. (2021), specific dialogues and utterances were used on purpose to discriminate against the Indonesian-Chinese descents who were not part of the majority group. In this case, the word *loleng* is the Javanese transliteration of the Hokkien word *láolóng*, or *lao lang* which means 'pig basket'. When a pig is confined within a basket, its mobility becomes restricted, hence rendering it susceptible to having its tail easily fried. The phrase *Tjina loleng* understandably elicited a strong sense of offense in Kwee and made him very insulted.

Further, in the article *Ben Jij Een Chinees?* 'Are You Chinese?' he explained his experiences with people from different backgrounds. The term *totok* refers to native Dutch, and they were fair enough in the fight, according to Kwee. When the bullied said *excuss* 'excuse' in the fight, they would stop their action. But it would be different when Indonesian children were having an advantage in the fight, when the opposing side said *excuss*, they would pretend not to hear them and continue hitting two or three more punches. This difference between both groups represents Kwee's self-identification as a non-Dutch. Indonesian children were portrayed as young and free souls, who are naughty but at the same time, they kept their dignity and pride.

14.5.3 Gaining Understanding, or Knowledge

Baker's (2011) third definition of translanguaging is gaining understanding or knowledge. In this section, we provided two examples to show the portrayal of the speaker's self-identification.

> (7) *Rumah sekolah jang pertama kali saja kundjungi jalah* **Eerste Europese Lagere School** *jang terletak diderekan rumah Assistant Resident Malang. Buat tahun 1907 sebenarnja hal itu djanggal, tidak mudah bisa terwudjud* **Eerste Europese Lagere School!** *Dikundjungi kebanjakan oleh anak2 jang rambutnja pirang dan bermata hidjau, jang bapaknja punja kedudukan istimewa tinggi dalam kalangan pemerintahan, perkebunan atau perusahan. Lebih djauh jang bisa diterima tentu sadja Bupati atau golongan priaji kelas atasan.*

> 'The boarding school I visited for the first time was **Eerste Europese Lagere School** which was located in the row of house Assistant Resident Malang. For the year 1907, it was actually strange and it was not easy to enroll in the **Eerste Europese Lagere** School! It is visited by a large number of children with blonde hair and green eyes, whose fathers have special high positions in government, plantation or corporate circles. Another of Indonesia's classes that will be accepted are district leaders or those in the upper classes.'

Excerpt (7) was taken from an article entitled *Ben Jij Een Chinees* 'Are You Chinese?' It depicts the Dutch education system which categorizes people by their classes. In the article, Kwee questioned his opportunity to go to school despite his minority status. He said, *sebenarnja hal itu djanggal* 'it was actually strange', because not everyone can pursue education. School was expensive and exclusive only for the middle and upper classes. This was against the modern notion that education is a basic human right that should be available to everyone. Colonialism shows that the basic human rights and needs of individuals are taken by force. The education system is one of the important things to control because it has the power to lead people to rebellion (Nwanosike & Onyije, 2011). Educated people would fight for Indonesian independence and this would endanger the Dutch government in Indonesia.

In ELS, educated people talked in Dutch. It shows that there was a language hierarchy. Not only language, people in the colonialism era also grouped people depending on the nation and race. The original Dutch descent was becoming the first class in the social hierarchy, because they led the country. Then, the second class was for people who had half Dutch blood. And, the rest was for the rich people from any nation or to indigenous people of Indonesia which involved the district head or *Bupati* or *priyayi* (Zentz, 2017).

> (8) *Si sobat dari Ngoenoet tahan napasnja. Dibandingkan dengan Hong Tjiang, ia dapet perasaan seperti djuga dirinja sendiri sama sekali tida ada artinja, teroetama dalem soal pindah-pindah roemah. Kerna selama hidoepnya ia tjoema pernah pindah satoe kali, jaitoe, abis kawin dari Toeloeng Agung* **"bojongan"** *ke Ngoenoet, sehingga sekarang ini.*

> 'The friend from Ngunut holds his breath. Compared to Hong Tjiang (Hong Tjiang), he feels that he is nothing, especially about relocating to another house, because during his life, he has only moved once, that is, after married from Tulung Agung *"boyongan"* (moved) to Ngunut, until now.'

Example (8) discusses the insecurity of the friend from Ngunut in a conversation with Hong Tjiang. In contrast to Hong Tjiang, he experienced a lack of emotional feeling about relocating to a new house as he recognized the complexity of such an undertaking. There are some reasons that contribute to people's decision to move from one place to another, such as job demands, educational pursuits, and marriage, among other things.

At that moment, the friend from Ngunut thought that Hong Tjiang was an important person in his job that required him to move from one city to another city in China. The friend from Ngunut only moved because of marriage reasons. In Javanese tradition, *boyongan* 'moving' is used for someone who moved to another city to stay after marriage (Wibowo, 2015). This tradition can take place in both the male and female side, but mostly, the female. Because after marriage, a woman is usually required to go with her husband and follow him. From a male perspective, *boyongan* 'moving' can be caused by the job or other factors.

The use of Javanese words within Malay structure helps the reader focus on something that is culturally specific. Shifting language leads to the complex understanding of both the author and reader. This is in line with Baker's (2011) definition of translanguaging, it is the way the speakers make the meaning, shape their experience, and gain the knowledge or understanding. Kwee, being a proficient multilingual speaker, demonstrates a remarkable mastery of multiple languages, effectively developed inside his cognitive skills. The themes in his writings indicated the reasons why Kwee used different languages as a bilingual to write in the newspaper, which was to share the stories with other people. He wanted to emphasize the state of Indonesia during the colonial era, wherein disparities existed across various ethnic and social groups, but people had a shared sense of belonging to their group identities. The novel portrayed the prevalent discrimination of the time period, and Kwee's articulation of his thoughts has the potential to enlighten readers, whether they belong to the same or following generations.

14.6 Conclusion

Throughout the article, we have looked at how polyglots in the colonialism era defined their identity through translanguaging, the shifting from one language to another without realizing the boundaries between languages. In general, the results of the analysis reveal various ways of framing self-identification. García and Wei (2014) explained the power of words which are produced by bilinguals as their privilege. We have focused on how Kwee framed his self-identity by making meaning, shaping experience, and gaining understanding or knowledge (Baker, 2011).

The meaning-making discussion underlines that Kwee's self-identity comes from emotions, feelings, sarcasm, connections to the community, convenience, and job or education. The shaping experience analysis encompasses two factors that can contribute to the construction of self-identification, namely the sense of national belonging and past discrimination. In addition, Kwee also performed translanguaging as he gained and spread the understanding of the Dutch government system and the indigenous tradition. The way Kwee aligns himself with Chinese, Indonesian, and Dutch identity indicates his hybrid identity.

The relationship between the colonial era and self-identity is influencing the decision-making of bilinguals. Kwee was shown to have more than one identity as he moved between Indonesian and Chinese in his speech. Even though Kwee regularly declared that he was Indonesian, his nationality is a complex matter. As Kwee lived in the colonialism era, he wanted to frame himself as an Indonesian citizen with the same sense of belonging as the indigenous who were equally colonized. Kwee thus stated his loyalty to Indonesia.

This paper has shown Indonesian writings in the colonialism era, how polyglots defined the use of translanguaging in determining self-identification through their sharing thoughts written in newspaper columns, and how colonialism had influenced the writer's self-identification. From this perspective, we have highlighted the richness of Indonesian newspapers' use of multiple languages during the colonial era. Kwee's writing is authentic evidence of the history of Indonesia and the Indonesian language.

References

Abas, H. (1987). Indonesian as a unifying language of wider communication: A historical and sociolinguistic perspective. *Pacific Linguistics Series, D*(73), The Australian National University.

Abduh, A., & Rosmaladewi. (2019). Language policy, identity, and bilingual education in Indonesia: A historical overview. *Xlinguae, 12*(1), 219–227.

Amelia, D. (2016). Indonesian literature's position in world literature. *Teknosastik: Jurnal Bahasa dan Sastra, 14*(2), 1–5.

Anderson, B. (1966). The languages of Indonesian politics. *Indonesia, 1*, 89–116.

Ang, I. (2003). Together in difference: Beyond diaspora, into hybridity. *Asian Studies Review, 27*(2), 141–154. https://doi.org/10.1080/10357820308713372.

Arifin, E. Z., & Tasai, S. A. (1995). *Cermat berbahasa Indonesia untuk Perguruan Tinggi (Accurate in Indonesian Language for College)*. Akademika Pressindo.

Baker, C. (2011). *Foundations of bilingual education and bilingualism* (5th ed.). Bristol, England: Multilingual Matters.

Balam, O. (2021). Beyond differences and similarities in codeswitching and translanguaging research. *Belgian Journal of Linguistics, 35*(1), 76–103.

Broadbent, J. T. & Vavilova, Z. (2015). Bilingual Identity: Issues of self-identification of bilinguals in Malaysia and Tatarstan. *3L; Language,Linguistics and Literature, The Southeast Asian Journal of English Language Studies., 21*(3), 141–150.

Chan, B. H. (2021). Translanguaging or code-switching? Reassessing mixing of English in Hong Kong Cantonese. *Chinese Language and Discourse, 13*(2), 167–196.

Dannari, G. L., Ulfa, M., & Ayundasari, L. (2021). *Dekolonialisasi : Menuju pembebasan materi pembelajaran sejarah di Indonesia abad 21* [Decolonization: Towards the liberation of History learning materials in Indonesia at 21st century], *1*(4), 425–436. https://doi.org/10.17977/um0 63v1i4p425-436.

Djati, A. W. & Anderson, B. R. O. (2010). *Menjadi Tjamboek Berdoeri: Memoar Kwee Thiam Tjing* [Becoming Tjamboek Berdoeri: Memoirs of Kwee Thiam Tjing]. Jakarta: Komunitas Bambu.

Dumadi, S. M. (1988). *Jakarta dari tepian air ke kota proklamasi* [Jakarta from the Waterfront to the Proclamation City]. Dinas Museum dan Sejarah.

García, O. & Wei, L. (2014). Language, languaging, and bilingualism. In O. García & L. Wei (Eds.). *Translanguaging: Language, Bilingualism and Education* (pp. 5–18). Palgrave Macmillan. https://doi.org/10.1057/9781137385765.

García, O. (2009). *Bilingual education in the 21st century a global perspective.* Blackwell Publishing.

Hapsari, D. E. (2014). Tionghoa's political standing points on Indonesian revolution in Tjamboek Berdoeri's Indonesia dalem Api dan Bara. In Fr. B. Alip, F. X. Siswadi, P. Sarwoto, A. B. Sri Mulyani, A. Fitriati, & H. H. Setiajid (Eds.). *Proceeding, Literary Studies Conference 2014 on De/Reconstructing Southeast Asian History through Literature* (pp. 38–43). Universitas Sanata Dharma, Yogyakarta, Indonesia 16–17 October 2014.

Hatta, M. (1979). *Mohammad Hatta: Memoir* (Mohammad Hatta: Memoirs). Jakarta: Tintamas Indonesia.

Ivanič, R. (1998). *Writing and identity: The discoursal construction of identity in academic writing.* John Benjamins Publishing Company.

Kurnia, N. I., Nurgiyantoro, B., & Fitri, C. E. (2021). The othering of majority and minority groups in Lessing and Ajidarma's literary works: A postcolonial analysis. *GEMA Online® Journal of Language Studies, 21*(1), 76–88. https://doi.org/10.17576/gema-2021-2101-05.

Lo, M. M. (2002). *Doctors within borders: Profession, ethnicity, and modernity in colonial Taiwan.* University of California Press.

Montolalu, L. R., & Suryadinata, L. (2007). *National language and nation-building: The case of bahasa Indonesia. In Language, nation and development in Southeast Asia* (Hock Guan). ISEAS–Yusof Ishak Institute Singapore. http://www.degruyter.com/view/books/9789812304834/9789812304834-007/9789812304834-007.xml.

Myers-Scotton, C. (2011). The matrix language frame model: Developments and responses. *Codeswitching Worldwide, Bd. II.* https://doi.org/10.1515/9783110808742.23.

Nwanosike, O. F., & Onyije, L. E. (2011). Colonialism and education. *Mediterranean Journal of Social Science, 2,* 108–118. https://doi.org/10.4324/9780203837450.

Otheguy, R., Garcia, O., & Reid, W. (2015). Clarifying translanguaging and deconstructing named languages: A perspective from linguistics. *Applied Linguistics Review, 6*(3), 281–307.

Pavlenko. A. (2014). *The bilingual mind: And what it tells us about language and thought.* Cambridge University Press.

Richardson, L. (2000). Writing: A method of inquiry. In N. K. Denzin & Y. S. Lincoln (Eds.), *Handbook of qualitative research* (2nd ed., pp. 923–948). Thousand Oaks, CA: Sage.

Setiono, B. G. (2008). *Tionghoa dalam pusaran politik: Mengungkap fakta tersembunyi orang Tionghoa di Indonesia* (Chinese in Political Maelstrom: Revealing the Hidden Facts of Chinese People in Indonesia). Jakarta: TransMedia Pustaka.

Shah, M., Pillai, S., & Sinayah, M. (2020). Identity construction through code-switching practices at a university in Pakistan. *GEMA Online® Journal of Language Studies, 20*(4), 1–17. https://doi.org/10.17576/gema-2020-2004-01.

Smith, K. E. I., & Leavy, P. (2008). *Hybrid identities: Theoretical and empirical examinations.* Brill.

Sneddon, J. (2003). *The Indonesian language: Its history and role in modern society.* University of New South Wales Press.

Streifeneder, E., & Missbach, A. (2008). *Indonesia- The presence of the past: A festschrift in honour of Ingrid Wessel.* regiospectra Verlag.

Sumadyo, B. (2013). Sekilas tentang bentuk umpatan dalam bahasa Indonesia [The Overview of Swearing Forms in Indonesian]. *2nd International Seminar on Quality and Affordable Education, Isqae,* 197–201. https://educ.utm.my/zh-TW/wp-content/uploads/2013/11/271.pdf.

Taylor, S. J., Bogdan, R., & DeVault, M. L. (2016). *Introduction to qualitative research methods: A guidebook and resource.* John Wiley & Sons, Inc.

Wahyuni, A. E., Yannuar, N., Basthomi, Y., & Suharyadi. (2023). The negotiation of identities in multilingual settings as depicted in Indonesia dalem Api dan Bara. *Linguistik Indonesia, 41*(2), 151–167.

Wei, L. (2011). Moment Analysis and translanguaging space: Discursive construction of identities by multilingual Chinese youth in Britain. *Journal of Pragmatics, 43*(5), 1222–1235. https://doi.org/10.1016/j.pragma.2010.07.035.

Wibowo, S. (2015). *Nilai-nilai pendidikan Islam dalam tradisi boyongan rumah di Desa Ngenden Kecamatan Ampel Kabupaten Boyolali Tahun 2014* [Islamic Education Values in the Boyongan House Tradition in Ngenden Village, Ampel District, Boyolali Regency in 2014]. http://e-repository.perpus.iainsalatiga.ac.id/id/eprint/537.

Yannuar, N. (2022). "Keep original": Translanguaging and identity construction among East Javanese football supporters. In S. H. Mirvahedi (Ed.), *Linguistic Landscapes in South-East Asia: The Politics of Language and Public Signage* (pp. 185–207). Routledge. https://doi.org/10.4324/9781003166993.

Yasmis. (2007). Jepang dan perjuangan kemerdekaan Indonesia [Japan and the struggle for Indonesian independence]. *Jurnal Sejarah Lontar, 4*(2), 24–32.

Zentz, L. (2017). *Statehood, scale and hierarchy history, language and identity in Indonesia.* Multilingual Matters. https://doi.org/10.21832/ZENTZ8460.

Open Access This chapter is licensed under the terms of the Creative Commons Attribution 4.0 International License (http://creativecommons.org/licenses/by/4.0/), which permits use, sharing, adaptation, distribution and reproduction in any medium or format, as long as you give appropriate credit to the original author(s) and the source, provide a link to the Creative Commons license and indicate if changes were made.

The images or other third party material in this chapter are included in the chapter's Creative Commons license, unless indicated otherwise in a credit line to the material. If material is not included in the chapter's Creative Commons license and your intended use is not permitted by statutory regulation or exceeds the permitted use, you will need to obtain permission directly from the copyright holder.

Part V
Clinical Linguistics

Chapter 15
Superstructure of Discourse and Cohesion in Narratives Spoken by People with Alzheimer's

Nailah Azkiya and Untung Yuwono

Abstract Alzheimer's is part of dementia, a symptom of memory loss commonly known as senility. Alzheimer's will initially distract memory, then disrupt language skills. The disruption in language skills is mainly due to reduced memory of the language form and vocabulary. In addition, memory disorders also affect the reduction in language skills because people with Alzheimer's lose things they have remembered and understood to the point of being unable to express their thoughts in the language form. This study analyzes the superstructure and cohesion in narratives spoken by people with Alzheimer's. The purpose of this study is to explain the narrative superstructure and cohesive device used by people with Alzheimer's in their narratives. This research uses a qualitative method. The subjects in this study were elderlies with Alzheimer's who live in a nursing home in East Jakarta. It was a large government-owned social institution that accommodated large numbers of patients from various backgrounds. The data were collected by conducting open interviews to elderlies with Alzheimer's in several levels of seriousness based on the results from the Mini Mental Status Exam (MMSE) test; namely, those with mild Alzheimer's and serious Alzheimer's. Those who match the criteria were randomly chosen, resulting in three selected respondents with Alzheimer's as the samples. Then they were given two questions as the trigger for their stories, which are, "What was the most happily experience in your life?" and "What was the most sinister experience in your life?" It is found that narratives produced by people with mild Alzheimer's have a complete narrative structure, which are orientation, complication, evaluation, resolution, and coda. On the other side, people with serious Alzheimer's could not produce narratives without guidance. Narratives about unpleasant experiences are more remembered than narratives about pleasant experiences. In addition, the cohesion that is commonly used by people with Alzheimer's are references, substitutions, and conjunctions. The research result shows the aspects of language that can be maintaned by people with mild Alzheimer's. It gives an implication in how medical

N. Azkiya · U. Yuwono (✉)
Indonesian Study Program, Faculty of Humanities, Universitas Indonesia, Jakarta, Indonesia
e-mail: untung.yuwono@ui.ac.id

N. Azkiya
e-mail: nailah.azkiya@ui.ac.id

practioners handle the language maintenance of the people with mild Alzheimer's. The decreased ability of mild Alzheimer's to narrate and use cohesive device can signalize the worsening of Alzheimer's. Furthermore, by continuously encouraging people with Alzheimer's to tell memorable things in their lives, it would be possible to slow down the degeneration process as they are invited to recall their memories perpetually.

Keywords Alzheimer's · Cohesion · Discourse analysis · Narrative · Superstructure

15.1 Introduction

Alzheimer's is senility that is chronic, persistent, and irreversible. Hitherto, the right medication for and the exact cause of Alzheimer's disease could not be ascertained yet. People with Alzheimer's disease first experience memory problems, and eventually become senile progressively (Fish & Cuthbert, 1994). In general, Alzheimer's disease attacks the elderly. The disease degenerates the brain so that it interferes with the language and memory function in particular. According to Lumbantobing (2006), the definitive diagnosis of Alzheimer's requires a post-mortem examination, or generally known as an autopsy. Certainly, this procedure cannot be applied to the patients while living. Hence, in that condition, the only diagnosis that can be made is an uncertain diagnosis. One of the techniques that can be done for such diagnosis is by using the Mini Mental Status Exam (MMSE). In the USA, a study that records the number of Alzheimer's sufferers is carried out annually. Such an attempt is done with the purpose of establishing a basis for taking preventive steps toward the development of the disease. In 2019 alone, there are approximately 5.8 million people with Alzheimer's, and 81% of them are aged 75 years and over (Alzheimer's Association, 2019).

Unlike the United States, there have been no scientific attempts to trace the number and distribution of people with Alzheimer's in Indonesia up until today. The data regarding this mental health condition are only generally stored in individual health records in social care homes or hospitals. These facts lead to the uncertainty regarding the number of Alzheimer's patients in this country. Therefore, this research will focus on a social home—which is Tresna Werdha Budi Mulia 1—that is located in East Jakarta.

As people with a healthy and functioning brain, Alzheimer's sufferers also record past activities or things that they consider valuable in their long-term memory. The memory can sometimes be recalled and retold through speech or writing. In terms of pleasant memories, most of the sufferers use narrative discourse as the media for retelling the events to others. Labov (1997) explains that narrative discourse is one of many ways for recounting past events. Structurally, Labov argues that the narratives consist of clauses that are delivered in chronological order; hence, referred to as narrative clauses. Presumably, the series of clauses that were spoken by the subjects represent (or are close to) the sequence by which the actual events happened in the past. Apart from that, discourse on its own can be understood as a semantic unity among parts in a language construction (Yuwono, 2009). As a holistic unity of meaning, discourse is maintained under a language production using cohesion. Cohesion is a grammatical and lexical language feature that is used to mark the semantic relations between elements within a discourse. In storytelling, speakers control the flow of the topic using cohesions. That feature creates interconnection between prepositions in a discourse so that it becomes a holistic unity.

This paper will examine the narrative discourse superstructure as well as the language features that serve as cohesions in spoken stories by Alzheimer's patients. The main purpose is to explain the superstructure of narrative discourse inside stories that are produced by people with Alzheimer's. In addition, this paper will also describe the types of cohesion markers within the spoken narratives. The research object for this analysis is the narrative discourse generated by Alzheimer's patients regarding to the way they met their life partners. The study is expected to be the cornerstone in understanding the way Alzheimer's patients construct stories. Subsequently, the results of this research are expected to be a reference for Alzheimer's patient care in terms of maintaining memory as part of one's cognitive abilities.

15.1.1 Literature Review

Several studies in the field of medicine and neural showed that people who actively use their brains in old age have a lower percentage of being attacked by Alzheimer's (Akbaraly et al., 2009; Verghese et al., 2003; Williams et al., 2010; Wilson et al., 2002, 2007). In other words, deploying our cognitive ability as long as possible could defend ourselves from Alzheimer's. The research is conducted by using the perspective of medical science. However, based on our literature study, we have not found any research that analyzes narratives by Alzheimer's patients regarding the superstructure of their narrative discourse.

Nevertheless, there are literatures with little similarity to the said study; which are 'Time Reference and Telicity in Agrammatic Aphasia in Bahasa Indonesia' by Suhardijanto (1993) and Anjarningsih (2012). Despite its somewhat similar topic, that research focused on examining grammatical defects in speech by people with Aphasia. Therefore, it is different with this study in terms of its focus—to examine the discourse superstructure and cohesion in speeches by people with Alzheimer's—even though the two mental health conditions are quite alike brain disorder-wise.

15.1.2 Theoretical Framework

Dementia is a series of symptoms including memory loss, cognitive difficulty, problem solving, and even disruption in the use of language. In general term, dementia is known as senility. Dementia happens when the brain is damaged with illness, such as Alzheimer's or stroke. Among all causes, Alzheimer's is the most common trigger for dementia. While the patient suffers from the disease, the chemicals and structure of the brain are shifting so that it leads to the death of brain cells. Alzheimer's, as first described by a German neurologist, Alois Alzheimer, is a physical illness that affects the brain. As time goes by, the kinked plaque and fiber protein that are developing kill the brain cells. Alzheimer's sufferers are also lacking several necessary chemical substances within their brains. Those chemicals are important for neural process (Curiel et al., 2019; Fish & Cuthbert, 1994; Sahyouni et al., 2016).

Because Alzheimer's is a progressive, chronologically gradual disease that causes increasing damage in brain parts, the symptoms that appear would get worse overtime. Precedent to this date, there is no single factor that is considered as the main cause of this disease. It is probable that the combination of several factors such as age, genetics, environment, lifestyle, and one's health condition could lead to Alzheimer's attack. In some people, this health condition could secretively flourish for years until the symptoms appear (Curiel, 2019; Fish & Cuthbert, 1994; Sahyouni et al., 2016).

Cohesion is the interrelation that is marked by an explicit lingual form. It is also the harmony of the relation between elements within a discourse so that a holistic and coherent meaning is constructed (Moeliono et al., 1993). A cohesion marker is a set of devices that are used for marking the whole and coherent connection between forms. Gutwinsky in Tarigan (1987) defined cohesion as a syntactic organization that acts as the container for sentences that are solidly and systematically arranged for generating utterances. That also means that cohesion is the intersentence connection in a discourse, in terms of either a certain grammatical or lexical level. In line to that, Tarigan (1987) summed up that cohesion is the way a component acts its role in relation to the other elements. The component could consist of several words with words, clauses with clauses, sentences with sentences, paragraphs with paragraphs according to the system of the language itself. Samsuri (1987) claimed that cohesive interconnection is formed when the interpretation of an element in utterances depends on the meaning interpreted from other utterance. This means that a single utterance could not be perfectly understood unless the other is present. An example of a good cohesion is causal relations. Mulyana (2005) explained that cohesion in discourse is defined as the structural cohesiveness that forms syntactical bond. Basically, cohesion as a concept is deeply linked with interrelation between forms; that is, elements in discourse (words or sentences) that are used for constructing a discourse have whole and cohesive linkages. Cohesion is included in the internal aspect of a discourse.

Halliday and Hasan (1976) differentiate two forms of cohesion, which are grammatical cohesion and lexical cohesion. The first is grammatical attachments between elements in discourse. Then, the latter is lexically bound between elements in discourse. While grammatical cohesion consists of reference, substitution, ellipsis, and conjunction, lexical cohesion only made up of reiteration and collocation. The five cohesion devices can be said as endophoric cohesion because of the location of their interpretation and function in forming solid bond in a text. Other than endophoric cohesion, there is also exophoric cohesion which interpretation is situated outside the text of which situational context do not influence the wholeness of the text.

Cohesion in discourse theorized by Halliday and Hasan (1976), Tarigan (1987), Moeliono (1993), and Mulyana (2005) departs from observations of linguistic data in general. In this study, the cohesive theory is used as a reference for our explanation of how Alzheimer's sufferers produce cohesiveness in their narratives. We suspect that cognitive impairment experienced by people with Alzheimer's causes impairments in producing discourse cohesion as has been studied in people with aphasia. Cognitive disorders that cause problems in generating cohesion are interesting to study descriptively qualitatively based on narrative speech data of Alzheimer's sufferers. Qualitative descriptive analysis will reveal the characteristics of cohesion production constraints at each level of seriousness of Alzheimer's symptoms.

15.1.3 Research Methods

Descriptive qualitative approach was used as the method for carrying out this research. The qualitative method was put into effect for analyzing narrative discourse data; thus, the method was meant for data analyzing and text interpreting. On the other hand, descriptive method is a research method that aims to illustrate and comprehend a study object as it is. This study was conducted by examining the data source, analyzing the data, and finally summarizing and explaining the patterns or rules of the behavior based on phenomenon encountered or collected (Creswell, 2008; Denzin & Lincoln, 2011). The author used the said procedures for this research.

The subjects of this study were elderlies with Alzheimer's who live at a social care home that is located at East Jakarta. Two respondents were chosen at random as a representation of the entire population. They were a grandfather and a grandmother who had been assessed using MMSE, thus were classified under the same category of mild Alzheimer's patients with a score of 18–22. The object of this research is the narrative discourse superstructure and cohesion in narration generated by people with Alzheimer's. The superstructure of the narrative discourse includes orientation, complications, evaluation, resolution, and coda. Second to that, cohesion markers consist of types and variations in their use in narratives.

The data was collected by deploying listening method and indirect note-taking technique (Sudaryanto, 1993). With the listening method, we listened and observed the subjects, which are elderlies with Alzheimer's in the social care home. The following is a gathering technique used to obtain the data in this study by recording and examining the research samples. After the listening activity, the author conducted an indirect note-taking attempt, which was done by transcribing the data recorder in a recording device. Data transcription was intended for facilitating the analysis and data attachment process as they have been converted into written forms.

The main instrument for this study was the researcher herself (Moleong, 2007). In being the instrument, the author based herself on her knowledge regarding the theories of cohesion markers along with their usage frequency and variety that are established upon conducted activities starting from planning, data gathering, analysis, interpreting, to reporting the research results. The focus of this research is type of cohesion markers in the narratives by people with Alzheimer's, and the unit of analysis is the paragraph within those narratives. In addition to the main instrument, a recording device that was utilized for data documentation and word-processing software for writing down the transcript of the recording were also used.

As for analyzing the data, a qualitative descriptive analysis technique was used. The author illustrated and described qualitative data that were selected on the basis of empirical facts. Consequently, the gathered data were filtered, reduced, identified, classified, then analyzed in accordance with the research topic.

15.2 Analysis

15.2.1 Narrative Structure

The findings obtained by the author at a nursing home in East Jakarta are narratives produced by people with mild Alzheimer's having a complete narrative structure, namely orientation, complications, evaluation, resolution, and code. The narrative structure of the narration spoken by mild Alzheimer's begins with orientation. The orientation is found in the introduction to the name and country of origin of the guest's wife. The next narrative structure found in the narratives uttered by Alzheimer's patients is complications. Complications were found on the part of the interviewees' children who fell in love with the speakers and stated this. The next narrative structure found in the narratives spoken by Alzheimer's sufferers is evaluation. Evaluation was found on the part of the interviewees' children who continued to give positive signals to the interviewees. The next narrative structure found in the narration spoken by Alzheimer's sufferers is resolution. The resolution found in the part of the resource persons' relationship with the work of their co-workers continues and is blessed. The next narrative structure found in the narration of Alzheimer's sufferers is coda. Coda was found in the interviewees married to a colleague's child and had three children (Table 15.1).

On the other hand, narratives produced by people with serious Alzheimer's have an incomplete narrative structure. They must be guided in producing narratives (Table 15.2).

Narratives produced by people with serious Alzheimer's have an incomplete narrative structure, namely orientation, complications, evaluation, resolution, and code. There is no orientation, complication, or evaluation in the narrative structure of the narration spoken by serious Alzheimer's. The resolution is found in a short verbal phrase which is expressed without any main idea. They just said *bilang sayang* (telling love), *dijak apa diantarkan* (to be asked or to be taken to a place), *dijak* (to be asked), *ke ibu* (to you), *diramuti di sana* (to be taken care there), *di kandang* (in the cage) to answer the question about the way they met their life partners. This short

Table 15.1 Narrative structure of mild Alzheimer's disease

Narrative structure	Data
Orientation	Yes. I have a wife, as I said before, Liza. That's what she was called, Liza Faizah. She was a Pakistani *Iya itu. Saya punya istri, sudah kasih tahu namanya ya, Liza. Panggilannya itu, Liza Faizah. Dia aslinya orang Pakistan*
Complication	We met, when I had a business with her father, then I went to her house. She saw me as a man, or she had feelings for me. She told me *Ketemunya, waktu saya ada urusan dengan Bapaknya, lalu Bapak main-main ke rumahnya. Nah nggak tahunya dia sebagai wanita, istilahnya jatuh cinta, kan. Dan itu dia ungkapkan*
Evaluation	After she confessed, I had another business with her father, then she kept attending to me *Udah dia ungkapkan, terus saya ada satu urusan dengan bapaknya, ya udah dia tetap melayani*
Resolution	After that, our relationship continued as her mother permitted us (2″), and her mother didn't mind having me as her son-in-law *Setelah itu, hubungan itu lanjut dan direstui oleh ibunya dan ibunya tidak keberatan mengangkat saya sebagai menantu*
Coda	It continued, until we have three children *Teruslah berjalan, hingga dapat anak tiga*

Table 15.2 Narrative structure of serious Alzheimer's disease

Narrative structure	Data
Orientation	–
Complication	–
Evaluation	–
Resolution	*Bilang sayang* *Dijak apa diantarkan* *Dijak* *Ke ibu* *Diramuti di sana* *Di kandang*
Coda	–

verbal phrase is a resolution mark in a narrative structure, which signifies problem-solving or decreases story tension. In the end of the narrative, there is no coda as a closing.

It is interesting to find dialectal vocabularies used by serious Alzheimer's. The respondents use Javanese words in his narrative, e.g., *dijak* "to be asked for" and *diramuti* "to be cared." It shows that the respondent still maintain the mastery of his mother language. This finding also shows the code-switch between Indonesian language and Javanese. In the code-switch, the Javanese use does not disturb the sentence structure.

15.2.2 Cohesion in Narratives Spoken by Alzheimer's

In maintaining narrative cohesion, Alzheimer's sufferers use cohesion. Common cohesions used by mild Alzheimer's sufferers to maintain speech are references, substitutions, and conjunctions. On the other hand, people with serious Alzheimer's cannot produce a complete narrative. They must be guided in producing narratives.

Alzheimer patients in mild stages can still use cohesion in the sentences they produce. The use of cohesion is functioning properly. Meanwhile, patients with serious Alzheimer's cannot use cohesion because they say either only a word or few short phrases in the narration they produce. People with serious Alzheimer's can't use cohesion because they speak some short sentences in the narratives they produce (Table 15.3).

The observation results showed language aspects that people with mild Alzheimer's could maintain. It implied the recommended way that medical practitioners should act in keeping Alzheimer's patients' language ability. As a degenerative disturbance in the brain, Alzheimer's will progressively decrease its victims' cognitive abilities, including language skills. By illustrating the superstructure and cohesion in narratives spoken by Alzheimer's sufferers step by step over time, medical practitioners could monitor the degree of reduction periodically.

Furthermore, by encouraging people with Alzheimer's to retell impressive experiences in their lives, it is possible to slow down the degeneration process because of the continuous memory repetition. This activity is a suggested exercise to inhibit Alzheimer's attack like several studies have showed beforehand; that people who utilize their brain up to old age have a lower chance to be attacked by Alzheimer's

Table 15.3 Cohesion in narratives with mild Alzheimer's

Cohesion type	Cohesion mark	Data
Grammatical cohesion	Reference	*nya*
	Substitution	*itu*
	Ellipsis	*saya*
	Conjunction	*lalu, terus, setelah itu, dan*
Lexical cohesion	Repetition	*ibunya*
	Reiteration	Synonym: - Antonym: - Meronym: - Hyponym: - Collocation: *jatuh cinta, hubungan, direstui, menantu*

disease (Akbaraly et al., 2009; Verghese et al., 2003; Williams et al., 2010; Wilson et al., 2002, 2007).

15.3 Conclusion

These are several preliminary points that can be concluded according to the initial observation of narratives spoken by elderlies with Alzheimer's in a nursing home in East Jakarta. First, there is a complete superstructure in narrative discourse that is produced by people with mild Alzheimer's. They produce a narrative with orientation, complication, resolution, and coda. Second, patients with severe Alzheimer's cannot produce any narratives without guidance. Interviewer should trigger them with several questions to produce a narrative. Third, narratives related to unpleasant experiences tend to have more deviations. For example, the experience of being cheated on by their partner is more difficult to remember in detail than the story of the first time they met their partner. Fourth, the cohesion marker types in narratives that are produced by people with Alzheimer's consist of grammatical cohesion (reference, substitution, and cohesion) and lexical cohesion (only collocation).

The results of this study have implications for how medical practitioners focus on narrative as a means of maintaining language for people with mild Alzheimer's disease. The decreased ability of people with mild Alzheimer's to tell stories and use cohesion markers may signal worsening of Alzheimer's. Furthermore, by continuing to encourage people with Alzheimer's to tell fun things, the possibility of the degeneration process will slow down because it is triggered to recall memories continuously.

The recommendation given by researchers for further research is that research on the language skills of Alzheimer's sufferers can be expanded by reaching out to Alzheimer's patients in hospitals or other health care centers. For this reason, it is advisable to conduct a preliminary study that takes an inventory of the number of Alzheimer's sufferers in an area or even in Indonesia so that the research conducted can include a representative sample.

References

Akbaraly, T. N., Portet, F., Fustinoni, S., et al. (2009). Leisure activities and the risk of dementia in the elderly: Results from the three-city study. *Neurology, 73*(11), 854–861.
Alzheimer's Association. (2019). Alzheimer's disease facts and figures. *Alzheimers Dementia, 15*(3), 321–387.
Anjarningsih, H. Y. (2012). *Time reference in standard Indonesian agrammatic Aphasia*. University of Groningen.
Cresswell, J. W. (2008). *Research design: Qualitative, quantitative, and mixed methods approaches* (3rd ed.). Sage Publication.

Curiel, R. E., et al. (2019). *Handbook on the neuropsychology of aging and dementia*. Switzerland: Springer Nature.
Denzin, N. K., & Lincoln, Y. S. (2011). *The SAGE handbook of qualitative research*. Sage Publication Inc.
Fish, S., & Cuthbert, S. (1994) *Penyakit Alzheimer: Bagaimana Menjaga Diri Anda dan Orang yang Anda Kasihi*. Jakarta: PT BPK Gunung Mulia.
Halliday, M. A. K., & Hasan, R. (1976). *Cohesion in english*. Routledge.
Labov, W. (1997). Further steps in narrative analysis. *Journal of Narrative and Life History, 7*(1–4), 395–415.
Lumbantobing, S. M. (2006). *Kecerdasan Pada Usia Lanjut dan Demensia*. Faculty of Medicine, Universitas Indonesia.
Moeliono, M. A., et al. (1993) *Tata Bahasa Baku Bahasa Indonesia*. Jakarta: Balai Pustaka.
Moleong, L. J. (1995) *Metodologi Penelitian Kualitatif*. Bandung: Remaja Rosda.
Mulyana. (2005) *Kajian Wacana: Teori, Metode, dan Aplikasi Prinsip-Prinsip Analisis Wacana*. Yogyakarta: Tiara Wacana.
Sahyouni, R., et al. (2016). *Alzheimer's disease decoded: The history, present, and future of Alzheimer's disease and dementia*. World Scientific Publishing Co., Pte. Ltd.
Samsuri. (1987). *Analisis Bahasa*. Jakarta: Erlangga.
Sudaryanto. (1993). *Metode dan Aneka Teknik Analisis Bahasa*. Duta Wacana University Press.
Suhardijanto, T. (1993). *Cacat Gramatikal Pada Keluaran Wicara Penderita Sindrom Afasia Broca: Sebuah Analisis Struktural dan Neurolinguistik Pada Lima Kasus Sindrom Afasia Broca di FKUI/RSCM, Jakarta*. Faculty of Humanities, Universitas Indonesia.
Tarigan, H. G. (1987). *Teknik Pengajaran Keterampilan Berbahasa*. Bandung: Angkasa.
Verghese, J., Lipton, R. B., Katz, M. J., et al. (2003). Leisure activities and the risk of dementia in the elderly. *New England Journal of Medicine, 348*(25), 2508–2516.
Williams, J. W., Plassman, B. L., Burke, J., et al. (2010). Preventing Alzheimer's disease and cognitive decline. *Evidence Report/technology Assessment, 193*, 116–117.
Wilson, R. S., Mendes De Leon, C. F., Barnes, L. L., et al. (2002). Participation in cognitively stimulating activities and risk of incident Alzheimer disease. *JAMA, 287*(6), 742–748.
Wilson, R. S., Scherr, P. A., Schneider, J. A., et al. (2007). Relation of cognitive activity to risk of developing Alzheimer disease. *Neurology, 69*(20), 1911–1920.
Yuwono, U. et al. (2009) *Pesona Bahasa: Langkah Awal Memahami Linguistik*. Jakarta: PT Gramedia.

Nailah Azkiya is an undergraduate student of Indonesian Studies in the Faculty of Humanities, Universitas Indonesia. She is interested in discourse studies.

Untung Yuwono is a lecturer of linguistics in the Linguistics Study Program, Graduate Program, Faculty of Humanities, Universitas Indonesia. In 2004, he finished his doctorate degree in Linguistics at the Faculty of Humanities with a dissertation titled "Asyndetic Construction in Indonesian Sentences." He is interested in discourse studies, morphology, syntax, semantics, Indonesian language for foreigners (BIPA), and forensic linguistics.

Open Access This chapter is licensed under the terms of the Creative Commons Attribution 4.0 International License (http://creativecommons.org/licenses/by/4.0/), which permits use, sharing, adaptation, distribution and reproduction in any medium or format, as long as you give appropriate credit to the original author(s) and the source, provide a link to the Creative Commons license and indicate if changes were made.

The images or other third party material in this chapter are included in the chapter's Creative Commons license, unless indicated otherwise in a credit line to the material. If material is not included in the chapter's Creative Commons license and your intended use is not permitted by statutory regulation or exceeds the permitted use, you will need to obtain permission directly from the copyright holder.

Chapter 16
Time Reference and Telicity in Agrammatic Aphasia in Bahasa Indonesia

Siti Eka Soniawati, Harwintha Anjarningsih, and Myrna Laksman-Huntley

Abstract Several cross-inflectional-language studies claim that reference to time and telicity marked by verbs are difficult for agrammatic speakers. Thus, the PADILIH claims that time reference referring to the past is difficult and AAM claims that the combination of argument structure (transitivity & telicity) and time reference is relatively difficult for agrammatic speakers. It is predicted that a similar phenomenon is observed in the agglutinative Indonesian. Furthermore, filling in the gap in rehabilitation method in the Aphasia Test for Diagnosis, Information and Rehabilitation (TADIR), which currently has no standard guidelines, it is interesting to examine telicity and time reference in addition to the accompanying deficit. BI verbs have the potential to indicate telicity through inherent meaning by referring to the two semantic parameters of time reference including dynamism and durativity, while time reference is simultaneously marked by aspectual adverbs and temporal lexical adverbs. Ten participants were divided into two groups, with one group comprised of agrammatic speakers and a second group comprised of five speakers without brain damage (NBDs) as controls. Agrammatism was determined based on the TADIR, and both groups of speakers were tested with the Test for Assessing Reference of Time (TART) and Verbal Sentence Production (SPP-verbal). The validated sentences have the patterns of subject + verb (intransitive) in basic and derived verb forms. The results of the study, in line with the PADILIH hypothesis both in production and comprehension tasks, show that referring to the past that requires discourse linking tends to be difficult. The performance of agrammatic speakers is lower than that of the controls in both temporal and lexical adverb tasks. However, the AAM hypothesis cannot be fully generalized. In both the production and comprehension tasks the atelic verbs are not difficult; however, telic verbs are difficult. Clinical contribution as a complement of rehabilitation method (TADIR) is the evaluation of the difficulty of derived verbs and time reference, and an adaptive method by manipulating a series of tests that involves three time frames and stresses on especially the forms of derived verbs. This finding has implications for efforts to develop the integrity of sentences

S. E. Soniawati · H. Anjarningsih (✉) · M. Laksman-Huntley
Linguistics Departement, Faculty of Humanities, Universitas Indonesia, Depok, Indonesia
e-mail: harwintha@ui.ac.id

triggered by a decrease in the lexical level and the development of the language potential of agrammatic speakers who may be indicated by memory disorders.

Keyword Indonesian agrammatism · Telicity · Time reference · Bahasa Indonesia

16.1 Introduction

Brain damage caused by cerebrovascular injury (Klebic et al., 2011) results in a person experiencing speech difficulties due to dysfunction in the left hemisphere (Gajardo-Vidal et al., 2018; Lukic et al., 2017). This condition causes a linguistic disorder which came to be known as aphasia and 80% of the most common causes are strokes (Doesborgh, 2004). In addition to influencing language skills in both production and comprehension, some affected individuals have problems with grammatical features (agrammatism). Usually, individuals with agrammatism can speak, but use incorrect grammar: they use incorrect affixes, and they use incorrect words (Kolk, 1998; Kusumoputro & Sidiarto, 2009). Sometimes it is difficult to understand the sentences or syntactic inaccuracies which are produced (Edwards & Tucker, 2006). Another deficit, for example, in cross-inflected-language research is that agrammatic individuals speak with a disruption to the verb.

Verbs have been reported to be difficult for people with agrammatism. This is found in studies investigating different languages including Dutch (Bastiaanse & Van Zonneveld, 2004), English (Cho-Reyes & Thompson, 2012), and Turkish (Faroqi-Shah & Friedman, 2015). This condition is a consequence of phonological coding disorders (Auclair-Oullet et al., 2019) and difficulty producing verbs in sentences (Faroqi-Shah & Thompson, 2007). As a result, not only is the problem of verb inflection found, but also time reference disturbances especially referring to past forms are also reported. Bastiaanse et al. (2011) note that there is a selective difficulty in Dutch agrammatic speakers regarding time reference mainly referring to the past compared to the form of inflection that refers to present and or future (PAst DIscourse Linking Hyphothesis/PADILIH). References to the future do not require discourse links, while verb forms that refer to the past are more complex and difficult for agrammatic speakers (Avrutin, 2006). Similar cases in Turkish (Yarbay Duman, 2009), Russian (Dragoy & Bastiaanse, 2010), and Serbian (Kljajevic & Bastiaanse, 2011) also confirm the same findings. Furthermore, involving the verb problem, Bastiaanse and Platonov (2015) try to examine the time reference problem including the time and aspect and its relation to the structure of the argument (transitivity and telicity). The combination of these three features has implications for the language skills of agrammatic speakers, as explained in the Aspect Assignment Model (AAM) hypothesis. This hypothesis claims that the perfective and imperfective aspects expressed through finite verbs are reported to be problematic in Russian.

Responding to some of the conditions above, in agglutinative Indonesian (Bahasa Indonesia [BI]; Larasati et al., 2011), agrammatic language performance is characterized by non-fluent speech and production of short sentences (Anjarningsih &

Bastiaanse, 2011). If in the inflected languages, the finite verb is found to be difficult, in agrammatic speakers of BI, main verbs (predicates) are relatively spared from disturbances. However, when it comes to time reference, in this case, verbs that are used together with aspectual and temporal lexical adverbs, are reported to be problematic. This fact has been confirmed by Anjarningsih et al. (2012) who found that there are obstacles mainly referring to the past form.

In this case, there are some interesting conditions in the BI to fill the gaps in rehabilitation methods in the Aphasia Test for Diagnosis, Information and Rehabilitation (TADIR; Dharmaperwira-Prins, 1996) that currently does not have standard guidelines for rehabilitation. First, BI verbs that are not bound by inflectional morphemes to show time reference (Sneddon, 1996) are relatively understood by agrammatic speakers. Separating the possible consequences of inflection, it is still necessary to conduct an assessment by filling in the research gap of the property in question, namely the verbs related to the accompanying semantic category (argument structure). To the best of our knowledge, there is no previous work that discusses the relationship between verbal predicates with telicity and time reference in BI. This is interesting to explore, to see whether there are difficulties due to inflection, semantic influence, or other reasons that are not yet known.

Second, related to the first condition, there is a possibility that a speaker is constrained by certain forms of verbs that are accompanied by telicity and transitivity. In general, Filip (2011) revealed that telicity can be divided into telic and atelic. Telic is a situation that has an end point while atelic is a situation that has no end point (Comrie, 1976; Smith, 1997). For example, 'He built a house' (telic) and 'She walked' (atelic). Thus, the telicity of the verb can be defined as an indicator of a verb in explaining events related to temporal meanings that are universal. In BI, Nurhayati (2011) mentioned that the forms of verbs independently have the potential to have end-point (telic) and those without (atelic) meaning by referring to two parameters, namely: semantic and syntactic. Semantic features include semantic timing characteristics with [+durative] and [+dynamic]. A dynamic verb can answer the question 'what does subject do?' or can be used to make an imperative sentence and a durative verb can answer the question 'how long does the situation happen?'; for example, *berlari* 'run' is a dynamic & durative verb because it can answer both of these questions. While the syntactic features (transitivity) include the form of BI verbs including basics or affixless forms such us *tidur* 'sleep', *makan* 'eat' and derived forms with affixes such us *ber-* + *jalan* or *berjalan* 'walk', *Meng-* + *cangkul* or *mencangkul* 'hoe' both to intransitive and transitive verb. Table 16.1 contains a list of BI verbs along with their individual characteristics.

Third, BI time reference and telicity are not complementary because the two components do not contrast (Montolalu, 2003). BI time reference is marked by lexical and aspectual adverbs (Anjarningsih et al., 2012), while telicity is characterized by the inherent meaning and constellation of verbs and arguments (argument structure). Based on these facts, the focus in this study is only to examine the forms of intransitive verbs. Tadjuddin (2005) specifies the use of aspectual adverbs by using particles 'sudah', 'telah', 'belum', and 'akan'. 'Sudah' is perfective, 'belum' is imperfect, and 'will' means future. For temporal lexical adverbs, Asmah Hj. Omar in Anjarningsih

Table 16.1 BI verbs with their telicity (Nurhayati, 2011)

Basic verbs				Derived verbs			
Transitive		Intransitive		Transitive		Intransitive	
[+tel]	[-tel]	[+tel]	[-tel]	[+tel]	[-tel]	[+tel]	[-tel]
lempar (throw)	makan (eat)	patah (break)	terbang (fly)	mem-buka (open)	memakai (wear)	menepi (pull over)	bersepeda (bike)
tutup (close)	minum (drink)	jatuh (drop)	tumbuh (grow)	menutup (close)	melihat (see)	mengering (dry)	berjatuhan (fall (of many small things))

Note [+tel]: telic, [-tel]: atelic

(2012) describes that BI time adverbs are classified into three, namely 'baru saja' marking the past, 'sekarang' marking the present, and 'sebentar lagi' marking future events. This condition is different from the concept of time reference in English or Dutch which is expressed by morphological changes.

Thus, based on the above review, if the PADILIH hypothesis (Bastiaanse et al., 2011; time reference referring to the past form is difficult) and the AAM hypothesis (Bastiaanse & Platonov, 2015; the combination of the structure of arguments (transitivity & telicity) and time reference tends to be difficult) are correct, similar phenomena will be observed in BI. Due to the fact that telicity and time reference in BI are not in contrast, two research questions are formulated. The first question is whether or not telicity affects the language ability of agrammatic speakers due to the fact that BI verbs are not bound by tenses, but affixes are employed to derive verbs. Separating the possible consequences of inflection, a study is necessary considering that BI verbs have a number of functional morphemes that mark different domains in the language, for example, the prefixes meN- and -ber (Jeoung, 2018). The second question is whether time reference marked by aspectual and lexical adverbs influences language modality in agrammatic speakers. In general, time reference referring to the past is reported problematic. By examining these two points, this study's clinical contribution is a proposal of a complementary form of rehabilitation methods in TADIR.

16.2 The Current Research

Participants in this study are ten people, divided into two groups, with one group comprised of agrammatic speakers and a second group comprised of five speakers without brain damage (NBDs) as controls. The inclusion criteria included: (1) five people who were diagnosed with Broca's aphasia based on the Aphasia Test for Diagnosis, Information and Rehabilitation (TADIR; Dharmaperwira-Prins, 1996) with a minimum onset time of three months; (2) each participant has relatively good hearing and vision; (3) active speakers of Indonesian language; and (4) the

16 Time Reference and Telicity in Agrammatic Aphasia in Bahasa Indonesia 295

backgrounds of NBDs are adjusted in terms of age, sex, education, and occupation with those of the speakers with agrammatism. Agrammatic speakers with dementia are not taken into account to prevent the effects caused by disorders caused by aging. The demographic profile of participants can be seen in Table 16.2 along with TADIR norm profile in Table 16.3.

Table 16.2 Demographic data of the speakers with agrammatism and non-brain damaged speakers (NBDs)

	Sex	Age	Handedness	Pendidikan	Pekerjaan	Time post onset	Bahasa
A1	M	62	Right	Secondary school	Retired employee	>2 years	BI
A2	M	58	Right	University	Retired civil servant	>1 years	BI
A3	M	47	Right	University	Member of the army	>1 years	BI
A4	F	48	Right	Secondary school	Homemaker	>1 years	BI
A5	M	53	Right	University	Retired civil servant	>2 years	BI
B1	M	55	Right	Secondary school	Self-employed	–	BI
B2	M	52	Right	University	Retired civil servant	–	BI
B3	M	40	Right	University	Civil servant	–	BI
B4	F	50	Right	University	Homemaker	–	BI
B5	M	51	Right	University	Retired teacher	–	BI

Note Speakers with agrammatism 'A1-A5'; NBDs 'B1-B5'

Table 16.3 Profile of language performance of speakers of agrammatism and Non-Brain Damaged Speakers (NBDs) based on the TADIR (Dharmaperwira-Prins, 1996)

	No. animal names produced in 1 min	Word-level picture naming (max. 8)	Words per minute	Auditory word and sentence comprehension (max. 10; word = 4, sentence = 6)	Word and sentence repetition (max. 4; word = 2, sentence = 2)	Severity
A1	4	7	40	6	2	Severe
A2	7	7	28	8	3	Mild
A3	9	6	25	7	2	Mild
A4	7	7	37	7	3	Moderate
A5	4	3	20	5	2	Severe
NBDs	>10	8	80–120	10	4	Normal

The participants are tested by adapting the Verbal Sentence Production Priming (SPP-verbal; Bastiaanse & Platonov, 2015) for production tasks and the BI version of the Test for Assessing Reference of Time (TART; Bastiaanse et al, 2008) in comprehension tasks. Both methods are arranged in the context of sentences that have been validated with subject + intransitive verb patterns. The breakdown of the number of verbs used in the three experiments is: five telic basic verbs, five atelic basic verbs, five derived telic verbs, and five derived atelic verbs (N = 20) which were then illustrated in the form of images. The preparation of this instrument uses A4-sized drawing paper, with details of 40 images to test the verb telicity and 120 images to test the time reference (60 aspectual adverbs and 60 lexical adverbs).

In production tasks (N = 160; 40 for telicity and 120 for time reference), participants were given two groups of images with different subjects but involved similar actions (see Figs. 16.1 and 16.2). Trial testing was carried out until participants understood the instructions, namely: 'I will describe the first picture, and then I want you to describe a similar event in the second picture'. Then, participants are required to complete the last sentence by completing the target verb in each sentence that is tested. The following are examples of testing procedures for participants.

In the comprehension tasks, (N = 160; 40 for telicity and 120 for time reference), participants were to choose between two contrasting images (telic vs atelic, perfective vs durative; future vs duratif). The binary options are modified to avoid drawing illustrations that have almost the same action in the three time frames, so the perfective and the future are not compared. The experiment begins with the researchers reading the sentence that is tested, and then participants are required to choose one of the two pictures that are considered correct. The following is an example (see Fig. 16.3) of the testing procedure for participants.

All responses given by participants were analyzed quantitatively and qualitatively based on data and tabulation of the answer sheets prepared before the administration of the experiments. Quantitative analysis is calculated statistically based on the provisions of the true and false scores of each participant's response. In the BI time reference production task, there are a number of possibilities that need to be considered, for example: the possibility of using synonymous aspectual adverbs, such as, 'akan' (future-asp) replaced by 'mau' (future-asp), 'sedang' (durative-asp) replaced by 'lagi' (durative-asp). This is a condition in BI that has a number of synonymous time-reference adverbs. Recognizing this condition, synonymous adverbs are scored

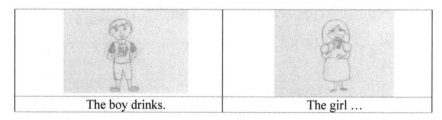

Fig. 16.1 Example of SPP-verbal to investigate telicity. Priming sentence 'Anak laki-laki itu minum' (The boy drinks), target verb, 'The girl...'

16 Time Reference and Telicity in Agrammatic Aphasia in Bahasa Indonesia

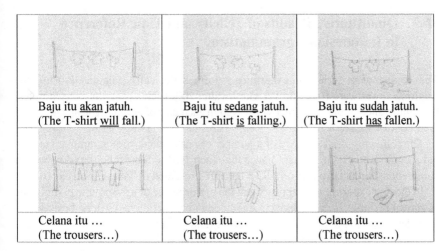

Fig. 16.2 Example of SPP-verbal to investigate time reference. The priming sentences are on the first line and the target verbs are on the second line

Fig. 16.3 Example of comprehension test item. (1) telicity comprehension task, target sentence 'Anak laki-laki itu <u>minum</u>'. (The boy drinks.) (2) aspectual adverb comprehension task, target sentence 'Anak laki-laki itu <u>sudah minum</u>'. (The boy has drunk.) (3) temporal lexical adverb comprehension task, target sentence 'Anak laki-laki itu <u>baru saja minum</u>'. (The boy drank just now.)

correct when they arise in participant responses. While in qualitative analysis, the errors include: (1) removal of affixes, for example for the target verb 'berjatuhan', participants produce 'jatuh,' (2) verb errors, in this case the response contains a verb that is different from the target, (3) substitution of adverbs of time reference, for example using the adverb 'sekarang' (now) instead of 'sudah' (perfective), and (4) other errors (responses), including no response.

16.3 Quantitative Results of Telicity and Time Reference in Indonesian Agrammatism

The results of a series of experiments were statistically calculated using the singlim.exe software (Crawford & Garthwaite, 2002). This program is used to test the significance of the differences observed in each pair of agrammatic speakers and their control speakers.

The following is a summary of a number of participants with agrammatism who have significantly poorer performance than their NBDs in the telicity tasks (both in comprehension and production). Raw data are presented in Tables 16.4 and 16.5.

In the first experiment, it appears that the performance of agrammatic participants as shown in Table 16.5 is relatively disrupted in production tasks (telic basic verbs, telic-derived verbs and atelic-derived verbs) and comprehension (telic basic verbs, telic-derived verbs, and atelic derived verbs). In the production tasks, 3 agrammatic speakers had significant difficulties with basic telic verbs compared to the NBDs (t = −4082, P = 0.005) and 5 agrammatic speakers had significant difficulties with telic-derived verbs (t = −3674.2, P = 0.005). Furthermore, the production performance of 5 agrammatic speakers also indicated disturbance to the atelic-derived verbs (t = −4082, P = 0.005). A similar tendency towards telic verbs both basic and derived was also reported to be constrained in comprehension tasks. Four agrammatic speakers had significant difficulties with basic telic verbs (t = −4082.4, P = 0.005) and 3 agrammatic speakers had significant difficulties for derived telic verbs (t = −2857.7,

Table 16.4 Summary of tasks conducted in the research

Experiment	Details
First experiment. Production and comprehension of telicity	5 telic basic verbs, 5 atelic basic verbs, 5 telic derived verbs dan 5 atelic derived verbs
Second experiment. Production and comprehension of aspectual adverbs	20 sentences with aspectual adverb *sudah* (perfective), 20 sentences with aspectual adverb *sedang* (durative), and 20 sentences with aspectual adverb *akan* (future)
Third experiment. Production and comprehension of lexical adverbs	20 sentences with lexical adverb *baru saja* (past), 20 sentences with lexical adverb *sekarang* (present), and 20 sentences with lexical adverb *sebentar lagi* (future)

Table 16.5 Number of agrammatic participants that have significantly poorer performance in production and comprehension tasks investigating effects of telicity

Production				Comprehension			
Telic		Atelic		Telic		Atelic	
Basic	Derived	Basic	Derived	Basic	Derived	Basic	Derived
3	5	0	5	4	3	0	1

P = 0.005). However, overall the agrammatic speakers (N = 5) are relatively spared in the comprehension tasks investigating atelic verbs (t = 0,000, P = 0.005). Only 1 of the 5 agrammatic speakers had a significantly lower performance in derived atelic verbs (t = −4490.7, P = 0.005). The raw data are presented in Figs. 16.4 and 16.5.

As shown in Table 16.6, time references in this case aspectual adverbs & temporal lexical adverbs are reported to be constrained in both production and comprehension tasks. The results of the second experiment, overall, the performance of speakers with agrammatism (N = 5) in production tasks were significantly different from that of the NBDs' (for sudah 'perfective', t = −18,779.4, P = 0.005; sedang 'durative', t = −13,063.9, P = 0.005, akan 'future-asp', t = −14,696.9, P = 0.005). Similar results, in the comprehension tasks 5 speakers with agrammatism had significant difficulties with aspectual adverbs (for sudah 'perfective', t = −13,472.1, P = 0.005, sedang 'durative', t = −6531,973, akan 'future-aspt' = −9389.7, P = 0.005). Then in the third experiment, overall agrammatic performance in production and comprehension tasks were significantly lower than the NBDs' scores. All five speakers with agrammatism performed significantly lower in temporal lexical adverbs production task, for baru saja 'past', t = −21,228,911, P = 0.005, sekarang 'now', t = −15,513,435, P = 0.005, sebentar lagi 'future', t = −22,453,656, P = 0.005. A similar condition

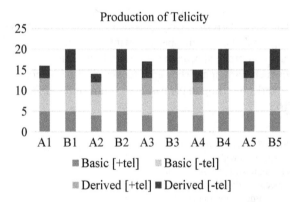

Fig. 16.4 Performance of the speakers with agrammatism (A1-A5) in the production of telic and atelic verbs compared with that of NBDs (B1-B5)

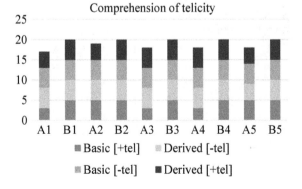

Fig. 16.5 Performance of the speakers with agrammatism (A1-A5) in comprehension of telic and atelic verbs compared with that of NBDs (B1-B5)

Table 16.6 Number of agrammatic participants that have significantly poorer performance in production and comprehension tasks investigating effects of time reference

	Aspectual lexical adverbs			Temporal lexical adverbs		
	Sudah (Pft)	Sedang (Imp)	Akan (Fut-asp)	Baru saja (past)	Sekarang (now)	Sebentar lagi (Fut)
Production	5	5	5	5	5	5
Comprehension	5	5	5	5	5	5

is found in the comprehension of the temporal lexical adverb task in which the five agrammatic speakers show significantly lower performance compared to that of the NBDs (for baru saja 'past', $t = -17,962,925$, $P = 0.005$, sekarang 'now', $t = -12,247.449$, $P = 0.005$, sebentar lagi 'will', $t = -17,146.428$, $P = 0.005$).

Therefore, based on the statistical results of the first experiment, telic verbs, both basic and derived, are shown to be difficult. As for the second and third experiments, all agrammatic participants face difficulties in time reference. Interestingly, the frequency of mistakes of all participants suggests that aspectual and temporal lexical adverbs referring to the past are impaired (see Figs. 16.1, 16.2, 16.3 and 16.4).

Thus, based on the statistical results of the first experiment, in general, telic basic and derived verbs are indicated to be difficult. While for the second and third experiments, overall, speakers with agrammatism experience difficulties to produce and comprehend reference to time. Interestingly, the individual frequency of errors in each participant showed a tendency that aspectual adverbs and temporal lexical adverbs referring to the past are significantly difficult (see Figs. 16.6, 16.7, 16.8 and 16.9).

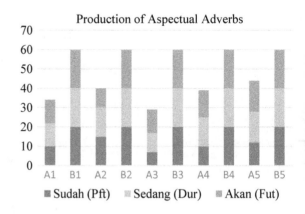

Fig. 16.6 The performance of speakers with agrammatism (A1-A5) in the aspectual adverbs production task compared with that of NBDs (B1-B5). Maximum score 20 per category. Pft = perfective, Dur = durative, Fut = Future-aspect

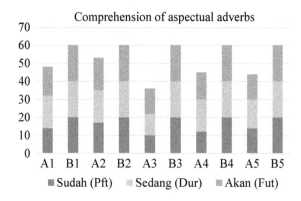

Fig. 16.7 The performance of speakers with agrammatism (A1-A5) in the aspectual adverbs comprehension task compared with that of NBDs (B1-B5). Maximum score 20 per category. Pft = perfective, Dur = durative, Fut = Future-aspect

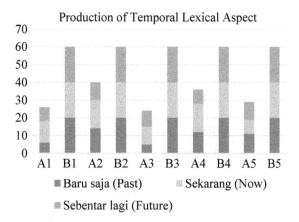

Fig. 16.8 The performance of speakers with agrammatism (A1-A5) in the temporal lexical adverbs production task compared with that of NBDs (B1-B5). Maximum score 20 per category

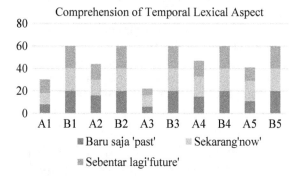

Fig. 16.9 The performance of speakers with agrammatism (A1-A5) in the temporal lexical adverbs comprehension task compared with that of NBDs (B1-B5). Maximum score 20 per category

Table 16.7 Total number (mean) and error types in the production of telicity

		Basic [+tel]	Basic [-tel]	Derived [+tel]	Derived [-tel]	Total errors
Production of telicity	Affix omissions	0	0	8	8	18
	Wrong verbs	3	0	0	0	3
	Other	0	0	1	1	2

Table 16.8 Total number (mean) and error types in production of time reference

	Aspectual adverbs			Total errors	Temporal lexical adverbs			Total errors
	Sudah (pft)	Sedang (dur)	Akan (fut-asp)		Baru saja (Past)	Sekarang (Now)	Sebentar lagi (Fut-asp)	
Aspect substitutions	29	12	15	56	23	10	19	52
Wrong verbs	13	9	11	33	7	13	14	34
Other	6	11	10	27	22	15	18	55

Note pft 'perfective', dur 'durative', fut-asp '*future*-aspect'

16.4 Qualitative Results of Telicity and Time Reference in Indonesian Agrammatism

While in the comprehension tasks for telicity and time reference, errors are only classified based on the calculation of correct and incorrect responses (see Table 16.5 and Figs. 16.5, 16.7, and 16.9) the response pattern in the performance of agrammatic speakers and NBDs in production tasks can be classified into three types of errors (see Tables 16.7 and 16.8). Table 16.6 shows that the majority of errors that occur in the telicity task are the removal of affixes in the telic and atelic verbs. In this case, the affixes me- and ber- tend to be constrained, and only basic verb forms can be produced. Furthermore, the pattern of errors in the production of time reference (Table 16.8), in addition to the nil response, is that agrammatic speakers tend to substitute the target adverb with another adverb.

16.5 Identification of Results of Production and Comprehension Performance of Speakers with Agrammatism Compared to NBDs

The purpose of this study is to identify the influence of telicity and time reference on the production and comprehension of speakers with agrammatism by conducting three experiments. Furthermore, the findings are explained in connection with the deficit of both features that affect language modality. Finally, by investigating the research problems a formulation of clinical implications can be drawn up.

The results of the first experiment in the tasks of production and comprehension show that telic verbs in general (both basic and derived) are difficult for speakers with agrammatism. In addition to involving endpoints and more prototypical categories (Romagno et al., 2012), the shape of telic verbs with past conditions and/or depictions of completed conditions (perfect aspects) tend to be difficult (Bastiaanse & Platonov, 2015; Torrence & Hyams, 2004). Furthermore, regarding the difficulty with derived verbs shown by 5 agrammatic speakers, it is speculated that this phenomenon has the tendency to be caused by integration between the verbs with the condition of past-perfect aspect with the derivation of BI verbs (Adriani et al., 2007). Most errors are failures in producing affixed morphemes that accompany basic verbs. For example, in the case of one speaker with agrammatis, the person failed to access affixes in the target verb 'berpelukan' (hug).

To sum up the results of the second and third experiments focusing on aspectual adverbs & temporal lexical adverbs as BI time reference markers, the performance of agrammatic speakers in production and comprehension tends to be constrained mainly referring to past forms. For example, the performance of speakers with agrammatism tends to be poor on aspectual adverbs that are 'perfective' and temporal lexical adverbs 'baru saja' (past) compared to markers that refer to 'durative' and/or ongoing activities. Interestingly, the number of errors in temporal lexical adverbs has a greater proportion than the errors in aspectual adverbs.

The difficulty with derived verbs that appeared in the first experiment implies a failure in producing and comprehending affixes. This condition is assumed to be related to the typology of BI verbs that have a number of different morphemes in one language, for example, the prefix meN- and BER (Jeoung, 2018), and can be caused by a failure to access affixes, which mark the continuity of a process in a derived verb. This pattern has similarities with Suhardiyanto's research (2003) that the tendency of errors in the lexical elements appears in the initial syllables and the last syllables. In contrast with the results of Anjarningsih (2012), the findings that telic verbs are impaired fills the gap left by Anjarningsih (2012) that has not yet specifically mapped the shape and dimensions of the verbs studied. Thus, completing the research gap as well as answering the first research question, the telicity in intransitive verbs tends to affect the production and comprehension of agrammatic speakers, with intransitive telic verbs more difficult to be produced and comprehended by speakers with agrammatism.

Furthermore, answering the second research question, it is noted that time reference referring to the past tends to be difficult to produce and comprehend by agrammatic speakers. Compared to future references, a time frame that refers to the past requires discourse links, so this condition is constrained. Avrutin (2006) also asserts that the form of verbs that refer to the past is more complex and that it becomes difficult for agrammatic speakers. In this case, difficulties with temporal lexical adverbs have a greater proportion than that of aspectual adverbs, in line with Anjarningsih (2012) who found that temporal lexical adverbs are more prone to be substituted by aspectual adverbs (e.g., 'baru saja' substituted by 'sudah'). Thus, separating the BI time reference and telicity because the two components are not in contrast (Montolalu, 2003), based on data, the two components are reported to be constrained, time reference referring to the past and telic verbs.

Based on the two findings above, contrasting with the two main hypotheses, Aspect Assignment Model (AAM; Bastiaanse & Platonov, 2015) and PAst DIscourse Linking Hyphothesis (PADILIH; Bastiaanse et al., 2011) there are some differences and similarities in the BI case. The results of the first experiment imply that the AAM hypothesis cannot be fully generalized. This condition is related to differences in language typology in that the BI time reference is not marked by dependent grammatical morphemes, while telicity is characterized by inherent meaning and the constellation of verbs and arguments (argument structure). Because transitivity in this study is limited by only involving intransitive verbs, the AAM hypothesis cannot be generalized. Regarding similarities with other, inflected languages, for example, Dutch (Bastiaanse et al., 2011) and Russian (Dragoy & Bastiaanse, 2010), the results of the current research are in line with the PADILIH hypothesis. Both production and comprehension of the time reference that requires discourse links tend to be difficult. The performance of agrammatic speakers is lower than that of the control group in both aspectual adverbs and temporal lexical adverbs. This pattern has also been found in non-inflected languages, for example, Chinese (Lin, 2003), where the three time frames are reported to be problematic (Bastiaanse et al., 2011).

16.6 Clinical Implications

The clinical contribution as a complementary form of rehabilitation method for the TADIR is an evaluation of the difficulty of derived verbs and time reference, and an adaptive method by manipulating a series of tests involving three time frames and stresses especially the forms of derived verbs. Jap and Arumsari (2017), for example, adapt the Token Test in BI as a form of refinement for the TADIR. As the difficulty with time reference may indicate the possibility of a disturbance in memory performance, it is necessary to evaluate the production ability and comprehension of agrammatic speakers by manipulating a series of tests involving three time frames. This finding has implications for efforts to develop the integrity of sentences triggered by a decrease in the lexical level (see Webster & Whitworth, 2012) and the development of the language potential of agrammatic speakers who may be indicated by memory disorders.

16.7 Conclusion

To conclude, this study examines the modality of production and comprehension of speakers with agrammatism on telicity and time reference marked by the inherent meaning of verbs and the use of adverbs in tenseless languages (BI). Compared to

Bastiaanse and Platonov (2015), which claim that the combination of the two features is influential, a similar case involving a series of experiments leads to two answered research questions. First, regarding the telicity of the BI verbs, referring to telic verbs is difficult. These constraints are found in basic and derived verbs. Second, BI time reference marked by aspectual adverbs and temporal lexical adverbs tend to be disrupted in three time frames (past, present, & future). Interestingly, these results are consistent with findings across inflected languages (Anjarningsih, 2012) and non-inflected languages (Bastiaanse et al., 2008). Collectively, references to the past are difficult. Thus, the current findings show that the linguistic typology of each language has a tendency to integrate so that it can cause certain difficulties. In this case, involving the morphological process that accompanies verbs and time reference is difficult for speakers with agrammatism in BI. This finding has implications as a TADIR refinement method, namely an evaluation of the morphemes that accompany the verbs and treatment manipulation involving three time frames.

Acknowledgements This work was supported by Universitas Indonesia's Research Grant (PITMA B 2019) managed by DRPM UI.

References

Adriani, M., Asian, J., Nazief, B., Tahaghoghi, S. M., & Williams, H. (2007). Stemming Indonesian: A confix-stripping approach. *ACM transactions on asian language information processing*, Vol. 6, No. 4.
Alwi, H., Dardjowidjojo, S., Lapoliwa, H., & Moeliono, A. N. (2010). *Tata Bahasa Baku Bahasa Indonesia*. Jakarta: Balai Pustaka.
Anjarningsih, H. Y., & Bastiaanse, R. (2011). Verbs and time reference in standard Indonesian agrammatic speech. *Aphasiology, 25*, 1562–1578.
Anjarningsih, H. Y., Haryadi-Soebadi, R. D., Gofir, A., & Bastiaanse, R. (2012). Characterising agrammatism in standard Indonesian. *Aphasiology, 26*, 757–784.
Anjarningsih, H. Y. (2012). *Time reference in standard Indonesian agrammatic aphasia*. Groningen (NL): Grodil.
Auclair-Oullet, N., Pythoud, P., Koenig-Bruhin, M., & Fossard, M. (2019). Inflectional morphology in fluent aphasia: A case study in a highly inflected language. *Language and Speech, 62*(2), 250–259.
Avrutin, S. (2006). Weak syntax. In Y. Grodzinsky & K. Amunts (Eds.), *Broca's region* (pp. 49–62). Oxford University Press.
Bastiaanse, R., & van Zonneveld, R. (2004). Broca's aphasia, verbs and the mental lexicon. *Brain and Language, 90*, 198–202.
Bastiaanse, R., Jonkers, R., & Thompson, C. K. (2008). *Test for assessing reference of time (TART)*. University of Groningen.
Bastiaanse, R., Bamyaci, E., Hsu, C.-J., Lee, J., Duman, Y., & Tuba & Thompson, Cynthia. (2011). Time reference in agrammatic aphasia: A cross-linguistic study. *Journal of Neurolinguistics, 24*, 652–673.
Bastiaanse, R., & Platonov, A. (2015). Argument structure and time reference in agrammatic aphasia. In R. G. de Almeida, & C. Manouilidou (Eds.), *Cognitive Science Perspectives on Verb Representation and Processing*. Oxford University Press.

Cho-Reyes, S., & Thompson, C. (2012). Verb and sentence production and comprehension in aphasia: Northwestern assessment of verbs and sentences (NAVS). *Aphasiology, 26*, 1250–1277.
Comrie, B. (1976). *Aspect.* Cambridge University Press.
Crawford, J. R., & Garthwaite, P. H. (2002). Investigation of the single case in neuropsychology: Confidence limits on the abnormality of test scores and test score differences. *Neuropsychologia, 40*, 1196–1208.
Dharmaperwira-Prins, R. (1996). *TADIR: Tes Afasia untuk Diagosis, Informasi, Rehabilitasi.* Penerbit Fakultas Kedokteran Universitas Indonesia.
Doesborgh, S. J. C. (2004). *Assessment and treatment of linguistic deficits in aphasic patients.* PhD dissertation, Erasmus Universiteit Rotterdam.
Dragoy, O., & Bastiaanse, R. (2010). Verb production and word order in Russian agrammatic speakers. *Aphasiology, 24*, 28–55.
Edwards, S., & Tucker, K. (2006). Verb retrieval in fluent aphasia: A clinical study. *Aphasiology, 20*(7), 644–675.
Faroqi-Shah, Y., & Friedman, L. (2015). Production of verb tense in agrammatic aphasia: A meta-analysis and further data. *Behavioural Neurology, 2015*(1), 1–15.
Faroqi-Shah, Y., & Thompson, C. K. (2007). Verb inflections in agrammatic aphasia: Encoding of tense features. *Journal of Memory and Language, 56*(1), 129–151.
Filip, H. (2011). Aspectual class and Aktionsart. In C. Maienborn, K. von Heusinger, & P. Portner (Eds.), *Semantics: An international handbook of natural language meaning* (pp. 1186–1217). Mouton de Gruyter.
Gajardo-Vidal, A., Lorca-Puls, D. L., Hope, T. M., Parker Jones, O., Seighier, M. L., Prejawa, S., & Price, C. J. (2018). How right hemisphere damage after stroke can impair speech comprehension. *Brain, 141*(12), 3389–3404.
Jap, B. A. J., & Arumsari, C. (2017). Adaptation of the token test in standard Indonesian. *Makara Human Behavior Studies in Asia, 21*(1), 44–51.
Jeoung, Helen, N. (2018). Optional elements in Indonesian Morphosyntax. *Publicly Accessible Penn Dissertations.*
Klebic, J., Salihovic, N., Softic, R., & Salihovic, D. (2011). Aphasia disorders outcome after stroke. *Medicinski Arhiv, 65*(5), 283–286.
Kljajevic, V., & Bastiaanse, R. (2011). Time reference in fluent aphasia: Evidence from Serbian. In A. Vatakis, A. Esposito, M. Giagkou, F. Cummins, and G. Papadelis (Eds.) *Multidisciplinary aspects of time and time perception*, number 6789 in Lecture Notes in Artificial Intelligence, pages 258–274, Heidelberg etc., 2011. COSTS TD0904 International Workshop, Springer.
Kolk, H. H. J. (1998). Disorders of syntax in aphasia. In B. Stemmer & H. Whitaker (Eds.), *Handbook of neurolinguistics* (pp. 249–260). Academic Press.
Kusumoputro, S., & Sidiarto, L. D. (2009). *Afasia Gangguan Berkomunikasi Pasca Stroke Otak.* Penerbit Universitas Indonesia.
Larasati, S. D., Kubon, V., & Zeman, D. (2011). *Indonesian morphology tool (morphind): Towards an Indonesian corpus.* Springer.
Lin, J.-W. (2003). Temporal reference in Mandarin Chinese. *Journal of East Asian Linguistics, 12*, 254–311.
Lukic, S., Barbieri, E., Wang, X., Caplan, D., Kiran, S., Rapp, B., & Thompson, C. K. (2017). Right hemisphere grey matter volume and language functions in stroke aphasia. *Neural Plasticity, 2017*, 5601509.
Montolalu, L. R. (2003). Teori Dwikomponen: Sebuah Parameter Untuk Mengukur Aspek. *Makara Sosial Humaniora,* Vol 7, No.1. Universitas Indonesia.
Nurhayati. (2011). Telicity in Indonesia. Diterbitkan dalam *Jurnal Ilmiah Linguistik Indonesia* Terakreditasi: SK Dirjen Dikti No.64a/DIKTI/Kep/2010 Tahun ke 29, Nomor 2 Agustus 2011. ISSN 0215-4846.
Romagno, D., Rota, G., Ricciardi, E., & Pietrini, P. (2012). Where the brain appreciates the final state of an event: The neural correlates of telicity. *Brain and Language, 123*(1), 68–74.
Smith, C. (1997). *The parameter of aspect.* Dordrecht. Kluwer. 2 nd ed.

Sneddon, N. J. (1996). *Indonesian: A comprehensive grammar*. Routledge.
Suhardiyanto, T. (2003). Agramatisme pada Afasia: Kajian Singkat Terhadap Empat Penderita Afasia Broca. *Universitas Indonesia. Linguistik Indonesia, 21*, 309–320.
Tadjuddin, M. (2005). *Aspektualitas dalam Kajian Linguistik*. Bandung: Alumni.
Torrence, H., & Hyams, N. (2004). On the role of aspect in determining finiteness and temporal interpretation in early grammar. In J. van Kampen & S. Baauw (Eds.), *Proceedings of GALA 2003: Vol 2. Generative approaches to language acquisition*. Utrecht: LOT.
Webster, J., & Whitworth, A. (2012). Treating verbs in aphasia: Exploring the impact of therapy at the single word and sentence levels. *International Journal of Language and Communication Disorders, 6*, 619–636.
Yarbay Duman, T. (2009). Turkish agrammatic aphasia: word order, time reference and case. *Groningen Dissertations in Linguistics, 73*.

Siti Eka Soniawati a student in the Linguistics study program, the Faculty of Humanities, Universitas Indonesia, Depok. Born in Salatiga, 1 August 10, 1994, now still completing her Master's Degree with the final project with the theme of aphasiology. Her research interest is in morphology, syntax, pragmatics, psycholinguistics, neuropsycholinguistics, and children's language development. E-mail: s.ekasonia@yahoo.com.

Harwintha Anjarningsih born in Kebumen, March 2, 1981, completed her doctoral study in Neurolinguistics/Aphasiology at the University of Groningen, the Netherlands. A faculty member in the English Study Program and Linguistics Department, the Faculty of Humanities, Universitas Indonesia, her research interests span from phonetics/phonology, morphology, syntax, psycholinguistics, language impairments across ages, bilingual language processing, and education for children with special needs. Website: harwintha.blogspot.com. Email: wintha_salyo@yahoo.com.

Myrna Laksman-Huntley born in Jakarta, Januari 5, 1961, obtained her doctorate degree in *communication parlée* (phonetics) from Université Stendhal, France. Since 1990, she has been a Lecturer and Researcher in the French Section and Linguistic Department of Universitas Indonesia. She has been and is the Director of undergraduate and graduate research projects presented in several international symposiums and conferences in different places in Indonesia. Her research interests include phonetics and phonology, morphology, syntax, semantics, sociolinguistics, discourse analysis, and teaching French as a foreign language. Email: laksman.huntley@gmail.com

Open Access This chapter is licensed under the terms of the Creative Commons Attribution 4.0 International License (http://creativecommons.org/licenses/by/4.0/), which permits use, sharing, adaptation, distribution and reproduction in any medium or format, as long as you give appropriate credit to the original author(s) and the source, provide a link to the Creative Commons license and indicate if changes were made.

The images or other third party material in this chapter are included in the chapter's Creative Commons license, unless indicated otherwise in a credit line to the material. If material is not included in the chapter's Creative Commons license and your intended use is not permitted by statutory regulation or exceeds the permitted use, you will need to obtain permission directly from the copyright holder.

Printed in the USA
CPSIA information can be obtained
at www.ICGtesting.com
CBHW050943311024
16618CB00003BA/79